With Us Always

NATIONAL UNIVERSITY
LIBRARY   SAN DIEGO

With Us Always

A History of Private Charity and Public Welfare

Edited by
Donald T. Critchlow
and
Charles H. Parker

ROWMAN & LITTLEFIELD PUBLISHERS, INC.
Lanham • Boulder • New York • Oxford

YTIƧЯƎVINU JAИOITAИ
OƎIO ИAƧ

ROWMAN & LITTLEFIELD PUBLISHERS, INC.

Published in the United States of America
by Rowman & Littlefield Publishers, Inc.
4720 Boston Way, Lanham, Maryland 20706

12 Hid's Copse Road
Cumnor Hill, Oxford OX2 9JJ, England

Copyright © 1998 by Rowman & Littlefield Publishers, Inc.

"Claiming the Poor" © 1998 Elizabeth McKeown.

The editors are grateful to the Center for Medieval and Renaissance Studies at Saint Louis
University for underwriting the expenses of reproduction and copyright permission for the cover
photograph.

All rights reserved. No part of this publication may be reproduced, stored in a retrieval system, or
transmitted in any form or by any means, electronic, mechanical, photocopying, recording, or
otherwise, without the prior permission of the publisher.

British Library Cataloguing in Publication Information Available

Library of Congress Cataloging-in-Publication Data

With us always : a history of private charity and public welfare / edited by
    Donald T. Critchlow and Charles H. Parker.
        p.   cm.
    Includes index.
        ISBN 0-8476-8969-7 (cloth : alk. paper). — ISBN 0-8108-8970-0 (pbk. :
    alk. paper)
        1. Charities—History. 2. Poor—Services for—History. 3. Public welfare
    —History. 4. Non-governmental organizations—History. I. Critchlow,
    Donald T., 1948–. II. Parker, Charles H., 1958–.
    HV16.W58   1998
    361.7'632'09—dc21   97-40121

ISBN 0-8476-8969-7 (cloth : alk. paper)
ISBN 0-8476-8970-0 (pbk. : alk. paper)

Printed in the United States of America

♾™ The paper used in this publication meets the minimum requirements of American National
Standard for Information Sciences—Permanence of Paper for Printed Library Materials, ANSI
Z39.48–1984.

Contents

United States Relief and Welfare
in the Nineteenth and Twentieth Centuries

DONALD T. CRITCHLOW
CHARLES H. PARKER

Introduction

To the biblical injunction that "You shall have poor with you always" (Matt. 26:11) might be added, "and in caring for the poor, you will suffer many trials and tribulations." Surely the historical record reveals, as these essays illustrate, a consistency in Western societies confronting similar problems in relief and charity: provision of aid for the poor, indigent, and sick without inducing permanent dependency; appropriation of funds to care for those left destitute by economic displacement, illness, or personal infirmity; distinction between the "deserving" and "undeserving" among the indigent; acclivity of mercy and control; and accommodation between private voluntarism and government activism. Although certain scholars have maintained that a universal theme of "social control" can be found in these efforts of charity and welfare, others have challenged this perspective as imputing a greater consciousness and far too deliberate intentions to state, church, and welfare authorities, who have often displayed profound sentiments of benevolence and religious motivation in their work.[1]

Whatever the motivation evident in the care of the poor and the indigent, continuity itself can be overstated. Certainly, religious motivation played a more significant role in early modern European relief than it has in the modern period, especially the twentieth century, where a bureaucratic impulse characterizes welfare organization. This is not to demean the importance of religious beliefs in modern welfare; clearly religious philanthropic organizations—Jewish, Protestant, and Catholic—remain integral to the modern welfare state. However, in our time, bureaucratic government on the local, state, and national levels predominates in health and welfare care in both European and American countries.[2]

If Western societies in the early modern period have displayed a certain preoccupation with the poor, to a large degree that compulsion has grown out of the religious mandates of medieval Christianity. For centuries the

Catholic Church had established the "seven works of mercy" as an obligation for all Christians, or at least for those who concerned themselves with the state of their souls and salvation in the afterlife. Protestants in the sixteenth century may have repudiated any salvific merit for charitable work, but they retained the motivation of charity as a primary Christian responsibility. In drafting new poor relief ordinances for Wittenberg, Martin Luther wrote in 1522 that beggars brought shame to a Christian society.[3] And, just over half a century later, a Dutch Calvinist pastor in Holland exhorted his congregation to give liberally to the poor, "so that the poor member of our Lord Jesus Christ will not be neglected."[4]

Despite all the waves of welfare reform in Europe from the sixteenth century to the present day, religious charity has continued to play an important role in social provision for the poor. Even though the aim of helping the poor move out of poverty is often expressed today as a moral (if not religious) obligation, this ideal comes from a long tradition of Christian religious charity.

Unfortunately, the current historical model of poor relief in early modern Europe has largely neglected the influence of religious charity in the development of welfare policy. The reason for this omission is that, until very recently, historians have assumed that the poor relief reforms of the sixteenth century introduced a sharp dichotomy between religious charity and civic welfare. For example, W. K. Jordan claimed that the motivation for philanthropy in seventeenth-century England became more social than spiritual. Analyzing over 50,000 wills, he argued that charitable bequests for the poor supplanted pious bequests for the repose of one's soul, which for Jordan indicates that English benefactors became more concerned with social problems in this world than with spiritual anxieties about the afterlife.[5] Institutional studies of poor relief have underscored this pattern. As governments developed a sense of social responsibility, they established rational (i.e., nonreligious) systems of provision. In his recent synthesis of early modern poor relief, Robert Jütte claimed that the Protestant Reformation "paved the way for the development of a new social policy which favoured secular systems of poor relief."[6]

Consequently, according to this model, public assistance prevailed over religious charity, which ultimately led to the inevitable triumph of the modern welfare state. Freed from the motivations of religious charity and ecclesiastical restraints, municipal and national governments experimented with institutions and laws meant to deal with poverty. From the seventeenth through the nineteenth centuries, workhouses, asylums, and prisons confined the "undeserving" poor, while proscriptive laws and workfare programs attempted to force people to work. In the twentieth century, national governments became the custodians of the poor through massive welfare programs.

The articles in this volume on European poor relief demonstrate that the reigning historical model is problematic because a strict dichotomy between public assistance and private charity is far too simplistic for the early modern period. In the early Dutch Republic, which was rapidly becoming the commercial center of Europe, Calvinist poor relief agencies were an integral component of municipal welfare, despite thorny conflicts between religious and political leaders. With respect to motivation, the religious and social values of a predominately Counter Reformation society inspired testators in Grenoble well into the eighteenth century. Later in eighteenth-century France, religious and lay leaders still believed that providing work for the poor was, in and of itself, a charitable work. Likewise, notions of the civic "public good" and religious "good works" went hand in hand in shaping charitable institutions in northern Italy. And, traditional altruistic incentives mitigated the local effects of the 1834 Poor Law in Victorian England. Thus, a high degree of collaboration between religious charity and public assistance marked the development of social welfare in various areas of Europe from the sixteenth to the nineteenth centuries.

Integrating religious charity into the historical analysis of early modern poor relief will enable scholars to explore the cultural framework that encased social provision in a more comprehensive way. Since the poor constituted the socio-economic margins of a society, decisions about who merits what type of assistance bring the boundaries of a community into clear focus. In the lands of early modern Europe, sacral ideals and civic values provided the framework of community life. Enveloped within this cultural ethos, poor relief measures conformed to the ideal that all inhabitants of the city were bound together in a sacred and civic community under the authority of the magistracy. These essays indicate several ways in which religious ideals and civic values in early modern Europe played themselves out in different cultural contexts.

The unusual character of the Reformed Church of the Dutch Republic led to conflicts over poor relief that reveal two antithetical visions of Christian community. Calvinists intended to reserve church deacons for the "household of faith," whereas city magistrates held to the unity of religious and civic community. As a result, they expected church poor relief agencies to serve all the inhabitants of the city as the Catholic Church had done for centuries. While confessional and civic values collided in this decentralized Protestant Republic, Tridentine Catholicism reinvigorated traditional concepts of community in areas where the Counter Reformation ultimately succeeded. Private charitable giving actually increased with the establishment of public poor relief institutions in Grenoble. The liberal bequests of Catholic elites to municipal relief agencies show their adoption of Counter Reformation ideals and their understanding of the sacral unity of civic society. An embattled minority in Grenoble, Protestants contributed to the maintenance of their confessional community.

Over the course of the late seventeenth and eighteenth centuries, clerics and lay officials in France relied increasingly on public assistance, in the form of workhouses and public work projects, to discipline the poor and to provide them with the means to sustain themselves. Contemporaries, however, viewed this effort as a form of charity that would enable the poor to incorporate themselves more positively into the local community. Work reinforced the community by providing entrance into it. Similarly, institutions like the Monti di Pietà in Italian cities loaned money to poor artisans, based on the religious conviction that such an undertaking was an act of Christian mercy. The diverse urban charitable institutions in eighteenth-century Italy functioned to preserve civic order, to perpetuate good works, and to solidify the Christian community.

As industrial capitalism began to alter the fundamental social structures of European society in the nineteenth century, Evangelicals, Utilitarians, and Malthusians in England reinaugurated a debate over how to deal with the poor. Set in a very different context, these competing views, nevertheless, point to disparate conceptions of the poor in relation to the national community. Should society use charity for the moral regeneration of the poor, restructure welfare to serve the greatest good for the greatest number, or simply dispense with all forms of assistance? The ways in which various English advocates answered these questions reveal their distinctive views of society as it was undergoing industrialization.

These essays point to problems with conventional scholarship and call for a reappraisal of the relationship between religious charity and public assistance in early modern Europe. Collectively, they argue that assistance to the poor in early modern Europe, no matter when, where, and in what form, was rooted in a tacit vision of an ideal society and the place of the poor in that society.

Similarly, the development of the American welfare state, as illustrated by these essays, reveals the continued importance of voluntarism, religious involvement, and private philanthropic activity in the modern welfare state. While a fierce debate concerning the role of the state in modern welfare arose in the twentieth century, beginning with the Great Depression in the 1930s, and taking on particular ideological poignancy following the war, especially beginning in the late 1970s, the record of private philanthropic involvement has been uneven. While private charity activity in the treatment of orphans reveals considerable success compared to governmental support of orphaned children, the role of the nonprofit sector in the Great

Society provides a counter-example of bureaucratic entanglement, frustrated policy achievement, and dashed hopes.[7] However one weighs the achievements of private philanthropy and government welfare programs, reappraisal of the traditional dichotomy between the two appears to be in order.

The modern welfare system of the United States emerged in the late nineteenth century from efforts to solve an American version of the "welfare problem" that appeared in all major Western nations during that time. The growing inability of private charity organizations to address the perceived needs of societies being transformed by new technologies and the workings of commercial markets led many reformers to call for new state involvement.

In a society in which individualism and free market ideology gained an exceptionally strong foothold, Americans in the nineteenth century developed a complex of specialized charity organizations and philanthropic institutions to care for their dependent and deviant populations. At the same time, government involvement overlays this private-voluntaristic system with a politicized benefit program that emerged to protect disabled soldiers and dependent mothers.[8] By the late nineteenth century, many Americans came to believe that this traditional system was working badly, as evidenced by mounting social distress and social conflict, the spread of political corruption and discontent, and the perceived gap between welfare needs and the capacity of families, churches, and other components of the traditional system to meet those needs.

Beginning in the early 1900s, public officials, encouraged and led by reformers, began to experiment with new government programs on the local, state, and federal levels. Prescriptions for new government involvement sparked sharp and continued debate concerning the balance between federal and local jurisdictions; public and private welfare; the role of trained and credentialed experts; and voluntaristic, nonstatist alternatives to statist welfare bureaucracies. As these debates continued, Americans developed in the first two decades of twentieth century a complex array of welfare agencies for the rehabilitation of the dependent and the deviant, increasingly overseen by professionalized social workers who sought to apply the latest scientific and social science research to the administration of these programs.

In the 1920s, Herbert Hoover sought to rationalize this involvement of private and public welfare activities through an "associative" state that offered an alternative to a Prussian-style bureaucracy or the British dole. This associative state placed responsibility on private groups and local communities supported by expert federal advice and minimal federal funding and involvement.

Hoover's program offered an alternative to a national welfare system as found in Germany and Britain. Indeed, the period's resurgent individualism and heightened faith in private and corporate business voluntarism thwarted further attempts to give the United States a comprehensive social welfare system based on national social insurance.

The depression crisis in the 1930s, however, discredited Hoover's vision and provided an impetus for major innovations in the welfare system. Franklin D. Roosevelt's New Deal created a "modern" welfare state—certainly incomplete, in comparison with those abroad, but still one in which an expanding public-sector bureaucracy administered national old age insurance and assistance, unemployment compensation and relief, aid to dependent groups, and fair labor standards. While political debate continued concerning the extent of the federal government's role in this new system, few believed that the new welfare state could or should be completely dismantled. The modern welfare state had arrived, rather belatedly, in America.

Yet to see the development of the modern welfare state simply in teleological terms as an inevitable response to industrialism and technological advancement is to misperceive the peculiar nature of the American welfare system. Its federal structure relies on state and local governments to set standards, allocate funds, and administer programs. Moreover, the peculiarity of the modern American state is revealed by the continued expression of strong antistatist sentiments found in the polity. Moreover, to see the "evolution" of the American welfare state as a movement from private to public, local to national, religious to secular, communitarian to bureaucratic is to misread history and the nature of what was created.

Much of the historiography of the modern welfare state accepts the dichotomy between the private voluntary welfare system and the public welfare state that emerged with the New Deal. Yet divisions between private charity and public assistance remain less clear upon closer examination. A strong antistatist tradition continued to find expression in both the nineteenth and twentieth centuries. In the late nineteenth century the major federal social welfare program was the pension system for Civil War veterans, a highly politicized system that by the turn of the century provided two out of three native white persons over the age of sixty with a federal pension. In general, however, relief remained localistic, private, and primarily centered around the poorhouse and charity organizations that reflected a deep ideological antistatist bias that relief of the poor was best handled by private organizations and local officials who were better able to check the abuse of relief by "loafers," while imparting aid to the "deserving poor." Although the line between private and public charity was often blurred through the nineteenth century, the development of specialized institutions for dealing with crime, poverty, disease, mental illness, and other afflictions shifted policy away from care in the home to public, albeit local, institutions.

Following World War I, policymakers, led by Herbert Hoover, promised a "New Era" in which enlightened businessmen, responsible labor representatives, knowledgeable experts, and government leaders would work together to serve the public interest. This vision, however, continued to embody a deep belief in traditional American values of individualism, voluntarism, and local initiative. The New Era, therefore, is portrayed by historians as a transitional period that ultimately failed and was replaced by the New Deal and the creation of the modern welfare system, which was centered around a national social security system.

The Great Society in the 1960s extended this system through the development of new welfare programs with medicare and medicaid that provided health insurance to the elderly, the poor, and the disabled. Only in the late 1990s would conservatives successfully challenge this statist solution and call for a return to local community involvement and private voluntarism. This schema that divides voluntaristic pre-New Deal charity organizations from New Deal statism, while correct in many ways, neglects the important fact that voluntarism and antistatist ideology remained continuous, even as the federal government assumed great responsibility for the care of the poor, the elderly, the sick and disabled, and the unemployed.

This understanding that the nonprofit sector and local, community organizations remained integral to the modern welfare state casts a different perspective on the history of welfare in the United States. Moreover, the debate over welfare reform appears different once it is understood that the nonprofit, voluntaristic system remained an essential part of federal programs. Federal programs relied on the nonprofit sector, which, in turn, became increasingly dependent on public funds to continue their work. As a result a symbiotic relationship developed between the federal government and the nonprofit sector; the two depend on each other for program implementation on one hand, and funding on the other. Thus, for partisans to speak of only strengthening federal funding, or on the contrary replacing federal efforts with local community and private voluntary effort, misconstrues the relationship between the two. While debates over the balance of federal involvement with local, community involvement will continue as important policy issues, any replacement of one sector, public or private, seems unlikely, if not impossible, given the nature of their relationship in the American federalist system.

Still, the distinguishing characteristic central to both public and private agencies involved in the modern welfare state is the critical role played by policy experts. Both government and private agencies rely on highly trained, specialized policy experts for policy innovation, administrative management, and program implementation. In this way, expertise, bureaucracy, and technique have replaced religious sentiment and the humanitarian impulse of the premodern charity and relief efforts of the medieval Catholic Church and the Reformation Protestant churches. Religious and humanitarian ideals continued to find expression in the modern period, but clearly Catholic and Protestant officials in the sixteenth century would have been startled by the amount of data, social science analysis, and administrative information that sets the parameters of welfare discourse today.

These essays suggest continuity in how Western societies have faced the problems of caring for the poor, sick, and indigent, but the contributors to this volume illustrate that the role of experts, the vast array of welfare programs, and the bureaucratic nature of the modern welfare state marks a sharp break with the premodern age. Yet these essays propose that historical reappraisal is in order for scholars who seek to understand the relationship between the premodern and modern eras. In turn, these essays invite policymakers to reconsider the relationship of private and local voluntarism to the public sector. In doing so, scholars and policymakers will develop a deeper appreciation of the injunction that we will have the poor with us always (it seems), and the travail of determining the best means to care for them. Most assuredly, however, the history of relief and charity remains essential to any discussion of welfare reform.

Notes

1. Francis Fox Piven and Richard A. Cloward, *Regulating the Poor* (New York, 1971). Seymour Drescher, *Capitalism and Anti-slavery: British Popular Mobilization in Comparative Perspective* (New York, 1987).

2. There is an abundant, indeed nearly overwhelming, literature on the modern welfare state. For the development of the modern American welfare state, see Edward D. Berkowitz, *American's Welfare State: From Roosevelt to Reagan* (Baltimore, 1991); Michael Katz, *In the Shadow of the Poor House* (New York, 1986); Katz, *Poverty and Policy* (New York, 1983); and Katz, *The Undeserving Poor: From the War on Poverty to the War on Welfare* (New York, 1989). Also, provocative interpretations of the modern welfare state are found in James T. Patterson, *America's Struggle Against Poverty: 1900–1980* (Cambridge, 1981); James Leiby, *A History of Social Welfare and Social Work in the United States* (New York, 1978); and Walter I. Trattner, *From Poor Law to the Welfare State* 4th ed. (New York, 1978). For the important role of the Social Security system in American welfare, see Martha Derthick, *Policymaking for Social Security* (Washington, D.C., 1979); Andrew Achenbaum, *Social Security: Visions and Revisions* (New York, 1986); Jill S. Quandagno, *The Transformation of Old Age Security: Class and Politics in the American Welfare State* (Chicago, 1988); and Carolyn L. Weaver, *The Crisis in Social Security* (Durham, 1982). The bureau-

cratic nature of health care is recounted in Paul Starr, *The Social Transformation of American Medicine* (New York, 1982); Edward Berkowitz, *Disabled Policy: America's Programs for the Handicapped* (New York, 1987); and Deborah Stone, *The Disabled State* (Philadelphia, 1984). Medicare is discussed by Theodore Marmar, *The Politics of Medicare* (Chicago, 1973). The importance of women in creating the modern welfare state in the United States is found in Theda Skocpol, *Protecting Soldiers and Mothers, The Political Origins of Social Policy in the United States* (Cambridge, 1992). A comparative perspective of the American welfare state is offered by Daniel Levine, *Poverty and Society: The Growth of the American Welfare State in International Comparison* (New Brunswick, 1989); and Gaston V. Rimlinger, *Welfare Policy and Industrialization in Europe, America, and Russia* (New York, 1971). Histories of individual European welfare systems are similarly abundant. A good beginning to this literature is found in P. Flora and A. Heidenheimer, *Welfare States in Europe and America* (New Brunswick, 1981). For Latin America, James M. Malloy, *The Politics of Social Security in Brazil* (Pittsburgh, 1979); and for the British Commonwealth countries, Francis G. Castles, *The Working Class and Welfare: Reflections on the Political Development of the Welfare State in Australia and New Zealand, 1880–1980* (London, 1985). For Great Britain, see Derek Fraser, *The Evolution of the British Welfare State* 2nd ed. (London, 1984).

3. See Carter Lindberg, "'There Should be no Beggars among Christians': Karlstadt, Luther and the Origins of Protestant Poor Relief," *Church History* 46 (1977): 313–333.

4. Gemeente Archief te Delft: Archief van de Kerkeraad van de Nederlands Hervormd Gemeente: Verzameling van Arent Corneliszoon Crusius., nr. 100.

5. W. K. Jordan, *Philanthropy in England 1480–1660: A Study of the Changing Pattern of English Social Aspirations* (London, 1959), 15.

6. Robert Jütte, *Poverty and Deviance in Early Modern Europe* (Cambridge, 1994), 108. See also, Natalie Zemon Davis, "Humanism, Heresy, and Poor Relief in Sixteenth-Century Lyon," in *Society and Culture in Early Modern France* (Stanford, 1975), 56–60; Jean-Pierre Gutton, *La Société et les pauvres en Europe (XVIe–XVIIIe siècles* (Paris, 1974), 104–106; Fernand Braudel, *Civilization and Capitalism, 15th–18th Century* 3 vols., trans. by Sian Reynolds (New York, 1981), 2: 506–511. Immanuel Wallerstein, *The Modern World-System I: Capitalist Agriculture and the Origins of the European World-Economy in the Sixteenth Century* (New York, 1974), 254–255; Catharine Lis and Hugo Soly, *Poverty and Capitalism in Pre-industrial Europe* (Sussex, 1979); H. Soly, "Economische ontwikkeling en sociale politiek in Europa tijdens de overgang van middeleeuwen naar nieuwe tijden," *Tijdschrift voor Geschiedenis* 88 (1975): 584–597; R. H. Tawney, *Religion and the Rise of Capitalism* (New York, 1926), 262–264.

7. For an argument that federal involvement in child dependency is needed, see Leroy Ashby, *Endangered Children: Dependency, Neglect, and Abuse in American History* (New York, 1997).

8. Theda Skopol, *Protecting Soldiers and Mothers* (Cambridge, 1992).

9. Walter Dean Burnham, *Critical Elections and the Mainsprings of American Politics* (New York, 1970), 71–90.

Charity and Poor Relief
in
Early Modern Europe

CHARLES H. PARKER

Poor Relief and Community in the Early Dutch Republic

Over the course of the sixteenth century, city governments in western Europe began to reorganize the patchwork of charitable foundations that had alleviated poverty for centuries into a comprehensive network of poor relief. In response to rising levels of poverty and social instability, a strong movement emerged in the 1520s that called on urban magistrates to reconstitute charitable institutions in keeping with the economic realities of the early sixteenth century.[1] The key features of this reform program included eliminating begging, consolidating all parish foundations under the authority of a municipal agency, laicizing charitable institutions, and establishing rigid criteria to identify the "deserving" poor. Although individual features of this plan had actually originated in the late middle ages, the aggregate character of the sixteenth-century program, along with its widespread acceptance, marked a new approach to urban poverty in western Europe.[2] By the end of the century, most cities in Europe had either completely reorganized parish charity along these lines or had adopted many of these principles.[3]

These dramatic changes have produced a great deal of scholarship over the motivations that led to the reorganization of charitable institutions. Until the late nineteenth century, most historians regarded Protestantism to be the singular force behind poor relief reform.[4] According to this view, the Protestant condemnation of the Catholic penitential system desacralized charity and thereby destroyed the rationale for begging and for the fragmented ecclesiastical foundations that provided benevolence. These historians also called attention to the fact that Martin Luther was an influential advocate of poor relief reform in Protestant areas of Germany.[5] From this viewpoint, the new welfare programs manifested a distinct Protestant social vision.[6]

Most scholarship in the twentieth century, however, has undermined the direct relationship between Protestantism and the origins of social welfare reform.[7] In the 1920s, Paul Bonenfant argued that the Catholic cities in the Low Countries that centralized poor relief in the 1520s did not recognize

anything Lutheran about these reforms.[8] Much more recently, Natalie Davis
has demonstrated that the fear of social instability inspired Protestants and
Catholics in Lyon to work together to create the aumône général (general
almshouse) in 1534.[9] And, Brian Pullan's massive study of charitable institutions in Venice has demonstrated that many components of the relief programs of the 1520s and 1530s predated the Protestant Reformation.[10] Consequently, Pullan has stressed the gradual evolution of sixteenth-century
reform and argued that there were few practical differences in charitable
institutions in Protestant and Catholic lands.[11]

Since the pioneering works of Davis and Pullan, most scholars no longer
consider Protestantism as the single factor in the formation of sixteenth-
century poor relief.[12] Yet it also remains clear that Protestantism was a powerful force in the development of centralized poor relief in many areas of
Europe. Eschewing the penitential incentive of traditional charity, Ulrich
Zwingli, like Luther, supported a centralized system of poor relief under the
aegis of lay magistrates in Zurich.[13] Likewise in Geneva, John Calvin gave
his approval to a centralized system that had been put in place before his
arrival.[14]

Given the Protestant support for centralized welfare under civil administration, it may appear surprising that Calvinist leaders in the province of
Holland opposed a fully centralized poor relief system that entailed merging
the diaconate (the church college responsible for charity) into a municipal
structure. To be sure, these Calvinists roundly condemned begging just as
they denounced the salvific motivations in Catholic charity. And in principle, they welcomed greater magisterial involvement in parish poor relief.
But they strongly resisted subordinating church deacons to municipal control and centralizing the revenues allotted for the poor. For Dutch Calvinists, incorporating the diaconate into an aggregate welfare network violated
the apostolic model of an independent diaconate that cared for those within
"the household of faith."

The reason that Calvinists advocated this exclusive agency for church
members was that the historical circumstances in which Dutch Calvinism
arose fostered a vision of Christian community that was distinct from civil
society. This Dutch Calvinist model stood in opposition to the traditional
understanding of the civic corporation promoted by urban magistrates and,
therefore, produced conflicts over the relationship between the Reformed
diaconate and municipal welfare institutions. The tensions in poor relief
organization sheds light of the divergent visions of Christian community
that came to the fore as a result of the Dutch Reformation. The ideals of
Calvinist charity came into conflict with the civic vision of magistrates in
three cities, Leiden, Delft, and Amsterdam. Despite varied institutional settle-

ments, the outcomes point to the distinct blend of religious pluralism and confessional identity in early modern Holland.

I. Poor Relief in the Municipal Community

Parish foundations, such as almshouses, hospitals, orphanages, and outside relief agencies (managed by lay regents known either as masters of the Holy Ghost "Heilige Geestmeesters" or as masters of the house poor "huiszittenmeesters") were the most extensive charitable institutions in the cities of late medieval Holland. Together with monastic cloisters, guilds, and confraternities, parish institutions formed a fragmented network of charity. Two primary ideals shaped the benevolent activity of parish relief in pre-Reformation Holland: charity was a sacred work and municipal residents constituted an organic spiritual and civic community. Informed by the religious ideals of medieval Catholicism, charity bound benefactor and recipient together in a sacred relationship.[15] Giving to the poor provided spiritual benefits to the donor as well as material assistance to the recipient. Although charitable giving was a spiritual work, prosperous laymen played the most central role in parish foundations

Burgers and residents in these cities understood themselves to be part of an indivisible Christian community that pursued eternal salvation and material welfare collectively. That is, urban elites promoted the ideal that their city was a corporate Christian community that served the spiritual and material interests of all residents.[16] In this cultural context, urban charity primarily served the poor of the municipal community and, thereby, reinforced its communal character. Thus, charity in the late middle ages reflected the cultural ethos of a corporate civic and spiritual community.

Compared to other cities in Europe, the towns of Holland began to centralize the poor relief institutions in their parishes at a very late date. It was not until 1577 that Leiden became the first city government to undertake poor relief reorganization; Delft and Amsterdam followed suit in 1597 and 1598, respectively.[17] The primary reason that centralization came later to these cities was that parish charity in each city was already well organized. Since the fourteenth century, magistrates in all of these cities had superintended almost the entire range of parish charity. They appointed the parish officers who distributed outside relief as well as the regents who managed the financial affairs of almshouses, hospitals, and orphanages.[18] Although magistrates had controlled almost every aspect of parish charity for a very long time, they did not possess the legal authority to centralize these institutions until 1575. In the aftermath of the Revolt against Spain, the States of Holland in March 1575 authorized magistrates to consolidate all charitable revenues at their discretion.[19]

II. Poor Relief in Dutch Calvinism

The late centralization of municipal poor relief in Holland was contemporaneous to the Revolt against Spain and the Calvinist Reformation in the United Provinces. Rewarding Calvinists for their unwavering support for the rebellion, the States of Holland and Zeeland declared in 1572 that the Reformed faith would be the official, "privileged" church of the rebellious provinces. In order to placate the opposition of city magistrates, most of whom had little sympathy for Calvinism, the States did not make the Reformed Church a formal state church, at least in the usual European sense. City governments paid the salaries of ministers, and Reformed worship services were held in the parish churches. But church membership was strictly voluntary, and the former properties of the Catholic Church (parish and monastic) came under the control of civil authorities.[20] Thus, citizenship, or residency in civil society, was not synonymous with church membership in a Reformed eucharistic community. Furthermore, the closed oligarchies that governed the cities of Holland sought to expand their political power and to keep a close check on the affairs of the local Reformed Church.[21]

This ambiguous settlement produced widespread disagreement and considerable negotiation over the role of the Reformed Church in Dutch society. Throughout the political turbulence of the 1560s and 1570s, magistrates were keen to protect their local privileges and liberties from outside influences, whether it was a Hapsburg government, a provincial stadholder, the States of Holland, or a Calvinist synod. Many city magistrates found common cause with a small, but vocal, cadre of ministers who also opposed the strong Calvinist character of the Dutch Reformed Church.[22] This faction, which Calvinists derisively labeled "Libertine," envisioned the new church to be a public church for all people.[23] Their vision of Dutch society was a Protestant version of the old medieval corporation. That is, they believed that the new Reformed Church, purged of clerical political pretensions, should support the needs of the city and its residents regardless of their own private religious inclinations. These opponents of Calvinism made it clear that the magistracy, as the "Christian authority," should govern most church affairs and should even select ministers and church officers of local congregations. Accordingly, Libertines worked to undermine an independent ecclesiastical structure (such as synods and presbyteries),[24] eliminate church discipline by the clergy, and place the diaconate under municipal control.[25]

Orthodox Calvinists, the dominant force in the Dutch Reformed Church since the early 1570s, understood their church to be a supralocal eucharistic community that was distinct from local civil society. To protect the purity of the community, ministers and elders regulated access to communion and disciplined members, while deacons distributed alms to the poor within "the household of faith." This ideal was reinforced by the fierce religious persecution that had taken place in the Low Countries from 1566 to 1572, the formative years of Dutch Calvinism.[26] During this period, Reformed leaders fled to London, Emden, the Palatinate, and Geneva, while others took their chances living clandestinely "under the cross." The Duke of Alba's bloody reign in the Low Countries fostered an exile mentality among Dutch Calvinists that led them to understand Christian community as primarily a eucharistic body and not a civil one.[27]

Under the leadership of Johannes a'Lasco, the exiled churches in London and Emden put into practice the ministries that would later become a staple of the Reformed Churches of the Netherlands. The members of this cohesive body were mutually interdependent and responsible before God for supporting those within the religious community. Care for the poor members was basic to the task of the church and a sacred duty for deacons. In holding on to this apostolic example, the community would honor God and serve as a witness to those outside the faith.[28] Under the supervision of the consistory (the governing church college of ministers and lay elders), deacons were to collect alms, keep a financial account of receipts and distributions, inquire into the needs of the congregation, visit the sick, and distribute assistance to those in distress. A'Lasco also stipulated that deacons should ferret out those recipients who conducted themselves dishonorably and cast shame onto the congregation.[29] Poor relief and its disciplinary mechanisms were a dual-pronged attempt to forge a self-sustaining and pure religious community in the exile churches.[30]

The practices of the Reformed Church in exile became prescribed in the synodal protocols of the Dutch Reformed Church during the 1570s and 1580s.[31] These synods unified the doctrine, offices, and ministries of the Reformed Churches of the Netherlands.[32] In terms of church governance, the consistory had the authority to regulate all internal church affairs, such as the preaching of the gospel, administering the sacraments, disciplining wayward members, and overseeing the work of the deacons. The synods established the diaconate as a distinct ecclesiastical office and designated it as the only relief agency for members of the Dutch Reformed Church.[33]

The synodal representatives also set forth the Reformed perspective on the relationship between the diaconate and municipal charitable organizations. They regarded diaconal charity as a function of an independent eucharistic community, a condition that necessitated independence from municipal control. Based on their view of the apostolic church, Calvinists placed the highest priority on the needs of church members and tried to make sure that recipients followed the moral dictates set forth by the Reformed Church. The ideal condition was for an independent diaconate to receive a portion of its revenues from the income of parish poor relief agencies without any municipal interference. Traditional parish foundations such as the Table of the Holy Ghost should care for the "general" poor and the church should limit its relief efforts to church members. While the synods held to an independent diaconate, they also recognized that cooperation with parish or municipal agencies might be necessary. Yet even in these circumstances, the consistory and not the city government was to have direct authority over the deacons. Moreover, the deacons were still to maintain a distinct fund for poor members and to create a separate register of relief recipients.[34]

In disparate political circumstances in the cities of Holland, Reformed consistories attempted to implement the communal ideal of Reformed charity by defending an independent diaconate for church members. Given the economic hardships in the late sixteenth century, magistrates were not necessarily averse to a new charitable agency. At the same time, many local officials were less than enthusiastic about an ecclesiastical agency over which they had little control and any favoritism for church members. For them, clerical independence in discipline and poor relief smacked of an ecclesiastical tyranny that Netherlanders were fighting to overthrow.[35]

These disputes over authority connoted a deeper conflict over what actually constituted a Christian community during this critical period in Dutch history. Holding to the ideal that the city was a unified corporation, magistrates expected deacons to contribute to the welfare of all residents without distinction. Calvinists, however, rooted their understanding of poor relief in the eucharistic community, and they attempted to reserve the deacons for needy church members.

III. Three Trends in Poor Relief Organization

The settlements in Amsterdam, Leiden, and Delft represented the prevailing three trends of poor relief organization in the cities of Holland. For Calvinists, the most preferable arrangement took place in Amsterdam, which allowed the deacons to assist only church members, while municipal almoners provided charity to the city poor. The most unwelcome organization was a merger between the diaconate and a city poor relief agency under the authority of the magistracy. This situation occurred in Leiden in 1582 and eventually in Delft in 1614. Before 1614, a third type of settlement characterized poor relief in Delft. This arrangement permitted the deacons to care for church members but also required that these church officers assume most of the burden for outside relief in the city.

The poor relief arrangements in Amsterdam represented the highest aspirations of Reformed charity in Holland. In Amsterdam, a consistory dominated by uncompromising Calvinists had close ties with Reform-minded leaders in the city government. As a result, the Amsterdam diaconate was able to maintain its independence without the burden of providing outside relief to nonmembers. By virtue of wealthy lay benefactors and municipal subsidies, the deacons administered an enormous chest that was unrivaled throughout the Netherlands.[36]

Calvinists dominated the Amsterdam city government from 1578 to 1620. Shortly after joining the side of William the Orange in 1578, the magistracy in Amsterdam was purged of the uncompromising Catholic faction (known as the *Dirkisten*, after its leader Hendrik Dirkz), who had held power since 1538.[37] Ten of the fifteen Protestant leaders who had opposed Dirksz in 1564 (known as the *Doleanten*) served as burgomasters between 1578 and 1588. In addition, Protestants filled all four burgomaster positions after the "Alteration." In the new thirty-six member city council, thirteen members were strong Calvinists who had fled Amsterdam in 1567 after the city chose to remain loyal to Phillip II. Thirteen other members were moderate Protestants who had not been implicated in the tumultuous events of 1566 and 1567, and ten members were Catholics who had supported the rebellion.[38]

The new magistracy proved to be wholly sympathetic to the Amsterdam consistory and diaconate. Like most cities in Holland, the Amsterdam city government was for all intents and purposes a closed oligarchy that continued to hold the reins of power throughout the sixteenth century by coopting family members into the *vroedschap*. Sixteen members of the 1578 city council were succeeded by family members, while thirteen of the seventeen burgomasters from 1578 to 1590 were sons or sons-in-law of previous burgomasters.[39] At the turn of the century, a number of magistrates even more concerned with confessional orthodoxy than their predecessors assumed leadership in the city government. These magistrates came to power during the period in which theological disputes over predestination became intertwined with hotly contested political issues.[40] Regents such as Reynier Pauw, Gerrit Jacob Witsen, Barthold Cromhout, Frans Hendricksz Oetgens, and Claes Fransz Oetgens allied themselves with an orthodox church council led by Pieter Plancius and Jacob Trigland.[41] These magistrates, in concert with the consistory, promoted the Contra-Remonstrant cause in the Republic, launched an East Indies trading company, and supported Maurice's opposition to prolonging peace with Spain.[42]

Although diaconal poor relief was not without its critics among Amsterdam regents, the dominance of the Calvinists in the city government enabled the deacons to confine poor relief to church members and to count on a good deal of financial assistance from the government. The Amsterdam consistory annually nominated a slate of candidates from which the congregation chose deacons for two-year terms. The six deacons met weekly to decide who merited relief and to distribute church alms to those poor members in good standing.[43] In addition, the deacons were required to visit poor members in order to ensure that their faith and lifestyle were in conformity with the church's standards, and that the recipients were not misusing their alms.[44] Those who were lacking in any of these areas jeopardized their subsidy. The diaconate concentrated its relief efforts on outside relief to members until later in the seventeenth century, when they also began to shoulder the burden of orphans in the city.[45]

The Amsterdam diaconate was also unique in Holland in that it operated from a substantial chest, despite the fact that municipal almoners continued to collect alms in the two central parish churches after the Reformation.[46] According to their annual accounts, they never operated in the red after 1578 and usually had a significant amount of residual revenues. The deacons obtained their revenues from voluntary donations and house-to-house collections from members. The Amsterdam diaconate received annual subsidies from the city government from a one-thousandth penny on VOC (Dutch East India Company) transactions.[47] In addition, the magistracy made annual grants to the diaconate.[48] For this reason, the Amsterdam diaconate was able to provide occasional assistance to a number of other poorer congregations in the Netherlands throughout this period. From 1578 to 1587, they sent relief to Reformed churches in Schoonhooven, Oudewater (both in 1578), Enkhuizen (1581), Brussels, Oosteinde, Utrecht (all in 1583), Antwerp, Dordrecht (both in 1584), and Arnhem (1587).[49] For the purposes of this study, providing assistance to Reformed congregations outside the city, the province, and the Republic suggests a distinctive Calvinist vision of community. They envisioned Christian community to be the supralocal "household of faith"; consequently they provided relief to help maintain that body throughout the Low Countries.

Because of the Reformed sympathies on the *vroedschap* from 1578 to 1620, the diaconate worked comparatively smoothly with city authorities in Amsterdam. In 1583, the city government proposed a union of the diaconate with the city almoners, but when the consistory objected to the plan, the deacons were allowed to continue to operate independently of the municipal almoners. The deacons cooperated with the municipal almoners to ensure that poor relief recipients did not receive relief from both agencies. The deacons supported poor church members, while city almoners distributed charity to the poor of the city.[50] In 1598, when magistrates completely consolidated all parish poor relief institutions in the city, the Amsterdam diaconate retained its independence.[51] Even in a situation where the Reformed congregation could count on the support of a sympathetic magistracy, the Calvinist ministers, elders, and deacons resisted merging its poor relief agency with a municipal one.

The cases of Leiden and Delft show, however, that Calvinists did not always have this option available to them. The magistrates in Leiden exhibited a bitter animosity toward Reformed Calvinism and the poor relief arrangement there also represented the most disagreeable outcome for Calvinists in Holland. Leiden's magistrates compelled the Reformed consistory to merge the diaconate with the centralized municipal agency in 1582. In Leiden this issue became part of a broader and highly rancorous dispute during the late 1570s and 1580s over the practice of consistorial discipline, the appointment of church officers, and the validity of the Dutch Confession of Faith in the Leiden church.[52]

After two years of siege and strife in Leiden, a city government finally emerged in 1574 that was loyal to William of Orange.[53] Although Leiden's Calvinists saw the hand of God in this triumph, they soon discovered that the magistracy's allegiance to the new order also meant the city government intended to exercise a great deal of authority over the new church.[54] While Calvinists could be assured of a city government more favorable to their concerns, this favor entailed more civil control than Reformers were willing to grant. The noted historian Robert Fruin has remarked that the Leiden city government "respected rather than loved the new order."[55] With a memory of the 1566 *beeldenstorm* (iconoclasm) and the destructive plundering of Beggar troops in 1572,[56] Leiden's regents actively resisted clerical claims to autonomy, a stance that made them infamous among the Calvinist ministers in Holland.

After the dust settled from the war in Leiden, the problem of poor relief had become an urgent matter. The collapse of the textile manufacturing, the most important industry in Leiden, brought unprecedented poverty to the city. It was a truism that "there were more beggars in Leiden than in the rest of Holland."[57] In order to deal with the acute economic difficulty, a commission of burgomasters in 1577 recommended that all incomes and properties devoted to poor relief were to be directed to a central fund and all beggars were to be deported.[58] The commissioners also proposed eliminating entirely collections during the church services because it interfered with the sermons and because many people, especially Catholics, refused to attend church.[59]

In the 1577 plan, the magistracy allowed the church to operate an independent diaconate that would only serve poor members. Perhaps this decision was a result of the presence of large numbers of religious refugees that would have overstrained municipal resources.[60] The strident Calvinists on the consistory believed that diaconal charity was an integral part of the confessional community; but for the burgomasters it was a way to unburden municipal charity from the weight of religious refugees.

Five years later, however, the Leiden magistracy reversed itself. In 1582 the magistrates forced the consistory to merge the diaconate with city almoners. According to this new ordinance, six deacons would serve alongside six almoners, thereby uniting ecclesiastical and municipal poor relief into one administrative unit. All revenues for poor relief, including church collections, city-wide collections, donations, propertied revenues, and testaments, went into a central chest. The city council limited the deacons' specific domain of service to outside relief. Both the city council and the consistory participated in the annual selection of deacons, who served for a term of two years.[61]

This decision came during fierce struggles between the magistracy and strong-minded Calvinists in the consistory over the role of the new church in post-Reformation Leiden.[62] The 1578 Synod of Dordrecht had stipulated that in cases where the municipal authority impeded the work of the diaconate, the consistory was to defend the activity of the diaconate and to call upon the classis (presbytery) for support.[63] For their part, Leiden Calvinists protested that a merger would oblige the deacons to give charity to "barbarians" and would short-change poor church members.[64] Nevertheless, above this protest and four subsequent years of opposition, the magistracy compelled the deacons to merge with municipal almoners under the authority of the city government. The diaconate lost its autonomy and undermined the confessional aims of Calvinist charity in Leiden.

Delft represented a third trend in poor relief organization as the diaconate there inadvertently became the primary charitable agency in the city. In the aftermath of the Beggar victory in Delft, the magistracy experienced very little displacement. Only six new members matriculated into the city council and all regents maintained their previous positions.[65] Throughout this period, Delft's city government was made up of a large number of regents who had Protestant inclinations but did not accept the rigid confessional stance of Dutch Calvinism.[66] As was the case in Leiden, many of these Delft magistrates displayed a strong aversion to Calvinist claims to independent self-governance.[67] Reminiscent of the Catholic Church's function in pre-Reformation Delft, these magistrates considered the new church largely a public institution that should serve the needs of the entire community.

Despite the continuity in the city government after 1572, there was a much greater degree of collaboration between the magistracy and the Calvinist-dominated consistory in Delft than in Leiden. In his comparative essay on these two cities, J. J. Woltjer has attributed this stability to the personal connections between the consistory and magistracy in Delft.[68] Between 1573 and 1621, at least thirty elders or deacons served in the city council.[69] Furthermore, Arent Cornelisz, the most prominent minister in Delft, expended a great deal of effort to nurture the consistory's relationship with the city fathers. The son of a Delft burgomaster, Cornelisz grew up in Delft and returned from exile in 1573 to shepherd the congregation there until his death in 1605. One of the most important Reformed ministers in Holland, Cornelisz became the consistory's primary delegate in its relations with the magistracy.[70] As a result of these personal connections, the Delft consistory enjoyed a cooperative, yet often precarious, relationship with the city government.

In the late fall of 1573, church leaders in Delft informed the magistrates that they intended to select its own elders and deacons without municipal interference. Warning the ministers to stay out of political affairs, the Delft magistrates treated this as a request to which they consented.[71] Yet the consistory's assertion of an independent diaconate for church members would ultimately carry a high price tag for ecclesiastical poor relief. Since the deacons received church collections and occasionally obtained a modicum of support from the city government, the Delft magistrates required that the deacons assume a primary role in providing outside relief to all of the domiciled poor in the city. Consequently, the Delft deacons shouldered the primary burden for outside relief in the city until 1614.

Until 1614, the Delft diaconate functioned as a universal charitable agency in the city. While the Reformed Church was not necessarily opposed to aiding nonmembers, its primary aim was to care for needy members in "the household of faith." In addition, church officers were rather ambivalent about taking over the burden of outside relief services in the city. But in 1574 the consistory decided that the deacons should also serve nonmembers in order to maintain an independent diaconate for church members.[72] In August 1580, Arent Cornelisz complained to the burgomasters that the deacons were assisting as many nonmembers as they were members, a condition that drained resources away from the church poor.[73] Throughout this period, the deacons kept a separate register of recipients who were members and attempted to raise additional revenue to support the poor within "the household of faith."[74]

The primary goal of the consistory, therefore, was to establish the diaconate as the exclusive charitable agency for members of their eucharistic community. The implementation of this ideal meant that the deacons would also have to provide charity to those outside the faith. This arrangement produced a great deal of financial adversity for the church; from 1584 to 1600 poor relief expenditures outpaced the receipts from church collections by a monthly average of 269 guilders.[75] Throughout this period, the consistory consistently appealed to the magistrates to help augment the incomes of the diaconate. While the city government occasionally granted assistance on a short-term basis, it did not establish a permanent means to offset the expenses of diaconal charity.

Due to the complaints of ministers, elders, and deacons, the burgomasters proposed in 1597 that the deacons merge with a newly created muncipal relief institution, the Kamer van Charitate. In the spirit of sixteenth-century poor relief reform, the Kamer would consolidate all charitable agencies in the city and provide work for unemployed men and orphans. Given the chronic deficits of the diaconate, this proposal presented a dilemma for church leaders. After some deliberation, the consistory rejected the merger because it would violate "the apostolic example" of Reformed charity.[76] Thus, the consistory and diaconate opted for apostolic integrity over financial security, revealing the tenacity with which they would cling to their vision of a poor relief agency rooted in the offices of the church. The magistrates made it clear to the consistory that they were not altogether happy with the consistory's decision, but nevertheless, they permitted them to remain independent.[77]

Unfortunately for Reformed charity, this decision saddled the deacons with even greater responsibility for outside relief. The deacon's poor relief register swelled from 499 recipients in 1602 to 633 recipients in 1607, three-fourths of which were not church members.[78] The rising number of recipients produced even greater deficits; monthly deficit of the deacons rose to an average of 715 guilders from 1600 to 1611.[79] The consistory consistently appealed to the burgomasters for a long-term basis of financial support. Despite the consistory's efforts, the burgomasters would only agree to periodic short-term grants, and they regularly criticized the deacons for bad management.[80]

Due to the religious tensions associated with the Remonstrant controversy and the weak financial base of Reformed charity in the 1610s, the Delft magistrates began to take a much harsher stance against an independent diaconate. Consequently, in January 1614, the city government issued an ordinance that merged the diaconate with the Kamer van Charitate under magisterial authority.[81] While there is no record of the consistory's response to this measure, in the ensuing negotiations the consistory fought tooth and nail to retain certain confessional characteristics of diaconal charity. The consistory sought to place the deacons on an equal footing with regents of the Kamer and to keep the church poor distinguished from non-members. Originally, the city government had stipulated in 1614 that eight deacons should serve alongside the twelve municipal regents. Shortly after the incorporation, the magistrates reduced the size of the Kamer's administration to four deacons and six regents.[82] By April 1617, however, the consistory was able to petition the magistrates successfully to balance the number of municipal regents with a diaconal equivalent. One month later, the magistrates agreed that six deacons should serve with six regents.[83]

To be sure, the Delft diaconate lost its autonomy in this merger. Yet the consistory was able to incorporate several characteristics of Calvinist poor relief in the Kamer. One deacon and one municipal regent were assigned to districts (*wijkjes*) which the consistory had devised in 1574 to investigate the needs and morals of the poor.[84] Like the old Reformed inspectors (*opsienders*), district masters (*wijkmeesters*) now assisted deacons and almoners by keeping watch over activities in their districts.[85] The six deacons and their six municipal counterparts distributed charity three times per week: Mondays and Fridays for nonmembers and Saturdays for church members.[86] The separate distribution for members suggests that the church leadership in Delft continued to maintain a distinction between the poor within "the household of faith" and the poor outside the religious community, even though it was largely symbolic.

IV. Concluding Summary

The historical framework that enveloped Dutch Calvinism in the late sixteenth century points to the conditions in which a Protestant denomination would resist the complete centralization of poor relief. From 1566 to 1572, persecution and exile reinforced the Calvinist understanding that the church was a gathered eucharistic community set apart from temporal society. For these Calvinists, the diaconate should primarily care for the poor within the "household of faith." After 1572, the ambiguous status of the Dutch Reformed Church placed this Calvinist vision at odds with most magistrates who expected the church to support the civic traditions of the municipal corporation. According to these magistrates, the diaconate should work under civil control and serve all the "deserving" poor in the city. The negotiations between city governments and Calvinist consistories over poor relief came out of the Holland's unique political and religious profile. While most other Protestant states in Europe were trying to standardize the new poor relief program, the cities of Holland were attempting to reconcile the overlapping demands of civic welfare and Protestant charity at the end of the sixteenth century. In this respect, the aims of Calvinist poor relief, despite profound theological differences, bore a closer resemblance to confraternal charity in Catholic countries than to the Protestant contributions to centralized social welfare.

Notes

1. Between 1522 and 1526, Protestant cities in the Empire (Wittenberg, Nuremberg, Strasbourg, and Augsburg) and Catholic cities in the Southern Low Countries (Ypres, Bruges, Mons) and Italy (Venice) were among the first to enact these reforms. Jean-Pierre Gutton, *La Société et les pauvres en Europe XVIe–XVIIIe siècles* (Paris, 1974), 104–106; J. Nolf, *La réforme de la bienfaisance publique a' Ypres au XVIe siècle* (Ghent, 1915), xl–xliii; P. Bonenfant, "Les origines et le charactère de la réforme de la bienfaisance publique aux Pays-Bas sous le règne de Charles-Quint," *Revue Belgique de Philologie et d'Histoire* 6 (1927): 219–220, 225–226.

2. Brian Pullan, *Rich and Poor in Renaissance Venice: The Social Institutions of a Catholic State* (Cambridge, 1971), 198–215. Brian Tierney, *Medieval Poor Law: A Sketch of Canonical Theory and Its Application in England* (Berkeley, 1959), 131–132. Robert Jütte, *Poverty and Deviance in Early Modern Europe* (Cambridge, 1994), 102.

3. For useful surveys of the implementation of these reforms across Europe, see Jütte, *Poverty and Deviance*, 105–125; Camille Bloch, *L'Assistance et l'état en France à la vielle de la Revolution* (Geneve, 1909), 44; Gutton, *La Société et les pauvres*, 105–109. Elements of these reforms also took place in Italian and Spanish cities, which until recently have been considered outside the realm of centralized poor relief. Pullan, *Rich and Poor*, 239–422; Linda Martz, *Poverty and Welfare in Hapsburg Spain. The Example of Toledo* (Cambridge, 1983), 61–158; Maureen Flynn, *Sacred Charity: Confraternities and Social Welfare in Spain, 1400–1700* (Ithaca, 1989), 75–141. This does not mean, though, that decentralized forms of poor relief became extinct at the end of the sixteenth century. In Catholic countries, confraternal charity existed well into the eighteenth century. And during the Counter Reformation, private religious foundations even made a comeback. Yet in most areas these religious institutions either worked alongside of centralized municipal agencies, cooperated with them, or took over the entire range of parish poor relief. Jütte, *Poverty and Deviance*, 125–139.

4. See Otto Winckelmann, "Über die ältesten Armenordnung der Reformationszeit," *Historische Vierteljahrschrift* 17 (1914/1915): 376–384.

5. Carter Lindberg, *Beyond Charity: Reformation Initiatives for the Poor* (Minneapolis: Fortress Press, 1993), 119–126.

6. Ernst Troeltsch, *The Social Teaching of the Christian Churches*, 2 vols., 2nd. ed., trans. by Olive Wyon (New York, 1960) I: 133–138; Winckelmann, "Armenordnung," 361–440. For this approach in later twentieth-century historiography, see Harold Grimm, "Luther's Contributions to Sixteenth-Century Organization of Poor Relief," *Archiv fhr Reformationsgeschichte* 61 (1970): 222–234; Carter Lindberg, "'There Should Be No Beggars Among Christians': Karlstadt, Luther, and the Origins of Protestant Poor Relief," *Church History* 46 (1977): 313–334; idem., *Beyond Charity*.

7. Franz Ehrle, *Beitrage zur Geschichte und Reform der Armenpflege* (Freiburg, 1881); George Ratzinger, *Geschichte des kirchlichen Armenpflege* (Freiburg, 1884); P. Bonnenfant, "Origines," 207–230; L. Feuchtwanger, "Geschichte der sozialen Politik und des Armenwesens im Zeitalter der Reformation," *Jahrbuch fhr Gesetzgebung, Verwaltung und Volkswirtschaft* 32 (1908): 167–204 and 33 (1909): 191–228.

8. Bonnenfant, "Origines," 220–223.

9. Natalie Zemon Davis, "Humanism, Heresy, and Poor Relief in Sixteenth-Century Lyon," in *Society and Culture in Early Modern France* (Stanford, 1975), 56–60.

10. Pullan, *Rich and Poor*, 198.

11. Pullan, *Rich and Poor*, 11–12, 104, 197. Pullan does note that Catholic charity continued to concern itself with the salvation of benefactor and recipient. Idem., "Catholics and the Poor in Early Modern Europe," *Transactions of the Royal Historical Society*, series 5, 26 (1976): 25–30.

12. Most scholars now agree that poor relief reform cut across confessional lines. For some of the most important local studies that take this approach, see Lee Palmer Wandel, *Always Among Us: Images of the Poor in Zwingli's Zurich* (Cambridge, 1990), 13–15; Davis, "Poor Relief," 56–60; Martz, *Toledo*, 7–34; Jütte, *Poverty and Deviance*, 100–105; Kathryn Norberg, *Rich and Poor in Grenoble, 1600–1814* (Berkeley, 1985), 61, 148.

13. Lindberg, *Beyond Charity*, 119–145; Wandel, *Always Among Us: Images of the Poor in Zwingli's Zurich* (Cambridge, 1991), 124–169.

14. Robert Kingdon, "Social Welfare in Calvin's Geneva," *American Historical Review* 76 (1971): 52–56.

15. Joke Spaans, *Haarlem na de Reformatie, stedelijke cultuur en kerkelijke leven* ('s-Gravenhage, 1989), 163; F.R.J. Knetsch, " 'De Armen hebt gij altijd bij U' Religieus gemotiveerde armenzorg in de stad Groningen, Enkele inleidende opmerkingen," in *Geloven in Groningen, Capita Selecta uit de geloofsgeschiedenis van een stad*, ed. Ds. G. v. Halsema Then, Jos. M.M. Hermans, F.R.J. Knetsch (Kampen, 1990), 11; Johannes Everts, *De Verhouding van kerk en staat in het bijzonder ten aanzien der armverzorging* (Utrecht, 1908), 4–8; W. P. Blockmans and W. Prevenier, "Armoede in de Nederlanden van de 14e tot het midden van de 16e eeuw: bronnen en problemen," *Tijdschrift voor Geschiedenis* 88 (1975), 4: 520.

16. Scholarship on many cities in northern Europe has shown that the collective nature of religious life reinforced the civic traditions promoted by municipal leaders. Some of the most important works taking this approach include, Bernd Moeller, *The Imperial Cities and the Reformation: Three Essays*, H. C. Erik Midelfort and Mark U. Edwards, eds. (Durham, N.C., 1982), 44–49; Thomas A. Brady, Jr., *Ruling Class, Regime, and Reformation in Strasbourg 1520–1555* (Leiden, 1978), 17–18; A. N. Galpern, *The Religions of the People in Sixteenth Century Champagne* (Cambridge, 1976), 17, 38–39, 102–103; Barbara Diefendorf, *Beneath the Cross: Catholics and Huguenots in Sixteenth-Century Paris* (New York, 1991), chapter two; Natalie Zemon Davis, "The Sacred and the Body Social in Sixteenth Century Lyon," *Past and Present* 90 (1981): 40–41. Adriaan H. Bredero, *Christenheid en Christendom in de middeleeuwen: over de verhouding van godsdienst, kerk, en samenleving*, 2nd. ed. (Kampen, 1987), 277; Spaans, *Haarlem*, 163; Herman Roodenburg, *Onder censuur, De kerkelijke tucht in de gereformeerde gemeente van Amsterdam, 1578–1700* (Hilversum, 1990), 65–71.

17. Christina Ligtenberg, *De Armezorg te Leiden tot het einde van de 16e eeuw* ('s-Gravenhage, 1908), 229–230; Gemeente Archief te Delft. Archief van de Kamer van Charitate; inv. nr. 43, ff. 7r, 1596; Gemeente Archief te Amsterdam. Archief van de Burgermeesteren; inv. nr. 5023, ff. 179r, April 27, 1597.

18. Jan Wagenaar, *Amsterdam, in zyne opkomst, aanwas geschiedenissen*, 3 vols.

(Amsterdam, 1760), 2: 262; Ligtenberg, *Armezorg te Leiden*, 159, 166; G. Verhoeven, *Devotie en Negotie, Delft als bedevaartplaats in de late middeleeuwen* (Amsterdam, 1992), 26. In addition, each of these cities had issued anti-begging ordinances since the fifteenth century, which aimed primarily at restricting begging by nonresidents.

19. Ligtenberg, *Armezorg te Leiden*, 298; J. F. van Beeck Calkoen, *Onderzoek naar den rechtstoestand der geestelijk en kerkelijke goederen in Holland na de Reformatie* (Amsterdam, 1910), 47–48.

20. A.Th. van Deursen, "Kerk of Parochie? De Kerkmeesters en de dood tijdens de Republiek," *Tijdschrift voor Geschiedenis* 89 (1976): 531–535. Numerically, the Reformed Church grew very slowly and only claimed about 20 percent of the population by 1620. J. J. Woltjer, "De plaats van de calvinisten in de Nederlandse samenleving," *Zeventiende eeuw* 10 (1994): 16.

21. James D. Tracy, "The Calvinist Church of the Dutch Republic, 1572–1618/19," in *Reformation Europe: A Guide to Research II*, William S. Maltby, ed. (St. Louis, 1992), 261–262.

22. Benjamin J. Kaplan, " 'Remnants of the Papal Yoke': Apathy and Opposition in the Dutch Reformation," *Sixteenth Century Journal* 25 (1994), 3: 659–662.

23. Benjamin J. Kaplan, *Calvinists and Libertines, Confession and Community in Utrecht, 1578–1620* (Oxford, 1995), 75.

24. The organizational structure of the Dutch Refomed Church followed a Presbyterian form of church government. Comprised of lay elders and ministers, the consistory governed the ministries of the local congregation. Consistories sent delegates to a larger regional body, the classis, which met regularly to resolve disputes, examine ministerial candidates, and discuss common concerns among local churches. Beyond the classis, synods were held at both the provincial and national levels to clarify doctrine and settle matters of church polity.

25. Kaplan, *Calvinists and Libertines*, 68–81.

26. Andrew Pettegree, *Emden and the Dutch Revolt: Exile and the Development of Reformed Protestantism* (Oxford, 1992), 228–229; see also idem., *Foreign Protestant Communities in Sixteenth-Century London* (Oxford, 1986).

27. Andrew Pettegree, "Exile and the Development of Reformed Protestantism," paper presented to the Sixteenth Century Studies Conference, Toronto, Ontario, October 29, 1994. Heiko Oberman has observed that Calvinists throughout Europe considered themselves to be perpetual refugees. This outlook gave them the "flexibility to dominate cities when they were in the majority and to survive as underground communities when they were in the minority." Heiko Oberman *"Europa afflicta*: the Reformation of the Refugees," *Archiv für Reformationsgeschichte* 83 (1992): 99.

28. Wilhelm Bernoulli, *Das Diakonenamt bei J.a Lasco* (Grifense, 1951), 12, 16.

29. Bernoulli, *a Lasco*, 15.

30. Heinz Schilling, "Reformierte Kirchenzucht als Sozialdisziplinierung? Die Tätigkeit des Emder Presbyteriums in den Jahren 1557–1562 (Mit vergleichenden Betrachtungen hber die Kirchenräte in Groningen und Leiden, sowie mit einem Ausblick ins 17. Jahrhundert)," in: *Niederlande und Nordwestdeutschland. Studien zur Regional- und Stadtsgeschichte Nordwestkontinentaleuropas im Mittelalter und in der Neuzeit*, ed. by Wilfried Ehbrecht (Cologne, 1983), 263, 273–275, 321.

31. Alastair Duke and Rosemary Jones: "Towards a Reformed Polity in Holland, 1572–1578," in *Reformation and Revolt in the Low Countries* (London, 1990), 223.

32. Due to conflicts over the relationship between political and religious jurisdictions, the Estates of Holland did not ratify any church order drawn up by the synods until the Synod of Dordrecht in 1618/1619. Nevertheless, the Reformed consistories in most cities of Holland attempted to follow the synodal resolutions.

33. The most important synodal decisions regarding the diaconate may be found in J. Reitsma and S. D. van Veen eds., *Acta der Provinciale en Particuliere Synoden, Gehouden in de Noordelijke Nederlanden gedurende de jaren 1572–1620*, vol. 2, Noord-Holland 1618–1620, Zuid-Holland 1574–1592 (Groningen, 1893), 127–156; F. L. Rutgers ed., *Acta van de Nederlandse Synoden der Zestiende Eeuw* ('s-Gravenhage, 1889), 25–31.

34. Reitsma and van Veen, *Acta*, 138–139, 261.

35. For crticisms of Calvinist practice see, Johannes Uytenbogaert, *Kerckelijcke Historie, vervatende verscheyden ghedenckwaerdige saken, in de Christenheyt voorgevallen. Van het jaer vier hondert af, tot in het jaer sesthien-hondert ende negenthien. Voornamelijck in dese Geunieerde provintien* (Rotterdam, 1647), 799. For the growing rift within the Reformed Church during the late sixteenth century, see Kaplan, *Calvinists and Libertines*, 28–110.

36. In 1578 the Amsterdam diaconate showed a surplus of 536 guilders, an amount that increased to 5,076 guilders in 1593, to 25,289 guilders in 1605, and 95,532 guilders in 1620. Casparus Commelin, *Beschryvinge van Amsterdam*, 2 vols., second ed. (Amsterdam, 1729), 2: 489–490.

37. James D. Tracy, "A Premature Counter Reformation: The Dirkist Government of Amsterdam, 1538–1578," *Journal of Religious History* 13 (1984), 2: 151–153.

38. Carl Bangs, *Arminius: A Study in the Dutch Reformation*, 2nd. ed. (Grand Rapids, Mich., 1985), 91–94. The leader of this party, Hendrik Dirksz never again sat on the *vroedschap* after 1578. Johan E. Elias, *Geschiedenis van het Amsterdamsche regentenpatriciaat* ('s-Gravenhage, 1923), 9–13, 19–20.

39. Elias, *Regentenpatriciaat*, 22–23, 28–29.

40. The two primary antagonists were the stadhouder, Prince Maurice of Orange, and Johannes Oldenbarnevelt, pensionaris of the States of Holland. Maurice backed the Contra-Remonstrants and advocated war with Spain at the end of the Twelve Year's Truce (1621), whereas Oldenbarnevelt championed the Remonstrant cause and resisted renewal of the war. Amsterdam stood at the center of these conflicts. And, the victory of Prince Maurice over Oldenbarnevelt in the Northern Netherlands and the Contra-Remonstrant triumph at the Synod of Dort owed a great deal to the support of the triumphant Calvinist party in Amsterdam. Jonathan Israel, *The Dutch Republic, Its Rise, Greatness, and Fall, 1477–1806* (Oxford, 1995), 403–485.

41. Johan E. Elias ed., *De Vroedschap van Amsterdam, 1578–1795*, 2 vols. (Haarlem, 1903), I: lv.

42. Elias, *Regentenpatriciaat*, 50. The Remonstrants, however, also had support in the Amsterdam magistracy. The burgomaster Cornelis Pietersz Hooft was one of the most vocal and prolific critics of confessional Calvinism. Hooft condemned an independent diaconate because he believed that it favored the church poor over those who had to make do with allotments from municipal institutions. Cornelis Pieterzoon Hooft, *Memorien en Adviësen* (1616; repub., Utrecht, 1871), 54. Working alongside Hooft were Lauren Jacobsz Real, Jacob Arminius' father-in-law, P. C. Boom and C. van Teyligen, friends of Arminius. Bangs, *Arminius*, 235. These magistrates believed

that asserting governmental control over the church would promote the measure of religious freedom necessary for a merchant city. Consequently, they became strong supporters of Oldenbarnevelt and fierce adversaries of confessional Calvinism.

43. Gemeente Archief te Amsterdam. Archief van de Nederlands Hervormd Gemeente; Protocollen van de Bijzonderen Kerkeraad, May 24, 1578, July 1, 1578, August 15, 1579, November 14, 1579 (hereafter cited as GAA. Kerkeraad, according to date); R. B. Evenhuis, *Ook dat was Amsterdam. De kerk der hervorming in de Gouden Eeuw*, 5 vols. (Amsterdam, 1965–1978), 2: 74; Commelin, *Amsterdam*, 2: 489.

44. GAA. Kerkeraad (April 7, 1579, November 14, 1579, January 9, 1597).

45. Evenhuis, *Ook dat was Amsterdam*, 2: 75.

46. The deacons did win the concession to take collections in Reformed churches that were built after 1578. Evenhuis, *Ook dat was Amsterdam*, 2: 21, 77.

47. Evenhuis, *Ook dat was Amsterdam*, 2: 75; Charlotte A. van Manen, *Armenpflege in Amsterdam in ihrer historischen Entwicklung* (Leiden, 1913), 50.

48. The city treasury records mention in 1621 that the annual subsidy to the deacons would be raised from 3,120 to 3,600 guilders, indicating the level of support the diaconate received from the city government. Gemeente Archief te Amsterdam, Archief van de Thesaurien Ordinaris, 1490–1824; #1 Resolutien, Notuleringen en Verbalen, ff. 76v February 19, 1621. In addition to these subsidies, the Reformed deacons received 100 ponden vlaems from the kerkmeesters of the Oude Kerk and 1,200 ponden vlaems from the kerkmeesters of the Nieuwe Kerk in 1602. Wagenaar, *Amsterdam*, 2: 151.

49. On some occasions the consistory did appeal to the burgomasters to help them raise funds for these churches. GAA. Kerkeraad (October 9, 1578, December 30, 1578, January 6, 1581, April 28, 1583, October 4, 1583, December 18, 1583, January 24, 1584, November 7, 1584, and February 21, 1587).

50. Evenhuis, *Ook dat was Amsterdam*, 2: 74, 78; Van Deursen, *Bavianen*, 106; Van Manen, *Armenpflege*, 52.

51. Gemeente Archief te Amsterdam. Archief van de Vroedschap; inv. nr. 5025, Resoluties van de Vroedschap, vol. 8, 450, March 11, 1598.

52. For a discussion of these issues in Leiden, see Christine J. Kooi, "The Reformed Community of Leiden, 1572–1620" (Ph.D. thesis, Yale University, 1993), 75–190.

53. Sterling Lamet, "The *vroedschap* of Leiden 1550–1600: The Impact of Tradition and Change on the Governing Elite of a Dutch City," *Sixteenth Century Journal* 12 (1981), 1: 19, 25. Lamet has argued that the pre-1572 ruling elite was able to retain political power after 1574 through the cooperation of younger family members. Recently, Dirk Noordham has cast doubt on the ability of these old families to retain their political influence after the 1572–1574 period. He argues that from 1574 to 1618, two-thirds of the *vroedschap* were recruited from families who had obtained power during 1572–1574. In Noordham's view, the Leiden *vroedschap* in the late sixteenth century became dominated by up-and-coming local families who displaced an older patriciate. Dirk Jaap Noordham, *Gerende buffels en heren van stand, Het patriciaat van Leiden, 1574–1700* (Hilversum, 1994), 28–29, 103. Regardless of these different views, the Leiden magistracy pursued a very consistent policy with respect to the Reformed Church.

54. Kooi, "Leiden," 48–49.

55. R. Fruin, *The Siege and Relief of Leyden in 1574*, trans. Elizaeth Trevelyan (The Hague, 1927), 37.

56. Rosemary Jones, "De Nederduitse gereformeerde gemeente te Leiden in de jaren 1572–1576," *Leidse Jaarbookje* 66 (1974): 126.

57. J. Prinsen, ed., "Armenzorg te Leiden in 1577," *Bijdragen en mededeelingen van het Historisch Genootschap* 26 (1905): 143.

58. The sheriff (*schout*) was charged to apprehend and punish all beggars. Foreign beggars could stay in the city for one day and one night, but could not beg. After deliberations in 1577, the *vroedschap* voted not to merge the almshouses at this time, although they also became consolidated by 1583. Ligtenberg, *Armezorg te Leiden*, 228–230, 299–305.

59. Prinsen, *Armezorg te Leiden*, 154. Even before 1577, Leiden's city government had attempted to exert its influence over Reformed charity. In 1576, the minister Pieter Cornelisz complained to Arent Cornelisz in Delft that the city government was trying to prescribe how much and to whom church alms should be given. Kooi, "Leiden," 63.

60. Kooi, "Leiden," 63–64. Unfortunately, diaconal records do not exist for this period, making it difficult to ascertain how the deacons managed to care for poor church members.

61. Ligtenberg, *Armezorg te Leiden*, 231.

62. H. C. Rogge, *Caspar Janszoon Coolhaes, de voorloper van Arminius en der Remonstranten*, 2 vols. (Amsterdam, 1865), 1: 102–105.

63. Reitsma and van Veen, *Acta*, 267.

64. The merger led to further disputes in 1586 and 1587 over the joint administration of poor relief. In December 1586, the municipal almoners complained to the city council that the consistory wanted the deacons to give higher rates of assistance to members. The magistrates responded by informing the consistory that it had no authority in poor relief matters. The following February, the consistory protested that the deacons were forced to give charity to those outside "the household of faith." In the winter of 1587 it appears that the city council was inclined to divide the deacons and almoners once again, although by April 1587, the magistrates decided to reissue the 1582 ordinance that united the deacons and almoners. Ligtenberg, *Armezorg te Leiden*, 231–233.

65. J. C. Boogman, "De Overgang van Gouda, Dordrecht, Leiden, en Delft in de Zomer van het Jaar 1572," *Tijdschrift voor Geschiedenis* 57 (1942): 110. Reinier Boitet, *Beschryving der Stadt Delft* (Delft, 1729), 83. After the changes of 1572, a number of municipal officers remained Catholic. Even Christian van der Goes, the sheriff (*schout*) who had prosecuted a number of heresy cases against Protestants in Delft, retained his post until his death in 1577. J. H. van Dijk, "Bedreigd Delft," *Bijdragen voor vaderlandsche geschiedenis en oudheidkunde*, zesde reeks 6 (1928): 185. M. A. Kok, "Opkomst van het Protestantisme," *De Stadt Delft: cultuur en maatschappij tot 1572*, 3 vols. (Delft, 1979), I: 108; Boitet, *Delft*, 131–132.

66. For an extended discussion of the religious makeup of Delft's city government during this period, see P.H.A.M. Abels and A.Ph.F. Wouters, *Nieuw en Ongezien, kerk en samenleving in de classis Delft en Delftland 1572–1621*, 2 vols. (Gouda, 1994) 1: 388–414, 2: 119–123.

67. Delft joined Leiden and Gouda in blocking approval of the 1578 national Synod of Dordrecht in the Estates of Holland, because these magistrates believed that the Synod granted the clergy far too much authority in the public church. Delft regents also defended the rights of Catholics to worship and attempted to check the confessional ambitions of the local Reformed leadership throughout this period. *Resolutiën van de Staten van Holland* (August 28, 1579): 108.

68. J. J. Woltjer, "Een niew ende onghesien dingh: Verkenningen naar de positie van de kerkeraad in twee Hollandse steden in de zestiende eeuw" (Afschiedscollege, Rijksuniversiteit, 1985), 12.

69. Abels and Wouters, *Nieuw en Ongezien* 1: 397.

70. The most influential minister in the Delft church, Arent Cornelisz played a leading role in trying to establish a Calvinist Church Order in the Reformed Churches of Holland and the Netherlands. He was one of the primary architects of the Calvinist protocols at the Provincial Synod of Dordrecht in 1574, the National Synod of Dordrecht in 1578, and the National Synod of Middleburg in 1581, all of which sought to limit political encroachment in church affairs, including diaconal poor relief. R. H. Bremmer, *Reformatie en rebellie. Willem van Oranje, de calvinisten en het recht van opstand tien onstuimige jaren: 1572–1581* (Franeker, 1984), 88, 176. Also see, H. J. Jaanus, *Hervormd Delft ten tijde van Arent Cornelisz (1573–1605)* (Amsterdam, 1950), 94–95.

71. Gemeente Archief te Delft, Archief van de Nederlands Hervormde Gemeente te Delft, #1. Handelingen van de Algemene Kerkeraad, November 9, 1573 (hereafter cited as GAD. Kerkeraad, according to date). A summary of the deacons' duties in Delft may be found in Gemeente Archief te Delft. Archief van de Kerkeraad van de Nederlands Hervormd Gemeente; Kerkeraad reglementen en instructie #314 (hereafter cited as GAD. Regle).

72. Abels and Wouters, *Nieuw en Ongezien*, 2: 215.

73. GAD. Kerkeraad (August 22, 1580).

74. GAD. Kerkeraad (December 26, 1574, December 31, 1578, November 12, 1581).

75. Church officers and wealthy members of the congregation often had to make up these deficits through loans or outright donations. But the primary strategy the consistory used to increase the deacon's revenues was to petition the magistrates for financial help. Charles H. Parker, "The Reformation of Community: The Reformed Diaconate and Municipal Poor Relief in Holland, 1572–1620" (Ph.D. thesis, University of Minnesota, 1993), 375–383.

76. GAD. Kerkeraad (September 26, 1597).

77. GAD. Kerkeraad (September 29, 1597).

78. Abels and Wouters, *Nieuw en Ongezien*, 2: 238–239.

79. Parker, "Reformation of Community," 375–383.

80. GAD. Kerkeraad (January 20, 1597, February 3, 1597, December 12, 1608, September 27, 1610, October 25, 1610, November 1, 1610); Gemeente Archief te Delft, Resolutieboeck van Veertigen, 3 vols., 3: ff. 195v December 23, 1608; Gemeente Archief te Delft. Archief van de Vroedschap, Keurboek 5, ff. 257, January 4, 1609.

81. Gemeente Archief te Delft. Archief van de Vroedschap; #2001 Resolutien van de Heeren van de Wet, 2 vols., 1609–1719: 1, ff. 10v-11r January 28, 1614. Unfortunately, consistorial records between 1613 and 1616 are uncharacteristically meager,

making it difficult to ascertain the attitude of church leaders. To my knowledge there is not even one entry in the consistorial records mentioning the 1614 incorporation.

82. Gemeente Archief te Delft. Archief van de Vroedschap, Resolutien van de Heeren van de Wet; ff. 12v, May 9, 1614.

83. GAD. Kerkeraad (April 24, 1617); GAD. Wetresoluties, ff. 16v, May 17, 1617.

84. GAD. Regle, #312.

85. D. Wijbenga, *Delft een verhaal van de stad en haar bewoners*, 2 vols. (Elmar, 1984), 2: 82.

86. GAD. Kerkeraad (August 25, 1617).

KATHRYN NORBERG

Religious Charity and Cultural Norms in Counter-Reformation France

Sometime on the afternoon of April 16, 1685, Francois de la Croix de Chevrières, marquis of Ornacieu and president of the Parlement of Grenoble, sat down to dictate to master Froment, his notary, his last will and testament. He did so, his will tells us, because "the hour of our death is uncertain and it is imprudent to leave the disposition of one's estate to the end of life and the pain and confusion that accompany a grave illness." Thus "to avoid the conflicts which may arise over the division of my estate," and "while still in good health and full possession of (his) senses, will and faculties," the marquis set about providing for his heirs. First, however, he provided for himself, for his immortal soul, and for the poor, both in Grenoble and at his rural estates.

He instructed his heirs to have a thousand masses said for the repose of his soul immediately after his death by the priests of the Hospital General, the principal charitable institution of the town and in whose chapel the marquis wanted to be buried "without the slightest pomp or display." He also bequeathed 1,000 livres to the Hospital General for a monthly mass in perpetuity and an additional 100 livres each to the Augustinian, Carmelite, Capuchin and Recollect monasteries, and Poor Care convent so that these religious would take a communion in his honor.

Having provided for his own salvation, the marquis now looked to that of the poor. To the Congregation for the Propagation of the Faith (which maintained an orphanage in Grenoble) he left 100 livres. To the inhabitants of the community of Marisolles (a part of the marquisat of Ornacieu) he bestowed the income from a tax, the *vingtaine du vin* for the "establishment and maintenance of a schoolmaster so that the youth there may be raised in the fear of God." In addition, he instructed his heirs to distribute 200 livres to the poor of his other estates. To the destitute of Grenoble, he left 100 livres to be distributed by the directresses of the Providence hospital. To the

Hospital de la Charité (also in Grenoble), he left 100 for the establishment of a bed, to which his family's coat of arms would be affixed and which would be filled from time to time by a sick pauper "nominated" by his heirs.

At this point, the marquis turned to his immediate dependents. He left two years wages to the domestics in his service at the time of his death and 1,000 livres to his widowed mother. To his sons, Gabriel and Jean, he left 21,000 livres to be paid on their twenty-fifth birthday and the same to any child that either might father in the future. He nominated as his principal heir his wife, Marguerite Vidaud de la Tour, with the provision that she turn the bulk of his estate over to their eldest son at the time of her death. Numerous clauses of substitution followed designed to keep the Ornacieu estate intact even if virtually all his relatives died. Having foreseen every possible disaster, the marquis closed his will and signed it. Seven witnesses— Froment's five clerks, the marquis' lawyer, Dumolard and the notary himself—signed the document. Sometime later Froment had one of his clerks copy the will into his register or *minutier* where it can still be found today, sandwiched in between hundreds of other notarial registers in the Archives départementales de l'Isère.[1]

What does this will (or the hundreds of others like it) tell us about charitable giving in seventeenth-century France? To be sure, charity was not the testament's sole purpose. When the marquis wrote his will, he thought about death, about his funeral, about the fate of his immortal soul, and about his family. One might argue that these considerations weighed more heavily on him than his obligations to the poor. One might also argue that the charitable gifts were shaped by the anxieties of the moment, by the marquis' fear of death, by his concern for his soul or by his desire to sustain his lineage. Moreover,the marquis' will tells us nothing about the charitable gestures that punctuated his life. He was a generous director of the local Hospital General and a fervent patron of the Propagation of the Faith orphanage but he makes no reference to these activities in his will. Testaments are just a snapshot, not the full picture, of the poor. They must be supplemented with confraternity records, municipal documents, and hospital account books. At the same time, wills are cursed with the same flaws as so many other seventeenth-century documents: they are formulaic, sometimes fragmentary, and always less informative than one would like.[2]

Still, wills are an invaluable source. They are in fact one of the very few sources that allow us to analyze individual, private charity and to confront the donor personally. We can examine the donor's motives closely and determine to what degree public charity frustrated or encouraged—his or her private generosity. And because both Catholics and Protestants made wills, the Grenoble documents have an additional advantage: they allow us to test the traditional interpretations of Catholic and Protestant charity. Wills can help us determine if Catholic charity was "selfish," "indiscriminate" and archaic (as one traditional interpretation would have us believe) while its Protestant counterpart was "rational" and "forward-looking." The notions of community and responsibility that underlay Protestant and Catholic charity can be outlined and the differences and similiarites between the two confessions highlighted. Of course, testaments are far from perfect; like all historical sources they must be used carefully. They must also be supplemented with data on the organization and evolution of public poor relief. They may not be, as Brian Pullan has argued, "the whole story," but they are a very important part of it.[3]

My study deals with some of the testaments drawn up by the elite of one French, provincial town, Grenoble. Why Grenoble? Located in the foothills of the Alps, Grenoble was the capital of the province of Dauphin and a town of some 20,000 people. In the seventeenth century, the law was its principal industry, for it was the home of the Parlement of Dauphin, one of the so-called sovereign courts as well the Bailliage du Grésivaudan and Justice de Grenoble. The magistrates of the Parlement (like Chevrières) dominated life in the city. They had political clout and great prestige, for they combined ancient lineage (all were nobles by birth) with wealth (all owned estates in rural Dauphin). Grenoble also possessed a small but prosperous Protestant minority, the legacy of its Reformed past. During the sixteenth century, civil war had ravaged the city, and Grenoble was by turn Protestant or Catholic depending on the army outside its gates. In the early seventeenth century, the Bourbon monarchs began to reassert their authority bringing with them post-Tridentine Catholicism. By 1700, the Catholic Church (under the dynamic Bishop Etienne Le Camus) had vanquished its Protestant rival and inspired unprecedented fervor among the faithful. In this regard, as in most others, Grenoble was an unexceptional French provincial. It was an administrative, as opposed to manufacturing center, and it had a wealthy elite (the magistrates of the Parlement of Dauphin), some stubborn Protestants (also magistrates at the Chambre de l'Edit), and a large number of indigent artisans, unwed mothers, orphans, the old, the sick, and the hungry—in short, the poor.

Because by 1660 Catholics constituted the majority of Grenoble's inhabitants, we will begin with their wills. Did Grenoble's Catholic testators provide for the impoverished? My sample of 2,272 wills made between 1620 and 1729 indicates that many did.[4] A quick look at the percentage of Catholic Grenoblois making charitable bequests reveals an overall upward trend (Table 1). The rate of charitable giving increased from 32 percent in the 1620s to 55 percent in the 1680s and then peaked at 66 percent in the 1690s.[5]

TABLE 1. PERCENTAGE OF CATHOLIC TESTATORS MAKING
CHARITABLE BEQUESTS

DECADE	NOBLES	MAGIS-TRATES	BASOCHE*	BOUR-GEOIS	MERCHANT	OTHER	TOTAL
1620–1629	33 (9)	86 (7)	44 (34)	46 (13)	28 (29)	17 (87)	32 (179)
1630–1639	75 (12)	33 (12)	29 (41)	13 (8)	28 (25)	8 (100)	22 (198)
1640–1649	41 (29)	88 (24)	48 (33)	29 (14)	22 (32)	20 (138)	37 (270)
1650–1659	62 (26)	66 (29)	49 (39)	61 (18)	42 (38)	15 (124)	38 (274)
1660–1669	54 (46)	76 (34)	51 (35)	44 (16)	48 (23)	16 (77)	43 (232)
1670–1679	50 (44)	82 (39)	41 (56)	56 (26)	52 (21)	4 (186)	41 (265)
1680–1689	54 (46)	82 (39)	69 (49)	61 (36)	55 (29)	20 (55)	55 (254)
1690–1699	79 (34)	72 (32)	69 (59)	69 (32)	63 (32)	47 (49)	66 (238)
1700–1709	61 (33)	74 (27)	51 (69)	55 (20)	43 (46)	18 (77)	44 (272)
1710–1719	55 (33)	72 (36)	68 (47)	52 (25)	31 (55)	20 (89)	44 (285)
1720–1729	66 (41)	80 (40)	45 (66)	33 (3)	33 (58)	16 (97)	41 (305)
TOTAL	58 (353)	75 (319)	52 (528)	53 (210)	39 (388)	18 (974)	42 (2,272)

Basoche is an old French expression for a group of individuals—lawyers, barristers, *huissiers* and
    notaries—whose livelihood was the law and whose place of work was the Parlement. How-
    ever, they had neither the wealth or breeding of their superiors the magistrates.

Note: Testators for whom no occupation is given and soldiers and peasants have been omitted from
    this table. The figures in parentheses are the absolute numbers of testators in each category.

The overall upward trend is interesting, for it coincides with the creation
of a number of public poor relief institutions. Between 1620 and 1725,
Grenoble's authorities created nine new charitable institutions which provided housing, food, emergency financial assistance, and medical care to
orphans, domestic servants, prostitutes, foundlings, and the old and infirm.[6]
The most important of these institutions was the Hospital General, a workhouse which provided indoor relief to foundlings, the sick, and the elderly
and outdoor relief via bread distributions to between 10 and 20 percent of
the population. All of these institutions were municipal entities, that is "public" institutions.[7] But "private" individuals were responsible for creating
and sustaining these hospitals. The city's elite, its magistrates, and their
cousins, the nobles, staffed the boards and confraternities that administered

and funded the hospices. Public charity did not discourage private giving among the elite. Grenoble's magistrates had an extremely high rate of charitable giving, one that approached 80 percent in the latter part of the century (Table 1).

Then in the period 1690–1729, a puzzling decline occurs in the rate of charitable giving: it drops from 66 to 41 percent (Table 1). Did the Grenoblois' altruism flag during these years? Hardly: of Grenoble's nine charities, five were created at this time and donations by the living to the Hospital General increased tenfold.[8] Difficult economic times probably explain some of the decline in charitable bequests.[9] Repeated subsistence crises aggravated by the nearby Savoyard war and frequent floods plagued Grenoble in these years probably making benefactors wary of giving to the poor at the expense of their families.[10]

TABLE 2. PERCENTAGE OF CATHOLIC TESTATORS MAKING
RELIGIOUS BEQUESTS

DECADE	NOBLES	MAGIS-TRATES	BASOCHE	BOUR-GEOIS	MER-CHANT	OTHER	TOTAL
1620–1629	44 (99)	86 (7)	47 (34)	38 (13)	21 (29)	21 (87)	30 (179)
1630–1639	58 (12)	92 (12)	34 (41)	25 (8)	28 (25)	16 (100)	29 (198)
1640–1649	69 (29)	88 (24)	42 (33)	43 (14)	34 (32)	35 (138)	44 (270)
1650–1659	73 (26)	86 (29)	51 (39)	50 (18)	37 (38)	22 (124)	41 (274)
1660–1669	67 (46)	97 (34)	86 (35)	81 (16)	57 (23)	37 (78)	64 (232)
1670–1679	80 (44)	85 (39)	70 (56)	68 (26)	52 (21)	41 (80)	63 (265)
1680–1689	72 (46)	85 (39)	69 (49)	61 (36)	69 (29)	35 (55)	62 (254)
1690–1699	62 (34)	81 (32)	68 (59)	75 (32)	66 (32)	49 (49)	65 (238)
1700–1709	70 (33)	81 (27)	71 (69)	75 (20)	78 (46)	58 (77)	70 (272)
1710–1719	73 (33)	81 (36)	77 (47)	68 (25)	60 (55)	50 (89)	67 (285)
1720–1729	75 (41)	90 (40)	83 (66)	100 (3)	74 (58)	68 (97)	76 (305)
Total	70 (353)	86 (319)	65 (528)	63 (210)	55 (388)	3 (974)	57 (2272)

Note: Testators for whom no occupation is given and soldiers and peasants have been omitted from this table. The figures in parantheses are the absolute numbers of testators in each category.

But the explanation for the decline in charitable bequests may lie in another sort of legacy—the gift for religious purposes. If we were to graph bequests for religious purposes along the same axis as charitable bequests, both curves would follow the same path until 1690 when they would diverge (Tables 1 and 2). Tables 1 and 2 suggest two possible interpretations: first, religious and charitable bequests were linked and sprang from the same sources; second, religious and charitable bequests competed with each other, and religious institutions "stole" funds that otherwise would have gone to charities. To some extent, the second explanation is correct and appears to be sustained by the evolution of both forms of giving in the years between 1680 and 1719: at this time pious gifts outstrip charitable bequests. But a closer look at the size and composition of the sample reveals that the divorce between religious and charitable giving is not a reflection of diminshed altruism, but a product of new notarial habits. Between 1680 and 1720, Grenoblois of relatively modest means began making wills and carrying more weight in the overall sample. These artisans, day laborers, and domestics could not make numerous or large donations, if they could make any at all. When we eliminate the effects of shifts in sample composition by using a more sophisticated statistical tool, we find that the marriage between charity and piety is still strong. Multivariate regression analysis shows that all other things being equal a Catholic Grenoblois who made a pious bequest was 17 percent more likely than one who did not to remember the poor in his will.[11]

Before we conclude that religious belief, in this case post-Tridentine Catholicism, encouraged altruism, we must take a closer look at the pious bequests in wills. Most—75 percent—were for masses to be sung for the redemption of the testator's soul, either in the church where he was buried or in Grenoble's "four convents" the Recollets, Capuchin, Augustinian, and Reformed Carmelite churches. Because these masses accompanied or followed swiftly upon the heels of the testator's funeral, bequests for such purposes could be construed as proof of a particular attitude toward death.[12] Or they might be narrowly interpreted as evidence of belief in purgatory and no more. I would argue that these bequests constitute an endorsement of Counter Reformation Catholicism and an affirmation of belief in the intercessory powers of the Catholic Church and its clergy. Belief in the efficacy of the Mass was central to post-Tridentine Catholicism; bequests for masses indicated adherence to the church in the face of Protestantism.[13]

At the same time, not all religious bequests were for masses. Devout Grenoblois—particularly magistrates and urban nobles—also left money to religious houses that did not specialize in the liturgy, houses like the Jesuits or the collegiate church, St. André. Sometimes the magistrates provided long-term endowments to the convents like the Visitation, where their daughters had taken the veil. Most popular of all were bequests to rebuild and embellish the Grenoble Church in a very literal sense. Gifts for the "ornamentation" of sanctuaries, that is the purchasing of vestments, candles, and ciboria were popular as were bequests for silver chalices and tabernacles to celebrate and dignify the miracle of the Host. This preoccupation with the Eucharist sprang from the very heart of post-Tridentine Catholicism. The Grenoble testators who professed "a very special respect and affection for the very Holy Sacrament" partook of the "christocentrism" and the emphasis on the sacraments that scholars believe distinguished post-Tridentine Catholicism from its medieval predecessor.[14]

The group most likely to make such pious bequests was also the group most likely to give to charity—the magistrates. Along with their wives, the magistrates had formed the vanguard of militant Catholicism. In the secret company of the Holy Sacrament and the anti-Protestant congregation for the Propagation of the Faith, they agitated for reform of the Church, the moralization of the poor, and the destruction of the Protestant "heresy."[15] Like their wives, they were deeply involved in the city's charitable institutions and served as directors of the Hospital General and champions of the confinement of the poor.

In both domains—charity and religious giving—the magistrates were the most consistent and generous testators. But during the years 1690–1719, a few magistrates refused to include bequests in their wills. The result was a slight but significant decline in religious giving among magistrates. This decline is particularly puzzlingly because it coincided with the episcopate of reforming Bishop Etienne Le Camus, who enjoyed the enthusiastic support of the magistracy.[16]

A change—not a decline—in religious belief appears to have occurred in the years 1680–1719. If we look more closely, we find that many magistrates chose to shift their religious giving from masses to other religious purposes. Some left money to the local seminary or their rural parish church. Others moved their patronage to charitable institutions, like the Hospital General or the orphanage of the Propagation of the Faith, with a religious mission. Consequently, the rate of charitable giving among magistrates was, for the first time, superior to the rate of religious giving. At the same time, other magistrates made no religious bequests at all and gave generously to the poor.[17] One is tempted to label this piety "Jansenist" because it coincides with the episcopate of proto-Jansenist Bishop Etienne Le Camus and denotes a preference for austerity over display. There are other indications of the emergence of a new sensibility. For the first time, the Hospital General received numerous anonymous donations.[18] And some testators eschewed all religious and charitable institutions saying that "they had seen to their charitable gifts in life."[19]

Whether one calls it Jansenist or not, this new religious sensibility suggests that the connection between Catholic belief and charitable impulse is more complex than the tables imply. In fact, the distinction between religious and charitable bequests is problematic, if only for the simple reason that most charitable donations had religious purposes. Not that the donor sought only to save his own soul; the charge of "selfishness" leveled against Catholic charity seems both simplistic and naive. Certainly, every testator knew that some good might accrue to his soul, but his principal goal was not his own salvation but that of the poor. One should remember that seventeenth-century Catholics, including Grenoble's elite, believed that poverty and sin were equated. Grenoble's benefactors thought that material want chained the soul to sin: "unfortunate necessity" (that is poverty) encouraged begging, blasphemy, and other forms of "disbelief."[20] Consequently, the sick pauper received both medical care and spiritual assistance in the Hospital General and the most extreme form of sin—Protestantism—was also regarded as a species of material need. Grenoble's elite sincerely believed that no more than fear of poverty or isolation bound the Protestants in their midst to heresy. Such gestures as money, food, and asylum in Grenoble's hospice of the Propagation of the Faith sufficed to free a Protestant from want, thereby liberating him from heresy.[21] Bequests to more conventional charities were no different: when the marquis d'Ornacieu left money to establish rural schools, he aimed to have children "raised in the fear of God," that freed them from disbelief and imbued them with post-Tridentine Catholicism.[22]

The marquis had a religious purpose in mind when he made his charitable bequests, but that does not mean that his gesture constituted (as the traditional critique of Catholic giving would have it) indiscriminate "casual almsgiving." Grenoble's testators were neither casual nor indiscriminate in their charity. They were quick to specify that only the "most deserving" or "most in need" receive their gifts and they left strict instructions to their heirs or the directors of the Hospital General that their largesse be carefully and regularly distributed to the "truly needy," not the beggars or *gueux*. Nor were these donors indifferent to the material circumstances of the poor. Grenoble benefactors wanted to alleviate pain and improve the lot of the poor. They endowed "beds" at the Providence hospital thereby providing medical care to sick paupers. They paid for a pharmacy at the Providence hospital, so that the poor who were ill could receive appropriate drugs. And they gave money to fund the Hospital General's outdoor relief effort—its distributions of bread and sometimes clothing. Some of these bequests aimed to affect a permanent improvement in the lot of the poor. A few specified that the young inmates of the Hospital General be taught to read and write (in conjunction with spiritual instruction, of course).[23] Other late seventeenth-century benefactors chose to endow apprenticeships and dowries, which would lift poor children out of absolute need.[24]

TABLE 3. COMPOSITION OF PROTESTANT AND CATHOLIC
SAMPLES OF WILLS

SOCIAL GROUP	PROTESTANT (%)*	CATHOLIC (%)	T-STATISTIC
Nobles	11.7 (39)	11.5	–
Magistrates	3.9 (13)	10.4	10.62
Basoche	18.8 (63)	17.2	–
Bourgeois	4.5 (15)	6.9	2.02
Merchants	20.1 (67)	12.6	3.55
Artisans	21.3 (71)	11.1	4.44
Plowmen	1.2 (4)	4.6	5.22
Workers	5.1 (17)	13.8	7.15
Domestics	0.6 (2)	2.1	3.67
Soldiers	6.0 (20)	3.8	–
Unknown	6.8 (23)	6.0	–
Total	100.0 (334)		
GENDER			
Male	61.4 (205)	61.0	
Female	38.6 (129)	39.0	
Total	100.0 (334)		

Note: The t-statistic measures the significance of the difference between Protestant and Catholic percentages. If the t-statistic is larger than 1.96, there is a significant difference.

*The numbers in parentheses are the number of wills in each caetgory in the smaller Protestant sample analogous numbers for Catholics can be found in Table 1.

TABLE 4. PERCENTAGE OF PROTESTANT TESTATORS MAKING
CHARITABLE BEQUESTS

DECADE	NOBLES	MAGIS-TRATES	BOUR-GEOIS	MER-CHANT	ARTISAN/WORKERS	UNKNOWN	TOTAL
1620–1629	75 (4)	57 (7)	75 (4)	78 (9)	75 (20)	50 (2)	72 (46)
1630–1639	100 (3)	100 (2)	0 (0)	100 (5)	58 (12)	33 (3)	72 (25)
1640–1649	63 (8)	56 (9)	100 (2)	79 (14)	50 (22)	60 (5)	61 (60)
1650–1659	63 (16)	75 (20)	–	59 (17)	70 (20)	20 (5)	63 (78)
1660–1669	44 (9)	70 (10)	83 (6)	60 (10)	17 (12)	33 (6)	49 (53)
1670–1679	38 (8)	42 (12)	33 (3)	60 (10)	63 (19)	100 (2)	53 (54)
1680–1689	25 (4)	0 (3)	0 (0)	0 (2)	60 (5)	0 (0)	29 (14)
Total	56 (52)	60 (63)	73 (15)	67 (67)	58 (110)	43 (23)	59 (330)

Note: Peasants have been omitted from the table. Figures in parantheses are the absolute number of
    testators in each category.

Such forward-looking bequests underscore just how little the traditional critique of Catholic charity as "other-worldly," "casual," or "ineffective" applies to Grenoble. This criticism usually springs from an unflattering comparison to "secular," "rational" Protestant charity, which is conceived of as "progressive" and somehow more comprehensive and effective.[25]

That this interpretation is based upon a comparison of charity in very different geographical (England vs. Italy) and social settings (monarchy vs. city state) does not enhance its credibility. Fortunately, data from Grenoble allows us to draw a closer comparison between the two confessions. While the records of Grenoble's Protestant consistory have disappeared, hundreds of Protestant wills remain and these documents, like their Catholic equivalents, contain charitable bequests.

In 1627, some fifty years before the Marquis d'Ornacieu with whom, we began this analysis, made his will, noble Laurent de Martinet sat before notary Froment. Like Ornacieu, Martinet was a magistrate and like him he began his will by remarking "that the hour of death is unpredictable" and the "disposition of one's estate too important to be delayed." Then, like the Catholic Ornacieu, the Protestant Martinet elected his place of burial (in the Reformed cemetery) and set aside money for the poor. Not unlike Ornacieu, Martinet asked that his universal heir give 50 livres to the poor of Grenoble and 50 to the paupers in his hometown, Gap. Martinet did specify that the paupers be of the "reformed faith" and he left their selection to his heirs. Martinet then bequeathed 1,600 livres to his sister and named his older brother as his universal heir. There followed numerous clauses of substitution, a necessity in an era of epidemic disease. Thereafter, Martinet signed and sealed the document, and the notary's clerks witnessed it.

Obviously, there were broad similarities between the wills dictated by Catholic Ornacieu and Protestant Martinet. Both were made under similar circumstances (while the testator was in good health) for not dissimilar ends (the orderly disposition of the testator's estate). In fact, testamentary practices were remarkably similar among Grenoble's Protestants and Catholics. Protestants, like their Catholic neighbors, didn't wait for death to "surprise them," they all made their wills on average between two months and two years before their demise. Wealthy Protestants, like elite Catholics, were more likely than their poorer cousins to go to a notary. Protestant or Catholic, relatively few Grenoblois beneath the level master artisan bothered to dispose of their estate legally. Similarly, Protestant men, like Catholic men, were more likely to visit the notary. Indeed, the percentage of men and women who made testaments, whether Catholic or Protestant, was identical—61 percent and 39 percent respectively (Table 3).[26] These similarities suggest that despite some variations, a valid basis for comparison between Protestant and Catholic exists.

Were Protestants more likely than their Catholic neighbors to remember the poor in their wills? The answer appears to be yes: 72 percent of the wills made by Grenoble's Protestants in the 1620s contained bequests of clothes, bread or most often money for the Reformed poor (Table 4). This rate did tend to decline, especially after the 1660s when royal persecution accelerated and many Protestants fled or converted. But on the whole, the Protestant's rate of charitable giving was astonishingly high: 59 percent as compared with a mere 39 percent rate of beneficence among Catholics during the same years.

These figures suggest that in the Protestant community charitable giving was not, as among Catholics, limited to the elite but spread up and down the social scale.[27] Statistical analysis confirms that virtually all Protestants— rich or poor—remembered the "poor of the Reformed Religion" in their wills. As one might expect, the average size of these bequests did vary from one social group to another with the elite—the magistrates and nobles— tending to be more generous than their social inferiors (Table 5). But here too the differences are only slight by comparison with the enormous disparities that characterized the size of Catholic bequests. Nor did those traditionally disadvantaged groups—women and rural folk—prove less apt to remember the poor in their wills. Be they journeymen clock makers, like Alexandre Cochet, or rural carpenters like Michel Pupin from Cornillon, most Protestants made donations to the poor.[28] Country Protestants were slightly more generous than their city cousins, and some like the wife of a flax comber proclaimed themselves too poor to make charitable gifts.[29] On the whole, Protestants whatever their origin, gender, or place of residence, no matter how rich or poor, remembered to provide for "their" poor.[30]

TABLE 5. COMPARISON OF AVERAGE PROTESTANT AND CATHOLIC
DONATIONS TO CHARITY (IN LIVRES)

	PROTESTANTS	CATHOLICS
Nobles & Magistrates	110.69	480.58
Basoche	49.66	112.27
Merchants	32.78	21.50
Master artisans	29.88	40.20
Overall Average	46.34	262.57

AVERAGE FAMILY BEQUESTS 1620–1689

	PROTESTANTS	CATHOLICS
Nobles	6,534	5,164
Basoche	1,222	3,668
Merchants	1,941	1,391
Master Artisans	1,693	981

Because everyone in the Reformed community made charitable bequests, Protestantism appeared to have been very successful in stimulating the social conscience, more successful than its Catholic rival. But every Protestant also gave about the same amount, which suggests that no one gave too much. In fact, the average Protestant donation totaled 46 livres, whereas the average Catholic bequests for charitable purposes amounted to over 262 livres. A comparison of the size of gifts made by Protestants and Catholics of the same social group bears out this picture of relative parsimony (Table 5). Only Protestant merchants exceeded their Catholic counterparts in generosity, and Reformed nobles, lawyers, and artisans lagged far behind (Table 5). These differences could, of course, stem from inferior means, not lack of altruism. Considering the hardships experienced by Protestants, it would be surprising if they were not economically handicapped. The lack of data which plagues the study of Grenoble Protestantism as a whole make any comparisons between Protestant and Catholic incomes difficult. Dowries, usually a good index of wealth, are not helpful here, for Protestants tended to marry Protestants so the Reformed marriage market was separate and distinct from the Catholic marriage market. Family bequests, contained in wills provide a better basis for comparison. When the relationship between charitable bequests and family bequests are expressed as a ratio, Catholics do appear more generous: whereas the ratio among Protestants never exceeded 2 percent in the whole seventeenth century, that among Catholics climbed to 4 percent at the height of the Counter Reformation.

TABLE 6. PERCENTAGE OF PROTESTANTS WHO MADE RELIGIOUS BEQUESTS

DECADE	NOBLES/ MAGIS- TRATES	BASOCHE	BOUR- GEOIS	MERCHANT	ARTISAN/ WORKERS	UNKNOWN	TOTAL
1620-1629	0 (4)	29 (7)	25 (4)	11 (9)	10 (20)	0 (2)	13 (46)
1630-1639	67 (3)	0 (2)	–	20 (5)	20 (12)	33 (3)	20 (25)
1640-1649	38 (8)	22 (9)	0 (2)	21 (14)	23 (22)	0 (5)	21 (60)
1650-1659	50 (16)	20 (20)	0 (0)	29 (17)	15 (20)	0 (5)	25 (78)
1660-1669	33 (9)	20 (10)	33 (6)	50 (10)	25 (12)	17 (6)	30 (53)
1670-1679	38 (8)	42 (12)	33 (3)	30 (10)	5 (19)	50 (2)	25 (54)
1680-1689	50 (4)	33 (3)	0 (0)	0 (2)	0 (5)	0 (0)	21 (14)
TOTAL	40 (52)	25 (63)	27(15)	27 (67)	14 (110)	13 (23)	23 (330)

Note: Peasants have been omitted from the table. Figures in parantheses are the absolute number of testators in each category.

Protestants gave less money than Catholics to the poor. They also gave less money to their church, the consistory (Table 6). Only 23 percent of the Protestant testators made bequests for religious purposes, that is "for the support of the ministry."[31] These gifts were larger than bequests to the Protestant poor: the average gift to the consistory exceeded 200 livres whereas the average bequest to the poor amounted to only 46 livres. And legacies to the consistory tended to preclude gifts to the poor: few Protestant testators included both kinds of bequests in their wills. Generally they opted for one or the other and the consistory tended to prevail as the Revocation of the Edict of Nantes drew nearer. Consequently, charitable and religious giving were negatively correlated among Protestants—just the opposite of the situation among Catholics. This negative correlation suggests that while Protestantism encouraged charity (as the Protestants high rate of giving testifies), it did not stimulate the social conscience in the same way as its Catholic rival.

To define how Protestantism encouraged charity, we must consider not just what appears in Protestant wills, but also what is omitted. The charitable clauses in Protestant wills tended to be shorter and more concise than those in Catholic wills: most Reformed benefactors simply assigned a sum of money to the Protestant poor and then hastily, without comment or explanation, proceeded to the division of their estates. Lacking the elaborate stipulations concerning the administration of the gift, Protestant bequests seem terse, unvaried, and formulaic. Perhaps this impersonality indicates a lack of concern for the administration of the bequest. Maybe Protestant almsgiving was truly casual. Or maybe Protestants had more faith in the heirs and did not feel compelled to spell out just how the bequest should be administered. Or maybe Protestants had a different attitude toward death. The reformed religion certainly encouraged a certain indifference to what happened after death because it offered no promises of postmortem redemption (unlike its Catholic rival). As far as their own salvation was concerned, Protestants had less of a personal stake in charitable bequests so they could afford to be parsimonious in both words and funds.

Of course, Protestants did not need to waste their time distributing alms to an array of hospices, asylums and confraternities. By 1640, no public institution catered to their poor, so most Reformed testators had to rely on their relatives or much less frequently the consistory when it came to the distribution of their alms. Protestants had once—albeit briefly—been served by Grenoble's municipal institutions. In 1627, the Hospital General distributed bread to the Reformed and Catholic alike and allowed Calvinist ministers to visit its sick wards. But this period of peaceful coexistence was relatively short. Conflict between Protestants and Catholics broke out in the hospital wards in 1632, and thereafter reformed ministers were banned from the hospital buildings.[32]

While Catholic bequests could go to prostitutes' asylums, orphanages, hospitals, and confraternities, Protestant gifts had only one possible destination—the poor. Like their Catholic neighbors, Protestants might specify paupers from a certain place, most often Grenoble, but sometimes rural villages where the testator had lived or maintained an estate. But they never identified the poor, as did their Catholic counterparts, as prostitutes, prisoners, orphans, or peasants. For Protestants, the poor were an undifferentiated group whose only distinguishing feature was membership in the Protestant community. For Catholics the poor took on many identities, and religious confession was not foremost among them. Catholics could reach outside their own faith to assist the unfortunate of the rival confession, but Protestants never did: they felt responsible only for "their" poor.

What was at issue was differing notions of the community. For Catholics, the community consisted of all individuals, good or bad, sinners or saints, Protestants or Catholics, albeit usually in a particular locale. For Protestants, community was also defined by place, but it was further identified by confession. Dame Louise de Dorvoise, widow of the Seigneur of Villeneuve bequeathed money to the poor of Grenoble and of Lalbenc, her ancestral home, but she was careful to specify that only the "reformed" poor in these places should receive the benefit of her generosity.[33]

Of course, persecution may account for the Protestant's rather narrow sense of social obligation. In Grenoble, Calvinists were an embattled minority who were attacked on all sides by Catholic zealots and royal officials alike. Any affirmation of the testator's ties to the Reformed church, be it a legacy to the poor or the consistory itself, was a defiant, even brave gesture. But the narrow scope of the Protestant's altruism reflects more than persecution: it stems from key concepts in Calvinist belief. In an article on a quite different city, Lyon at a quite different time, during the Protestant heyday between 1562 and 1572, Natalie Davis has outlined the basic qualities of the Protestant social vision and contrasted them to Catholic social views.[34] In her examination of the two confessions' concepts of "urban body social," Davis found that Catholicism constituted (to simplify a subtle and complex argument) a "helping religion," which, through rituals, such as prayer for the dead and exorcism, encouraged the faithful to help one another achieve salvation. Protestants, on the other hand, vociferously denied the efficacy of such rites and proclaimed each true believer incapable of either giving or receiving spiritual aid. One hundred years later, these same qualities still characterized Catholic and Protestant social visions; indeed, they had become more pronounced. The whole purpose of Catholic charity was, as we have seen, the conversion of men and women. Whether it took the form of building a hospital or making testamentary bequests, Catholic charity always expressed this desire to save souls. Grenoble's Protestants, on the other hand, never sought to save either themselves or anyone else through their charitable activities. No souls were at stake in Protestant beneficence, which accounts, perhaps for its lack of urgency. A Protestant only aspired to strengthen the Reformed community symbolically by asserting his individual ties with the true faithful. A Grenoble Protestant could not, whether by his charity or anything else, actually save other souls, just—perhaps—his own. If Catholicism was a spirituality of "helping" others, then Protestantism was the religion of "self-help."

At this point, the "traditional" interpretation of Catholic and Protestant charity appears to be reasserting itself: Grenoble's Catholics look "selfish" (if not indiscriminate) in their almsgiving, while the city's Protestants seem individualistic and even secular. But I am not providing new wine in old wineskins. Protestants were by no means "secular" in their charity: they defined the poor by confession, and when they lacked heirs, they sought the help of the Protestant consistory in administering their alms. They also sought, if not to save souls, at least to perpetuate their religion. Moreover, while Reformed theology did throw the believer back on his or her own resources and create a kind of spiritual "individualism," it did not mean that Catholics automatically lacked such a quality. Quite the contrary: Catholics demon-strated in their wills the most thoroughgoing kind of individualism. They gleefully deprived their heirs in order to purchase Masses and to make chari-table bequests that would save their own souls. Selfish is certainly the only way to describe such behavior, for Catholic charity, however secular in na-ture, always carried with it the promise of spiritual benefit. But did this selfishness make the alms distributed to the Catholics any less effective? Catholics usually went to greater lengths than Protestants in framing their bequests so as to assure their correct administration. Did the self-serving quality of Catholic charity render it any less welcome to the poor or any less abundant? Probably not, for the selfishness decried by historians prompted Catholic benefactors to be more generous than their Protestant neighbors. Nor did the Catholic stress upon personal (private) initiative make the Catho-lics wary of municipal (public) solutions. On the contrary, the crusading zeal that animated so many Catholic benefactors made them ardent support-ers of innovations in poor relief, and they tended to support the new institu-tions like the Hospital General that sought to rationalize and reshape tradi-tional almsgiving. Catholicism, unlike its Protestant rival, successfully tied self-interest to the public welfare and made each good Catholic the steward not just of his own soul but that of his more unfortunate neighbor as well.

Still, it would be a mistake to conclude that Catholicism was somehow superior to its Protestant rival. Though they drew the boundaries of commu-nity variously and defined the rewards of charity differently, Grenoble's Protestants and Catholics were more alike than different. Both Catholics and Protestants faced the same problem, endemic poverty; both applied the same solution, voluntary donations administered by a large institution, be it the consistory or the Hospital General. Both groups were inspired by religion and both made charitable donations with the hope of perpetuating or extending their confession. Both Protestant and Catholic assumed that the rich would bear the burden of the poor, and neither (not even the Catholics) claimed that the state had that responsibility. To our knowledge, neither confession had much success in relieving the poor because both had inadequate resources. Grenoble's Protestants and Catholics operated in a world where poverty was more common than prosperity, and the poor more numerous than the rich. Both confessions made the best of their limited resources and tried to provide effective relief. For all their differences, Protestant and Catholic testators took their responsibilities toward the poor seriously, and they reached deeply into their own pockets to do so.

Notes

1. Archives départmentales de l'Isère, Froment III E. 1.470 (20) pp. 70–71v. Most wills can be found in the notarial archives. But wills by the elite are most easily located in the records of the *beluga* court of the Grésivaudan and Grenoble's own *Justice*, courts before which these wills were proved.

2. Of course, not all seventeenth-century Frenchmen or women made wills. Only the elite appear to have done so. This poses no serious problem for the study of charity since only those with money to give away concern us here. On notarial practices in old regime France, see Jean-Paul Poisson, "La Pratique notariale au XVIIIe siècle," *Revue d'histoire économique et sociale* 50 (1980): 231–254.

3. Brian Pullan, *Rich and Poor in Renaissance Venice: The Social Institutions of a Catholic State to 1620* (Cambridge, 1971), 14.

4. Because the Grenoble notarial archives consist of 1,731 thick, unindexed registers, I searched only selected registers. This was not a random sample: I searched all the registers of prestigious notaries (like master Toscan) because I was most interested in the group most likely to give money to the poor, the rich. I did choose other notaries randomly. And I supplemented the notarial sample with wills proved before the Baillage de Grésivaudan and the Justice de Grenoble. By this means, I constituted a total sample of 5,012 wills made between 1620 (when wills become relatively plentiful) and 1789. I calculate that there are 500,000 acts in the Grenoble notarial archives of which 2 percent are wills. Consequently, my sample constitutes approximately 50 percent of the extant wills. For the period 1620–1729, the percent is probably higher, as Grenoblois became more likely to make wills as time went on. For more information about my sampling techniques see Kathryn Norberg, *Rich and Poor in Grenoble* (Berkeley, Calif., 1985), 115–116.

5. Multivariate regression analysis confirms this impression. When religious giving is included as an independent variable in the regression equation for the percent-

age of Grenoblois making charitable gifts, the resulting coefficient is 0.173 with a t-statistic of 8.08, Norberg, *Rich and Poor in Grenoble*, 119.

6. These institutions were the Hospital General (1627); the Magdalene hospice for prostitutes (1638), the Orphans asylum (1638); the hospice of the Congregation for the Propagation of the Faith (1647); the Providence hospital for the sick (1676); the Pret Charitable, a charitable pawnshop or *mont de piété* (1699); Bureau de l'Aide Judiciaire (1699); the Filles de Service; Notre Dame de Refuge (1712).

7. I place public and private in quotes because there was no clear distinction in the seventeenth century between the public and private domains. The King of France, for example, was at once a private and public person. The poor relief institutions of the period were also at once public or official (funded by market taxes and created by municipal officials) and private (funded by private donations and governed by private persons).

8. Norberg, *Rich and Poor in Grenoble*, 84. On the acceleration of charitable activity in the period 1690–1720 see Norberg, *Rich and Poor in Grenoble*, 81–112.

9. In the years 1680–1729, merchants and laborers (categorized under "other" in Table 1) constitute a larger portion of the sample. These groups were more economically vulnerable than the magistrates, lawyers (*basoche*), or rentiers and more likely to feel the pinch in hard economic times.

10. On the economy in Dauphiné in the years 1680–1720 see Pierre Léon, *La Naissance de la grande industrie* (Paris, 1954) 1: 93–132. Other evidence in wills suggests that diminishing resources produced the diminution in charitable giving. In particular, the dowries mentioned in the wills (our best indicator of wealth) grew much smaller in this period. The elite Grenoblois, who in the 1660s could afford to give his daughter an average dowry of 9,061 livres, could only manage in the 1720s to provide her with 2,224 livres, Norberg, *Rich and Poor in Grenoble*, 117.

11. When religious giving is included as an independent variable in the regression equation for the percentage of Grenoblois making charitable gifts, the resulting coefficient is 0.173 with a t-statistic of 8.08, Norberg, *Rich and Poor in Grenoble*, 127.

12. Some bequests for Masses were designed to complement the testator's funeral and they were clearly evidence of the seventeenth-century's taste for extravagant funeral display. But the taste for "baroque" funerals was relatively rare in Grenoble (much rarer than in Provence), and some Grenoblois (like the marquis d'Ornacieu) made a point of discouraging their heirs from wasting money on their funerals. The magistrate Jullien, for example, instructed his heirs to suppress "all superfluous funeral expenses which do my soul no good and have masses said instead." Some testators even distinguished between their funeral and their spiritual needs , A. D. Isère, B. 1008 (1639). On attitudes toward death in seventeenth-century France see Michel Vovelle, *Mourir autrefois: Attitudes collectives devant la mort aux XVIIe et XVIIIe siècle* (Paris, 1974); Roger Chartier, "Les arts de mourir," *Annales* 31 (1976): 51–75.

13. Here, I'm following Michel Vovelle, whose study, *Piété baroque et déchristianisation en Provence aux XVIIIe siècle* (Paris, 1973) had a great deal of influence on my work.

14. A. D. Isère, B. 1012 (1714); B. 1018 (1721); B. 1013 (1672); on eucharistic piety in Counter Reformation France see Brémond, *Histoire littéraire du sentiment*

réligieux (Paris, 1903).

15. On the role of magistrates and their wives in seventeenth-century charity see Norberg, *Rich and Poor in Grenoble*, 20–81.

16. On Le Camus in Grenoble, see Bernard Bligny, ed. *Histoire du diocèse de Grenoble* (Paris, 1979); on Le Camus, see Jean Godel, ed. *Le cardinal des montagnes: Etienne Le Camus, Jveque de Grenoble, 1671–1707* (Grenoble, 1974).

17. In 1680, the rate of charitable giving among the magistrates was 82 percent whereas only 79 percent of the magistrates made bequests for Masses. In the following years, the rate of charitable giving was only slightly lower than the rate of giving for Masses. For wills that demonstrate a new sensibility see A. D. Isère, B. 1015 (1684); B. 1015 (1714); Aubert III E.1.185 (36), 15v.

18. See A. D. Isère, Archives hospitalières, F.31.

19. For a more detailed discussion of religiosity in Grenoble in the period 1680–1720, see Norberg, *Rich and Poor in Grenoble*, 128–131.

20. Pere Guévarre, *La Mendicité abolie* (Grenoble, 1712) Bibliothèque municipale de Grenoble, Fonds Dauphinois, O.7735, 1.

21. For more information on the "charitable" activities of the Grenoble branch of the Congregation for the Propagation of the Faith, see Norberg, *Rich and Poor in Grenoble*, 65–81.

22. For similar donations to schools see A. D. Isère, Froment III E. 1.420 (20) p.70v; A.D.B. 1016 (1682).

23. A. D. Isère, Froment III E. 1.420 (20), 70v; A. D. Isère, B.1013 (1672).

24. A list of these benefactors appears in the Archives hospitalières F.31 in the Archives departementales de l'Isère.

25. This view of Catholic charity is expressed in W. K. Jordan, *Philanthropy in England 1480–1660* (New York, 1958).

26. Of course, there are differences in the social composition of Protestant and Catholic wills: in the Protestant community master artisans and merchants appear to be disproportionately represented, while simple artisans and day laborers appear strangely absent. These differences appear to reflect not differing notarial habits but the social composition of Grenoble Protestantism in the mid-seventeenth century. Persecution had driven many Protestants at the lower end of the social scale out of the city, while only the most independent (master artisans) or financially secure (magistrates) could resist incentives to convert. On Grenoble Protestantism, see Pierre Bolle, "Le Camus et les Protestants," in *Le Cardinal des montagnes*, ed. Jean Godel (Grenoble, 1974), 143–159.

27. Multivariate regression reveals that only one group—merchants—were more likely than other Protestant groups to make bequests and the coefficient is just barely significant see Norberg, *Rich and Poor in Grenoble*, 143.

28. A. D. Isère, Patras III E 1.438 (36), 256; (22), 160.

29. A. D. Isère, Merle III E 1.099 (11).

30. One might wonder just how these bequests were administered. We know from the bequests themselves that the consistory dispensed aid to destitute Protestants. But beyond this, we know virtually nothing. The documents which might have been helpful disappeared shortly after the Revocation of the Edict of Nantes in 1685. All that is left is an inventory of these documents which reveals that the consistory, like the Catholic charities, frequently found itself at odds with heirs and had to press its

case in court.

31. A. D. Isère, Blanc III E 1.346 (32).

32. A. D. Isère, Archives hospitalières, E.4.

33. A. D. Isère, Patras III E 1.438 (39), 312.

34. Natalie Zemon Davis, "The Sacred and the Social Body in Sixteenth-Century Lyon," *Past and Present* 90 (1981): 40–70.

THOMAS M. ADAMS

The Provision of Work as Assistance and Correction in France, 1534–1848

"...WHETHER BY INVITING THEM TO WORK OR FORCING THEM TO IT."
—Étienne Charles de Lomenié de Brienne

On December 30, 1776, the subdelegate in the Norman town of Lisieux wrote to his superior, the royal intendant at Alençon, that on a recent visit to inspect repairs at the local dépôt de mendicité (where beggars were locked up under royal authority) he and the royal engineer had heard three girls lustily singing merry songs.[1] He had subsequently asked the three of them whether they did not wish to receive aid so that they might return home. The upshot of his conversation was the following:

> Two of them were from Saint-Lô and the vicinity—they answered me that they did not at all want to return home; that they had been in dépôt de mendicité before, but they had not been so well off as at Lisieux where they were in a well-aired warm room for which they paid no lodging; that they had a good pound and a half of bread; that they had work that earned them enough for extra things to eat, with still some money left over. This said, they began singing an air with a natural gaity and in fact I think they would be sorry to leave— they are pillars of the dépôt.[2]

The scene of inmates singing "*chansons gaillardes*" hardly fits the pious routine typically prescribed for institutions that traditionally housed the poor. One expects a quasi-monastical round of prayer, liturgical singing, and the reading of edifying texts in workrooms and refectories.[3] Here, the subdelegate appears bemused by the girls' good spirits—perhaps even entertained by their lyrics. In fact, he seems to report this interview to the intendant, Jullien, with a nod or a wink. Jullien's earlier correspondence with Jacques Turgot in the two years of that philosopher-statesman's tenure as finance minister reveals that both attributed the prevalence of public begging primarily to economic causes. Both rejected the arguments that had justified the estab-lishment of the royal dépôts a decade earlier. Both judged that the most effective remedy was to expand public works. For Turgot, the use of *ateliers de charité* to provide employment and wages complemented his liberal plan to abolish the use of forced labor (the *corvée*) in maintaining royal highways, replacing it with a tax paid by all landowners. He had promoted textile workshops as an additional means for employing women.[4] In 1774, Turgot had launched a review of measures to combat mendicity; by his fall from office in May 1776 he had shut down all but a few of the dépôts. If beggars committed crimes, they would be arrested. Those unable to work because of illness, age, or infirmity required care in hospitals or in their parishes. Since the only inmates remaining in the dépôts would be a small hard core of "dangerous" beggars, it was unreasonable to expect that the general contractors could extract useful labor from them—accordingly Turgot also abrogated the contract that had linked provisioning with the correctional workshops established in the dépôts.[5]

The duality of work as a freely accepted benefit or as a sanction endured under coercion is perhaps nowhere more sharply stated in the eighteenth century than in a formulation of the role of "administration" and "law," in a memoir prepared as part of Turgot's review of royal policy on "mendicity." The author of the memoir, Lomenie de Brienne, Archbishop of Toulouse and chairman of Turgot's Commission on Mendicity, was particularly intrigued by special quasi-military work companies that the intendant of Paris had set up to enroll youths who might otherwise fall into dissolute ways. Although all these "pioneers" were subject to a quasi-military discipline, some were bound over from the dépôts, and some were foundlings. Coercion was more severe in special disciplinary units, while outstanding pioneers could be promoted to the regular military companies that kept the others in order. Brienne sought an institutional arrangement that could overcome the disjuncture between work as penalty and work as the prerogative of worthy citizens. With apologies for lingering over the details of the "pioneers," he offered a summation of what he wished to see happen: "The law will punish only in order to turn over to administration those whom it has condemned; their common vigilance must at last return beggars to society, whether by inviting them to work or by forcing them to it."[6]

What was troublesome for those in the circle of Brienne and Turgot was that their liberal ideology required them to emphasize the positive association between free labor, prosperity, social integration, and, ultimately, citizenship. To institutionalize labor as a form of punishment stigmatized it as slavery. The logic of confinement took various forms, but the harsher rationale was that those guilty of idleness and the vices associated with it would be purged of their offense through a strict chastisement. Accustomed to work or inured to it, they might be trained in certain skills, habits, and techniques of labor. However, since the goal was to ensure that they would not return to idleness, the medicine was intended to be distasteful. They would appreciate the fact that work outside the workhouse, however demanding, was to be preferred to the rigor of confinement. In a nutshell, this was the argument for "less eligibility" that would be refocused in the 1834 reform of the poor law in England, and that found expression throughout Europe in many writings about workhouse management.

A subtler logic of confinement reserved the notion of "less eligibility" for dealing with intractable inmates. Some found they could most effectively "correct" idle habits by manipulating the modest cumulative rewards for labor, in the order spelled out by the young women of Lisieux. First there was food and shelter, then air and warmth, and then the incentive of a small wage for labor, allowing the pleasures of consumption (on a modest scale, to be sure) and the possibility of accumulating some savings. This rationale was elaborated institutionally and in print by the abbé de Montlinot, a protégé of Jacques Necker who oversaw the operation of the dépôt de mendicité at Soissons through the 1780s. At one point Montlinot was under fire for using such extravagant phrases as *"le luxe du dépôt"* and saying that inmates would be rehabilitated by accustoming them to a state of ease (*aisance*) and a decent way of life attainable only through steady labor. He resolved this situation by continuing to operate the dépôt exactly as before, but changing the terms of his description to emphasize the frugality and sternness of every provision by comparison with standards of maintenance in the typical urban hôpital. The underlying positive reinforcement worked as before, we may be sure; the inmates at Soissons were cajoled and manipulated into working by an elaborate pattern of control and reinforcement—but above all by the inducements identified by the young women at Lisieux.[7]

During the Revolution, Montlinot served as a consultant to the Committee on Mendicity (1790–1791) and the committee's reports adopted his conception of the value to be placed on work in the context of assistance and repression. The integrative function of work was affirmed, while forced labor in confinement was drastically limited to a penal and correctional setting. Houses of correction where inmates were kept under duress were, in theory, to be distinct from the workhouses and *ateliers de charité* that provided opportunities for unemployed workers to earn their subsistence. Penal rehabilitation through hard labor, mixed with positive incentives for those who were showing signs of reintegration, was meanwhile provided in a new criminal code introduced by Le Peletier de St. Fargeau. The important point was that the notion of work as reward was expanded (in theory) and strictly segregated in its institutional and juridical locus from the imposition of work as penalty. In fact, the positive methods of behavior modification were similar for both categories. The negative were mostly reserved for the penal side (with controls on any use of corporal punishment); the threat of deprivation still hung as an implicit negative sanction over any free worker who failed to produce within the norms. While the Assembly, advised by Necker, shied away from making it a citizen's right to have work or, alternatively, to receive support from the state, it adopted a policy of government responsibility for ensuring the same result in the aggregate.[8]

In effect, then, there was a consensus of enlightened opinion, shared at least by Liancourt, Montlinot, Turgot, Brienne, Jullien, and his subdelegate at Lisieux, that the only "correction" most beggars needed was the opportunity to make a decent living. The three young women of Lisieux were quite willing to put up with the official charade of confinement if they were given this opportunity. But would the remedy work better without the charade? That was the point of the subdelegate's letter.

Charity and Discipline at the Aumône-Générale of Lyon

How do these late-eighteenth-century developments fit in the longer evolution of provision for the poor through work in France? Here, I would like to demonstrate how the positive pole of the duality of work found institutional expression in the provision of relief on the municipal level before 1789. Then, I would like to suggest an important continuity between this hierarchically bound vision and the formulation of a "right to be useful" during the Revolution, a potent idea now again revived by those discontent with an excessively passive construction of social rights in the contemporary welfare state.

The case of Lyon is perhaps ideally suited to highlight the positive dimension of work in a municipal setting. Natalie Zemon Davis demonstrated how Protestants and Catholics alike supported the establishment of the Aumône-Générale to promote social peace following the 1529 hunger riots known as La Rebeine. While all categories of need were addressed, the Lyonnais focused especially on the upbringing of abandoned children to ensure that they would find a place in the adult world of popular trades. Étienne Turquet, one of the merchants who launched the silk trade in Lyon, served as rector and treasurer of the Aumône-Générale in 1536. He and his fellow board members established a close connection between the education of the poor and the growth of an industry which was to become a staple of Lyon's trade for the next three centuries.[9]

Early in the seventeenth century the institution of the Aumône-Générale was expanded by the addition of a new facility, the Hôpital de la Charité, adjoining the convent of the nuns of St. Elizabeth on the banks of the Rhône.[10]

The decision to confine large numbers of the poor of Lyon in these new quarters might seem to have signaled a shift toward the repressive pole in the valuation of work. Hovever, the introduction to the regulations of the Aumône-Générale, published in 1632 with an account of how the Hôpital de Notre-Dame de Charité, was managed, conveys a vision that is anything but punitive or repressive.

The author of the introduction begins with an impassioned sermon on the theme that Charity is the greatest of the three supernatural virtues. In exercising charity toward others, "the poor are the principal object." The argument from Matthew that what is done for the poor is done for Christ is lined out in clarion tones. The civil implications of charity are universal, but Lyon has been chosen "to serve for all as a first example of charity." Triumphalist rhetoric and civic pride converge in the hyperbolic claim that "as the peak of honor and holiness [God] has established in this [city] the first throne of this divine virtue."

The perception that the work of La Charité is indeed a work of assisting the poor in their greatest need takes more specific form in the claim that through the institution's actions "fourteen or fifteen thousand poor . . . escaped or were preserved from the scourge of desolation with which this city was so grievously afflicted in the year 1628, at which time they exceeded nineteen thousand and were charitably succored there." The provision of work is seen throughout this text as a form of "succor"; the correction of idleness is placed at the end of a series of acts of providing aid:

> The orphan is adopted, the young child instructed, the young woman dowried, the widow assisted, the old man fed, the invalid served, the naked clothed and the traveller comforted; and none is seen to beg by necessity or otherwise but without our knowledge and through idleness, which is there charitably corrected.[11]

The text of the regulation again evokes the Counter Reformation virtue of "order" as a divine sequel to disorder, just as the Resurrection was the sequel to the Crucifixion. Following the disorder of famine, charity made her triumphal entry. The new buildings of La Charité in the Bellecourt quarter served "to shut up the poor of the town, whose own industry, strength, and means were wanting, and who were no longer able to live from the distributions made to them, and to prevent beggary" There, we learn, they are fed, clothed, and warmed with admirable care and economy. In describing their activity, the regulation emphasizes their prayers (1) in praise of God, (2) for the health of the king, and (3) for their benefactors. In second place comes their work, "which is not excessive, but only such as to keep them from idleness." Indeed, the text continues, "Poverty here feels none of the 'incommodities' that were harrowing her." The word for "harrowing" in the French was from the verb *travailler*, which, as Lucien Febvre pointed out, could have the negative connotation of a form of scourging or torture, just as the English word "travail" in the King James translation of the Bible conveys affliction.[12]

To be sure, one of the rectors is responsible for ensuring that the inmates have always enough silk to work upon, so that they are not left idle, which, the text notes, leads to "divisions" among a multitude assembled in close quarters. The inmates are expected to reciprocate the benevolence shown toward them by working for their keep. However, the practice of providing a positive incentive to make them work with a will is recognized as a natural way of inspiring the desired attitude. This rector is charged to see to it,

> that all the poor be obliged to work with a will to the profit of the house in which they are fed, albeit if they had no hope to draw some profit from it, they would go laggardly to the task. For this reason the Rector must pay them one quarter of the amount he brings in from their work.[13]

The point of quoting such language is not to prove that all was affection and gentleness in treatment of inmates in the municipal workhouse of Lyon. What the text demonstrates is that the function of the workshops, as broadcast publicly to an audience that was expected to support the operation with their gifts, was primarily to enable the poor to maintain their station and their worthiness in the community when circumstances threatened them with "misery" and the ensuing danger of "disorder."

Over a century later, in 1765, the organization of the institution is essentially unchanged. It still houses those too old and infirm to work, orphans and abandoned children, and those "who are confined solely on account of having plied the trade of mendicity."[14] This later regulation lacks the impassioned articulation of a theology of charity, but it demonstrates how finely the practices of the institution had been calibrated to function as a household economy, while articulating smoothly with the social policy objectives of the municipality on the one hand and the economic structure of the city's textile industry on the other.

The personal linkage of the eighteen rectors of the hospital with the governing elite of Lyon is represented throughout the hierarchy of the rectorate, "chosen among the principal citizens of this city," all of whom advance large sums of their personal worth to supply the institution with a revolving capital. The fourth-ranking rector (after the representative of the seigneurial overlords of the city, of the church, and of the courts) is an "ex-consul," who has served as an alderman (*échevin*) on the city council. The commentary at this point indicates that service to the hospital is a normal step in the *cursus honorum* of municipal offices both preceding and following service on the council: "Although the place of alderman has always been regarded in this city as the recompense for services rendered to the *patrie*, and that, among such services, several years devoted to this house hold first rank; this honor does not hoewever extinguish the indefatigable zeal of the Citizens who have enjoyed it; they make it a rule for themselves to be of service to the poor."[15] This rector has in his province anything relating to maintenance or repair of the physical plant of the hospital.

Work is not only imbedded in every phase of the institution, it is articulated in the crosscutting duties of the eighteen rectors, and each category of inmate is assigned work according to his or her capacity. The rector responsible for the silk manufacture, an establishment "as old as the house," has a prominent role, to be sure, because he has the reponsibility for setting orphans on a path that will make them useful "in a city notable for its productions." The order to be established within will be made known without, "by the perfection of the work." The rector is thus the educator of the orphans, and their taskmaster.[16] He must also inspect the machinery and authorize expenses for maintenance. The rector is cautioned "not to expect silks that are too long or too difficult to produce" but to choose, where possible, "that which is better suited to still novice hands."

Another rector supervises the wool manufacture and has responsibility for clothing all inmates. Several thousand are thus clothed, a trained workforce is maintained, and idleness is occupied. The rector must inspect the work being conducted in all parts of the house, with the cooperation of rectors responsible for each wing or "community" in the house in order to maintain productivity and discipline, and to detect any inmate selling directly "outside." This operation has its long-established customs and standards. The rector buys at shearing time, usually seeking the best wool from the nearby region of the Valentinois, completing the appropriate paperwork to avoid paying those duties from which the hospital enjoys special exemptions. Details of organization and staffing are spelled out for each operation—spinning, weaving, dyeing, finishing—and again the rector is cautioned to assort workers according to the strength and skill appropriate for each operation.[17] In the provision of clothes to the inmates, the rector is counseled to choose always "solidity over fineness (*finesse*)" and to try to arrange to the extent possible to time the provision of new outfits for the Easter procession to Fourvières (the site of the cathedral).

The rector in charge of linens and weaving operations sees to it that the old women are employed mending linens. The young also learn simple tasks from the old women before being set to work making new cloths. The old women's spinning can also help bring down the cost of the fabrics woven in the house. Those best at sewing should be employed in mending the better fabrics.

Yet another rector is in charge of shoemaking. A shoemaker must commonly be hired in town, but the old men who can assist this artisan should be employed, "in order to draw them out of idleness." Here as elsewhere, the quasi-manorial function of work comes out in related instructions on how various employees and inmates are to be shod. In particular, the young women who are married off shall receive new shoes on their wedding. In the winter, the house supplies a pair of repaired old shoes to the *galériens* and soldiers who pass through Lyon. Their leave passes are to be stamped, presumably to ensure that no one receives more than the allotted pair. This provision tells volumes about the relationship between charity and social integration. The recipients of charity are themselves involved in carrying out one of the symbolic Seven Mercies, the provision of the needs of prisoners and of passing strangers.[18]

The rector in charge of the sacristy also organizes production of the large draperies used to drape the walls of churches for funerals. Producing these cloths is a privilege of the house. Repair of robes and cloaks for the sacristy can be attended to in the slack time following the procession to Fourvières at Easter.[19]

As these details indicate, work functions as a measure of good discipline, as a contribution to the provisioning of the house, and as a means of bringing income to the house. The marketing of goods is seen not only as a means of producing revenue, but, through recognition of the quality of its products, as a recommendation for the skills of the inmates, especially the orphans, who are being trained to local trades. With all its interlaced functions, work thus has a positive valuation in the Lyon regulations.

A telling paragraph toward the end of the regulation of 1765 signals a conflict with royal authority over the mission of the Lyon work arrangements that will come to a head in bitter disputes throughout the last two decades of the Old Regime. The spokesman for the house complains that it has been obliged to take part in the boundless task of proscribing mendicity throughout the kingdom. A separate building, given the name "Bicêtre" after the portion of the Paris hôpital-général devoted to confining sturdy male beggars, will be governed separately under five of the administrators of La Charité, and the costs of operating this house for the confinement of beggars foreign to the city of Lyon will be monitored separately. The Lyonnais defend the function of their institution and its independence. Although it is right, they say, to confine beggars who take away food and sustenance from the true poor of this city, it would be contrary to the views of the public good that have led the Administrators to determine that this establishment must never be envisaged as a *maison de force*—as the asylum for all the beggars of the Kingdom—that this same establishment could ever be subordinated to an authority other than that of the Bureau; the endeavor would soon collapse under the burden with which it is overloaded.[20]

Questions of finance undoubtedly play a part in explaining the dialogue of the deaf that took place between municipal and royal authorities—not only in Lyon—over the task of policing the sturdy beggars who did not "belong" in the place of their arrest. In 1680, Louis XIV had insisted that nonresident beggars were not to be excluded from the Hôpital-Général of Paris.[21] However, the royal aid that was supposed to accompany this mandate was provided only in fits and starts. A few solid results in establishing workhouses were obtained in a decade of royal funding pursuant to the royal Declaration of 1724, notably in the généralités of Riom and Caen, where the intendants took a hand in promoting manufactures, but the shifts and uncertainties of royal support encouraged local boards to use royal funds to extend their activities in support of their "own" poor, usually those unable to work.[22] Inspecting the records of La Charité at Lyon, Jean-Pierre Gutton was surprised to find that no inmates were listed under the heading of *engagés*, the able-bodied beggars who were to be farmed out for public works according to the Declaration of 1724. A note in the register explained, however, that any beggar found fit to work was moved from the roll of beggars and was paid wages in return for work along with the "resident" Lyonnais.[23] It was as if the Lyonnais preferred to count some of the strangers as their own than to become mere agents of a royal mandate.

In 1769, the dépôt at Bicêtre was supplemented by a separate house, La Quarantaine, dedicated solely to confining the beggars arrested by the royal constabulary (the *maréchaussée*). In 1783, a regulation was formally approved by the royal inspector of hospitals, *maisons de force*, and prisons of the kingdom, Jean Colombier, placing the *dépôt royal de la Quarantaine* strictly under the intendant and his subdelegate. Throughout the kingdom, the royal inspector consistently questioned the utility of workshops for the poor managed by hospitals. He also refused to allow expenses for special workshops intended to serve as halfway houses for former inmates of dépôts.[24]

Enlightened Opinion and Municipal Tradition

In 1769, as the Lyonnais found themselves under increasing pressure to operate a *dépôt de mendicité* in consonance with royal views on correctional labor, the *avocat-recteur* of the Aumône-Général, Prost de Royer, placed announcements in various French and foreign journals, including the April 19 issue of the *Petites Affiches de Lyon*, inviting memoirs in answer to the question, "What is the simplest, most advantageous, and, if possible, most uniform, way to occupy the poor confined in hospitals, beggars in particular?"[25] A review of a bundle of memoirs retained in the archives reveals a considerable fund of expertise on the typical challenges of employing the poor in workhouses; most of them include textile operations as a major option. If some suggestions, such as crushing rocks to prepare cement or rasping wood, seem to indicate a focus on arduous and relatively unproductive labor, at least one writer was alert to the potential of "new machines," for employing unskilled labor and producing a variety of types of cloth. All seem to be aware of the importance of skilled management and marketing. One writer suggests that the key to success for any workhouse is the direction of a wholesale merchant draper.

Two memoirs are of particular interest for what they say about the necessity of maintaining a positive, honorable status for the inmates who work. The author of one of these memoirs is identified within as "Brisson, Inspecteur du Commerce et des Manufactures de la Généralité de Lyon."[26] Brisson states at the outset that the "wisest laws that men have made [are those] that have for their object the love of work," and blames legislators who are too far from poverty to see its effects for taking severe measures toward the poor. They should rather seek to bring back to the duty of labor those who have been turned from it by age, infirmity, or extreme need. "I say extreme need," he continues, "because far from exciting to work, it discourages, and produces most often the greatest indigence." There follows a lengthy argument on the necessity of houses of charity, leading specifically to the importance of providing work for the able-bodied beggar, often a hardworking peasant who lost out to the hazards of the elements, or a city-dweller whose wages depend on the vagaries of trade.

For each category Brisson creates a scenario, evoking the *tireuses de cordes* subject to occupational ailments, and journeymen dyers (*compagnons teinturiers*) whose annual budgets can allow no savings for hard times. Contrasting the lifestyles and habitations of rich and poor, Brisson argues that when manufactures languish, the worker has no choice but to die, steal, or expatriate himself. Work is thus the remedy for "an involuntary mendicity." The excuse for vagrancy and crime must be removed. Rather than turning loose desparate, uprooted citizens on their peaceful fellow citizens, Brisson argues it is wise policy to keep open at all times a refuge where the poor may subsist and earn at least part of their keep.

Answering the objection that a charitable refuge removes the spur to labor, Brisson argues for a far more important moral effect on civic life: the corps of administrators of a house of charity have the power to calm a popular tumult, because they are respected by the people. In any case, the regime of a house of charity can be fixed in such a way that it offers no special attraction. The rectors of the Aumône-Général, Brisson argues, have done this. He subscribes wholeheartedly to their stand on the proper mission of the house:

> Our house of charity will not be, for involuntary beggars, a *maison de force*, a redoutable dwelling, but it will always be a workhouse. The idle person will have only the indispensable physical necessity. Wine and better food will be reserved for those who occupy themselves, and these may even receive a wage.[27]

Addressing the challenge of the "new orders of the King" that the Aumône-Général "take care of all the city's beggars," Brisson notes that the Dutch found ways to employ even the most handicapped. In any case, the object of confinement is not primarily to make money. Quoting Josiah Child, Brisson argues that the point is to keep the poor from starving, "to accustom them to work and to an orderly life, so that they may become useful members of the state." However, Brisson argues that with all the privileges a house of charity enjoys, and needing only to pay workers half a wage, there is something wrong if they cannot break even on the work of inmates. The most common mistake, he suggests, is to employ inmates on tasks beyond their ability.[28]

The remainder of Brisson's memoir provides abundant detail on the management of various operations already established at the Aumône-Général, with further suggestions on how to avoid key problems—in particular how to avoid putting tradesmen out of work through unfair competition. One strategy was to export youths to the countryside, as the Aumône-Général had always done, but with a variety of skills that could provide alternative employment to agricultural labor, such as carpentry, masonry, and blacksmithing for boys and weaving and needlework for women. Such skills would constitute their most valuable asset, worth more than any tiny property they might obtain. Here Brisson borrows a phrase from Montesquieu, with an additional point of emphasis: "A man is not poor because he has nothing, but because he is not working, and can earn nothing."[29] In addition to providing reflections on various types and stages of cloth production, Brisson ended with some observations on how best to maintain the highest levels of productivity among inmates. Setting aside a share of the proceeds was most important. For the young, especially, it was important for each to have a book in which earnings were entered—the accumulation would undoubtedly be a matter of pride upon a youth's release, and a spur to the others. Brisson also argued for breaking up workers into small teams of five, with one of them leading the group. Older workers could supervise the work of several groups, receiving compensation for their oversight, to be docked in case of negligence. Personal interest might be harnessed in various ways. Rather than directly supervising the distribution and collection of silk to be spun, the sisters and brothers might confide this role to one of the poor inmates, who would become a subcontractor on a small scale.[30]

Another memoir by an unidentified author is particularly interesting for its concluding remarks on how the inmates should be treated.[31] His list of "General Rules of Conduct for the management of an Hôpital Général," begins with the precept, "Win over the poor and especially all the beggars with the instruction that they have lacked since childhood; treat them with gentleness and humanity." To be sure, the second point affirms the need for firm discipline and punishment. The third deals with the need to separate the sexes, but suggests that the men can be spurred to greater effort by competition with the women. The fourth speaks forthrightly of "maintaining them in honest cheerfulness (*gaieté honnête*) without dissipation" through religious readings and song. The fifth formulates the positive approach to "inspiring a love of work" through distinctions distributed with justice and impartiality.[32] The end result conveys a systematic goal of integration through work:

> To give back to the public as day-laborers those who have again found a taste for work, and as masters those who have made themselves proficient in some type of workmanship; to give to them a gratification on leaving the hôpital; to recommend and sponsor them after their leaving.[33]

While the overall tone of this memoir, like Brisson's, is in tune with eighteenth-century humanitarian rhetoric, citing as its authorities the *Journal Œconomique* and the *Éphémérides du citoyen*, it ends with an elliptical citation of St. Paul (1 Corinthians 13:7): "Charitas patiens est; benigna est . . . omnia sperat, omnia sustinet (Charity suffereth long, and is kind . . . hopeth all things, endureth all things)."

In his study of charity and society, focused on Lyon, Jean-Pierre Gutton offered a nuanced corrective to Michel Foucault's version of "the Great Confinement." He showed how the strategy had evolved in Lyon as an incremental adaptation of earlier practices, and he traced an intellectual counter-current matched by the persistence of traditional charitable practices. In his discussion of the eighteenth-century ideology of *bienfaisance*, Gutton also showed that confinement came to be seen as a subordinate element in an increasingly systematic approach to the challenge of providing assistance to those who were in need through no fault of their own.[34]

The interpretation offered here points to a significant continuity in the positive valuation placed on work as a means of assistance, extending to the theory and practice of confinement. The Aumône-Général of Lyon focused on the goal of enabling the working poor to maintain their status in the social and economic fabric of the city, with only a secondary concern for segregating and chastising the reprobate. It was indeed exceptional in the scope of its action (and even then it fell far short of its ideals). However, it established an influential pattern by which municipalitiés elsewhere measured their own efforts. An instance of this influence appears in a memoir written by an *avocat* of the *parlement* of Bordeaux 1783, offering reflections on the published abstract of the essays received by the Academy of Châlons-sur-Marne in response to its essay contest in 1777 on the subject, "How to make beggars useful to the state, without making them unhappy." Lamenting the injustices perpetrated by the royal *dépôts* and the vicissitudes of Bordeaux' own hôpital-général, established in 1624 as a manufacture for employing the poor, M. de Beaufleury offered a detailed account of the operation of the Aumône-Général of Lyon, "to pique the amour-propre of my compatriots."[35]

By and large, municipal *hôpitaux-généraux* focused their limited resources on providing for their own with relief and a measure of work-discipline.[36] Many of these institutions focused on children and their upbringing. For the period of children's maintenance within the institution, their education included not only manual training, but basic literacy. Among the *adoptifs* who were the legitimate sons of Lyonnais, some benefited from the opportunity of being selected for further education in the collége, and recited their lessons upon their return.[37] At the Aumône-Général in the seventeenth century, some children received music lessons from Augustin Dautrecourt, known as "Sainte-Colombe" (the subject of the film *Tous les matins du monde*). Perhaps the new attitude that music and singing were frills and not in the best interest of inmates was the surest sign of a transition to a new gospel of utility as the foundation of citizenship.[38]

Work as a Social Right

The Committee on Mendicity articulated for the National Constituent Assembly a remarkably "modern" concept of social rights to be shared by all citizens. For the social welfare historian, it is equally remarkable how long it took for these ideas to become part of the citizens' daily reality.

Ideologically, the support for the idea that a right to assistance was bound up with the rights and obligations of citizenship was as much a product of municipal "patriotism" as of a new unitary nationalism. In the Lyon regulation of 1765 cited earlier, it is a telling sign that the author refers in the course of his account to the inmates of the Aumône-Général as "this multitude of citizens."[39]

During the Revolutionary decade from 1789, the social ideal of the poor but thriving *sans-culottes* briefly found itself in harmony with the ideals of an enlightened elite regarding work, utility, and civic identity.[40] But the very effort to provide work as a form of public assistance during the Revolution opened up a fissure that became a chasm in 1848. The great public works around Paris for men were disbanded for reasons of public order as well as finance, and the massed armies of the unemployed were ordered to return to their homes. Those responsible for managing the public *ateliers* for women, which continued to operate well after the fall of Robespierre, broke with municipal charitable traditions and insisted on labor standards comparable to those prevailing in private manufacturing establishments. The women resisted these measures all along. Finally, the authorities decided it was cheaper and more manageable to provide assistance only to women who did spinning in their homes.[41] Workshops for women were revived in Paris in the early nineteenth century as an economical means of providing relief to the indigent but, in general, public efforts to provide work for men paled into insignificance in proportion to the vast fluctuations of an expanding industrial labor market.[42]

In 1831, a worker poet in the insurgent city of Lyon wrote the line that was to be inscribed on the banner of the *canuts* (silkworkers) in 1834 and again on those raised by the insurrectionary workers of 1848 in Paris: "to live working or die fighting."[43] In their struggle to obtain a *tarif* for their products that would guarantee a living wage, the well-educated silkworkers married a new republicanism to a long corporate and municipal tradition. Their way of life had suffered a series of blows and challenges since the 1770s. Their guild organization had been dismantled, the technology of their trade had been transformed by the introduction of the Jacquard loom, and they had been forced by high rents and prices to regroup into new neighborhoods, especially on the slopes of the Croix-Rousse. But they still represented the main source of Lyon's wealth. In the second struggle of 1834, the political goal of maintaining workers' rights of association was linked to the social rights of labor.[44]

In 1848, that idea of the *canuts* appeared to have been realized in the "national workshops" announced by the leaders of the Second Republic.

But those established in Lyon were limited primarily to unskilled labor on public works. Belatedly, the unemployed silkworkers benefited from a large order for silk flags for the new republic. The hasty organization of projects led to outbreaks of violence and eventually to the closing of worksites, as in Paris. The workers, bloodied in two previous uprisings, avoided confrontation with army units and modern artillery.[45]

Meanwhile, the administrators who reorganized the hospitals of Lyon in the early decades of the nineteenth century failed to revive their traditional functions of educating and moralizing the poor.[46] Hospitals were rapidly transforming themselves into institutions providing the benefits of a new scientific medicine. At the same time, the city's elite came to believe that private and municipal charity should primarily serve those physically unable to work.[47]

The weakening of traditional paternalistic measures of support for a stable labor force began early in the century. Municipal encouragement of savings banks and mutual aid societies reflected a view that workers should be thrifty as individuals and inure themselves to the discipline of an impersonal labor market. In 1837, as Timothy Smith notes in a recent article, the municipal Commission de Travail et de Prévoyance expressed concern whether actions taken to relieve workers would, "as a question of political economy," distort the functioning of the market in regulating the labor supply. As Smith notes, this commission was set up as a means of taking more visible and concerted action to allay the impact of unemployment and to avert a repetition of the uprisings of the *canuts* in 1831 and 1834.[48]

The decisive drop in commitment by Lyon municipal leaders to welfare for unemployed workers occurred finally in the 1880s, when the excess population drawn to the city made it pointless to subsidize a labor force. Not only had the labor supply changed (the key factor in Smith's analysis) but the structure of the urban economy and its population had also changed profoundly. From about 1850, the centuries-old pre-eminence of the silk trade gave way to heavy industry.[49]

French commentators on charity and assistance in the early decades of the nineteenth century reserved some of their most enthusiastic praise for private philanthropic enterprises that would employ the poor, and the idea of "agricultural colonies" experienced a particular vogue. There was perhaps a common inspiration underlying these projects and the utopian variants of voluntary communities of labor, in which production would be organized without oppression and work would be fulfilling or at least not degrading. Their utopian character derived undoubtedly from the fact that the nature of factory labor in the early nineteenth century came to be seen by many commentators as a physically and morally disfiguring experience. Some thought the problem could be solved by elevating the morals of the worker, but many thought that work itself had to be transformed.[50]

In 1910, a writer surveying the history of assistance through work in France argued that the "economic necessities" of the nineteenth century had thrown off track the consistent development of the previous four centuries. It was a law of 1515, Cormouls-Houlés claimed, that launched the idea that work should be used by the state as a form of "preventive assistance" rather than "an afflictive penalty." It gave work to those that did not have it and paid them wages—the idea that was defeated when demanded as a right in 1848. Cormouls-Houlés hoped that the idea might still be vindicated, since it "follows from the principle of solidarity and from the idea we hold of the social debt."[51]

In 1995, in the midst of a substantial discussion of work as a right (*le droit au travail*) in France, Pierre Rosanvallon observed: "A century and a half after the Revolution of 1848, reflection on work as a right has again become timely."[52] In the contemporary scene, Rosanvallon points to the resurgence of questions about the ability of a citizen to engage in work or socially valued activity. Today, those who cannot find work are effectively isolated while being guaranteed a *"revenu minimum d'insertion."* The determination of what work is, how it shall be valued, and how everyone shall be empowered to participate in it, he concludes, calls for a new "right of integration."

Is it too Proudhonian to imagine a "self-disciplined society"? If the idea of "discipline" can be rehabilitated as something conscious and positive, then the "pedagogical" dimension of work found in early modern charitable provision may have something to say to us in its unfamiliar language. Perhaps this is what Robert L. Heilbroner had in mind when he concluded a lecture on "The Act of Work," at the Library of Congress in 1985 with the questions:

> Can work, the first and perhaps most basic form of social subordination, become the first and perhaps most emancipatory form of social responsibility? Can men and women, by regulating their own relationships and obligations of work, establish a foundation on which will rest a similar self-regulation of other aspects of the human condition?[53]

Acknowledgments

The author would like to acknowledge the support of an Independent Staff Research and Development award of 240 hours of released time in 1994–1995 from National Endowment for the Humanities to pursue research on "Problems of Synthesis in Social Welfare History." An earlier version of this paper, broader in scope, was prepared for the 1996 meeting of the Social Science History Association: "Correction or Assistance?—Work as Penalty and Reward in European Poor Law History (16th–19th Centuries)." The author would like to thank the two commentators at that session, Jonathan Zeitlin and Michael Hanagan, as well as Charles Parker and Don Critchlow, organizers of the Saint Louis University Conference, for their thorough and helpful comments. Of course, they and the Endowment bear no responsibility for the views expressed by the author.

Notes

1. Archives départementales de l'Orne, C.284. The French vocabulary evokes freedom and spontaneity—the girls were described "en gaieté chantant des chansons gaillardes." The word "gaieté" is defined in the *Petit Larousse* as "bonne humeur, disposition à rire, à s'amuser," with an added note that the expression "de gaieté de coeur," refers to speech that is "délibéré et sans être contraint." "Gaillard" conveys vigorous health and means "un peu libre, en parlant des paroles." It can refer to someone adroit and perhaps malicious. On the *dépôts de mendicité*, see Thomas McStay Adams, *Bureaucrats and Beggars: French Social Policy in Age of the Enlightenment* (New York, 1990) and its bibliography.

2. Ibid. The text in French is as follows: "Il y en a deux de Saint-Lô et des environs, elles me repondirent qu'elles ne me demandoient point à retourner chez elles, qu'elles avoient déjà été dans des déposts de mendicité, mais qu'elles n'étoient pas si bien qu'au Lisieux, qu'elles étoient dans une chambre bien aérée et bien chaude dont elles ne payoient pas le giste, qu'elles avoient une bonne livre et demie de pain, qu'elles avoient du travail qui les raportait de quoy avoir du friant et encore de l'argent de reste, cela dit, elles se mirent à chanter un air de gayeté naturelle et en effet je pense qu'elles seroient faschés de sortir, ce sont des piliers du dépôt."

3. See for example the *Règlement concernant la nourriture et le travail des pauvres à l'hôpital de Notre-Dame de la Charité, établi en la ville de Dijon* (Dijon, 1752), 25. A regular cycle of liturgy for the daughters of Saint Anne included the *Veni Creator*, the *O salutaris hostia* or the *O panis* or *Ego sum* at the elevation of the Host, *O sacrum convivium* or the *Pange lingua* for Sundays and Thursdays, and others for the feast of the Holy Virgin and other days of the liturgical calendar. That inmates might sing in a more worldly vein if left to their own devices is suggested by the provision of an earlier regulation, *Fondations, construction, oeconomie et règlements des hôpitaux du Saint-Esprit et de Nostre-Dame de la charité en la ville de Dijon* (Dijon, 1649), 15. The staff overseeing the inmates were to lead them in singing hymns during Mass and at work, "not ever permitting them to sing lewd songs (*chansons deshonnêtes*) nor to engage in unseemly conversation (*tenir mauvais propos*)." See also the prescribed use of music and the prohibition on lewd songs in Hannes Stekl, "'Labore et fame'— Sozialdisziplinierung in Zucht- und Arbeiterhäusern des 17. und 18. Jahrhunderts," in Christoph Sachsse and Florian Tennstedt, eds., *Soziale Sicherheit und soziale Disziplinierung* (Frankfurt-am-Main, 1986), 119–147, loc. cit. 135–136. It should be noted that the dépôts provided little in the way of religious liturgy; instructions to intendants suggested that priests might be asked to conduct Mass on Sundays (usually with portable altars) and provide for the spiritual needs of inmates.

4. Adams, *Bureaucrats*, 142; 153.

5. Ibid., 155.

6. Ibid., 139.

7. Ibid., 201.

8. Ibid., 247.

9. Natalie Zemon Davis, "Poor Relief, Humanism, and Heresy," in idem, *Society and Culture in Early Modern France* (Stanford, 1965), 17–64, *loc. cit.*, 28, 35. Richard Gascon, *Grand commerce et vie urbaine au XVIe siècle: Lyon et ses marchands (environs de 1520-environs de 1580)* (Paris, 1971), 798–801. Jean-Pierre Gutton, *La Société et les pauvres: l'exemple de la généralité de Lyon, 1534–1789* (Paris, 1971), 229, 277.

10. *Institution de l'aumosne générale de Lyon, ensemble l'oeconomie et reiglement qui s'observe dans l'hôpital de Notre Dame de Charité* (Lyon, 1632). This and several other sources cited in this paper were consulted at the Bibliothèque de l'Assistance Publique in Paris. The author is grateful to its staff for their prompt and gracious assistance. On the founding of the new hospital and its significance in the history of the confinement of the poor, see Gutton, *La Société et les pauvres*, 298–303.

11. *Institution de l'aumosne-général*, introduction.

12. Ibid., 3; see Lucien Febvre, "Travail: évolution d'un mot et d'une idée," originally published as an article in 1948 and republished in Lucien Febvre, *Pour une histoire à part entière* (Paris, 1962), 649–658. The abbé de Montlinot used the word "travailler" in the same negative sense when he remarked that he knew several inspectors at the dépôt of St. Denis "qui travaillent St. Denis," a play on the martyrdom of the saint and the workshops in the dépôt. Cited in Adams, *Bureaucrats*, 205. For a biblical example, see Romans 8:22, "For we know that the whole creation groaneth and travaileth in pain together until now."

13. *Institution de l'aumosne-général*, 37: "Et encore que tous les pauvres soient obligés de travailler avec affection au profit de la maison, dans laquelle ils sont nourris, néantmoins s'ils n'avoient l'espérance d'en tirer quelque profit, ils iroient laschement au besogne. C'est pourquoi le Recteur leur doit payer le quart du profit qu'il retire de leur travail."

14. *Statut et Règlements de l'Hôpital Général de la Charité et Aumône Générale de Lyon* (Lyon, 1765), viii.

15. Ibid., Chapter 7. For a comparative view, see the discussion of charitable management and social promotion among elites in Marco H. D. van Leeuwen, "Logic of Charity: Poor Relief in Preindustrial Europe," *Journal of Interdisciplinary History* 24:4 (Spring 1994): 589–613, *loc. cit.*, 596.

16. *Statuts* (Lyon 1765), 67. This rector must also make the rounds in each ward where inmates are occupied in the *dévidage* of the silk (part of the preparation between spinning and weaving) to see if the work is being done properly, "si les enfants ne gâtent pas l'ouvrage, ne font point trop de déchet, faute d'être veillés et instruits par des personnes à ce destinés, s'ils ménagent les outils dont ils se servent afin de les faire punir, s'ils rompent par leur faute les campans, ou s'ils égarent et brûlent les roquets."

17. *Statuts* (Lyon, 1765), 50. In particular, the hospital has developed the practice of reserving certain skilled operations that are disrupted by frequent turnover in the workforce to inmates suffering from infirmities that prevent them from serving masters but who can still perform the work in question.

18. Ibid., 65.

19. Ibid., 78.

20. Ibid., 116.

21. Robert M. Schwartz, *Policing the Poor in Eighteenth-Century France* (Chapel Hill, 1988), 17.

22. Jean-Pierre Gutton, *L'État et la mendicité dans la première moitié du XVIIIe siècle: Auvergne, Beaujolais, Forez, Lyonnais* (Lyon, 1973), 148–155; Schwartz, *Policing the Poor*, 81, 128.

23. Gutton, *L'État et la mendicité*, 146.

24. Adams, *Bureaucrats*, 246.

25. Archives des hospices civils de Lyon, Archives de la Charité, G 350. The author is grateful to the director of the archives, Mme. Jacqueline Roubert, for locating this dossier and providing copies of the two memoirs in question.

26. He further identifies himself as "académicien de Villefranche et de la Société économique de Berne." Harold T. Parker, *The Bureau of Commerce in 1781 and its Policies with respect to French Industry* (Durham, N.C., 1979), 116, refers to Brisson's efforts to promote technical improvement in the bleaching process in the 1760s.

27. Archives de la Charité, G. 350, page 8 of Brisson's manuscript memoir. One instance of the argument that the Aumône-Général promoted mendicity rather than reducing it was Lord Kames' warning to English policymakers not to follow its example, noting that the poorhouse had grown from forty beds, half unoccupied, to eight hundred, "insufficient for those who demand admittance." This critique is cited in Donna T. Andrew, *Philanthropy and Police: London Charity in the Eighteenth Century* (Princeton, 1989), 140.

28. Ibid., 13–14.

29. Ibid., 24. Few sentences of Montesquieu are more frequently invoked than his statement in the chapter *"Des hôpitaux"* of *De l'esprit des lois* (Book 22, Chapter 29): "Un homme n'est pas pauvre parce qu'il n'a rien, mais parce qu'il ne travaille pas."

30. Ibid., 34; note the context of the word "liberté" in the description of how the inmates are to be motivated: "Une personne veut faire filer des fleurets à l'hôpital. Au lieu de remettre la bourre de soie à la soeur ou au frère chargé de cette partie, elle les confie à un pauvre qu'elle connait, et fait avec lui son marché dont elle lui laisse une note signée. Je dis qu'on pourroit donner à ce pauvre la liberté d'engager des fileuses de la maison à faire avec lui cette petite entreprise, dont l 'exécution ne coûteroit aucun embarras aux régisseurs de la maison. On retiendra cependant toujours quelque chose à son profit, mais moins que si elle eut été chargée des évenemens de la filature de cette bourre de soye."

31. Archives de la Charité, G 350. The author of this memoir, who is not identified, wrote in haste because he had not seen the announcement printed in the *Journal Œconomique* until November 20, and the deadline for receipt of entries was 1 December 1769. The memoir begins: "S'il est des vices contagieux dans la société, il est aussi des vertus qui se communiquent par sympathie."

32. Ibid., last page of unpaginated manuscript, "Établir des distinctions et de récompense pour leur inspirer l'amour du travail et l'émulation. Diviser chaque atellier en différentes classes pour faire monter d'une class inférieure à une supérieur ceux qui se seront distingués par leur addresse, leur assiduité au travail, leur application,

et leur habileté. Des prix de peu de valeur suffiront pour les animer à bien faire, et les rendre touts contents, quand ces prix seront décernés avec justice et impartialité."

33. Ibid., last page of manuscript.

34. Gutton, *Société et les pauvres*, 298, 415, 432.

35. *Projets de bienfaisance et de patriotisme pour la ville de Bordeaux et pour toutes les villes et gros Bourgs du Royaume, par M. L.F.D. B[eaufleury] avocat au Parlement, de l'Académie des Arcades de Rome...vendu au profit des Pauvres du Diocèse de Bordeaux* (Paris, 1783), 42. Other cities that Beaufleury found worthy of emulation were Vienna, Nuremberg, Bruges, Ath (in Hainault), Paris (St. Sulpice), Tours, Dijon, Marseilles, and Nîmes.

36. See for example, Kathryn Norberg, *Rich and Poor in Grenoble, 1600–1814* (Berkeley, 1985), 91–92; Colin Jones, *Charity and bienfaisance: the treatment of the poor in the Montpellier region, 1740–1815* (New York, 1982), 61–63; Nicole Patureau, "L'Assistance à Tours au XVIIIe siècle: la fondation de l'hôpital général de la charité," *Assistance et Assistés de 1610 à nos jours. Actes du 97e Congrès national des sociétés savantes, Nantes, 1972. Histoire Moderne et Contemporaine, tome 1* (Paris, 1977), 431–443, loc. cit. 441.

37. In the Lyon regulation of 1765 (p. 163), there is a *Règlement particulière pour les Enfans de la Chanal qui vont au Collège*, requiring that the children prepare their homework before going to class, and that the children report back to the master of their ward, "et au cas que quelqu'un d'eux étudie en philosophie, il lui montrera ses cahiers et la dictée du jour." The original sixteenth-century regulation, *La Police de l'Aumosne*, provided that youths cared for would be taught to read and write, according to Gutton, *Société et les pauvres*, 277. For an excellent account of the education of children at La Charité, see Jacqueline Roubert, "L'Instruction donnée aux enfants de la Charité de Lyon jusqu'à la Révolution," in *Assistance et Assistés de 1610 à nos jours. Actes du 97e congrès national des sociétés savantes, Nantes, 1972. Histoire moderne et contemporaine, Tome 1* (Paris, 1977), 277–297. On the role of hospitals in the early development of elementary education, see also René Grevet, "Le rayonnement scolaire de l'hôpital général Saint-Louis de Boulogne-sur-mer (1687–1789), *Bulletin de la Société française d'histoire des hôpitaux* 66 (1992), 31–40.

38. J. Roubert, "Instruction," 290; by a decision of 1740, the teaching of music was curtailed, not only because of the impropriety of introducing a male among the young girls, but also on the utilitarian grounds that "it is not at all suitable to give this education to poor orphan girls, who must only be incited to a love of work, inasmuch as they can hope for no other establishment befitting their station but that of wife or servant of a worker, and consequently that the talent of music would be prejudicial to them rather than useful." On utility and citizenship, see Philippe Sassier, *Du bon usage des pauvres: histoire d'un thème politique, xvie–xxe siècle* (Paris, 1990), 195.

39. *Statut et Règlements* (1765), 9. A similar pattern of civic tradition combining with "enlightened" social policy is traced in Mary Lindemann, *Patriots and Paupers: Hamburg, 1712–1830* (Oxford, 1990), 139–144.

40. The Commune of Paris heard a suggestion that a Comité des Arts be set up to place unemployed workers from each of the Sections, and that assistance through work was a basic principle: "Il est donc de l'essence de toute administration raisonable d'avoir de grandes atteliers toujours ouvertes," in *Mémoire sur les moyens de donner*

du travail aux ouvriers et aux artistes de la capitale, et sur l'Hôpital de la Salpétrière, lu dans l'Assemblée général des représentants de la Commune, le 10 juillet 1790, par M. Cousin (Paris, 1790), 5.

41. Lisa Di Caprio discussed these developments in a paper delivered at the March 1996 meeting of the Society for French Historical Studies in Boston. "From Corporate to Individual Rights of Citizenship: Women Workers and the 'Right to Subsistence' During the French Revolution." I am grateful to her for sharing with me a revised version of this paper that she is submitting for publication.

42. Frances Gouda, *Poverty and Political Culture: The Rhetoric of Social Welfare in the Netherlands and France, 1815–1854* (New York, 1995), 217. Assistance through work was often the instrument of choice for the *bureau de bienfaisance*, a nineteenth-century reincarnation of the *bureau de charité* of the Old Regime. See André Gueslin, "L'évolution du Bureau de Bienfaisance en France jusqu'en 1914," in *Le Social dans la ville en France et en Europe, 1750–1914*, ed. Jacques-Guy Petit and Yannick Marec (Paris: les éditions de l'atelier/éditions ouvrières, 1996), 239–249.

43. Robert J. Bezucha, *The Lyon Uprising of 1834: Social and Political Conflict in the Early July Monarchy* (Cambridge, Mass., 1974), 105. On the significance of the phrase in the evolution of working-class consciousness, see William H. Sewell, Jr., *Work and Revolution in France: The Language of Labor from the Old Regime to 1848* (New York, 1980), 207.

44. Bezucha, *Lyon Uprising*, 134.

45. Mary Lynn Stewart McDougall, *The Artisan Republic: Revolution, Reaction, and Resistance in Lyon, 1848–1851* (Kingston, Ontario, 1984), 57, 63. See also George J. Sheridan, Jr., "The Political Economy of Artisan Industry: Government and the People in the Silk Trade of Lyon, 1830–1870," *French Historical Studies* 11 (Fall 1979): 215–238.

46. Olivier Faure, *Genèse de l'hôpital moderne: les hospices civils de Lyon de 1802 à 1845* (Lyon, 1982), 106.

47. Timothy B. Smith, "Public Assistance and Labor Supply in Nineteenth-Century Lyon," *Journal of Modern History* 68 (March 1996): 1–30

48. Ibid., 12, 15.

49. Bezucha, *Lyon Uprising*, 195.

50. Pierre Rosanvallon, *La Nouvelle question sociale: repenser l'état providence* (Paris, 1995), 148; Sassier, *Du bon usage des pauvres*, 241. The vogue of agricultural colonies in the Low Countries, following the failure of many attempts to establish "factories for the poor," is treated in Herman Diederiks, "La politique économique et sociale à Amsterdam et Leyde, 1750–1850," in *Le social dans la ville en France et en Europe, 1750–1914*, eds. Jacques-Guy Petit and Yannick Marec (Paris: Les éditions de l'atelier, 1996), 253–269.

51. Édouard Cormouls-Houlès, *L'Assistance par le travail* (Paris, 1910), 214. The book is introduced by Léon Bourgeois, and cites as epigraphs both Liancourt's formula "Keep me alive—Give me your labor," and Bossuet's argument, "Before punishing the beggar, he must be furnished work, if he is able-bodied; help, if he is sick; a retreat, if he is frail." Cormouls-Houlès' beliefs were shared by others such as Ferdinand Dreyfus who turned to history in building a republican consensus for social welfare legislation.

52. Ronsavallon, *La Nouvelle question sociale*, 165

53. Heilbroner, Robert L., *The Act of Work* (Washington, D.C., 1985), 24. The pedagogical emphasis of "social discipline" in early modern Europe is discussed in Robert Jütte, "Disziplinierungsmechanismen in der städtischen Armenfhrsorge der Frühneuzeit," in Christoph Sachsse and Florian Tennstedt, eds., *Soziale Sicherheit und Soziale Disziplinierung* (Frankfurt am Main, 1986), 101–118. I am grateful to Joel F. Harrington for the reference to this collection.

BRIAN PULLAN

Good Government and Christian Charity in Early Modern Italy

In 1723, Ludovico Antonio Muratori, librarian to the Duke of Modena and priest in charge of the impoverished town parish of Santa Maria Pomposa, succeeded in the face of some opposition in publishing a treatise which affirmed the crucial importance of charity to the living poor as the first duty of a Christian.[1] In the course of this substantial work, he acknowledged, only to reject, a possible distinction between Christian charity and public policy toward the poor. Reviewing the institutions for poor relief most commonly found in Italian cities, he came in due course to the Monti della Canapa and della Seta which appeared to be a special invention of Bologna. These, he explained, were funds designed to advance money to poor artisans working on hemp or silk, on the security of the material they were handling, so that importunate creditors should not force them to sell it or prevent them from accumulating a new stock. "Certainly it may seem," he continued, "that such institutions are concerned only to enhance the glory of good government and not included within the sphere of Christian charity. But it is not so. Since these funds are of appreciable benefit to poor working folk, and of the trade by which so many poor creatures are maintained, an establishment directed to this end succeeds in becoming a splendid work of mercy. The less the interests of the fund are pursued, and the more the benefit and assistance of others are promoted, the more will it be so. For I say again that to open, or to keep open, to the poor, the means of earning their bread, whether by encouraging honest trades or by giving them opportunities to labor and to flee from laziness and an idle life, so long as it is done for that lofty purpose of benefiting the poor for the love of God—this will, without fail, receive its reward from God."[2]

Muratori offered an all-embracing vision of charity, of the love of God and one's neighbor, of the recognition of God in human beings who, so long as they belonged to the ranks of the deserving poor, must be served as if they were Christ. Hence even the harshest acts toward vagrants and undesirables could be represented in his pages, not as measures of discipline and punishment, but rather as deeds of charity either towards the individual or the body politic. "If we show little indulgence towards defective members, this becomes charity towards the whole body—though it cannot even be said that those who lead so unstable a life are true members of a body politic." True charity was not to be confused with liberal almsgiving. Deny alms to a wastrel beggar, and this refusal, since it might force him to lead a better life, became an act of charity.[3]

By Muratori's reckoning, therefore, few forms of poor relief lay absolutely outside "the sphere of Christian charity," though their charitable status would always depends on the altruistic spirit in which they were undertaken. But his remarks suggested that in other people's eyes there was a separate field of action ruled by secular and pragmatic considerations, one that could be described as the province of "good government" and was the proper concern of the state or commune rather than the Church. True, there was nothing new about the notion that poor relief could depend on virtues and sentiments other than that of Christian charity. In the late fifteenth century the Neapolitan humanist Giovanni Pontano had formulated notions about constructive giving to deserving people that rested on the concept of a disinterested "liberality" or "beneficence" which would seek no recompense other than a clear conscience for the giver and the receiver's gratitude. It would have no aspirations to the hundredfold return on good works promised on God's behalf by a legion of eloquent preachers. There was, said Pontano, a particular need to give to people who were worthy and of service to the state, and not consumed by idleness. "Beneficence," which offered help by actions rather than by donations of money, and could therefore be practiced by the poor as well as by the rich, was desired by nature itself, and by humanity, which was part of nature.[4] But the humanist was not hostile to well-established forms of Christian charity, such as the maintenance of hospitals, the dowering of poor maids, the support of poor scholars, or the care of distressed gentlefolk.[5] His aim was solely to place them within a different intellectual framework, to recognize social rather than religious virtues as the inspiration for discriminating poor relief.

Responding to these texts, this essay will describe certain forms of assistance to the poor, practiced in Italy between Pontano's time and Muratori's, that departed to some extent from traditional concepts of charity, mercy, and almsgiving. For the purposes of the argument, such "traditional" charity may be said to depend on the seven works of corporal mercy done to the deserving poor as if they were the representatives of Christ—on outright giving to poor people, or on performing unconditional services to them at one's own discretion, in response to moral pressures and scriptural exhortation rather than legal coercion. To qualify as true charity, such acts, directed toward individuals rather than toward a body politic, must be expressions of the love of God and deeds of genuine compassion; they must be done with a view to acquiring merit in the sight of God and to saving one's own soul and perhaps that of the recipients of the gift or service. Ideally, acts of charity are reciprocal transactions: no material contribution to them is expected of the receiver of alms, but he is expected to reward his benefactor with his prayers as well as his thanks.

Much, perhaps most, poor relief was at least formally administered in the name of these time-honored principles, but they did not account for everything, and it is worth paying attention to certain developments which arguably fell outside them—for example:

(a) to schemes intended to keep the working poor working, by tiding them over economic crises and stoppages of work, or by enabling them to support themselves at an advanced age, without resorting to begging or being compelled to enter hospitals or to address petitions to charitable brotherhoods;

(b) to associations which offered some form of social insurance, in which specific benefits, precisely calculated, could be obtained as a matter of right, as a result of paying contributions or rendering services;

(c) to institutions which offered loans rather than outright donations, either to meet the urgent needs of consumers, or to promote economic activity;

(d) to arrangements which made moneys available for poor relief by appealing to the convenience of lenders, rather than enticing givers with promises of heavenly rewards;

(e) to programs for poor relief which were financed by taxation, or by forced loans, or by other forms of large-scale public borrowing, rather than by successful appeals to the generosity of individual donors or charities;

(f) to organizations or schemes for the benefit of the poor which were avowedly administered by public authorities, be they states or communal councils, for the public good or in the interests of the commune.[6]

There is no intention, in pointing to these relatively sophisticated arrangements, to imply that they were necessarily better, or more efficient, or more progressive than the traditional forms of charity; but only to show that they were present, to inquire into their importance, and to show how they related to church and state.

It follows that most of the poor who figure in this essay will be the ordinary working poor, people who had no reserves or savings to cushion them against illness, accident, stoppages of work, or eventual old age. Later centuries would call them the "laboring classes" or the "crisis poor" (*pauvres conjoncturels*). Less attention will be given to the other kinds of poor who formed part of the hierarchy of poverty in Catholic countries—to the "shame-faced" poor, whose genteel or at least respectable origins prevented them from openly seeking alms; to the "poor of Christ," who might be pilgrims or clergy or widows or orphans or foundlings or simply patient victims of mis-fortune, of illness or accident or disability; or to the outcast poor, such as vagrants or harlots, who were candidates either for expulsion from the community or for a redemptive regime applied to them within a closed institution.[7]

Three topics will be explored here. First will be an examination of the forms of social insurance offered by religious confraternities and working men's associations in one particular city-state, the Republic of Venice. This will be followed by a discussion of the public loan banks known as Monti di Pietà which were established in virtually all major Italian towns other than Venice. Lastly, there will be some consideration of the reactions of states and cities to the most terrible of the natural disasters which regularly visited the peninsula. Outbreaks of bubonic and pneumonic plague brought about the disintegration of all routine arrangements for almsgiving and dissolved the very sentiment of charity itself, creating a climate of terror and suspicion in which human compassion and decency were subjected to extraordinary tests which they often failed.

To set the scene, a sketchy account of the whole system of poor relief in Italian cities is needed. At first it may seem an impossible task to provide one, because in principle every town made its own arrangements, and there were no central authorities capable of imposing a standard pattern even across particular territorial states, let alone throughout the whole peninsula. In practice, however, since towns learned from each other and were exposed to similar exhortations from Lenten preachers, the formal structure in most large centers of population (say, towns of 5,000 or more inhabitants) rested on four types of institution: religious fraternities, which were mostly broth-erhoods, with a few sororities; hospitals; conservatories and quasi-religious houses for orphans and for the protection and restoration of female honor; and Monti di Pietà.[8] All four of these were for the most part organizations with an avowed religious purpose, administered by lay officers with some degree of advice or guidance from clerics, who served them as chaplains and spiritual directors and sometimes held seats on their governing bodies. For financial support they depended overwhelmingly on voluntary contribu-tions, occasionaly supplemented by public subsidies or the personal gener-osity of princes. But their administration was a matter of public concern. Given their mixed character, authorities in both church and state could claim to supervise them, to approve their statutes, to conduct visits of inspection, to scrutinize their accounts, to ensure that they were not engaged in subversive activities, and to make certain that they were discharging the responsibilities laid on them by the testators.

Although the system, if it was one, appeared to be highly decentralized and uncoordinated, and there was nothing that quite corresponded with the Common Chests of towns in Germany and the Netherlands, institutions were linked both by the presence of the same prominent local figures on several of their managing committees,[9] and by the fact that they performed overlapping functions and offered services to each other. In the fifteenth and sixteenth centuries many cities in central and northern Italy consolidated most of their hospitals into one large organization. In the sixteenth century powerful confraternities engaged in the promotion of Catholic values, such as the Company of Divine Love in Genoa, the Companies of San Paolo in Turin and Lodi, or the Company of the Azzurri in Messina, and founded and managed a range of other institutions, including hospitals, conservatories and Monti di Pietà.[10] Existing charities, including hospitals, contributed to the working capital of Monti di Pietà.[11] These public charity banks, forbidden to make a profit, disposed of their annual surpluses by giving to other charities or by general almsgiving to the poor.[12] Though parish relief existed in Italian cities, it was less prominent than in Tudor and Stuart, England. More important than the limited fiscal capacity of the parish was the role of its priest as intermediary between his flock and the well-endowed city charities to which they might apply for assistance.

Such charities were often designed to serve not only residents in the city, but inhabitants of its subject district. They had modest equivalents in some townships and villages, not only small hospitals and confraternities, but also Monti Frumentari, a rural counterpart to the urban Monti di Pietà, dealing in seed and grain rather than in money. However, the distribution of organized charities throughout the countryside was often uneven, their unequal provision sometimes causing alarming displacements of population, with peasants making for the cities in a desperate search for relief in times of hardship.[13] Direct intervention in poor relief by the councils and magistracies of the state or commune was generally a response to dire emergencies, to famines or epidemics of plague or typhus. However, permanent boards of public health, and public grain stores designed to provide against future catastrophes, became increasingly common features of urban life from the fifteenth century onward.

Up to a point, the innumerable religious fraternities provided a kind of social insurance. They were voluntary associations for mutual aid and support, both spiritual and material, formed by people in the same trade or profession, or by co-nationals living in a foreign city, or by fellow-parish-

ioners, or by seekers of alms, or simply (and perhaps most commonly) by
people devoted to the same religious cult.[14] There were huge variations both
in their social standing and in the extent of their material resources. The
most prestigious bodies among them, such as the Scuole Grandi of Venice,
acquired a high reputation as executors of wills, as trustees, and as administrators of properties and investments.[15] Their charities became highly sophisticated, involving elaborate selection procedures, and included the distribution of marriage portions to young women of proven virtue, the provision of almshouses to artisans with large families and arrears of rent, and
the grant of alms payments at regular intervals which amounted to very
modest pensions.

It was true that the elements of a voluntary security system in microcosm
were present here, in that members paid subscriptions and performed services for the brotherhood at the time of life when they were fit and prosperous (or at least able to work), and in return for these could expect a sympathetic hearing if they sank into destitution. Seldom, however, at least in the
larger religious brotherhoods which had no strong professional or occupational identities, was there an exact relationship between what was put in
and what was taken out. Applicants for relief were cast in the role of humble
petitioners and not in that of beneficiaries claiming an entitlement.[16] Any
grant they might be afforded was at the discretion of the bench of officers.
Take, for example, the case of Marco Antonio Agostini, aged eighty, "an
honorable citizen of the middling sort," who in 1560 applied to his frater-
nity, the Scuola Grande di San Marco in Venice, for a "charitable subsidy."
He claimed to be confined to his home, probably lying low indoors to escape
arrest for unpaid debts; he had incurred considerable expenses, had a large
family to support, and exorbitant rents to pay for his house and shop. He
was forced, or so he said, to sell his own clothes to buy his daily bread. He
did not fail to remind the Scuola that on several occasions he had been "one
of the twelve," that is, one of the officers of the bench, and had never failed,
as custom demanded, to draw on his own purse to assist the poor and to
contribute to marriage portions for "donzelle da pacientia" (girls who proved
unsuccessful in the contest for dowries and drew from the lottery a slip
marked "Be Patient"). No precise figures were mentioned; despite his past
services, he could not claim a specific sum of money. A proposal to grant
him 15 ducats was narrowly defeated, but another to offer him 10 was passed
by a substantial majority.[17] When, later in the century, Paolo d'Anna, a
former Guardian of the Scuola Grande di San Rocco, left his widow destitute and responsible for a crippled son, her desperate petition to be allowed
the use of a squalid little house without paying any rent was answered, not

by the Scuola itself, but by the personal generosity of one of its prominent members, the mercer Bartolomeo dal Calice.[18]

Charity rather than social security was the business of the Scuole Grandi. They expected services not only from rich, but also from poor members, who were expected to attend funerals and diligently perform other ceremonial duties. But these were conditions for receiving benefits, and did not create a right to them. The only brothers who could in a sense claim such rights were men who had served the state in the reserve fleet of galleys which was called out in wartime; by a Senate decree of 1539, campaign veterans were entitled to be preferred over others in the distributions of regular alms payments, dowries for daughters, and almshouses, as opportunities and vacancies arose.[19]

Working men acting on their own initiative, within a far less hierarchical structure, came closer to providing pure mutual insurance with fewer religious trappings. In 1524 a body of thirty-seven Venetian sawyers, not the whole of the sawyers' craft but a group within it, formed an association to provide against sickness or industrial injuries, involving entrance fees, weekly contributions, and an exact entitlement to sick benefit.[20] Left to themselves, workers in Venice and elsewhere sometimes took a cavalier attitude toward religious ceremonies. Indeed, in 1583 an ecclesiastical visitor who had been scrutinizing the affairs of the Company of the Poor in Bologna, founded by street porters and others, complained that its members cared only about mutual assistance and not about works of spiritual mercy: "the intention of the founders was to provide material assistance . . . It seems that they care for nothing else." And "whereas a large number of poor persons enter to enjoy these hand-outs . . . there are only eight or ten at Mass and sometimes even fewer, and few people go to processions and funerals." But the Company could not maintain its original character for very long, since people of higher standing began to join it, and it developed into an organization of a more traditional and easily recognizable type.[21]

Beyond the structure of traditional charitable institutions in Venice lay other kinds of provision for workers particularly valued by the Venetian state, especially in the vast, publicly owned shipyard which built and equipped galleys for the Venetian navy. Anxious to forestall the emigration of craftsmen vital to the state's defenses, the Venetian government attempted to offer them, not charity, but a secure employment which would extend into old age. By the mid-sixteenth century, ship's carpenters, caulkers, and oarmakers all enjoyed in varying degrees a right to work in the Arsenal; moves to curtail this, as in 1581, provoked rioting.[22] During the seventeenth century Arsenal workers were moderately paid in comparison with shipwrights in the free market, but the promise of a job for life was a major compensation for a slenderer wage packet.[23] Since the early fifteenth century, work gangs of caulkers had been obliged to employ veterans, defined as men of over fifty-five, and to pay them the same wages as younger and quicker workers—a duty which at one time they preferred to commute into cash payments that effectively became old age pensions.[24] At least after 1600, undemanding and less strenuous jobs in the Arsenal were used either as a form of relief for accident victims who had worked in the Arsenal itself and were now appointed warehousemen and supervisors, or to provide employment for retired sailors thought to have deserved well of the Republic.[25]

In other trades vital to the city's well-being, especially those expected to provide skilled labor for the reserve fleet, government laws and guild regulations pursued a similar policy of reserving at least some of the less physically demanding jobs to men above a certain age. Hence, in the fifteenth and early sixteenth centuries, places in the boatmen's co-operatives which performed the relatively simple task of ferrying passengers across the city's waters were reserved to men over the age of forty. On reaching the point at which feebleness finally prevented them altogether from working, they were legally permitted by the rules of the ferry station to rent their coveted places to substitutes who would row for them, and thus provide a little security in their declining years.[26]

In the fishing trade, the occupation of fishmonger, organized into a separate guild, was jealously reserved to men over the age of sixty, born and bred in the fishermen's quarter, who had manned the fishing boats for a stretch of at least twenty years. Such regulations, passed by a government committee in 1481, were designed both to provide for the elderly and to restrict the number of middlemen purchasing fish in bulk and imposing themselves between the fishermen and the consumers. They did not please everyone; indeed, there were signs in the late eighteenth century that some of the workers would have preferred more traditional forms of relief and were yearning for a hospital for the aged.[27]

It seems, therefore, that at least one Italian government was capable of promoting, in certain restricted areas, a policy which sought to eliminate the need for almsgiving by offering guaranteed employment which would continue into old age. Although the notion of paid retirement from all work scarcely existed, the possibility of reserving light, paid work to the mature or elderly undoubtedly did. However, Italian cities can scarcely be regarded as welfare states, because such benefits were not open to the population at large. They were peculiar to particular trades, and reserved to groups of favored workers whose skills were recognized as vital to the maintenance of the economy and the defense of the state.

Monti di Pietà first sprang, in the mid-fifteenth century, from the moral criticisms of contemporary urban society and its excesses voiced from the pulpit by the Mendicant orders, and especially by the strict or observant Franciscans. Among their targets were usurers. Arising in Umbria and Tuscany from 1462 onward, the Monti di Pietà spread with time to most Italian towns, and marked an imaginative attempt to draw moneylending into the sphere of Christian charity. Nonprofitmaking pawnshops were to be established, drawing on capital furnished by charitable donors and by depositors who would generally expect no recompense for the use of their money. Over two hundred such institutions arose within the first century of their existence, though not all proved capable of sustained growth and some foundered after a few years of faltering life.[28]

In most places (Genoa was a prominent exception to the rule) the campaign for their introduction formed part of a concerted attack on the presence of Jews in or close to Christian communities, enthusiastically supported by those who feared Jewish competition in spheres of activity other than moneylending, such as the grain and textile markets. Jewish lenders were sometimes taxed, as in Sixtus IV's bull authorizing the erection of a Monte di Pietà in Savona in 1479, with tempting people of means into unwise borrowing, into applying the funds they borrowed to "evil uses," and into reducing themselves to "extreme misery."[29] In theory at least, a more provident and strictly controlled system of borrowing and lending on sound moral principles was to be introduced.

Customers of the Monte in Pistoia in the 1470s would be required to swear that they did not intend to use the money "to gamble or to incur any unnecessary and wasteful expense." Paternal control would be reinforced, as children of the house would be permitted to borrow here only with the express consent of parents or guardians.[30] Monti di Pietà were intended to be more inquisitorial and censorious than the Jewish banks, which often and quite understandably survived by their side, since some communes (in the Marches, for example) preferred to hedge their bets and not put all their faith in a new-fangled and often struggling institution.[31]

In some cities the Monti di Pietà enabled the commune to take over the direct management of the small loan business, rather than subcontract it to Jewish lenders. It was common enough for city councils to found them in response to the promptings of preachers, and for rulers or viceroys to take a personal interest in their organization or send their own delegates to join committees of management. They could also be established by individuals (ranging from friars through bishops to counts), or by associations of citizens formed for the purpose, or by fraternities.[32] But from the early days there was often a direct connection between the commune and the Monte di

Pietà, a recognition of the Monte as a fund toward which the commune directed cash, and on which it would draw in emergencies. It could partly be traced to the role of princely or civic authorities in licensing the Jewish banks, in granting the privileges which enabled bankers and their co-religionists to escape the general ban on Jews being permitted to live among or close to Christian communities.[33] Hence it fell to the prince or commune to provide or supervise the organizations which replaced or provided a partial substitute for the services of Jews.

Though intimately related to secular authorities, the Monti di Pietà were never free of clerical supervision and criticism. Churchmen were often, though not invariably, represented on their governing bodies, which usually included deputies from the principal social orders or estates within the commune—not only its patrician rulers, but also commoners of high standing, jurisconsults, merchants, and sometimes artisans.[34] Since the activities of the Monti raised many questions, first about the ethics of charging interest to clients and then about the propriety of paying it to depositors, they were exposed to ecclesiastical pronouncements, from local bishops or from the Papacy, on the legitimacy or otherwise of their operations. Particularly after the Council of Trent, and particularly in regions subject to the uncompromising authority of Carlo Borromeo, Archbishop of Milan, Monti di Pietà were faced with severe constraints. Despite the general approval of their interest charges by Pope Leo X in 1515,[35] it was still being claimed in the later years of the sixteenth century that all individual Monti needed to obtain papal authority for their arrangements. This was no mere formality, and might well (as in the Lombard city of Bergamo) result in demands that rates of interest be reduced to unacceptably low levels.[36] Open quarrels could well break out between diocesan bishops and the lay governors of Monti di Pietà, as in the small town of Lugo in the Romagna in the late seventeenth century, where the coat of arms of the Bishop of Imola was pointedly removed from the façade of the Monte's headquarters to celebrate a successful appeal against his intrusive authority.[37]

Some scholars have argued that the Monti di Pietà were not charities but rather banks, since their main function was not to give outright, since they made extensive use of moneys that had not been given to them absolutely, and since they charged borrowers for their services. If so, they were banks with a difference, because they were generally forbidden to make profits and plough these back into their accumulated capital.[38] Their business was to make credit available by lending small sums of money on pledges at very modest rates of interest, giving priority to poor borrowers. The charges they levied arose in part from their bureaucratic character, in that they were administered from the beginning by salaried officers rather than unpaid volunteers, and incurred considerable expenses in record keeping as well as in the rent of premises and the storage of pledges.[39]

Interest was generally low (seldom more than 7 to 8 per cent, and generally less), but this was in one sense immaterial; it was important to prove the principle that the poor were not being charged for the use of money itself, and that no advantage was being taken of their distress. Hence from the early days the rate was justified on the grounds that there was a contract of "placing work" between the borrowers and the staff of the Monte, who were distinguished from the Monte itself.[40] It was true that some idealists, such as Friar Michele of Acqui, had tried to avoid interest charges altogether, and that the Milanese Monte di Pietà would at first have nothing to do with them, only to be forced to bring in a charge in 1506 and abolish it again for theological reasons in 1542.[41] But the eloquence of the energetic Friar Bernardino of Feltre had favored the interest charge. This generally remained on the understanding that, should the officials accidentally make a profit, they must distribute it to the poor or to charities of their choice, and must in due course take steps to reduce the rate to the lowest possible level. During the seventeenth century the well-run Monte of Lugo succeeded in lowering this from 5 percent in 1624 to a mere 1 percent in 1681. Rome's Monte di Pietà could boast of lending gratuitously sums of up to 10 crowns from 1615 onwards, and up to 30 crowns from 1659.[42]

It was axiomatic that the poor, seldom if ever precisely defined, were intended to be the primary beneficiaries of the Monte di Pietà, but it did not serve the totally destitute. There is ample evidence that nobles, religious houses, employers and landed proprietors all resorted to Monti di Pietà when they needed ready cash.[43] Italian charity was always tender to genteel or respectable persons who were poor in the sense that they could not afford to live according to their station in life, and faced, not starvation, but loss of honor. And all transactions depended on having possessions of some kind to pawn, so that most clients were likely to be at least of the status of artisans or small tradesmen or farmers. Objects pawned included household linen, clothing, jewelry, and utensils of copper and iron; in the early sixteenth century books were surprisingly prominent among objects stored in the pawnshop of Siena; at Savona the single object most frequently pawned was a gold ring. This was no doubt, as an Italian scholar has written, "the first little bit of surplus capital surrendered in case of acute need."[44]

Regulations commonly stressed that the function of Monti di Pietà was to provide cash to cover pressing needs, to promote consumption rather than trade. But the rules were not always so strict. At first borrowers in Milan in 1496 had to swear that they wanted the money "for need, and for a respectable reason, and not to trade, or to gamble, or for any other depraved purpose." However, the ban on employing the loan in business was dropped the following year, when only the veto on gambling was retained.[45] In the same decade Annio di Viterbo, who was a supporter of the Monti di Pietà (unusual for a Dominican), justified interest charges on the grounds that they stimulated borrowers to harder work. No longer the passive recipients of unconditional handouts, they were expected to bestir themselves to pay the interest and save the pledge from forfeiture. Poor people, he argued a shade hyperbolically, would be made good citizens, and with the disappearance of "neediness and idleness" their "civic virtues" would be cultivated.[46]

If the Monti di Pietà broke with outright giving, they also departed from tradition in their methods of raising capital to lend. It was true that at the outset a fair proportion of their funds came from appeals to the local population, who were promised that their alms would be perpetually recycled and forever devoted to the seven works of corporal mercy, since the coffers ought never to be depleted. However, most of the larger charity banks relied heavily on sums which were not given outright, but deposited with them for safe keeping. Certain deposits were directed toward the bank by government or communal decree, many of these consisting of sums paid into court by litigants, or awards made to young women and intended to form contributions to their dowries, should they ever decide to marry or take the veil. Of immense value to the nascent Monte di Pietà of Florence, a by-product of political upheaval and an ornament to Savonarola's moral citadel, was the commune's decision to place at its disposal the proceeds of the confiscated goods of Pisan rebels, and later those of the confiscated estates of the exiled heirs of Lorenzo de Medici. It was thereby promoted to the status of a public bank charged with the care of some of the commune's most valuable assets.[47]

Deposits free both of interest rates and bank charges were also made by individuals and by corporations. Numerous depositors were attracted by the Monte's offer to keep money safely and provide highly convenient means of payment. In Naples especially, during the sixteenth and seventeenth centuries, the Monte di Pietà and other charities which imitated its practices allowed citizens to open accounts, even for very trifling sums of money, and issued against them certificates known as *fedi*. These developed into an important paper currency which supplemented the limited supply of coins in circulation and commanded enough confidence to be declared acceptable even when paying debts to the state. Extended even to people who themselves had very little money, this facility acted as an incentive to make cash available for loan to the poor, not because the bank's customers were moved by any avowedly charitable purpose, but because the institution offered services for their convenience. Among much else it acted as a giro bank, since debts could now be paid to anyone by means of transfers on its books.[48]

From an early date, however, some Monti di Pietà were prepared to pay interest on deposits. Indeed, in 1475, without going to any lengths to justify the practice, regulations from Pistoia authorized the payment of interest at 7.5 percent on deposits of up to 300 florins.[49] Not surprisingly, such practices seemed questionable in so far as they offered gains to persons making money available for loan to the poor. Justifications for the practice were found in the argument that to take interest was legitimate so long as the lender was making some form of self-sacrifice and not exploiting the distress of poor people. Lenders prepared to forgo the high gains offered by forms of lawful enterprise in agriculture, manufacturing, or trade, or by making other, legitimate forms of personal loans, would be entitled to partial compensation for their self-denial. At Udine and Vicenza in the late sixteenth century, the rates paid to depositors were intended to represent about half the returns available locally on contracts of *livello* or *censo*, which were forms of mortgage.[50] In theory, therefore, the modest gains offered by the Monti di Pietà should have served, not only to soothe the consciences of investors and silence the misgivings of churchmen, but also to protect the interests of economic enterprise. Inevitably, though, certain Monti (as in Florence in the late 1620s) were taxed with providing too safe and seductive an alternative to more profitable but more risky forms of investment, and thereby diverting capital from uses that would generate more employment. Hence, a commission of experts reporting to the Grand Duke of Tuscany favored reducing the Monte to its original role as a mere pawnshop which had nothing to do with deposit banking.[51]

From the early days of the Monti di Pietà, there was an expectation that their capital, since the commune had contributed to it, could properly be employed in lending to the commune on the security of communal property, to enable the local government to deal with natural disasters, extraordinary fiscal demands, or other emergencies which could not be met by uncoordinated private charity. This principle was expressly recognized by Pope Sixtus IV in the foundation bull of the Monte at Savona in 1479, which provided that "in case of need, and especially of a shortage of victuals," the commune might on certain conditions avail itself of the moneys of the Monte di Pietà.[52] In subsequent centuries, city governments were to call on their charity banks, not only to finance regular purchases of grain (as in Naples, every August and September), and not only to finance the notoriously expensive quarantine measures against the plague, but also, as in seventeenth-century Brescia, to provide for defense and the recruitment of troops.[53] Almost any kind of public need could be invoked to justify the raising of loans which were not always scrupulously repaid, so that Monti di Pietà were often in grave danger of depletion in the wake of disaster.

In Florence there were at least plans during the 1620s to use loans from the Monte di Pietà to deal with profound depression in the textile industries, both silken and woolen, in which looms were lying idle and unemployment was rife. In September 1621, when eight hundred people, artisans and their families, were said to be in deep distress, there was a proposal to make a loan of 40,000 crowns available to manufacturers who would get looms working again. One thousand ducats worth of interest-free credit would be granted for every five looms restored to activity.[54] Toward 1630 there was a similar ambition to rescue textile workers from beggary, not by simple handouts, but by injecting working capital into a half-paralyzed industry. In the words of a government commission, every effort must be made to restimulate industry, "so that they do not remain idle, but work and get something done, and earn a living for themselves and their families—if not a complete living, then the greater part of one. Above all we must ensure, as far as we are able, that they are not forced out of sheer need to go begging on the streets in such great numbers, and we must avoid the need to maintain them by alms alone, both men and women alike. And this would benefit them too, by contributing to their welfare [*ben essere*] and to their own interests, and by diverting them from vagrancy, which is the worst path of all to take."[55]

In one sense the Monti di Pietà were located within the field of Christian charity, proclaiming their pious intentions and sacred character, seeking ecclesiastical approval and generally submitting (albeit with occasional bursts of defiance) to episcopal visitation. To make credit available to poor persons, at low rates unlikely to be offered on the open market, and certainly far less than those offered by most Jewish bankers, was in theory at least an act of charity. But such credit was not a straightforward form of almsgiving. A pledge, an incentive to strive to pay small interest charges in order to prevent its loss, a duty to pay for the services rendered, an undertaking not to waste the sum lent on drink or dicing: all these things were implied in the transaction between the Monte and its clients. In its operation there was undoubtedly a notion of the public good or of the general welfare—of a fund to be kept perpetually available for use in the interests of the community as a whole, at times when the demand for poor relief had swelled to the point at which it could not be met by ordinary charity or person-to-person almsgiving.

In the face of an epidemic of plague, ordinary charity threatened to disintegrate, and normal standards of decent behavior and concern for fellow creatures lapsed. As the councilors of Oristano in Sardinia remarked during the great plague of the 1650s, "other citizens, having turned their backs on their civic duties, are shut up in their houses and concerned only with their own survival, not wishing to see corpses in the street or listen to cries and lamentations."[56] Or, as the board of public health in Milan put it with restraint in 1630, "all current problems make it impossible for many to give to charity."[57] A feature of virtually all epidemics was the mass flight of rich citizens to country retreats, paying off their servants and workpeople and abandoning the city to the poor, so that all pretense of reciprocal obligation between rich and poor began to lapse. Widespread unemployment also arose from the disruption caused by the decisions of trading partners to ban goods exported from suspect or infected regions, an unhappy consequence of the development of more efficient intelligent services concerning the whereabouts of plague. Hence a chronicler of Busto Arsizio, near Milan, reflected in 1630 that cotton produced in the area had been banned from every part of Italy "just as the Devil is banned from Paradise."[58] Equally damaging to ordinary economic life, as well as notoriously expensive to the public purse, were quarantine regulations which called for the prolonged confinement of plague suspects. Such measures sometimes culminated in calls for a general segregation of a large section of the populace—of all women and children, as was proposed in Florence in 1630, or of all the inhabitants of a poor and plague-ridden quarter such as the Roman Trastevere in 1656.[59]

In these circumstances, three sovereign remedies were needed, which all called for action by local or central government, and they were fire, gold, and the gallows. This maxim, traceable to a Palermitan physician in 1576, was often repeated.[60] Gold was needed, not only to pay spies and guards, but also for poor relief, and perhaps to provide compensation for poor people who had lost all their scanty possessions through the destruction of suspect or infected property by fire.[61] Vagrants and the disorderly poor, notoriously insouciant in the face of danger and bold in defiance of regulations, were prime candidates for the gallows. Should segregation orders be enforced, poor persons deprived absolutely of any chance of earning a living would become entirely dependent on public subsidies. Since plague could be associated with malnutrition or diagnosed as a form of food poisoning, there were incentives to make food rations as generous as possible. Such subsidies were sometimes declared, as they were by administrators in Florence in 1630, to be princely, as though the poor had never had it so good and they were making positive gains from the epidemic. But their supposed inadequacy could equally well be, as in Rome in 1656, the subject of bitter popular protest.[62]

Even with rising demands for public intervention, there was a reluctance to abandon the principle that contributions to the support of segregated persons, to the pesthouses, and to measures against the plague in general, ought to be voluntary and still depend upon charitable impulses. But beyond it loomed the threat that taxation would have to be imposed and that it would be justified by the overweening argument of "necessity." In plague-ridden Venice, the principle of the "voluntary tax," supposed to be voted on by parishioners according to a Senate law of 1529, died hard. During the terrible epidemic of 1630–1631, the Senate passed a decree to the effect that each head of household in Venice should "voluntarily pledge himself to disburse in the next five weeks as large a sum as he thinks he can afford, since the work is so charitable and so urgently needed."[63] In Florence, however, the Grand Duke spelled out the principles more clearly, according to the admiring commentator who testified that he "invited, begged and exhorted by public proclamation all persons of any rank who had the means to do so to offer a charitable subsidy to the needy, leaving each person to tax himself of his own good will, it being understood, however, that the Prince can and may tax him, in that necessity justifies any kind of impost. For everything vital to the state is just, and everything profitable to it is necessary, and nothing is of greater profit than the safety of subjects."[64]

In most epidemics the responsibility for raising funds rested with city authorities, even where the state (as in the Veneto or in Sardinia) was trying to put into effect a centrally directed policy for the control of plague, for the restriction of human movement, and for the provision of vital commodities such as food and fuel. Monti di Pietà might act up to a point as disaster banks which could provide cash advances, but they expected to be repaid, and the transition from calling on voluntary donations and services to exacting taxes or forced loans proved to be almost inevitable. According to Sporrin, a Sardinian magistrate of the seventeenth century, should the island committee for defense against the plague prove unable to raise adequate funds, then "the money can be taken by force, and those who have it can be compelled to give it, since in the face of such urgency there can be no privilege for the rich man."[65] True, there was a practical difficulty in resorting to taxation, since the forces which suspended almsgiving and stifled compassion also threatened to reduce taxpaying capacity, and it was hard to extract either loans or dues from persons who had fled into rural fastnesses. There was an inherent contradiction in the attempts sometimes made to provide for the poor by laying additional excises on food or wine, since these were almost certain to weigh more heavily on the poor, in whose budgets they bulked larger, than on the rich.[66] But whatever the difficulties there was in times of crisis a marked change in the process by which provision was made for the unemployed—a shift, however reluctantly and briefly accomplished, from the voluntary principle to one of compulsion.

This essay began with Muratori, and has probably ended by arguing laboriously that he was right. Few forms of aid to the poor in early modern Italy were expressly divorced from Christian charity or impossible to justify in terms of its rhetoric. The state and the prince were entities that needed, as much as individuals, to court divine favor by acts of piety, for the prosperity of the state and community depended on God's goodwill, and this could only be attracted by performing meritorious actions and suppressing sinful and blasphemous behavior.[67] Governments might be capable of invoking the concepts of the "public good" and the "safety of the people," using them to justify radical measures in the interests of the poor, but they did not, save in extraordinary situations, override or replace the sentiment of charity. As Muratori implied, charity was present wherever there was a disinterested intention, an earnest desire to benefit the poor in the name and love of God. Motives, of course, are difficult to fathom, and pure charitable impulses must often have been mixed with earthier considerations. No doubt charity was often influenced by a benefactor's desire to acquire status, respect, and even a modicum of power, to build up reserves of patronage, or to achieve a degree of personal mortality on earth through monuments commemorating his or her generosity (anything from a building to a well-placed bust or plaque).[68] Giovanni Pontano wrote of "largesse," a corruption of true liberality which consisted of self-interested giving on the part of persons of demagogic inclination, designed to form clienteles of grateful recipients and advance political ambitions.[69] Some assistance, as Marxist historians have argued, was inspired by the ambition to secure cheap, workhouse labor to perform the most rudimentary tasks in the textile industries.[70] Fear of riot by the "mean people," and even of discontent within a partially impoverished ruling order, could be a powerful incentive to provide relief, not always straightforwardly offered in the form of alms.

What can be done, however, is to identify certain activities which did not depend on simple gifts, but attempted to preserve independence and to stimulate work and productivity outside the walls of closed institutions or specially devised schemes for public works. Some organizations, including the Monti di Pietà, were closely tied to the commune and to the concept of a general "public good" which complemented the notion of "good works" performed for the benefit of individuals—of lending, not only to hard-pressed people in need of cash, but also to a community, to serve its collective needs for defense against foreign invasion, famine, and epidemic. Though supposedly undertaken in a spirit of charity, their paid administration was supported by clients' interest payments rather than by profiting from the prayers of grateful beneficiaries. Under normal circumstances, the burden of poor relief was carried by individuals and organizations that depended heavily on voluntary contributions. But great natural catastrophes could bring about a reluctant transition from private charity to public poor relief, visibly marked by elements of discipline and coercion. Words such as "welfare" (a reasonable translation of *"ben' essere")* were not unknown. Communities might at times be concerned with a general welfare, but sometimes this took the form of making special provision for trades deemed to be of particular benefit to the state. Public intervention on behalf of the poor in general tended to be spasmodic and reactive, rather than regularly forthcoming. It would be wrong to imply that charity, which at its best was not a chilly, patronizing agency that sapped the independence of the poor, but rather a kind of divine fire that burned up the love of self, was an old-fashioned concept from which poor relief needed to be cut loose in the name of progress. Impersonal and bureaucratic structures, financed by taxation and offering to guarantee rights rather than exercise sympathy and compassion, have not always worked better than schemes which claim to be inspired by the love of God. The important thing is to recognize the many guises in which charity could present itself and the complexity and variety of the motives and methods which underlay the practice of poor relief.

Notes

1. Ludovico Antonio Muratori, *Trattato della carità cristiana e altri scritti sulla carità,* ed. Piero G. Nonis (Rome, 1961). For the publishing history of the treatise, see Nonis's Introduction, separately paginated, 33–48.

2. Muratori, *Trattato,* 744–745.

3. Ibid., 631–632, 642.

4. See Giovanni Pontano, *I trattati delle virtù sociali. De Liberalitate, De Beneficentia, De Magnificentia, De Splendore, De Conviventia,* ed. Francesco Tateo (Rome, 1965). See *De Liberalitate,* Latin text, 4–5, 23–25, 33, Italian translation, 160–161, 178–181, 187; *De Beneficentia,* Latin text, 68, 76–78, Italian translation, 216, 224–225.

5. Pontano, *De Liberalitate,* Latin text, 34–37, Italian translation, 187–189; *De Beneficentia,* Latin text, 78–79, Italian translation, 226.

6. For illuminating remarks on this subject, see Massimo Maragi, "Istituzioni sociali non-caritative," in *e Forme e soggetti dell' intervento assistenziale in una città di antico regime* (Bologna, 1986), 145–162.

7. For some attempts to describe this hierarchy, see Brian Pullan, "Poveri, mendicanti e vagabondi (secoli XIV–XVII)," in *Storia d'Italia. Annali I. Dal feudalesimo al capitalismo,* eds. Corrado Vivanti and Ruggiero Romano (Turin, 1978), 981–1047.

8. For attempts to characterize the system of relief in major Italian cities, see Brian Pullan, " 'Support and Redeem': Charity and Poor Relief in Italian Cities from

the Fourteenth to the Seventeenth Century," in *Continuity and Change* 3 (1988): 177–208; Brian Pullan, "Povertà, carità e nuove forme di assistenza nell' Europa moderna," in *La città e i poveri. Milano e le terre lombarde dal Rinascimento all' età spagnola* (Milan, 1995), 26–33.

9. See, for example, Nicholas Terpstra, "Death and Dying in Renaissance Confraternities," in Konrad Eisenbichler ed., *Crossing the Boundaries: Christian Piety and the Arts in Italian Medieval and Renaissance Confraternities* (Kalamazoo, 1991), 190–191, 195; Nicholas Terpstra, "Women in the Brotherhood: Gender, Class and Politics in Renaissance Bolognese Confraternities," in *Renaissance and Reformation/Renaissance et Réforme* 26 (1991): 200–201.

10. For Genoa, see Rodolfo Savelli, "Dalle confraternite allo stato: il sistema assistenziale genovese nel Cinquecento," *Atti della Società Ligure di Storia Patria*, new series, 24 (1984), 177, 180, 182–184, 188–189, 192; for Turin, "Istituto bancario San Paolo di Torino: cenni storici," in *Archivi storici delle aziende di credito* (2 vols., Rome, 1956), I: 573–598, and Sandra Cavallo, *Charity and Power in Early Modern Italy. Benefactors and their Motives in Turin, 1541–1789* (Cambridge, 1995), 109–110, and see the index under "Compagnia di S. Paolo"; on Lodi, Marco Bascapè, "Confraternite e società a Lodi tra Quattro e Cinquecento," in *I Piazza da Lodi: una tradizione di pittori nel Cinquecento*, ed. Gianni Carlo Sciolla (Milan, 1989), 80–82; on Messina, Angelo Sindoni, "Le confraternite in Sicilia in età moderna," in *Sociabilità religiosa del Mezzogiorno: le confraternite laicali*, special issue of *Ricerche di storia sociale e religiosa*, new series, *anno* 19 (1990), 324, 329, 331, 334–335.

11. For examples, see Carol Bresnahan Menning, *Charity and the State in Late Renaissance Italy: the Monte di Pietà of Florence* (Ithaca, 1993), 51; Paola Massa Piergiovanni, "Assistenza e credito alle origini dell' esperienza ligure dei Monti di Pietà," in *Banchi pubblici, banchi privati e Monti di Pietà nell' Europa preindustriale*, in *Atti della Società Ligure di Storia Patria*, new series, 31 (Genoa, 1991), 605–606.

12. For examples, see Luigi da Rosa, "Banco di Napoli: cenni storici," in *Archivi storici*, I, 452–453; Mino Martelli, *Storia del Monte di Pietà in Lugo di Romagna (1546–1968)* (Florence, 1969), 111–112, 140–141, 302–304, 314–315; Brian Pullan, *Rich and Poor in Renaissance Venice: The Social Institutions of a Catholic State, to 1620* (Oxford, 1971), 584.

13. On these subjects, see Brian Pullan, "Charity and Poor Relief in Early Modern Italy," in *Charity, Self-interest and Welfare in the English Past*, ed. Martin Daunton (London, 1996), 65–89.

14. For a comprehensive survey of Italian fraternities, see Christopher F. Black, *Italian Confraternities in the Sixteenth Century* (Cambridge, 1989).

15. On the Scuole Grandi, see Pullan, *Rich and Poor*, 33–193.

16. The point is stressed by Armando Sapori, "I precedenti della previdenza sociale nel Medioevo," in his *Studi di storia economica medievale* (Florence, 1946), 422–423.

17. Archivio di Stato, Venice, Scuola Grande di San Marco, vol. 21, f. 192, 12 March 1560.

18. Archivio della Scuola Grande di San Rocco, Venice, Registro delle Terminazioni 3, f. 230v., 2 June 1593; an English translation appears in *Venice, A Documentary History 1450–1630*, ed. David Chambers and Brian Pullan (Oxford, 1992), 319–320.

19. For the Senate's decree, see Archivio di Stato, Venice, Senato, Mar, registro

25, f. 46r.–47r., 20 June 1539.

20. See Frederic C. Lane, *Venetian Ships and Ship-builders of the Renaissance* (Baltimore, 1934), 76–79.

21. See Mario Fanti, *La Chiesa e la Compagnia dei Poveri in Bologna. Una istituzione di mutuo soccorso nella società bolognese fra il Cinquecento e il Seicento* (Bologna, 1977), 43–44, 56–57; Maragi, "Istituzioni," 153–154.

22. Lane, *Venetian Ships*, 177–182; *Venice*, ed. Chambers and Pullan, 289–291.

23. See Robert C. Davis, *Shipbuilders of the Venetian Arsenal. Workers and Workplace in the Preindustrial City* (Baltimore, 1991), 20, 22, 25–26, 29–36.

24. Sapori, "I precedenti," 427–429; Lane, *Venetian Ships*, 76–79.

25. Davis, *Shipbuilders*, 40–41, 66, 72.

26. See, for example, the statutes of the ferry station of San Tomà on the Grand Canal: Sidney Jones University Library of Liverpool, Mayer MS. 20.9.83.37. Extracts in English translation appear in *Venice*, ed. Chambers and Pullan, 286–287.

27. Roberto Zago, I *Nicolotti: storia di una comunità di pescatori a Venezia nell' età moderna* (Abano Terme, 1982), 144–145, 153–157, 172 n. 44.

28. For a comprehensive survey, see Vittorino Meneghin, *I Monti di Pietà in Italia dal 1462 al 1562* (Vicenza, 1986). On the earliest Monte di Pietà, at Perugia, Stanislao Majarelli and Ugolino Nicolini, *Il Monte dei Poveri a Perugia: periodo delle origini (1462–74)* (Perugia, 1962). For a general discussion, Paolo Prodi, "La nascita dei Monti di Pietà: tra solidarismo cristiano e logica del profitto," *Annali dell' Istituto Storico Italo-germanico in Trento*, 8 (1982), 211–224.

29. Massa Piergiovanni, "Assistenza e credito," in *Banchi pubblici*, 595–596; Michele Luzzati, "Ruolo e funzione dei banchi ebraici dell' Italia centro-settentrionale nei secoli XV e XVI," ibid., 744–745.

30. Ilvo Capecchi and Luciana Gai, *Il Monte di Pietà a Pistoia e le sue origini* (Florence, 1976), 77–78, 146.

31. See Attilio Milano, "Considerazioni sulla lotta dei Monti di Pietà contro il prestito ebraico," *Scritti in memoria di Sally Mayer (1873–1953): saggi sull' ebraismo italiano* (Jerusalem, 1956), 214–217; Viviana Bonazzoli, "Monti di Pietà e politica economica delle città nelle Marche alla fine del '400," in *Banchi pubblici*, 570–573; Prodi, "La nascita," 223.

32. See, in general, Mario Maragi, "Cenni sulla natura e sullo svolgimento storico dei Monti di Pietà," in *Archivi storici*, I, 296–8. For details on Genoa in 1483, see Massa Piergiovanni, "Assistenza e credito," 605–606; on Florence in 1495, Guido Pampaloni, "Cenni storici sul Monte di Pietà di Firenze," *Archivi storici*, I, 530–34, and Bresnahan Menning, *Charity and the State*, 42–47; on Milan in 1496–1497, Giuliana Albini, "Sulle origini dei Monti di Pietà nel Ducato di Milano," *Archivio storico lombardo*, anno 111 (1985), 92–102; on Pistoia in 1473, Capecchi and Gai, *Il Monte*, 17–23.

33. Cf. Robert Bonfil, *Jewish Life in Renaissance Italy*, trans. Anthony Oldcorn (Berkeley-Los Angeles, 1994), 23–25.

34. For useful examples, see Albini, "Sulle origini"; Angelo Ventura, *Nobiltà e popolo nella società veneta del '400 e '500* (Bari, 1964), 421–439; Pullan, *Rich and Poor*, 581–583.

35. For the text of the bull, *Bullarium diplomatum et privilegiorum sanctorum romanorum pontificum taurinensis editio locupletior facta* (24 vols., Aosta, 1857–

1872), V, 621–623.

36. See Daniele Montanari, "I Monti di Pietà bergamaschi (secoli XVI–XVIII)," *Studi veneziani,* new series, 27 (1994), 176–184: Daniele Montanari, "I Monti di Pietà della Lombardia (secoli XV–XVIII). Prime riflessioni," *Annali di storia moderna e contemporanea* 2 (1996), 9–43.

37. Martelli, *Storia del Monte di Pietà,* 140–150.

38. For the best-known statement of this thesis, see Giuseppe Garrani, *Il carattere bancario e l'evoluzione strutturale dei primigenii Monti di Pietà: riflessi della tecnica bancaria antica su quella moderna* (Milan, 1957). Cf. Bresnahan Menning, *Charity and the State,* 86–87.

39. For early examples, Capecchi and Gai, *Il Monte di Pietà,* 63–64, 176–177; Bresnahan Menning, *Charity and the State,* 62; Bonazzoli, "Monti di Pietà," 582.

40. See Rodolfo Savelli, "Aspetti del dibattito quattrocentesco sui Monti di Pietà: *consilia* e *tractatus,*" in *Banchi pubblici,* 552–555.

41. Albini, "Sulle origini," 71–73, 88–89, 95, 100; Montanari, "I Monti di Pietà della Lombardia," 11–12, 19.

42. Martelli, *Storia del Monte di Pietà,* 150–152, 302–304; Carlo M. Travaglini, "Il ruolo del Banco di Santo Spirito e del Monte di Pietà nel mercato finanziaro romano del Settecento," in *Banchi pubblici,* 624, 631, 638.

43. Capecchi and Gai, *Il Monte di Pietà,* 77–78, 79–80, 85, 159; Martelli, *Storia del Monte,* 87–88; Paolo Ulvioni, *Il gran castigo di Dio. Carestie ed epidemie a Venezia e nella Terraferma, 1628–1632* (Milan, 1989), 140, 179.

44. Martelli, *Storia del Monte,* 87–88, 127–129; Capecchi and Gai, *Il Monte di Pietà,* 83–84, 128–129, 223–247; Massa Piergiovanni, "Assistenza e carità," 602–603; Bresnahan Menning, *Charity and the State,* 92–94.

45. Albini, "Sulle origini," 97, 99–100.

46. Savelli, "Aspetti," 556–557.

47. See Pampaloni, "Cenni storici," 536; Bresnahan Menning, *Charity and the State,* 84–85, 96. See also Pullan, *Rich and Poor,* 588; Travaglini, "Il ruolo," 624.

48. Luigi De Rosa, "Banchi pubblici, banchi privati e Monti di Pietà a Napoli nei secoli XVI–XVIII," in *Banchi pubblici,* 499–505, 511; Ennio di Simone, "I banchi pubblici napoletani al tempo di Carlo di Borbone: qualche aspetto della loro attività," ibid., 527, 530. For similar practices in Rome, see Travaglini, "Il ruolo," 624–627, 628–629.

49. Capecchi and Gai, *Il Monte di Pietà,* 41, 167. Cf. Pampaloni, "Cenni storici," 540–543; Massa Piergiovanni, "Assistenza e carità," 606–608.

50. Pullan, *Rich and Poor,* 589–595.

51. Daniela Lombardi, "1629–31: crisi e peste a Firenze," *Archivio storico italiano,* anno 137 (1979): 6–7; Ulvioni, *Il gran castigo,* 206, notes a similar complaint from the Venetian province of Friuli.

52. Massa Piergiovanni, "Assistenza e carità," 610–611.

53. On Naples, Di Simone, "I banchi pubblici," 520–521; De Rosa, "Banca di Napoli," I, 457; De Rosa, "Banchi pubblici," 508–509. On Brescia, Maurizio Pegrari, "L'immagine e la realtà. Attività di credito e vicende dei Monti di Pietà bresciani (secoli XV–XIX)," in *Per il quinto centenario del Monte di Pietà di Brescia (1489–1989),* (2 vols., Brescia, 1989), I, 118–120. See also Pullan, *Rich and Poor,* 605–609; Pampaloni, "Cenni storici," 551; Martelli, *Storia del Monte,* 156–157.

54. Carlo M. Cipolla, *I pidocchi e il Gran Duca. Crisi economica e problemi sanitari nella Firenze del '600* (Bologna, 1979), 24.

55. Lombardi, "1629–31," 16–17.

56. Quoted in Francesco Manconi, *Castigo de Dios. La grande peste barocca nella Sardegna di Filippo IV* (Rome, 1994), 227; cf. also 289–291, 326–331.

57. Carlo M. Cipolla, *Public Health and the Medical Profession in the Renaissance* (Cambridge, 1976), 42.

58. Ibid., 39–41.

59. For Rome, see Alessandro Pastore, "Tra giustizia e politica: il governo della peste a Genova e Roma nel 1656–7," *Rivista storica italiana, anno* 100 (1988), 140–141. For Florence, Dante Catellacci, "Curiosi ricordi del contagio di Firenze nel 1630," *Archivio storico italiano,* 5th series, vol. 20 (1897), 387–389; Lombardi, "1629–31," 43–49.

60. Extensively quoted in Giulia Calvi, "L' oro, il fuoco, le forche: la peste napoletana del 1656," *Archivio storico italiano* 139 (1981), 458; cf. also Carlo M. Cipolla, *Cristofano and the Plague: A Study in the History of Public Health in the Age of Galileo* (London, 1973), 89–90, and Manconi, *Castigo de Dios,* 127–128.

61. Catellacci, "Curiosi ricordi," 389; Calvi, "L'oro," 447; Manconi, *Castigo de Dios,* 206–208, 217.

62. Catellacci, "Curiosi ricordi," 388–389; Pastore, "Tra giustizia e politica," 140–141.

63. See Ulvioni, *Il gran castigo,* 80. The Venetian statute of 1529 appears in English translation in *Venice,* ed. Chambers and Pullan, 303–306.

64. Catellacci, "Curiosi ricordi," 384.

65. Manconi, *Castigo de Dios,* 126–127.

66. Ibid., 381–384.

67. For remarks on this theme, see Brian Pullan, "Plague and Perceptions of the Poor in Early Modern Italy," in *Epidemics and Ideas: Essays on the Historical Perception of Pestilence,* eds. Terence Ranger and Paul Slack (Cambridge, 1992), 101–103.

68. This theme is brilliantly expounded by Sandra Cavallo in, *Charity and Power.*

69. Pontano, *De Liberalitate,* Latin text, 36–37, 61–62; Italian translation, 189, 211–212.

70. See Catharina Lis and Hugo Soly, *Poverty and Capitalism in Pre-industrial Europe* (London, 1979), especially 88–96.

ANTHONY BRUNDAGE

Private Charity and the 1834 Poor Law

Historians of the English poor laws have paid relatively little attention to the parallel history of philanthropy.[1] Most poor law histories make passing reference to a supposed phase of benevolence in the eighteenth century, characterized by compassionate private giving, before concentrating on the efforts to transform and tighten up public relief beginning in the 1790s, leading to the enactment of the New Poor Law in 1834. Private charity tends to be largely ignored until the emergence of the Charity Organization Society in 1869 and its partnership with poor law authorities in the campaign to terminate outdoor relief. Overall, the public sector has drawn considerably more scholarly attention than the private. Frank Prochaska has noted the reluctance of historians to study "practices redolent of hierarchical values and now unfashionable pieties" and has further detected a certain Whiggishness in histories of charity, "a tendency to see philanthropy as a stage in the history of the welfare state."[2] Geoffrey Finlayson has recently amplified the latter criticism, making the Whiggish tendency to view philanthropy as a passing phase on the way to ever expanding public services the major fallacy to be attacked in his revisionist account of the history of public and private provision for the poor.[3]

Both writers make a strong case for studying philanthropy in order to better comprehend the history of modern British society. It might be added that the history of the poor law itself can be better understood by integrating with it the history of charitable giving. While it is true that the Royal Commission on the Poor Laws of 1832–34 and the resulting Poor Law Amendment Act of 1834 had relatively little to say on the subject, charity and public relief were in fact closely intertwined in the complex intellectual and social background to the New Poor Law, as well as in the implementation of the statute. This paper will explore some of these connections, and consider how they might illuminate the current debate over social policy.

The English Poor Law, born at the end of the sixteenth century out of a socioeconomic crisis engendered by the transition to early modern capitalism, had become a time-honored fixture of local government by the eighteenth century. Each parish was responsible for the maintenance of its settled poor, with oversight by the magistrates of the district. In the absence of central government supervision (the activist Privy Council of Charles I's day having fallen into disuse), a great variety of relief practices were to be found throughout the country. In spite of this variety, there was general agreement that the central purpose of public relief was the maintenance of a well-ordered society and a reduction in numbers of those vagrants and "masterless men" whose proliferation had first moved Elizabeth's parliament to act. The private charities of the era, though driven by a wide array of personal, humanitarian, and pious motives, shared the poor law's concern with social control. Many of them also sought to strengthen the sinews of national power. A mercantilist, pre-Malthusian concern to foster an increase of a healthy population and thus augment the labor force and military is a marked feature of the voluntary charities of the eighteenth century. Institutions like Thomas Coram's Foundling Hospital and Jonas Hanway's Marine Society, in addition to saving lives and reforming character, also sought to add to the number of "useful hands," especially in the merchant marine and navy.[4]

As mercantilism came under increasing fire in the latter half of the century, there was a corollary movement to reform both the poor laws and charity. Adam Smith's *Wealth of Nations*, while certainly the best-known assault on mercantilist economics, did not represent a radical assault on either the poor laws or philanthropy. Smith had no quarrel with a system of mandatory public relief, his strictures being confined to the inhibition of labor mobility represented by the laws of settlement.[5] Attacks on both the poor laws and philanthropy, however, became a marked feature of the period after 1780. Edmund Burke's condemnation of the poor laws, in his *Reflections on the French Revolution*, was based on the premise that mandatory assessment deadened the spirit of voluntary giving, thus undermining social virtue.[6] Burke's argument, although anticipated almost a century earlier by Sir Francis Brewster,[7] had much greater resonance in the 1790s because of the specter of revolutionary upheaval.

Counterrevolutionary anxieties also contributed to the fervent acceptance of Thomas Malthus's views, though Malthus went considerably beyond Burke by condemning charity as well as poor relief for fueling a demographic catastrophe. The *Essay on Population* (1798), by injecting a supposedly scientific rigor into the discussion, became the major text brandished by those seeking to reduce if not eliminate both poor relief and charity. While Malthus was somewhat more cautious than many of his avid disciples in his condemnation of the poor laws in general and the allowance system in particular, and moderated his views considerably for the revised edition of 1803, the pessimistic message was the one that stuck.[8] The Malthusians came to believe that poor laws and charity alike were bad policy, and that the de-moralizing of political economy was the necessary antidote to harmful laws and sentimental giving.[9]

The trajectory of thinking represented by the work of Smith, Burke, and Malthus seemed to point to abolition of the poor law and a severe curtailment of philanthropy. Indeed, during the first two decades of the nineteenth century this seemed the most likely outcome, at least in regard to the poor laws. Abolitionism was the most prominent strain in the numerous publications devoted to the topic, as well as in parliamentary discussions.[10] That this did not occur is due to many factors. One is the recognition that too dramatic a reduction in traditional relief, public or private, might trigger revolution. Mitchell Dean may well be correct in his assertion that a foundationalist defense of the right of the poor to adequate relief, found in writers like William Paley, was of quite recent origin, and emerged only in response to abolitionist arguments.[11] Nonetheless, it was an argument quickly embraced by spokesmen for the poor like William Cobbett.[12] It was also an argument brandished by such Establishment propagandists as Hannah More, who pointed out that English workers had no need of revolution because they enjoyed a well-established right to sustenance under the poor laws as well as being beneficiaries of a sturdy tradition of gentry paternalism.[13]

As an Evangelical, Hannah More was concerned not only to keep the poor quietly in their place, but to engage with them and bring about their moral regeneration. Evangelicalism was profoundly activist, fueling the campaign for the abolition of evils like slavery and working for the expansion of a certain kind of charitable activity. Evangelicals were devoted to the reformation of character and tended to believe that traditional almsgiving was a bounty on idleness and profligacy, but their critique of philanthropy was significantly different from that of the Malthusians. The latter were disposed to consider all giving as pernicious, to distance themselves from the poor and to allow market forces to effect a wholesome discipline. Evangelicals, with their intense Christian emotionalism, were eager to increase their involvement in the lives of the poor. This attitude tended to spill over into poor law reform, thus blunting the thrust of the abolitionist movement.

If Evangelicalism was loathe to withdraw from the lives of the poor, so, in a very different way, was Utilitarianism. In considering the impact of this intellectual system, it is useful to look beyond the work of Jeremy Bentham and his disciples. While Benthamism provided the central ideological core, there were many eighteenth-century writers and political figures who demonstrated a similar concern to reform government and law along rational lines. An example is the poor law reformer and MP Thomas Gilbert. Gilbert's Act of 1782 (22 Geo. III, c. 83) allowed the grouping of parishes into unions in which workhouses were to be used exclusively for children, the aged, and the infirm. Though often cited for its humanitarian provisions,[14] Gilbert's Act was even more important in expanding the area of pauper management and attempting to bring the gentry into closer involvement in poor relief administration.[15] His statute of 1786 (26 Geo. III, c. 58) supplemented an act of the same session (22 Geo. III, c. 56), requiring that parishes furnish accurate figures on both poor law expenditure and charitable payments to the poor during the previous three years.[16] These Gilbert Returns are of considerable significance, both because they denote the close connection in the minds of reformers between public and private giving, and because they represent the attempt to legislate on the basis of quantifiable data. The figures were widely cited by reformers, and the entire Gilbert Returns were reprinted in 1810 and 1816.[17] An accumulating body of more-or-less reliable statistics, coupled with a belief in the efficacy of reforming legislation, served further to thwart the momentum of poor law abolition.

Bentham's ideas offered the most original, if not necessarily the most practical, way of legislating the country forward to a sound system of poor relief. Many of his contemporaries were intrigued by his assertion that the reformational functions of a new kind of workhouse (Panopticon) could operate in harness with money-saving methods of organization, a squaring of the circle that pointed away from the gloomy quietism of hard-core Malthusianism. His original scheme called for a farming-out of poor relief functions by government to a private contractor, which he of course intended to be his own company. It was a plan that combined governmental and free-market activity, interweaving public and private sectors of giving. It was no accident that Bentham called his proposed run-for-profit poor relief organization the National Charity Company.[18] In any event, a skeptical parliament and ministry balked at such an innovation, and Bentham's later plans for poor law reform were more along the lines of establishing new government agencies to superintend more rigorous methods of relief. In spite of this reversion to somewhat less unorthodox ideas of reform, Benthamism retained some of its earlier visionary quality, inspiring an activist legislative program.

The first decades of the nineteenth century saw key Benthamites pressing for reform in both charity and the poor law system. Henry Brougham, barrister, Whig MP, and one of the founders of the reformist *Edinburgh Review*, campaigned aggressively for a rational reordering of the centuries-old jumble of testamentary and voluntary philanthropy. Brougham's campaign, based in part on the recently reprinted Gilbert returns, exemplified the utilitarian spirit—the determination to avoid all sentimentality in the drive to fashion institutions suitable to a modern commercial, industrial society. His early focus was on educational charities, and in 1816 he moved for a Select Committee on the Education of the Poor in the Metropolis. The original Select Committee gave way to the Charity Commissioners in 1818, and the inquiry quickly burgeoned into a great survey covering all endowed charities, an enterprise that would take twenty years and fill forty volumes.[19] An example of the ill-conceived endowments brought to light by the Commissioners, resulting, it was claimed, in flagrant abuses and demoralization of the poor, was the Jarvis Bequest. In 1793 George Jarvis, piqued by his daughter's marriage, left a fortune of over £100,000 to the poor of three Herefordshire parishes, whose total population was under 900. It took many years of legal and political wrangling before even a partial solution to this abuse was worked out by special legislation in 1852.[20] Their untiring efforts show that the Benthamites, sometimes derided for their excessive individualism, saw themselves as defenders of the public interest against eccentric individuals like George Jarvis.

The Charity Commissioners, under the control of Brougham and other reformers, used their annual reports to promote bringing system and rigor to charitable giving. On the surface, some of their comments appear very close to the Malthusian mistrust of the philanthropic impulse. Their 1823 report, for example, declared:

> A person may be endowed with a heart "overflowing with the milk of human kindness," and be the occasion of much more extensive mischief than the most hardened villain. The laws in any tolerably governed state limit the powers of the latter, but the former unfortunately is often encouraged in his career by the approbation of all in whose opinion he desires to stand well. Such a man by an indiscriminate alms-giving may be the promoter of idleness and beggary, the patron of deception and vice, and so far as he holds out a premium for what is bad, an actual diminisher of the sum of good.[21]

Yet, while the report does go on to express some alarm about philanthropy's inducement to the growth of surplus population, there is also a guardedly hopeful belief in the efficacy of education operating in harness with discriminating, well-informed giving. Most importantly, the Commissioners strove to remove the dead hand of ill-advised or obsolete testamentary bequests, redirecting substantial sums to more useful charitable purposes. Such a program required strong government, not a retreat into laissez-faire platitudes.

In addition to the work of the Charity Commissioners, there were in the early nineteenth century numerous local initiatives to bring order out of the chaotic world of private charity. The most important strategies adopted in these years were the relief ticket and district visiting. One of the earliest organizations to employ the ticket system was the Mendicity Society. To counter the sometimes menacing importunings of London's beggars, subscribers were given relief tickets to distribute. These in turn had to be presented at the society's headquarters in Red Lion Square, upon which a close inquiry would be made into the pauper's circumstances. Only after satisfying themselves that relief would have a salutary effect would the society's officer proceed to grant relief, often in kind. Not surprisingly, many of the indigent refused to submit to such scrutiny.[22] Systematic inquiry into the character of relief applicants, which was to be such a marked feature of mid-Victorian organized charity, was thus becoming established a couple of generations earlier. So was district visiting, an even more rigorous and intrusive method of investigation.

The most significant figure in the development of the visiting movement was the Rev. Thomas Chalmers. As minister of St. John's, Glasgow, in the early 1820s, Chalmers instituted a system in which visitors penetrated every street and alley and came to know many of the inhabitants of one of the worst slums in the country. Only with such detailed firsthand knowledge, he argued, could wise and socially responsible decisions be made about the granting of relief. The Select Committee on the Irish Poor Law in 1830 asked him to present evidence concerning his methods, which by that time had begun to spread to other philanthropic bodies. In 1828, a variety of Evangelical organizations joined in a General Society for Promoting District Visiting, which in a short time boasted 573 visitors making 165,000 calls annually.[23]

Another Scotsman to exercise great influence on questions relating to poverty and poor relief was Patrick Colquhoun. A Glasgow merchant and founder of the Chamber of Commerce in that city, Colquhoun became a London police magistrate and wrote on a wide array of social issues. In his *Treatise on Indigence* (1806), he stressed the difference between poverty and indigence, pointing out that the former was the natural state of mankind and the source of wealth and civilization. Undiscriminating charity, far from alleviating indigence, had simply wasted vast sums and demoralized the poor.[24] Colquhoun's stress on more rigorous relief under the poor law, coupled with his call for a professional police, make him an important forerunner of Edwin Chadwick and the reformers of the 1830s.[25]

The crucial influence of Chalmers and Colquhoun was part of a wider pattern in which Scotland came increasingly to be looked to as a model for wholesome practices in the treatment of indigence. The Scottish Poor Law recommended itself to English reformers because it avoided the evils of mandatory assessment and relief. In Scotland, a poor relief fund was gathered by voluntary donations in each church, sometimes supplemented by parochial assessments, and was dispensed by a committee of the kirk sessions and the principal heritors (landowners). Paupers in Scotland could thus lay no claim to a foundationalist right to relief, and complete discretion was accorded to those administering the fund.[26] In the eyes of reformers, it was a well-nigh perfect blend of discriminating private charity and local authority, further enhanced by giving a key role to major landowners. When poor law reform was being debated in 1817, Lord Castlereagh, a leading member of the cabinet, told the House of Commons that England should try to emulate Scotland, though he admitted that a wholesale adoption of the Scottish system would be tantamount to abolition and was therefore impracticable.[27] Nevertheless, the Scottish Poor Law influenced the fashioning of the Select Vestries Acts of 1818–19 (58 Geo. III, c. 69 and 59 Geo. III, c. 12) by which large landowners gained significant powers over poor relief in those parishes where the acts were adopted.[28]

That such piecemeal changes as the Select Vestries Acts gave way to the impetus for sweeping reform in the 1830s is due to two factors. One was the perception of widespread social breakdown in the countryside represented by the Captain Swing riots of 1830–31. The other was the coming to power of a Whig ministry, thus making it possible for Chadwick and other Benthamites to play a central role in fashioning the New Poor Law. Yet, while recognizing the pivotal role of Chadwick, as well as that of the economist Nassau Senior, on the Royal Commission for the Poor Laws, it is important to appreciate the influence of other commissioners—the Evangelical bishop of Chester (and later Archbishop of Canterbury) John Bird Summer, the bishop of London, C. J. Blomfield, an activist in the visiting movement, and the poor law reformer William Sturges-Bourne, architect of the Select Vestries Acts.

With such an array of Benthamites, Evangelicals, charity activists, and practical reformers drawn from the ranks of country gentlemen, reform of the poor laws was highly unlikely to be a purely ideological contrivance. This becomes more obvious when we consider that any bill would have to pass muster before an extremely aristocratic cabinet and a parliament in which the power of the landed interest was still preponderant. The continuing influence of Malthus's ideas led some contemporaries, as it later caused some historians, to assume that the New Poor Law was largely an act of applied Malthusianism. For example, William Otter, the Bishop of Chichester who published an appreciative "Memoir" to the second edition of Malthus's *Principle of Political Economy* in 1836, claimed that the *Essay on Population* and the New Poor Law "stand or fall together. They have the same friends and the same enemies, and the relations they bear to each other, of theory and practice, are admirably calculated to afford mutual illumination and support."[29] This is a considerable exaggeration. While a measure of Malthusian thinking was not incompatible with Utilitarian or Evangelical principles, the activist and sometimes ameliorative dynamic inherent in both systems cut the other way. Chadwick, the Benthamite voice of the Royal Commission, never tired of protesting the great gulf between his views and those of the Malthusians, even though many of the New Poor Law's opponents insisted that the act was designed to decrease the "surplus population."[30]

The Royal Commission concentrated its inquiries on the poor law system proper, drawing upon an abundance of evidence, both statistical and anecdotal. Private charity was not altogether ignored, but no single section of the Commission's Report of 1834 was devoted to the topic. Instead, there are scattered references to the evils of profuse, undiscriminating charity throughout the reports of some of the individual assistant commissioners.[31] The greatest amount of space accorded to philanthropy is found in the report of Chadwick himself, during his tenure as an assistant commissioner for London and Berkshire. He chose to highlight the alleged breakdown of family life and increase in social pathologies created by the Spitalfields charities, both endowed and voluntary, which served as a magnet for paupers from far and wide. Commenting on his findings a couple of years later, Chadwick noted:

> if any trustee of a public charity for the distribution of doles, instead of distributing the substance as intended, consumed it in good cheer for himself and friends; and . . . any trustee of a charity for foundlings, instead of applying the substance to those purposes, kept a mistress with it, [he] really produced less mischief with such a course of proceeding, as compared with a literal administration of the trust, and was *pro tanto* a benefactor to the public.[32]

Chadwick's report was the most prominent in the one-volume collection of extracts that the Whig government rushed into print in 1833 to help prepare the ground for legislative action.[33]

In spite of such material, when the time came to draw up their final report, the Royal Commission preferred to dodge the issue of what to do with the still sprawling mass of unreformed charities. After a couple of paragraphs describing in general terms the pernicious effects of many charitable trusts and voluntary funds, they concluded:

> These charities, in the districts where they abound, may interfere with the efficacy of the measures we have recommended [regarding the poor laws], and

on this ground, though aware that we should not be justified in offering any specific recommendation with respect to them, we beg to suggest that they call for the attention of the Legislature.[34]

The statute as finally approved by both houses and signed into law by the king in August 1834 (4 & 5 Will. IV, c. 76) contained only one section (Clause 85) pertaining to charity, giving the Poor Law Commissioners the power to call for returns of any charitable trust established for the relief of the poor.

The newly appointed three-man Poor Law Commission, with Chadwick, much to his dismay, as secretary rather than full commissioner, took office at the end of 1834. Their powers had been substantially reduced during the bill's passage, and the statute's implementation was necessarily often a matter of negotiation with local elites on such issues as poor law union boundaries, appointment of local poor law officials, and the regulation of outdoor relief.[35] Parliament had seen fit to grant the Commission only a five-year term. By the time that expired in 1839, it was renewed only on a year-to-year basis until the amending legislation of 1847, which transformed the Commission into the Poor Law Board, one of whose members was to have a seat in Parliament. Such reluctance grew out of the act's unpopularity, especially in the depressed north, as well as the desire of local elites to run their boards of guardians with as little interference as possible from London. Given their rather tentative status, the Poor Law Commissioners were not disposed to demand sweeping new powers, or even to press forward vigorously with the ones they possessed. Nonetheless, the dreaded workhouses spread across the land and were employed with deterrent rigor by local boards. Coupled with a policy of more discriminating outdoor relief, this resulted in a substantial reduction of expenditures in the first years of operation, to the delight of the nation's ratepayers.

In regard to governmental efforts at charitable reform, the New Poor Law served as something of a model. In 1835 a Select Committee on Public Charities recommended that all endowed charities be superintended by a three-man board similar in structure and authority to that of the Poor Law Commissioners, though this was not implemented for nearly two decades.[36] The Select Committee's final report, issued in six parts between 1837 and 1840, was quickly dubbed "Domesday Book" for its thoroughness.[37] In this it bore a close resemblance to the massive survey on the poor laws undertaken by the Royal Commission from 1832 to 1834. Finally, in 1853 a permanent supervisory body of four commissioners (three of them paid) was established by the Charitable Trusts Act (16 & 17 Vict., c. 137).[38] The powers of these new Charity Commissioners, however, were considerably more circumscribed than those of the Poor Law Commissioners, and only two inspectors were authorized by the legislation. In the halting, cautious manner of the early Victorian state, poor law and charity reform were operating on parallel tracks, though there was little cooperation between the agencies. Early on, friction developed when the Poor Law Commissioners authorized the sale of parish property held in trust for the poor, and subsequently they sought the approval of the Charity Commissioners in doubtful cases.[39]

Yet, while at the level of central administration, early Victorian poor relief and charity tended to be separate spheres, they were intertwined in the minds of many of those who administered the poor laws, especially at the local level. Not many able-bodied laborers were likely to have characterized the New Poor Law as paternalist. All too often, their application to a board of guardians was met by an "offer of the House." Even those who were kept on outdoor relief were apt to find it reduced in amount and offered partly in kind. However, large numbers of pauper applicants were aged, infirm, and children, and these were often treated humanely. Thus the workhouse wore two aspects: "Bastille" to some, place of refuge to others. As David Roberts puts it, the workhouse "combined that mixture of severe discipline and kindly benevolence in those local spheres where squire and parson thought they could distinguish between the unworthy and worthy poor."[40] Such discrimination was a far cry from the supposedly "self-acting" nature of the workhouse test, and represented a strategy that had much more in common with private charity than it did with Benthamite doctrines of poor relief.

Examples of poor law paternalism abound. In Sussex, local boards contrived, in the face of Poor Law Commission directives to the contrary, to take some children into the workhouse so that the rest of the family could remain in their cottage, to offer generous medical relief, and to serve roast beef and plum pudding to workhouse residents on Christmas Day.[41] Similar indulgences were granted in Wiltshire.[42] In Northamptonshire, several boards allowed daily excursions outside by workhouse inmates, improved upon the official dietaries, and allowed elderly couples to sleep together in the workhouse.[43] In Nottinghamshire, the doctrinaire Assistant Poor Law Commissioner for the area, Edward Gulson, tried to get the boards to stop outdoor relief altogether. Not only did they refuse, but a separate private relief fund was raised to offset the effects of trade depression, to which the chairman of the Basford Board of Guardians personally contributed £100.[44] On another occasion, Gulson tried unsuccessfully to prevent gifts of tea and tobacco from being given to workhouse inmates, exclaiming: "Charity and compulsory maintenance of the destitute ought never to be mixed together—each stands upon a different principle."[45] It is certainly important to keep in mind the deep hostility many of the poor felt toward the New Poor Law, not only in the agitated north, but even in relatively "quiet" rural areas.[46] Yet it is equally important to recognize the benevolent tendencies of some local officials, and their refusal to accept that absolute divorce of charity and poor relief urged by doctrinaire central officials like Gulson or Chadwick.

Close cooperation between local poor law authorities and charitable organizations was also a hallmark of the early Victorian period. It became an increasingly common practice, for example, for boards of guardians to place certain categories of pauper in specialist institutions run by private charities. The mentally ill and other classes of the indigent were thus being maintained at public expense in private facilities, with guardians periodically conducting inspection tours to ensure adequate treatment.[47] Representatives of charities also had some access to poor law institutions, the most notable activity being that of the Workhouse Visiting Society. The women visitors of this organization donated money and time to improve the internal arrangements and comforts of workhouses; their activities ranged from decorating to distributing toys to establishing libraries. Visitors also assisted in training workhouse girls for domestic service and finding employment for them when they reached puberty.[48] It is important also to bear in mind the considerable overlap in certain districts between the personnel on public and private agencies. As Norman McCord has commented:

> It would . . . give a misleading picture to suppose that the official Poor Law machinery and unofficial philanthropy existed in two different spheres . . . Those who sat as Poor Law guardians would very often be the same people who sat on the committees which controlled schools, hospitals, and dispensaries, and the other varied forms of charitable organizations.[49]

The massive and prolonged trade depression of the 1840s, coupled with the precariousness of the Poor Law Commission, ensured that there would be little tampering with the wide discretion allowed to local boards of guardians. Numerous exceptions were permitted to the prohibition on outdoor relief to the able-bodied, and an Outdoor Labour Test was used in place of the workhouse test in a number of unions, especially in the towns.[50] Even with the return of better times and their more secure footing after being transformed into the Poor Law Board in 1847, the central authority continued to display little initiative. Private philanthropy, meanwhile, continued a spectacular expansion. In London alone, 279 charities were established in the first half of the nineteenth century; a further 144 were added in the 1850s.[51] The royal family, always a major player in the philanthropic world, became even more central in the 1840s, thanks largely to the unstinting efforts of Prince Albert.[52]

That relatively little progress toward abolishing outdoor relief to the able-bodied had been accomplished by either the Poor Law Commission, or the Poor Law Board had a good deal to do with the economics of poor relief. Niggardly out-relief, at an average expenditure of about 2s. a head per week, cost only a third as much as maintaining someone in the workhouse. The 1860s saw outdoor relief rise by a further 25 percent, with the ratio of outdoor paupers to total population increasing from 1 in 27 to 1 in 25.[53] As Gareth Stedman Jones has shown, by 1860 the East End of London, with its demoralized and poverty-stricken masses, was seen as being in a state of crisis, exacerbated by the withdrawal of the middle class from the district. East End boards of guardians, mainly from the class of small shopkeepers, lacked vigorous leadership, while large charitable funds originating in the West End were squandered without any thought of the consequences.[54] A growing impatience with such a state of affairs make this decade an important watershed in the history of relief.

J. G. Fitch, an educational writer and inspector of schools, complained in 1869 that the poor law had utterly lost whatever deterrence it once possessed. The workhouse was no longer shunned, and the able-bodied made heavy use of the casual ward. These difficulties, he charged, were compounded "by professional almoners, and by the encouragement given to beggars."[55] Florence Nightingale had already made the same point more vividly by quoting with approval an unidentified French "administrateur":

We cannot understand your English laws—you have a Poor Law—you pay rates for your child paupers to be educated—for your sick paupers to be housed and doctored in places called workhouses, etc. etc. And then you subscribe to private charities to take your paupers out of the power of the Poor Law. If you do the one, why do you do the other? Would it not be cheaper to see that the two work in the same direction?[56]

Nightingale also praised Thomas Chalmers's administration at Glasgow, and the Scottish system in general—a hearkening back to early nineteenth century efforts to tighten up relief and coordinate the poor law and charity[57]

Such outcries clearly pointed the way to a new era of partnership between poor law authorities and charitable organizations to avoid working at cross-purposes. Close cooperation had indeed already begun on an ad hoc basis. During the 1862–1865 Lancashire cotton famine, occasioned by the Union's blockade of the South in the Civil War, the massive unemployment in the region produced a crisis. The Poor Law Board worked closely with charitable organizations in the cotton-spinning districts, dispatching a special commissioner, H.B. Farnell, to Lancashire to organize the relief efforts in conjunction with philanthropic leaders.[58] Initiatives to coordinate the welter of individual charities was also a marked feature of the decade. In Liverpool, William Rathbone's efforts resulted in the amalgamation of three relief agencies into the Central Relief Board. Similar coordination was achieved by the Edinburgh Society for Improving the Condition of the Poor (1867). The London Association for the Prevention of Pauperism and Crime (1868) reflected most accurately in its name the intense anxiety about the relationship between lax poor relief and social pathology.[59]

The Minute issued by G. J. Goschen, president of the Poor Law Board, at the end of 1869 brought many of these matters to a head. He sought to restart the campaign against outdoor relief by close cooperation with organized charity, initially in London metropolitan poor law unions.[60] Three East End Unions—St. George's in the East, Whitechapel, and Stepney—agreed to stop all outdoor relief immediately, with charitable agencies relieving only those applicants considered "redeemable."[61] That Goschen and the three boards of guardians were able to act so decisively is due to the fact that a major organizational breakthrough had been achieved earlier in 1869: the formation of the Charity Organization Society. The COS had already lobbied the Poor Law Board for such action and some of its members had secured election as poor law guardians. To underscore the new spirit of cooperation, Goschen himself became a vice-president of the COS.[62]

The ideas and methods of Thomas Chalmers provided the most important model for leaders of the campaign against outdoor relief. C. S. Loch, who became secretary of the COS in 1875, frequently invoked Chalmers's doctrine that social distress was caused by individual character flaws. To ensure that only the "deserving" poor would receive any relief outside the workhouse, the COS instituted the casework method, an important step toward the professionalizing of social work.[63] By coordinating their investigations with the local boards of guardians, the COS would ensure that the "house" was offered only to the undeserving. In effect, the COS would administer a test of character, which was provided by the case study, while the guardians would offer a test of destitution by a simple offer of the workhouse, as envisaged in Chadwick's original plan. The former would be the result of minute investigation into every aspect of the applicant's character and circumstances; the latter would be "self-acting."[64] Not only was COS casework much more thorough and intrusive than the investigations of earlier visiting societies, their definition of what constituted good character was much stricter.[65] It was no longer a question of weeding out the obviously dissolute, drunk, or work-shy. The 1876 annual report of the COS specified those contingencies that obligated the individual to make prudent provision for: temporary sickness, unemployment, early marriage, a large family, and old age.[66] Failure to make such provisions could be construed as evidence of character deficiencies, thus, in theory at least, consigning the applicant to the "undeserving" category and the tender mercies of the poor law.

In practice, the collaboration between poor law guardians and the COS was very uneven. It was quite close in Stepney, Whitechapel, Camberwell, and Marylebone; a number of Marylebone guardians were COS members. Outside London, too, certain unions were, in the eyes of the COS, models of strict administration and close cooperation: Newcastle, Darlington, Durham, and West Hartlepool. Unions in which there was little or no cooperation were, however, much more common.[67] The most striking characteristic to emerge from a study of poor law-COS relations in the northeast is the extreme variability, even in adjoining unions, and the modest achievements even in the most "advanced" unions.[68] A recent, comprehensive survey of COS activities outside London finds that provincial COSs were not only ineffective in the campaign against outdoor relief, but that, contrary to the claims of COS propaganda, they signally failed to assist the "deserving" poor.[69]

In the end, the campaign to abolish outdoor relief failed to achieve its objectives, though Karel Williams's work suggests that, for a considerable time, the campaign by poor law authorities was much more effective than is often recognized.[70] There are several reasons for the failure of the campaign. Most importantly, the policies being deployed were utterly unable to grapple with the effects of the trade cycles and mass unemployment of a mature capitalist system, or indeed with many of the "ordinary" crises of modern urban life. Other factors, however, were at work as well, including the impact of democratization and collectivism in the political sphere, professionalization of both the poor law and charitable services, and the persistence of nondoctrinaire habits and impulses among the public.

It is true that the working class entertained considerable suspicions about an activist state, and that their direct attempts to shape more liberal welfare policies began only after the formation of the Labour Party.[71] Yet Liberals and Conservatives themselves were undergoing ideological shifts after 1867. The Tories, inspired by Disraelian paternalism, embarked on new initiatives in social amelioration in such fields as housing. Within the Liberal Party, the development of the more activist New Liberals, inspired by the corporatist, communitarian values of T. H. Green and reflected in the Settlement House movement, pointed away from the orthodoxies of 1834 or the COS.[72] In relation to poor law administration, major changes were evident by the 1880s. Joseph Chamberlain, president of the Local Government Board in 1886, issued a circular calling on municipal councils to provide works programs for the unemployed, thus adding a third force to the poor law and

charity.[73] The Local Government Act of 1894 (56 & 57 Vict., c.73) democ-
ratized poor law elections, bringing about an end to strict policies in many
unions.[74] By the end of the century, Poor Law schools, hospitals, child care,
and medical treatment were often of a quite decent standard, with aggregate
spending per pauper head doubling between 1870–71 and 1905–6.[75] Moreover, the poor were quite knowledgeable about the various programs available to them and adept at selecting those most beneficial to their families.[76]
Legislation passed by successive Conservative and Liberal governments in
the years leading up to 1914 further undermined a deterrent poor law by
adding new programs for unemployment and pensions. The poor law was in
the process of being both transformed and superseded.

The strict charitable administration insisted on by the COS was also
being eclipsed. Even at the height of its influence, the COS had never been
the dominant force in the world of philanthropy. Enormous sums continued
to be raised and dispensed in a far looser fashion by a variety of charities,
drawing upon the emotional outpouring of donations by the public in hard
times. For example, the Mansion House Fund, started in response to the
exceptional distress of 1886, had no difficulty in raising (and squandering,
according to the COS), 79,000 in short order.[77] The great majority of those
contributing to charity (and this included many of the working class) had
little use for the close, suspicious scrutiny of COS casework. Cardinal Man-
ning no doubt spoke for many when he exclaimed, "As to the waste and
wisdom [of donations], I am content that many unworthy should share rather
than one worthy case be without help."[78] Moreover, COS visitors were tempting targets for satire. In Dickens's *The Mystery of Edwin Drood*,
Honeythunder is "an unpleasant bullying philanthropist" working for the
"Haven of Philanthropy," an organization whose approach seems remarkably like the COS.[79] Similarly, in *Bleak House*, Mrs. Pardiggle, a "friendly
visitor" to the poor, "seems to come in like cold weather."[80]

Yet the COS itself was undergoing substantial changes from the 1880s.
The casework of some visitors made them acutely aware of the complexity
of the problems faced by the poor, propelling them away from the individualistic, laissez-faire verities of the early COS—in some cases, to advocacy
of increased government action. Jose Harris has noted the gulf between older
members and a younger generation of COS workers with organicist and
"collectivist" values resembling those of the New Liberals.[81] That figures
generally associated with the foundation of the welfare state, like Beatrice
Webb and William Beveridge, should have started out with the COS (though
Webb was to develop a strong animus against it), indicates the nature of the
change. As Brian Harrison puts it: "The philanthropist does not supersede
the state, whatever his original intention; he skirmishes on its frontiers and

prepares the way for further advance."[82] This adaptation also helps explain the survival of the COS and its ability to raise twice as much money for charitable purposes on the eve of World War I as it had a quarter of a century earlier.[83] It was to transform itself into the Family Welfare Association in 1946 and to accept the Beveridge Report and the ensuing welfare state; it continues to be an important philanthropic agency.

The point here is that key aspects of this transformation were already evident by the early twentieth century. National and local legislation in areas like school meals and child care called for the direct involvement of voluntary bodies. The COS, though with some lingering reluctance, agreed to participate, as their annual report in 1908 shows:

> It will be noticed how heavy is the burden that the State is placing on its citizens in the execution of these new laws. If voluntary helpers do not come forward in large numbers to fulfil the obligation which the State imposes, there can be but one alternative, that these departments will be managed by officials, and must inevitably lose most of the characteristics that will make them useful to society.[84]

At this time, COS leaders were heavily engaged in the work of the Royal Commission on the Poor Laws, appointed in 1905 to study the effects of the public relief system that had been established in 1834 and to recommend reforms. The Majority Report of the Commission, signed by all the COS members on the body, far from being evidence of a negative attitude toward state intervention, reflected the new COS view that the state needed to provide an adequate base of social programs to sustain families in time of distress. The key to the success of these programs, of course, was to involve trained voluntary workers directly in their operation. As A.W. Vincent points out, the underlying philosophy of the Majority Report was that of T. H. Green's Philosophical Idealism, not Herbert Spencer's atomistic individualism.[85]

The Minority Report of the Royal Commission, written by Beatrice Webb, with its clarion call for total abolition of the poor law and its replacement by a cluster of specialist state services, has long seemed the herald of the modern welfare state. As a result, a "caricatured view"[86] of the Majority Report has persisted, still drawing heavily upon the Webb's indictment of it as little more than a reiteration of the "principles of 1834."[87] In fact, neither report provided a clear-cut blueprint. In the short term, the Liberal government chose to ignore both sets of recommendations. The poor law was ultimately allowed to pass from the scene in 1929, with the transferring of the functions of the old boards of guardians to the county and borough councils—a provision of the Majority Report of 1909. With the implementation of the Welfare State by Attlee's government after 1945, the array of services and the manner of their delivery did come more to resemble those advocated in the Minority Report, yet even here a significant level of cooperation between public and voluntary agencies was maintained. Indeed, William Beveridge, whose famous Report of 1942 was the real blueprint for the Labour government's new programs, published a book in 1948 stressing the importance of private philanthropy and the need for cooperation between it and the state.[88]

The close and complex interconnections between public poor relief and private charity examined in this paper will, it is hoped, help foster the move away from linear, Whig histories of the welfare state. Whatever the deficiencies of the Whig approach, however, they pale before the simplifications of history promoted by conservative leaders and theorists. In Britain, the "Thatcher Revolution" entailed an attempt to discredit and cut governmental social programs. The "nanny State," according to John Moore, Thatcher's Secretary of State for Social Services, had created "the sullen apathy of dependence."[89] Whatever merit there may be in the philosophical arguments brought forward by such reformers, the version of history they deploy in the campaign against welfare is, quite simply, false. It involves an assertion that throughout the nineteenth century there was a wholesome separation between philanthropy and a minimalist state, the latter operating on consistently deterrent principles. A recent article in a libertarian magazine on Thomas Chalmers and the Poor Laws, for example, depicts the Scottish reformer as the virtual architect of the 1834 Poor Law, which is said to have abolished outdoor relief, leaving the poor, wisely, to the many charities that "sprang up like flowers in the springtime." The twentieth century, with all its liberal, bureaucratic intrusiveness, saw the reversal of this wise system.[90]

A review and possible substantial reform of existing welfare practices is not something any society should seek to avoid. However, such a review must be grounded in the historical record; willful or naive misrepresentations of the past serve only polemical ends. An essential starting point for an informed debate on welfare reform is the recognition that both the public and private sectors of poor relief grew enormously in the nineteenth century. There was substantial cooperation between them, at the national and the local level. Similar attitudes and policies are to be found among the administrators of private and public agencies alike. Both became increasingly dependent upon experts. Both exhibited a harsh, deterrent aspect and a more benevolent one. Their underlying philosophies and relief strategies underwent major changes. Both sectors were, and are, vital to modern civilization. As is invariably the case in debates over social programs, simple dichotomies obstruct rather than facilitate understanding; bad history makes bad policy.

Notes

1. There is, for example, not a single reference to charity or philanthropy in my own book, *The Making of the New Poor Law: The Politics of Inquiry, Enactment, and Implementation, 1832–39* (New Brunswick, 1978).

2. F. K. Prochaska, "Philanthropy," in *The Cambridge Social History of Britain 1750–1950* (Cambridge, 1990), 3: 359.

3. Geoffrey Finlayson, *Citizen, State, and Social Welfare in Britain 1780–1930* (Oxford, 1994).

4. David Owen, *English Philanthropy, 1660–1960* (Cambridge, Mass.: Harvard University Press, 1960), 14–15.

5. Gertrude Himmelfarb, *The Idea of Poverty: England in the Early Industrial Age* (New York, 1984), 61.

6. Brian Harrison, "Philanthropy and the Victorians," in *Peaceable Kingdom: Stability and Change in Modern Britain* (Oxford, 1982), 229. See also Himmelfarb, *The Idea of Poverty*, 66–78.

7. M. J. Daunton, *Progress and Poverty: An Economic and Social History of Britain 1700–1850* (Oxford, 1995), 447–448.

8. Ibid., 457.

9. Himmelfarb, *The Idea of Poverty*, 100–132.

10. The fullest and best discussion of the reform literature of this era is in J. R. Poynter, *Society and Pauperism: English Ideas on Poor Relief, 1795–1834* (London, 1969).

11. Mitchell Dean, *The Constitution of Poverty: Toward a Genealogy of Liberal Governance* (New York: Routledge, 1990), 114–115.

12. See Ian Dyck, *William Cobbett and Rural Popular Culture* (Cambridge, 1992).

13. See especially the dialogue between Jack and Tom in her tract "Village Politics, Addressed to all the Mechanics, Journeymen, and Labourers in Great Britain," in *The Works of Hannah More: With a Memoir and Notes* (London, 1853), 2: 221–236.

14. See, for example, Raymond G. Cowherd, *Political Economists and the English Poor Laws: A Historical Study of the Influence of Classical Economics on the Formation of Social Welfare Policy* (Athens, Ohio, 1977), 5–7.

15. Brundage, *The Making of the New Poor Law*, 6–7.

16. Owen, *English Philanthropy*, 86.

17. Ibid., 182.

18. Charles Bahmueller, *The National Charity Company: Jeremy Bentham's Silent Revolution* (Berkeley, 1981).

19. Owen, *English Philanthropy*, 183–188.

20. Ibid., 76. The case, however, continued to plague the Charity Commissioners, who held a special inquiry into its administration as late as 1946.

21. Eighth Report of the Commissioners appointed by Parliament respecting Charities, 14 Feb. 1823, *Westminster Review* 2 (1824): 98. Reprinted in *Poverty in the Victorian Age*, ed. A.W. Coats (Farnborough, 1973), Vol. 3.

22. Owen, *English Philanthropy*, 106–113.

23. Ibid., 139–140. See also Frank Prochaska, *The Voluntary Impulse: Philanthropy in Modern Britain* (London, 1988), 44–45.

24. Owen, *English Philanthropy,* 100–102.

25. Dean, *The Constitution of Poverty,* 144–145.

26. R. A. Cage, *The Scottish Poor Law, 1745–1845* (Edinburgh, 1981). See also Daunton, *Progress and Poverty,* 463–467.

27. Hansard, *Parliamentary Debates,* 1st ser., 36 (21 Feb. 1817): 523–524.

28. Brundage, *The Making of the New Poor Law,* 9–11.

29. Quoted in Dean, *The Constitution of Poverty,* 100.

30. Anthony Brundage, *England's "Prussian Minister": Edwin Chadwick and the Politics of Government Growth, 1832–1854* (University Park and London, 1988), 37–38, 48.

31. See, for example, the reports of Assistant Commissioners C. H. Cameron and John Wrottesley, in *Report from His Majesty's Commissioners on the Administration and Practical Operation of the Poor Laws* (Shannon, 1971), 8: 452–453.

32. "The New Poor Law," *Edinburgh Review* 63 (1836): 495–496. Reprinted in *Poverty in the Victorian Age,* ed. A. W. Coats (Farnborough, 1973), Vol. 2.

33. *Extracts from the Information Received by His Majesty's Commissioners as to the Administration and Operation of the Poor Laws* (London, 1833), 201–339.

34. *Report from His Majesty's Commissioners on the Administration and Practical Operation of the Poor Laws* (Shannon, 1971), 17: 221.

35. Brundage, *The Making of the New Poor Law,* 75–144.

36. Owen, *English Philanthropy,* 191.

37. Ibid., 191–193.

38. Ibid., 202–203.

39. Richard Tompson, *The Charity Commission and the Age of Reform* (London, 1979), 207.

40. David Roberts, *Paternalism in Early Victorian England* (New Brunswick, 1979), 208.

41. Ibid., 123.

42. Adrian Randall and Edwina Newman, "Protest, Proletarians and Paternalists: Social Conflict in Rural Wiltshire, 1830–1850," *Rural History* 6 (1995): 218.

43. Anthony Brundage, "The English Poor Law of 1834 and the Cohesion of Agricultural Society," *Agricultural History* 48 (July 1974): 416.

44. Maurice Caplan, *In the Shadow of the Workhouse: The Implementation of the New Poor Law throughout Nottinghamshire, 1836–1846,* Center for Local History, Occasional Papers No. 3 (Nottingham, 1984), 15–16.

45. Ibid., 35.

46. See, for example, William Apfel and Peter Dunkley, "English Rural Society and the New Poor Law: Bedfordshire, 1834–47," *Social History* 10 (Jan. 1985): 37–68.

47. Norman McCord, "The Poor Law and Philanthropy," in *The New Poor Law in the Nineteenth Century,* ed. Derek Fraser (London, 1976), 102–103.

48. Frank Prochaska, *Women and Philanthropy in Nineteenth-Century England* (Oxford, 1980), 151, 178–79.

49. McCord, "The Poor Law and Philanthropy," 100.

50. For an overview of the various policies in practice between 1834 and 1847, see Sidney and Beatrice Webb, *English Poor Law Policy* (London, 1910), 21–87.

51. Robert Humphreys, *Sin, Organized Charity and the Poor Law in Victorian England* (New York, 1995), 52.

52. See Frank Prochaska, *Royal Bounty: The Making of a Welfare Monarchy* (New Haven, 1995).

53. Peter Wood, *Poverty and the Workhouse in Victorian Britain* (Wolfeboro Falls, N.H., 1991), 142–143.

54. Gareth Stedman Jones, *Outcast London: A Study in the Relationship between Classes in Victorian Society* (Oxford, 1971), 241–261.

55. *Frasers's Magazine* 80 (1869): 683. Reprinted in *Poverty in the Victorian Age*, ed. A. W. Coats (Farnborough, 1973), Vol. 2.

56. "A Note on Poverty," *Frasers's Magazine* 79 (1866): 287–288. Reprinted in *Poverty in the Victorian Age*, ed. A. W. Coats (Farnborough, 1973), Vol. 2

57. Ibid., 283–284.

58. Finlayson, *Citizen, State, and Social Welfare*, 105.

59. Owen, *English Philanthropy*, 220.

60. The text of the Goschen Minute is reprinted in Michael E. Rose, ed., *The English Poor Law, 1780–1930* (Newton Abbot, 1971), 226–28.

61. Owen, *English Philanthropy*, 222.

62. Humphreys, *Sin, Organized Charity and the Poor Law in Victorian England*, 159.

63. Owen, *English Philanthropy*, 236–237.

64. Wood, *Poverty and the Workhouse in Victorian Britain*, 46.

65. For an excellent discussion of casework in practice, see Judith Fido, "The Charity Organisation Society and Social Casework in London 1869–1900," in *Social Control in Nineteenth Century Britain*, ed. A. P. Donajgrodzki (London, 1977), 207–230.

66. Ibid., 45.

67. Finlayson, *Citizen, State, and Social Welfare*, 149.

68. Keith Gregson, "Poor Law and Organized Charity: The Relief of Exceptional Distress in North-east England, 1870–1910," in *The Poor and the City: The English Poor Law in its Urban Context*, ed. Michael E. Rose (New York, 1985), 93–131.

69. Humphreys, *Sin, Organized Charity and the Poor Law in Victorian England*, esp. 144–174. For a much more positive assessment, see Charles Loch Mowat, *The Charity Organization Society 1869–1913: Its Ideas and Work* (London, 1961).

70. Karel Williams, *From Pauperism to Poverty* (London, 1981).

71. Pat Thane, "The Working Class and State 'Welfare' in Britain 1880–1914," *Historical Journal* 27 (1984): 877–900.

72. Reba N. Soffer, *Ethics and Society in England: The Revolution in the Social Sciences 1870–1914* (Berkeley, 1978); see also Standish Meacham, *Toynbee Hall and Social Reform 1880–1914: The Search for Community* (New Haven, 1987).

73. Finlayson, *Citizen, State, and Social Welfare*, 150.

74. One of the most striking cases was in the Brixworth Union in Northamptonshire, where Albert Pell, a workhouse test doctrinaire, had succeeded in virtually eliminating outdoor relief. See Anthony Brundage, "Reform of the Poor Law Electoral System, 1834–94," *Albion* 7 (Fall 1975): 201–215.

75. Jose Harris, "The Transition to High Politics in English Social Policy, 1880–1914," in *High and Low Politics in Modern Britain: Ten Studies*, ed. Michael Bentley and John Stevenson (Oxford, 1983), 71–72.

76. Lynn Hollen Lees, "The Survival of the Unfit: Welfare Policies and Family

Maintenance in Nineteenth-Century London," in *The Uses of Charity: The Poor on Relief in the Nineteenth-Century Metropolis*, ed. Peter Mandler (Philadelphia, 1990), 68–91.

77. Maurice Bruce, *The Coming of the Welfare State* (New York, 1966), 107.

78. Finlayson, *Citizen, State, and Social Welfare*, 135.

79. Norris Pope, *Dickens and Charity* (New York, 1978), 246.

80. Robert H. Bremner, *Giving: Charity and Philanthropy in History* (New Brunswick, 1994), 116.

81. Jose Harris, *Private Lives, Public Spirit: A Social History of Britain, 1870–1914* (Oxford, 1993), 231.

82. Harrison, "Philanthropy and the Victorians," 236.

83. Gertrude Himmelfarb, *Poverty and Compassion: The Moral Imagination of the Late Victorians* (New York, 1991), 202.

84. Quoted in Mowat, *The Charity Organisation Society 1869–1913*, 154–155.

85. A. W. Vincent, "The Poor Law Reports of 1909 and the Social Theory of the Charity Organisation Society," *Victorian Studies* 27 (1983–84): 343–363.

86. Ibid., 362.

87. Sidney and Beatrice Webb, *English Poor Law Policy*, 274–295.

88. William Beveridge, *Voluntary Action: A Report on Methods of Social Advance* (London, 1948).

89. In a speech to the Conservative Constituencies Parties Association in September 1987. Quoted in Humphreys, *Sin, Organized Charity and the Poor Law in Victorian England*, 6.

90. Clifford F. Thies, "Thomas Chalmers and the Poor Laws," *The Freeman* 43 (Dec. 1993): 491–493.

United States Relief and Welfare
in the
Nineteenth and Twentieth Centuries

E. WAYNE CARP

Orphanages vs. Adoption: The Triumph of Biological Kinship, 1800–1933

In May 1994, soon-to-be House Majority Leader Newt Gingrich set off a national uproar when he proposed denying welfare payments to unwed mothers under the age of 21 and placing the children they were unable to support in orphanages. Congressional Democrats denounced Gingrich's proposal as callous and wrongheaded; Hillary Rodham Clinton declared the idea "unbelievable and absurd."[1] Gingrich invited the first lady to visit Blockbuster Video and rent the 1938 movie *Boys Town,* which depicts an idealized vision of orphanages.[2] Clinton advisor George Stephanopolous countered by promising to send Republicans a copy of *Oliver Twist.*[3]

Popular opinion has long favored the Democrats. Both Gilded Age and Progressive Era child-welfare reformers denounced orphanages, advocating instead that dependent, abandoned, or neglected children be placed in families. But a closer look at the historical record reveals a striking paradox: during this period of relentless criticism the number of orphanages and the number of children in them nearly tripled, while placing-out, foster care, and adoption increased only marginally. In the essay that follows, I shall try to explain this paradox by investigating the history of both orphan asylums and of child adoption during what I shall call, for lack of a better term, the long nineteenth century (1800–1933). Although I am well aware of the need to be careful in using history to address policy questions, this historical approach does shed light on the contemporary debate between Republicans and Democrats about whether to resurrect orphanages. The essay will attempt to show that politicians' ignorance of orphanages, coupled with America's emphasis on the primacy of blood kinship, have fundamentally distorted their understanding of care for dependent children.

Privately run orphanages have a long history in the United States.[4] The first one appeared in 1727, established by the French nuns of the Ursuline convent in New Orleans to care for the many children orphaned by an attack of the Natchez Indians. Eleven years later, in 1738, the first orphanage in the British colonies appeared when the Betheseda orphan house was founded in Savannah, Georgia. By 1800, there were six orphanages in the United States, mostly Protestant, in cities along the Eastern seaboard.[5] On the eve of the Civil War, under the impact of large-scale immigration, urbanization, and the advent of the factory system and wage-labor, urban poverty grew. Driven by this poverty, cholera and yellow fever epidemics, and evidence of child abuse in almshouses, humanitarian and religious child welfare reformers founded an additional 164 orphan asylums, 75 of them between 1831 and 1851.[6] By 1860 orphan asylums had become the primary method of caring for dependent children in America. Between 1860 and 1890, due primarily to the high mortality of the Civil War, the deepening of urban poverty caused by industrialization and large-scale immigration to the cities, state laws prohibiting children from being kept in almshouses, and sectarian competition, the number of orphanages more than tripled to 564, housing 68,011 children. Catholic institutions now outnumbered Protestant ones 173 to 111.[7]

As orphanages spread throughout the United States, they met increasing criticism. Complaints revolved around three interrelated issues: the excessive length of time children remained in institutions, parental abuse of public charity, and the detrimental effects of institutional child rearing. Whether for pecuniary, religious, or professional reasons, orphanage managers were criticized for admitting too many children and keeping them too long. According to child welfare reformers, this policy corrupted parents, who took advantage of public charity to send their children to orphanages either to save the expense of raising them or to provide them with a superior education.[8] But critics most commonly denounced the life children led in large, overcrowded orphanages. Believing strongly in the power of the environment to shape character, child reformers excoriated institutional life for its tendency to warp a child's initiative and individuality. Repeatedly, they bemoaned the monotonous, repetitive lives of inmates. The Reverend Hastings H. Hart, secretary of Minnesota's State Board of Corrections and Charities and nationally renowned child welfare leader, dolefully described the institutionalized regimen: "The bell rang for the child to rise in the morning, to say his prayers, to go to his meals, to return to his meals, to go to his studies and his play; all day long, the bell, the bell. What does that mean? It means that someone else is doing his thinking for him; someone else is planning his life for him. He is practically without a will of his own."[9] Moreover, the children were isolated from the community. Inculcated with useless knowledge, they were incapable of taking responsibility for their actions.[10] In 1881 at the National Conference of Charities and Correction, C. R. Lowell voiced a common sentiment when she said that she "should like to see every single institution in the country for dependent children closed tomorrow, if they could be."[11]

In the place of orphan asylums, child welfare reformers advocated placing dependent children "in a good family home, God's orphanage."[12] According to the critics of orphan asylums, home life had emotional, practical, and pecuniary advantages. Most obviously, families provided a nurturing environment: parents loved children and showered them with affection. As part of a family, children learned useful work habits and became "worldly wise in the art of living." They became self-reliant and self-supporting at an early age. They also interacted with the community at large. Best of all from the point of view of a cost-conscious public, placing children in families was less expensive than institutional care.[13] As one child welfare expert exuded: "The placing out of dependent children is by far the most economical, the most humane, and the most successful way of caring for them."[14] By 1899, foster care and adoption advocates had pronounced victory over the defenders of institutions. In that year, at the annual National Conference of Charities and Corrections, the delegates issued a unanimous report stating that "all workers agreed that the home is the natural place to develop the child."[15]

One might have thought that the two trends—reformers' denunciation of institutional care and their insistence on placing dependent children in families—would result in a steady decline in both the number of orphanages and children in institutional care *and* the increase in the number of children placed in some form of foster care or adoption. U.S. census data fail to justify that conclusion, however.[16] Between 1890 and 1910, the number of children's institutions almost doubled to 1,151, while the number of orphanages rose nearly 50 percent from 564 to 837. By 1910, approximately two-thirds of the nation's dependent children were living in institutions.[17] Thirteen years later, the number of children's institutions had risen 16 percent to 1,344, but the number of orphanages again climbed nearly 50 percent to 1,231. Although the percentage of children in institutions remained practically the same (64 percent), their numbers increased to 132,558.[18] A decade later, during the Great Depression, the number of children's institutions rose spectacularly to 2,280, while orphanages continued to multiply, but much more modestly, to 1,320. Although the number of dependent children resident in institutions also rose modestly to 140,352, they still constituted 58 percent of children living outside their biological families.[19] In sum, between 1890 and 1933 the number of orphanages more than doubled.

By contrast, the number of children adopted or in foster care grew slowly.[20] In 1910, the Census Bureau reported that 61,000 children received care in foster homes, two-thirds of whom were still under institutional supervision. They amounted to only 35 percent of the total dependent child population. Thirteen years later, the number of children receiving foster care or being adopted increased only 1 percent, climbing to 73,000 children. By 1933, foster and adopted children numbered 102,577 (42 percent). Not until the 1950s, when foster care and adoption became the dominant method of child care, did the proportion of children residing in institutions decline significantly (Table 1).

TABLE 1. Child Care in the United States By Selected Years and Type of Care [In Thousands]

Year	No. in Care	Institutions		Foster Care	
		No.	%	No.	%
1910	172	111	65	61	35
1923	214	132	64	73	36
1933	242	140	58	102	42
1951	223	95	43	128	57
1961	245	80	33	165	67

Sources: Adapted from Martin Wolins and Irving Piliavin, Institution or Foster Family: A Century of Debate (New York: Child Welfare League of America, 1964), Table 1, "Children in Foster Care in the United States—By Selected Years and Type of Care," p. 37. Figures for the years 1910, 1923, and 1933 were taken from the U.S. Census Reports.

How does one explain the continued vitality of orphanages in the face of child welfare reformers' hostility? One fundamental reason was that from the Civil War to the Great Depression orphan asylums provided important services to working-class parents, impoverished by the structural problems of an economy characterized by low wages, widespread unemployment, and job-related injuries.[21] This may sound like a contradiction in terms—how could orphans have parents, poor or otherwise? But Census Bureau records and recent studies are unanimous in concluding that there were few "true" orphans in orphan asylums. The 1890 Census Bureau, for example, found that of 68,011 orphans in "benevolent institutions" only 23 percent were missing both parents. Studies of individual orphanages tend to confirm these numbers.[22] The great majority of children were "half-orphans" brought to asylums by single parents, usually poor women who used the institutions as temporary shelters during economic hard times or because of the death or desertion of a family member.[23] Once the children were admitted, the orphanages fulfilled their primary mission to feed, clothe, shelter, and educate their young charges and return them to their families.[24] Few children spent long periods of time in an orphan asylum, though the average length of stay varied considerably.[25] Parents expected their children to return home and indeed, a large percentage of them did after several years of care. Between 1915 and 1919, for example, 66 percent of the children in Cleveland orphanages returned to parents or relatives. Orphan asylums did not disappear in the face of child welfare reformers' criticism in part because they gave impoverished working-class families the opportunity to become solvent again, which ultimately allowed them to keep their families intact. As Amos Warner noted in his magisterial survey, *American Charities*, "The institution is preferred by parents because they know where the child is, and can usually visit it, and frequently can retain the right to take it back again when they will."[26]

Orphanages not only provided relief when the working poor were impoverished, but also offered desirable service. In addition to providing their young charges with temporary shelter, food, and clothing, orphan managers made vigorous efforts to equip the children with a strong public school or vocational education. Children who enrolled in the more general curriculum took courses in English, arithmetic, geography, history, and literature. Girls who took the manual or vocational curriculum received training in drawing, sewing, and cooking, while vocational training for boys concentrated on courses like carpentry and carving. Both curricula emphasized practicality, seeking to make the children self-supporting.[27] Many poor parents, recognizing the educational advantages institutions offered their children, viewed orphanages as avenues of upward mobility and deliberately placed their children in them. Envisioning a better life for their children, one that might lift them out of the ranks of the laboring poor, parents enjoined their institutionalized children to " 'study hard to learn your lessons.' "[28]

During the Progressive Era, orphan asylums continued to increase their numbers by the various ways they maintained their attractiveness to the working poor. Many orphanages did so by reducing their size, reforming rigid policies, and becoming more homelike. Three private, Progressive era orphanages in Baltimore—the Hebrew Orphan Asylum (Jewish), the Samuel Ready School for Girls (Protestant), and the Dolan Children's Aid Society (Catholic)—illustrate this trend. Rather than languishing in large congregate institutions, the children in these Baltimore orphanages lived in small, clean, cottagelike buildings designed to encourage individualism and ensure privacy. Compared to the Baltimore slums where the children formerly lived, "the orphanages, by contrast, were healthy, safe, and spacious."[29] The children also received nutritionally adequate meals and enough clothing to remain neat and clean. These advantages were not lost on working-class parents. And the popularity of these Baltimore orphanages was responsible for their eventual demise. The orphanages responded to working-class demands by accepting more children than they could handle. By the 1930s, faced with "serious overcrowding, staff shortage, and financial strain," all three orphanages went into decline.[30]

Orphanages also stayed in business by selectively circumventing Progressive reforms. One scholar has detected a pattern of "resistance, indifference, and piecemeal reform" among most of Chicago's children's institutions. In particular, the Chicago Nursery and Half-Orphan Asylum's Board of Managers neither approved nor resisted Progressive reforms. Rather they made changes selectively. For example, they embraced Progressive reformers' public health measures—replacing dirty water pipes, providing regular check-ups for the children—thus reinforcing the older concept of asylum-as-refuge, while at the same time, fending off the Progressive reformers' efforts to replace institutional care with family placement or the homelike "cottage" system. In choosing which Progressive reforms to adopt their guiding light was the principle of autonomy from both state interference and the dictates of Chicago's private philanthropic community.[31]

In the face of intense criticism, orphanages prospered and multiplied because they performed a useful function for an impoverished working class. They maintained their usefulness by selectively reforming themselves. Meanwhile, adoption and foster care, defined as the irrevocable separation of parent and child, faced an uphill battle for acceptance. The great majority of the American people and child welfare experts were opposed to breaking up biological families permanently. As methods of child care, adoption and foster care ran afoul of the American belief that kinship is defined by the unalterable nature of blood ties. By definition, placing children into a family other than its original one violated, and continues to violate, Americans' cultural predilection for viewing the biological family as "a state of almost mystical commonality and identity."[32] The rest of this essay will describe how America's cultural kinship system, with its bias against breaking up biological families, affected nineteenth-century child placement practices and stigmatized adoption and foster care as an "unnatural," unsafe, and socially unacceptable method of caring for dependent children.

As early as the 1840s, child welfare reformers acted on their criticisms of orphan asylums and created organizations to place dependent children in foster families. The most influential of these charity organizations, New York's Children's Aid Society (CAS) was founded in 1853 by the Reverend Charles Loring Brace, a transplanted New Englander and graduate of Yale Divinity School, who began his much celebrated career as an evangelical missionary working with "street arabs" at New York City's Five Points Mission.[33] Upon arriving in New York City, Brace was appalled at the large numbers of impoverished immigrant children. To him they seemed a threat to the city's social order. His major goal during his forty-year tenure as secretary of the CAS was to rescue poor and homeless children from New York City's crowded, dirty streets and to place them out West in good Christian families where they would be cared for, educated, and employed. For Brace, "placing out" was superior to traditional antebellum institutional care because it promised to transform these "little vagabonds and homeless creatures" into "decent, orderly, industrious children."[34] When Brace quickly discovered that placing children individually in families was slow and expensive work, he turned to group placement, thus setting in motion the movement that became known as the orphan trains. In March 1854, the CAS sent the first large "train" of 138 children to western Pennsylvania.[35] In the following twenty years, the CAS placed out 20,000 Eastern children in the then western states of Michigan, Ohio, Indiana, Iowa, Missouri, and Kansas; by 1890 the number had climbed to 84,000.[36] In the four decades following the Society's founding, Brace enjoyed such great success that most existing charity organizations switched over to the CAS's placing-out system. Moreover, dozens of new children's aid societies replicating CAS methods sprang up in the 1870s and 1880s, and imitators also appeared in Great Britain and Australia.[37]

The boys and girls whom Brace placed out came under the authority of the CAS by a variety of routes. Critics of the child-placing system accused the CAS of stealing children. According to Marilyn Irvin Holt, the most thorough historian of the orphan trains, "the accusations were sometimes true, but it was a complex situation."[38] A small number of children were removed from asylums and prisons. Some came of their own volition to the CAS headquarters and volunteered for resettlement. Others were brought by their immigrant, working-class, poverty-stricken parents hoping to give them a better life, employing what historian Bruce Bellingham has called a "family strategy of economic calculation."[39] But there was much truth in the charges of child theft. Brace or a "Visitor" frequently roamed lower-class neighborhoods, going "from house to house," and recruited poor, destitute, and delinquent children for the program.[40] The net result of such recruitment was that a high percentage of Brace's clientele—some 47 percent by his own calculations—were not, in fact, orphans, but had one or both parents living. As Brace remarked, "the great majority were the children of poor and degraded people, who were leaving them to grow up neglected in the streets."[41]

Brace's comment reveals one of the most controversial aspects of the child-placement system: a decided preference for breaking up biological families in order to "save" children.[42] Brace broke families up to "rescue" the children from the evils of an urban environment. He assumed that a rural setting was morally superior and that the farm families desiring a child exemplified this rural virtue and would treat the children well. Brace's romantic optimism was reflected in the way the CAS placing-out system differed from the traditional idea of binding out: Brace did away with the written contract of apprenticeship. The CAS relied on a verbal agreement with the adult, while retaining custody of the child. Brace counted on the farmer's "sense of Christian duty and of affection" for his young charge to resist overworking or abusing the child. If farmers mistreated children, the CAS could reclaim them. If the children were unsatisfactory, they could be returned.[43] In addition to reducing the threat of social disorder in New York City and providing cheap labor for western farmers, Brace anticipated that the children would be "treated not as servants, but as sons and daughters."[44] This latter goal was often achieved. After several years, bonds of affection often sprang up between the family and child, which eventually led to, in Brace's words, "very many" of them being adopted.[45]

The large-scale placing-out movement inaugurated by the widely imitated CAS had enormous consequences for the history of adoption. The passage of more than twenty-five state adoption laws during the last quarter of the nineteenth century can be traced, in part, to the increase in the number of middle-class farmers desiring to legalize the addition of a child to the family.[46] More importantly, at least for the purposes of this essay, beginning in 1874 and continuing for the next half-century, Brace's reckless child-placing methods ignited a heated controversy in the annual meetings of the National Conference of Charities and Correction over the relative merits of institutionalization versus family homes for homeless children.[47] In the course of the debate, the child-placement system came under attack from a variety of groups highly critical of Brace's methods. Representatives from Midwestern states accused Brace of dumping into their communities "car loads of criminal juveniles, . . . vagabonds, and guttersnipes," resulting in a steep increase in vagrants and the state prison population.[48] Catholic authorities viewed the CAS child-placement system as an aggressive and covert form of Protestant proselytizing, equivalent to kidnapping.[49] Eastern child welfare reformers voiced concern that their states were losing valuable human resources that were needed closer to home.[50]

Child-welfare reformers also criticized the CAS for failing to investigate the families the children were placed with or supervising them afterward. As early as 1857, Brace himself admitted the inadequacy of placement procedures, noting that letters of references even from clergymen or magistrates were given "with too little care."[51] By 1882, at the ninth annual National Conference of Charities and Correction, the criticism reached new heights. J. H. Mills, the superintendent of an orphan asylum in North Carolina, accused the CAS of distributing large numbers of children to farmers "without asking any questions or obtaining any information regarding them or any security for their proper care or protection." The result, Mills stated, was that the farmers treated New York children like slaves.[52] Delegates from Ohio, Michigan, Wisconsin, and Pennsylvania followed with additional charges about the lack of supervision.[53]

Child welfare experts' criticism of the CAS's unsound child-placement practices led to the emergence of a "second generation" of child-placing experts who reformed the procedures surrounding the placing of orphaned, abandoned, and dependent children in families. Originating in the last quarter of the nineteenth century, this movement was initiated by Catholic leaders, state officials, and a new generation of child welfare reformers, who advocated abolishing many of the CAS child-placing practices, particularly the unnecessary breakup of families.[54] Second-generation child-savers like the Reverend Martin Van Buren Van Arsdale, a Presbyterian minister, led the way.[55] In 1886, Van Arsdale started his own state organization, the Illinois Children's Home and Aid Society (ICHAS) and instituted standards of child placing that reformed most of Brace's unsound practices. Like Catholic authorities, Van Arsdale made it a cardinal principle to investigate thoroughly each case in order to avoid "severing the bonds of blood relationship." ICHAS officials would accept children having parents or guardians only if a written surrender or commitment was given by the courts. To ensure a good home for the child, the ICHAS employed local advisory boards and trained agents to screen applicants requesting children. Officials began keeping exact records of all children placed out. ICHAS agents also made "visits of inspection" before and after the child's placement in a new home.[56]

By 1900, breaking up families had become practically taboo and family preservation had become a fundamental principle among all child-savers. This social work ideal would continue to be axiomatic among professional social workers up until World War II and beyond.[57] As Galen A. Merrill, a child welfare reformer, noted in 1900 at the twenty-seventh annual meeting of the National Conference of Charities and Correction, "the permanent separation of a child from its natural parents is such a grave matter that it should be permitted only when parents cannot be helped or compelled to meet their obligations as parents."[58] By the early twentieth century, a radical change had occurred in the meaning of the policy that all dependent children should be placed in families. In the effort to prevent Brace's reckless child-placing policies, child welfare experts and social workers went to the other extreme and stressed the cultural primacy of the blood bond in family kinship. While they extolled the family as superior to institutionalization, the "family" they now meant was the child's *biological parents*, the family of origin.[59]

It is this emphasis on the preservation of the biological family, above all, that explains why the number of adopted children or those in foster care failed to increase significantly. Rather than break up families, child welfare experts' new strategy was to emphasize the prevention of the causes of child dependency in the first place. To this end, they stressed that families should not be broken up merely because of poverty, but only for "inefficiency and immorality."[60] Taking their cue from President Theodore Roosevelt's 1909 appeal to help the widowed mother "keep her own home and keep the child in it," a coalition of child welfare experts, powerful women's organizations, and influential social workers lobbied state legislatures for mothers' pensions. Their lobbying campaign met with considerable success. In 1911, Illinois passed the first mothers' pension law. Other states rapidly followed. By 1920, forty state legislatures had passed similar statutes. They provided monthly grants for "deserving" widows that "ranged from $4.33 a month in Arkansas to $69.31 a month in Massachusetts; and the median grant was $21.78."[61] Historians have rightly emphasized the inadequacies and restrictiveness of these programs, especially toward minority mothers.[62] Nevertheless, as a result of these laws, the Children's Bureau in 1931 estimated that 93,600 families with 253,000 children were receiving mothers' pensions, more than twice the number of children adopted or in foster care.[63]

An aversion to adoption was the flip side of the popular and professional ideal that families should be kept together. Professional social workers made it a point of pride that they rarely recommended that children be adopted. Speaking before the prestigious National Conference of Social Work, Albert H. Stoneman, the Michigan Children's Aid Society's general secretary, noted approvingly that the twenty most respected child-placing organizations he studied all refused to receive children for adoption if it was possible for them "to be properly cared for by their own people."[64] Similarly, Children's Bureau researchers reported that the ten child-placing agencies they examined "were unanimous in their opinion that no child, whether of legitimate or illegitimate birth, should be placed for adoption if there were decent, self-respecting parents or other family connections who might later, if not at the moment, provide a home for him."[65] In teaching the art of child-placing, William H. Slingerland, special agent in the Russell Sage Foundation's department of child-helping, instructed social workers to conduct an intense investigation of the child's parents and especially "all near relatives, grandparents, brothers, sisters, uncles and aunts." Slingerland, noting that "blood is thicker than water" confidently predicted they would find some near relatives "fit, able, and willing to care for children whose parents have died, failed, or broken down."[66] Contrary to the assertion of some historians, adoption workers turned to adoption only as a last resort when other means to keep families together failed.[67] As a result, the number of children available for adoption remained small.

Americans' cultural definition of kinship had another important effect. It stigmatized adoption as socially unacceptable. Social workers had to overcome widespread popular prejudice toward adoption in order to convince would-be adoptors that taking a child into the home was not abnormal. During the late nineteenth and early twentieth centuries, a broad segment of the American public believed that adoption was an "unnatural" action that created ersatz or second-rate families. Most Americans would have agreed with Dr. R. L. Jenkins that "the normal biologic relationship of parent and child is more satisfactory . . . than an artificially created one."[68] They would have nodded their heads in agreement when hearing the opinion that "though it is better to be adopted than institutionalized, no adopted relation is likely to be as good as a natural one."[69] The very language underscored the inferior nature of adoption: in popular discourse, adoptive parents were always juxtaposed with "natural" or "normal" ones.[70] Discriminatory laws reinforced the notion that the adoptive relationship was inherently flawed. Jurists regularly ruled in inheritance cases, for example, that adoption violated the legal principle of consanguinity or blood ties. In practice, this meant that adopted children did not have the same inheritance rights as birth children. In 1881 an Illinois court ruled against a girl's right to inherit from her recently deceased intestate adoptive parents because she was "not a brother or sister in fact." In other cases dealing with disputed custody rights of adopted children, both courts and legislatures favored birthparents' appeals to restore their children to them.[71]

Medical science contributed to popular cultural prejudices against adopting a child by coupling the stigma of illegitimacy with adoption.[72] After 1910 the rise of the eugenics movement and psychometric testing led adopted children to be linked to inherited mental defects. Studies like Henry H. Goddard's *The Kallikak Family* (1912) claimed to demonstrate the tendency of generations of children to inherit the social pathology of their parents, particularly criminality and feeblemindedness.[73] Using the Yerkes-Bridges modification of the Binet-Simon intelligence test, psychologists and social workers uncovered a strong connection between unmarried mothers and the purported hereditary trait of feeblemindedness.[74] It was but a small conceptual step to include adopted children in the equation. As Ada Elliot Sheffield, director of Boston's Bureau of Illegitimacy, noted in 1920, "the children of unmarried parents, who doubtless make up a large number of adoptions, may turn out to show an undue proportion of abnormal mentality."[75] The purported link between feebleminded unwed mothers and their illegitimate children cast a pall over all adoptions; even popular magazines warned adoptive parents against the risk of "bad heredity."[76] Adopted children were thus burdened with a double stigma: they were assumed to be illegitimate and thus tainted medically *and* they were adopted, thus lacking the all important blood link to their adoptive parents. These cultural and medical stigmatic aspects of adoption made many potential adopters extremely wary.

Potential adoptive parents were also reluctant to adopt dependent children because the chaotic free market in child-placing, which sprang up at the beginning of the twentieth century, gave adoption a distinctly disreputable aura about it. Although the first generation of state laws provided a mechanism for legalizing adoption, they did not compel the state to regulate the transfers of children from one family to another. Consequently, the first private adoption agencies, created at the turn of the twentieth century, were largely unsupervised by federal or state agencies. Moreover, these amateur child-placing institutions were staffed by nonprofessional volunteers. Wealthy, socially prominent women, with little social work training, volunteered to care for homeless infants. They soon found themselves running adoption agencies, initially supplying their friends' requests for babies and later expanding their operations to meet childless couples' demands for infants.[77] Unlike professional social workers, these upper-class, female amateurs made little effort to keep families together and they vigorously recommended adoption for children born out of wedlock.[78]

A host of other institutions seeking to place for adoption children born out of wedlock engaged in similar dubious child-placing practices. These included private maternity homes, family welfare agencies, hospital social service departments, state court probation departments, child protective agencies, and legal aid societies. Doctors and lawyers also facilitated independent adoptions, acting as liaisons between childless couples and unmarried mothers trying to avoid social stigma.[79] Moreover, many birthparents succeeded in circumventing all established institutions by advertising in newspapers that their infants were available for adoption.[80] Adding to the notoriety of adoption were the commercial maternity homes and baby farms that sold infants born out of wedlock to childless couples.[81] A 1917 study, commissioned by Chicago's Juvenile Protective Association, investigated adoptions and confirmed the worst fears of Progressive reformers and prospective adoptive parents. It found that there was "a regular commercialized business of child placing being carried on in the city of Chicago; that there were many maternity hospitals which made regular charges . . . for disposing of unwelcome children; and that there were also doctors and other individuals who took advantage of the unmarried mother willing to pay any amount of money to dispose of the child. No name, address, or reference was required to secure the custody of a child from these people."[82] The combination of cultural, medical, and social stigma surrounding adoption during the first quarter of the twentieth century kept the number of potential adopted parents relatively low and thus depressed the number of children who were adopted or placed in foster care.

This essay has attempted to explain the paradox of why, despite intense denunciation by child welfare experts, the number of orphan asylums continued to increase from the Gilded Age to the Great Depression while the placement of dependent children in families, the method favored by these same experts, failed to catch on. Part of the explanation is that orphanages provided crucial services desired by the impoverished working class: they offered the working poor an opportunity to keep their families intact by temporarily caring for their children until the children could be reclaimed. Orphanages also provided the possibility of a better life through public school or vocational education. In addition, orphanage managers skillfully resisted reforms recommended by child welfare experts by incorporating selective changes that strengthened their attractiveness to the working class. The other half of the answer lies in Americans' cultural belief that the biological family is sacrosanct. Most Americans define kinship by the unalterable character of the blood relationship. During the late nineteenth century, child-placing methods that violated this cultural norm were replaced by practices that emphasized the preservation of biological families. To keep together biological families threatened with poverty, child welfare experts embraced the idea of mothers' pensions, resorting to foster care and adoption only as a last resort. But even if professional social workers wanted to promote adoption, they fought an uphill battle. Many Americans tended to look upon adoption as medically suspect, socially disreputable, second-class kinship. Not until the prosperous days of World War II and the pronatalism of the 1950s would a majority of Americans favor adoption, and only then would adopted children outnumber institutionalized ones.

What can a historical perspective add to the public policy debate on orphanages? Recent studies demonstrate that there is no such thing as "The Orphanage."[83] Rather, during the past century there have been many types of orphanages, differing with regard to their missions, policies, and clients. Working-class families have used orphanages to mitigate economic catastrophe and to advance educational opportunities for their children, while the powerful have used orphanages to control and socialize the less fortunate. Orphanages have inspired both appreciation and bitterness from their alumni. Given these conflicting conclusions, Democrats should think twice before rejecting orphanages outright. While there have been times in the nation's past when orphanages deserved condemnation, it is also clear that these institutions can serve useful purposes. They have served as temporary or even long-term shelters for children whose parents have fallen on hard times. It is paradoxical that Democrats, who advocate the use of tax breaks, food stamps, job training, and day care to help the working poor, will not even consider reviving an institution that in the past proved so useful to that constituency. Studies of orphanages also point up the fundamental contradiction in the Republicans' position. Though some may imagine that orphanages are a cheap substitute for welfare payments to unwed mothers, orphanages are in fact very expensive. That factor alone should be enough to make unlikely the revival of orphanages any time soon, no matter what their potential benefit to children in need. Given the dire condition of the current foster care system, however, politicians might be well advised to put aside their ideological predilections and consider any and all ways of bettering the lives of American children.

Acknowledgments

A number of individuals commented on earlier versions of this essay, including Mark K. Jensen, Paula B. Shields, Susan L. Porter, and Peter C. Holloran. I am grateful for their advice, criticism, and encouragement.

Notes

1. Tom Morganthau, "The Orphanage," *Newsweek* 124 (Dec. 12, 1994): 30.
2. Sara Collins, "There Are No Free Lunches," *U.S. News and World Report* 117 (Dec. 19, 1994): 56.
3. Morganthau, "The Orphanage," 30.
4. Traditionally, historians of the "social-control" school have generalized about orphan asylums by analogy with other nineteenth-century institutions, such as almshouses, penitentiaries, and mental hospitals. Recent scholars, however, have studied the case records of *actual* orphanages, seeking answers to the questions of how orphans and their families experienced and used these institutions for their own ends. Their conclusions have both confirmed and modified the social control thesis. For a brief historiographical overview, see E. Wayne Carp, "Two Cheers for Orphanages," *Reviews in American History*, 25 (June 1996): 277–284. No published, general history of American orphanages exists. But see Homer Folks, *The Care of Destitute, Neglected, and Delinquent Children* (New York, 1902). For this essay, I have consulted the following works: Catherine J. Ross, "Society's Children: The Care of Indigent Youngsters in New York City, 1875–1903" (Ph.D. diss., Yale University, 1977); Susan Whitelaw Downs and Michael W. Sherraden, "The Orphan Asylum in the Nineteenth Century," *Social Service Review* 57 (June 1983): 272–290; LeRoy Ashby, *Saving the Waifs: Reformers and Dependent Children, 1890–1917* (Philadelphia, 1984); Susan Lynne Porter, "The Benevolent Asylum—Image and Reality: The Care and Training of Female Orphans in Boston" (Ph.D. diss., Boston University, 1984); Priscilla Ferguson Clement, "Children and Charity: Orphanages in New Orleans, 1817–1914," *Louisiana History* 27 (Fall 1986): 337–351; Judith A. Dulberger,

"Refuge or Repressor: The Role of the Orphan Asylum in the Lives of Poor Children and Their Families in Late-Nineteenth-Century America" (Ph.D. diss., Carnegie-Mellon University, 1988); Peter C. Holloran, *Boston's Wayward Children: Social Services for Homeless Children, 1830–1930* (Rutherford, N.J., 1989); Marshall B. Jones, "Crisis of the American Orphanage, 1931–1940," *Social Service Review* 63 (Dec. 1989): 613–629; Marian J. Morton, "Homes For Poverty's Children: Cleveland's Orphanages, 1851–1933," *Ohio History* 98 (Winter/Spring 1989): 5–22; Gary Edward Polster, *Inside Looking Out: The Cleveland Jewish Orphan Asylum, 1868–1924* (Kent, Ohio, 1990); Hyman Bogen, *The Luckiest Orphans: A History of the Hebrew Orphan Asylum of New York* (Urbana and Chicago, 1992); Timothy Andrew Hacsi, "'A Plain and Solemn Duty': A History of Orphan Asylums in America" (Ph.D. diss., University of Pennsylvania, 1993); Nurith Zmora, *Orphanages Reconsidered: Child Care Institutions in Progressive Era Baltimore* (Philadelphia, 1994); Reena Sigman Friedman, *These Are Our Children: Jewish Orphanages in the United States, 1880–1925* (Hanover and London, 1994); Kenneth Cmiel, *A Home of Another Kind: One Chicago Orphanage and the Tangle of Child Welfare* (Chicago, 1995); Eve P. Smith, "Bring Back the Orphanages? What Policymakers of Today Can Learn from the Past," in Eve P. Smith and Lisa A. Merkel-Holguin, eds., *A History of Child Welfare* (New York, 1996), 107–134.

5. Folks, *Care of Destitute, Neglected, and Delinquent Children*, 9; Hacsi, "'A Plain and Solemn Duty,'" 27.

6. Hacsi, "'A Plain and Solemn Duty,'" Appendix A1.

7. Ibid., 74; Dulberger, "Refuge or Repressor," 17–21.

8. Dulberger, "Refuge or Repressor," 45–49.

9. Hastings S. Hart, "The Child-Saving Movement," *Bibliotheca Sacra* 58 (July 1901): 527.

10. Mrs. Lesley, "Foundlings and Deserted Children," *Proceedings of the National Convention of Charities and Corrections* (Boston, 1881), 284; hereafter cited as *PNCCC*; Homer Folks, "Why Should Dependent Children Be Reared in Families Rather Than in Institutions," *Charities Review* 5 (Jan. 1896): 140–144. See also Amos G. Warner, *American Charities: A Study in Philanthropy and Economics* (New York, 1894), 224–227.

11. Mrs. C. R. Lowell, "Debate on Placing Out Children," *PNCCC* (Boston, 1881), 302.

12. F. M. Gregg, "Placing Out Children, *PNCCC* (Boston, 1892), 415.

13. Folks, "Dependent Children," 140–144; quotation on 144.

14. Francis H. White, "Placing Out New York Children in the West," *Charities Review* 2 (Feb. 1893): 225.

15. Hart, "The Child-Saving Movement," 528. One child reformer noted that the year before at the annual meeting "the preponderance of opinion seemed to be in favor of placing the children in good homes." See J. M. Mulry, "The Care of Destitute and Neglected Children," *PNCCC* (Boston, 1899), 167. On the development of consensus, see Ross, "Society's Children," 154–158.

16. The basic census data are: Frederick H. Wines, *Report on the Defective, Dependent and Delinquent Classes of the Population of the United States as Returned at the Tenth Census, June 1, 1880* (Washington, D.C., 1888), issued as Volume 21 of the Tenth Census; Frederick H. Wines, *Report on Crime, Pauperism, and Benevolence in*

the United States at the Eleventh Census, 1890 (Washington, D.C., 1896), issued as Volume 3, Parts 1 and 2 of the Eleventh Census; Department of Commerce and Labor, Bureau of the Census, *Benevolent Institutions 1904*, Special Reports (Washington, D.C., 1905); Department of Commerce, Bureau of the Census, *Benevolent Institutions 1910* (Washington, D.C., 1913); Department of Commerce, U.S. Bureau of the Census, *Children Under Institutional Care 1923* (Washington, D.C., 1927); Department of Commerce, Bureau of the Census, *Children Under Institutional Care and in Foster Homes 1933* (Washington, D.C., 1935). The numbers cited in this and the next paragraph are only approximate. Census reports grossly underreported the number and size of institutions. Moreover, the Census Bureau used different classifications of institutions for each report, thereby obviating any consistency. For a more detailed discussion of the problems with census data, see Emma O. Lundberg, *Child Dependency in the United States: Methods of Statistical Reporting and Census of Dependent Children in Thirty-One States* (New York, 1931), 7–11; Dulberger, "Refuge or Repressor," 22–24.

17. *Benevolent Institutions 1910*, Table 17 and Table 19. In Chicago, during roughly the same period, children's institutions more than tripled. Cmiel, *Home of Another Kind*, 39. For the number of orphanages, I have relied on Hasci, "'Plain and Solemn Duty,'" Tables 3.1 and A7. Cf. Rachel B. Marks, "Institutions for Dependent and Delinquent Children: Histories, Nineteenth-century Statistics, and Recurrent Goals," in Donnell M. Pappenfort, Dee Morgan Kilpatrick, and Robert W. Roberts, eds., *Child Caring: Social Policy and the Institution* (Chicago, 1973), Table 1.1. The number of orphanages in Marks's article is higher than Hasci's due to her mislabeling of the phenomena she is describing. Drawing on U.S. census reports, Marks's data refers to *all* institutions not simply orphanages. For example, the number of orphanages Marks cites as existing in 1923—1,598—represents the number of all institutions including ones for delinquent children and for adults and children. See *Children Under Institutional Care 1923* (32), where the total number of institutions is given at 1,558 (not 1,598) and the total number of *children's* institutions is reported as 1,344. The point to be emphasized, however, is that whatever data set one uses the basic trend remains the same: institutional care for dependent children *increased* between 1890 to 1933.

18. *Children Under Institutional Care 1923*, 32; Hasci, "'Plain and Solemn Duty,'" Tables 3.1 and A7.

19. *Children Under Institutional Care and in Foster Homes 1933*, 2, Table 2.

20. The term "foster care" is fraught with misleading connotations. During the period under study, the term included children in free family homes and boarding homes. These terms, in turn, need to be clarified. As defined by the 1923 Census Report, some children in free family homes were to be adopted, some were indentured for small wages, and some were neither adopted nor paid wages. Likewise, the term boarding home needs to be used carefully because of the lack of a standard definition. While some institutions placed only one child in a boarding family home, others "place as many as five, or even eight or ten children, of different families in the same family home, making the home really a small institution." *Children Under Institutional Care: 1923*, 22.

To complicate the matter, the terms foster care and adoption were often used interchangeably. Before the 1940s, the terms "foster parent" and "adoptive parent," were synonymous. Thus, for example, the clause of the 1915 New York statute defin-

ing adoption stated "the person adopting is designated the 'foster' parent." Clarence
F. Birdseye, Robert C. Cumming, and Frank B. Gilbert, *Annotated Consolidated Laws
of the State of New York*, Supplement, 1915, ch. 352, clause 110 (New York, 1915),
159. For additional examples, see Illinois Children's Home Society and Aid Society,
Home Life for Childhood, new ser., 5 (Nov.-Dec. 1916), 4, 5; Cleveland Protestant
Orphan Asylum, *Annual Report* (Cleveland, Ohio, 1925), 10; Children's Home Finder
of Florida, *Annual Report* (1926), 1; Spence Alumnae Society, "Report of the Adoption Committee," *Annual Report* (New York, 1940), 7. The confusing interchange-
ability of the terms is nicely captured as late as 1944 in the title of the article, "The
Adoptive Foster Parent." See, Child Welfare League of America, *Bulletin* 23 (1944):
5–14; hereafter cited as CWLA, *Bull.*

21. For the economy, see James T. Patterson, *America's Struggle Against Poverty,
1900–1945* (Cambridge, Mass., 1986), 6–9; Morton, "Homes for Poverty's Children,"
5–11.

22. Wines, *Report on Crime*, 367; Cmiel, *Home of Another Kind*, 18–19; Morton,
"Homes for Poverty's Children," 17; Clement, "Children and Charity," 144; Dulberger,
"Refuge or Repressor," 142–144; Ross, "Society's Children," 45–46; Downs and
Sherraden, "The Orphan Asylum in the Nineteenth Century," 280–281. In 1993, only
about 10 percent of children in orphanages were true orphans. See Smith, "Bring
Back the Orphanages?" in Smith and Merkel-Holguin, eds., *History of Child Wel-
fare*, 125.

23. Cmiel, *Home of Another Kind*, 15, 17; Dulberger, "Refuge or Repressor,"
54–55, 157, 168–169; Morton, "Homes for Poverty's Children," 17; Ross, "Society's
Children," 35–36. For a variation on this point see Downs and Sherraden, "The Orphan Asylum in the Nineteenth Century," 275, who found that the users of the Protestant Orphan Asylum of St. Louis "were not simply the poor—they were the poor in
motion," and that the "child welfare problems of their families were related to their
transient condition as much as their poverty."

24. Hacsi, "'Plain and Solemn Duty,'" 7; Cmiel, *Home of Another Kind*, 14.

25. For example, at the low end of the spectrum, Cmiel found that in the Chicago
Nursery and Half-Orphan Asylum between 1865 and 1890 nearly "40 percent of the
children stayed less than three months; 57 percent less than six months. A full 74
percent of the children spent less than a year in the asylum; 86 percent spent less than
two years." Cmiel, *Home of Another Kind*, 22. For similar findings, see Dulberger,
"Refuge or Repressor," 162; Downs and Sherraden, "The Orphan Asylum in the Nineteenth Century," 287. At the high end of the spectrum, Zmora found that in the late
1880s children in three Baltimore orphanages had average stays of 3.56 years, 4.3
years, and 5.8 years. Zmora, *Orphanages Reconsidered*, 53.

26. Morton, "Homes for Poverty's Children," 17. See also Dulberger, "Refuge or
Repressor," 47, 56, 139–140, 150; Clement, "Children and Charity," 339, 345–347;
Warner, *American Charities*, 223.

27. Zmora, *Orphanages Reconsidered*, 97–105. In practice, many orphanages operated under severe fiscal restraints. Consequently, they did not always live up to
their promise of providing an excellent education. See Dulberger, "Refuge or Repressor," 116–118. Orphanage managers also valued education for its ability to inculcate
middle-class values of thrift and self-reliance and Americanize the children. See
Friedman, *These Are Our Children*, chap. 5; Ross, "Society's Children," 42.

28. Dulberger, "Refuge or Repressor," 149, 229–237; quotation on 231; Morton, "Homes for Poverty's Children," 13. It should be emphasized that working-class parents did not make these decisions lightly. Separation from their children, for whatever reason, was emotionally wrenching. See, Dulberger, "Refuge or Repressor," chap. 4, esp. 210–229; Hasci, "'Plain and Solemn Duty,'" 183–185, 260–262.

29. Zmora, *Orphanages Reconsidered*, 76.

30. Ibid., 181. During the first two decades of the twentieth century, Jewish orphanage directors also accommodated new trends in social welfare by liberalizing their operations. See Friedman, *These Are Our Children*, chap. 4.

31. Cmiel, *Home of Another Kind*, chaps. 2–3; quotation on 38.

32. David Schneider, *American Kinship: A Cultural Account*, 2nd rev. ed. (Chicago, 1980), 23–29; quotation on 25.

33. The most comprehensive and balanced account of Brace and the CAS is Marilyn Irvin Holt, *The Orphan Trains: Placing Out in America* (Lincoln, Neb., 1992). See also Miriam Z. Langsam, *Children West: A History of the Placing-Out System of the New York Children's Aid Society 1853–1890* (Madison Wisc., 1964); Kristine Elizabeth Nelson, "The Best Asylum: Charles Loring Brace and Foster Family Care" (D.S.W. diss., University of California, Berkeley, 1980); Bruce William Bellingham, "'Little Wanderers': A Socio-Historical Study of the Nineteenth-Century Origins of Child Fostering and Adoption Reform Based on Early Records of the New York Children's Aid Society," (Ph.D. diss., University of Pennsylvania, 1984); Ross, "Society's Children," 130–153. I have benefited from the extended attention given Brace in Thomas Bender, *Toward an Urban Vision: Ideas and Institutions in Nineteenth-Century America* (Lexington, 1975), chap. 6; R. Richard Wohl, "The Country Boy Myth and Its Place in American Urban Culture: The Nineteenth-Century Contribution," *Perspectives In American History* 3 (1969): 107–121; Joseph M. Hawes, *Children in Urban Society: Juvenile Delinquency in Nineteenth-Century America* (New York, 1971), chap. 6; Paul Boyer, *Urban Masses and Moral Order in America, 1820–1920* (Cambridge, Mass., 1978), 94–104.

34. "Fifth Annual Report" (1858), *Annual Reports of the Children's Aid Society, Nos. 1–10, Feb., 1854–Feb. 1863*, reprinted in David J. Rothman, ed., *Poverty, U.S.A.: The Historical Record* (New York, 1971), 55; hereafter cited as *CAS*; "Third Annual Report" (1856) CAS, 9; Henry Thurston, *The Dependent Child: A Story of Changing Aims and Methods in the Care of Dependent Children* (New York, 1930), 102.

35. Thurston, *Dependent Child*, 104; Nelson, "Best Asylum," 168.

36. Tiffin, *In Whose Best Interest*, 89; Holt, *Orphan Trains*, 48, 53.

37. Wohl, "The Country Boy Myth," 108–121; Hawes, *Children in Urban Society*, 107; Holt, *Orphan Trains*, chap. 3.

38. Holt, *Orphan Trains*, 129.

39. Bruce Bellingham, "Institution and Family: An Alternative View of Nineteenth-Century Child Saving," *Social Problems* 33 (Dec. 1986): 543.

40. "Third Annual Report" (1856), *CAS*, 7.

41. "First Annual Report" (1854), CAS, 9. The 47 percent figure comes from Holt, *Orphan Trains*, 128–129, who cites the 1893 CAS Annual Report statement that 39,406 of the 84,318 children the CAS placed out had one or both parents living.

42. Brace claimed it was a CAS principle to receive the parents' consent before taking the children. But misunderstandings often occurred. See the examples in Holt, *Orphan Trains*, 129–130.

43. Holt, *Orphan Trains*, 62; Thurston, *Dependent Child*, 101–102; Tiffin, *In Whose Best Interest*, 90; quotation from "Third Annual Report" (1856), *CAS*, 10.

44. "Third Annual Report," (1856), *CAS*, 9.

45. Charles L. Brace, "The 'Placing Out' Plan for Homeless and Vagrant Children," *Proceedings of the Conference of Charities and Corrections* (Albany, N.Y., 1876), 140. In 1861, Brace recorded the first account of a formal adoption: "Mr. F., who has A. W., told me he was glad that I brought him the papers of adoption, so that no one can now, at any time, might claim the object of my soul . . . In such an event, he thought he would take the child and run if he could not save it otherwise." "Eighth Annual Report" (1861), *CAS*, 71. See also Nelson, "Best Asylum," 334–335, n. 65.

46. State adoption statutes were designed to ease the burden on legislatures caused by the many private adoption acts and to clarify inheritance rights. For the legal history of adoption, see Jamil S. Zainaldin, "The Emergence of a Modern American Family Law: Child Custody, Adoption, and the Courts," *Northwestern University School of Law* 73 (1979): 1038–1089; Stephen B. Presser, "The Historical Background of the American Law of Adoption," *Journal of Family Law* 11 (1971–1972): 443–516.

47. Martin Wolins and Irving Piliavin, *Institution or Foster Family: A Century of Debate* (New York, 1964), 10–21; Langsam, *Children West*, chap. 5.

48. Quoted in Holt, *Orphan Trains*, 121; Langsam, *Children West*, 45, 57; Nelson, "Best Asylum," 234–235.

49. Holt, *Orphan Trains*, 134–136; Langsam, *Children West*, 45–55.

50. PNCCC delegates did not take this criticism seriously. Langsam, *Children West*, 58.

51. "Fourth Annual Report" (1857), *CAS*, 9.

52. Langsam, *Children West*, 58–59; Hawes, *Children in Urban Society*, 105.

53. *PNCCC* (Cincinnati, 1882), 147–148; Nelson, "Best Asylum," 236. Brace denied the charges and conducted several investigations by his own agents, which invariably exonerated the CAS of any wrongdoing. Charles Loring Brace, "The 'Placing Out' Plan for Homeless and Vagrant Children," *Proceedings of the Conference of Charities* (Albany, N.Y. 1876), 135–150; Holt, *Orphan Trains*, 142–143. However, in 1884, Hastings H. Hart, secretary of the Minnesota State Board of Corrections and Charities, conducted an independent investigation of 340 CAS children placed out in Minnesota and confirmed Mills's criticism: there were numerous hasty placements and inadequate supervision, which resulted in many abused and exploited children. Hastings H. Hart, "Placing Out Children in the West," *PNCCC* (Boston, 1885), 143–147; Langsam, *Children West*, 62–63; Nelson, "Best Asylum," 241–242; Thurston, *Dependent Child*, 114–115.

54. In addition, child welfare reformers sought to modify or abolish the casual solicitation of parental consent, poor investigatory procedures, inadequate supervision of the children placed, and deficient record keeping. This movement to reform child-placing practices faced an uphill struggle for the next seventy-five years. The implementation of its goals became the raison d'être of professional social workers in the field of adoption. E. Wayne Carp, *Family Matters: Secrecy and Disclosure in the History of Adoption* (Cambridge, Mass., forthcoming), chap 1.

55. By the 1890s, Children Home Societies had arisen in Iowa, California, Missouri, Indiana, Michigan, Minnesota, and Washington State; twenty years later there were twenty-eight Societies placing children in adoptive homes in thirty-two states.

Tiffin, *In Whose Best Interest*, 104–105; Ashby, *Saving the Waifs*, 39–41; Thurston, *Dependent Child*, 140–150; Elizabeth White, "The History and Development of the Illinois Children's Home and Aid Society," (M.A. Thesis, University of Chicago, 1934).

56. George Harrison Durand, "The Study of the Child from the Standpoint of the Home-Finding Agency," *PNCCC* (Indianapolis, 1907), 259–260; quotation on 259; Thurston, *Dependent Child*, 140–150; White, "The History and Development of the Illinois Children's Home and Aid Society." For Catholic leaders' opposition to Brace's system of placing out children, see Thurston, *Dependent Child*, 125–126.

57. E. Wayne Carp, "Professional Social Workers, Adoption, and the Problems of Illegitimacy, 1915–1945," *Journal of Policy History* 6 (1994): 161-184.

58. Galen A. Merrill, "Some Recent Developments in Child-Saving." *PNCCC* (Boston, 1900), 226.

59. Other historians have noticed this radical change in child-savers' strategies, but none have attributed it to Brace's child-placing practices. See, for example, Michael B. Katz, *In the Shadow of the Poorhouse: A Social History of Welfare in America* (New York, 1986), chap. 5; Molly Ladd-Taylor, *Mother-Work: Women, Child Welfare, and the State, 1890–1930* (Urbana and Chicago, 1994), 137; Dulberger, "Repressor of Refuge," 124–125. This does not mean that other factors were not at work. Katz attributes the change to "psychology, sentiment, anxiety, and male backlash." *In the Shadow of the Poorhouse*, chap. 5, esp. 124.

60. "Letter to the President of the United States Embodying the Conclusions of the Conference on the Care of Dependent Children," *Proceedings of the Conference on the Care of Dependent Children, 1909*, in Robert H. Bremner, ed., *Children and Youth: A Documentary History* (Cambridge, Mass., 1971), 2: 365

61. Theda Skocpol, *Protecting Soldiers and Mothers: The Political Origins of Social Policy in the United States* (Cambridge, Mass., 1993), chap. 8; quotation on 472; Linda Gordon, *Pitied But Not Entitled: Single Mothers and the History of Welfare* (New York, 1994), chap. 3; Ladd-Taylor, *Mother-Work*, chap. 5; Mark Leff, "Consensus for Reform: The Mothers'-Pensions Movement in the Progressive Era," *Social Service Review* 47 (Sept. 1973): 397–417; Tiffin, *In Whose Best Interest*, 121–130. Roosevelt quoted in Leff, "Consensus for Reform," 399.

62. While noting the historical importance of mothers' aid in the formation of the welfare state, both Gordon and Skocpol are highly critical of the legislation. Gordon, *Pitied But Not Entitled*, chap. 3; Skocpol, *Protecting Soldiers and Mothers*, chap. 8. For the travails of mothers' pensions recipients, see the case studies provided by Ladd-Taylor, *Mother-Work*, 152–159.

63. U.S. Children's Bureau, *Mothers' Aid, 1931*, Children Bureau Pub. 220 (Washington D.C., 1933), 8.

64. A. H. Stoneman, "Social Problems Related to Illegitimacy," National Conference on Social Work, *Proceedings* (Chicago, 1924), 148. In 1917, the National Conference of Charities and Correction changed its name to the National Conference on Social Welfare.

65. Katharine P. Hewins and L. Josephine Webster, *The Work of Child-Placing Agencies*, Children's Bureau Pub. 171 (Washington, D.C., 1927), 80.

66. W. H. Slingerland, *Child-Placing in Families: A Manual for Students and Social Workers* (New York, 1919), 88.

67. Carp, "Professional Social Workers," 169–173.

68. R. L. Jenkins, "On Adopting A Baby," *Hygeia* 13 (Dec. 1935): 1066.

69. "The Epidemic of Adoption," *Living Age* 294 (Sept. 8, 1917): 632.

70. On language see, Jenkins, "On Adopting a Baby," 106; "The Epidemic of Adoption," 632.

71. This paragraph draws heavily on the discussion in Peter Romanofsky, "The Early History of Adoption Practices, 1870–1930" (Ph.D. diss., University of Missouri, Columbia, 1969), 67–69; quotation on 68.

72. Even Progressive reformers, public health officials, and professional social workers assumed that many children born out of wedlock, if they survived, were adopted. How accurate these assumptions were is difficult to assess because of incomplete information. As late as 1937, Agnes K. Hanna, Director of the Social Science Division, U.S. Children's Bureau, observed, "as to the number of children born out of wedlock who are actually adopted, we have little information about them." Agnes K. Hanna, "The Interrelationship Between Illegitimacy and Adoption," CWLA, *Bull.*, 16 (Sept. 1937): 4. Whether the majority of adopted children were born out of wedlock or not, popular opinion believed that this was the case and that the incidence of illegitimacy was on the rise.

73. Henry H. Goddard, *The Kallikak Family: A Study in the Heredity of Feeble-mindedness* (New York, 1912); Hamilton Cravens, *The Triumph of Evolution: American Scientists and the Hereditary-Environment Controversy, 1900–1941* (Philadelphia, 1978), 47–48; William Haller, *Eugenics: Hereditarian Attitudes in American Thought* (New Brunswick, 1968), 106–107; Daniel J. Kevles, *In the Name of Eugenics: Genetics and the Uses of Human Hereditary* (Berkeley and Los Angeles, 1985), 77–78; James W. Trent, *Inventing the Feeble Mind: A History of Mental Retardation in the United States* (Berkeley, 1994), 155–166. For psychometric testing, see the essays in Michael M. Sokal, ed., *Psychological Testing and American Society, 1890–1930* (New Brunswick, 1987).

74. The belief that unwed mothers were feebleminded was widespread. See for example, Committee on Feeblemindedness, "The Menace of the Feeble-Minded," in *The Unwed Mother and Her Child: Reports and Recommendations of the Cleveland Committee on Illegitimacy* (Cleveland, 1916), 8; Jean Weidensall, "The Mentality of the Unmarried Mother," National Conference on Social Work, *Proceedings* (Chicago, 1917), 294; Ada Elliot Sheffield, "The Nature of the Stigma Upon the Unmarried Mother and Her Child," National Conference on Social Work, *Proceedings* (Chicago, 1920): 120; Katharine F. Lenroot, "Social Responsibility for the Protection of Children Handicapped by Illegitimate Birth," *Annals of the American Academy of Political and Social Science* 98 (Nov. 1921): 124, hereafter cited as *Annals*; "A Study of Unmarried Mothers," CWLA, *Bull.*, new ser., 5 (Nov. 15, 1926): 8; Charlotte Lowe, "The Intelligence and Social Background of the Unmarried Mother," *Mental Hygiene* 11 (Oct. 1927): 783–784.

75. Ada Elliot Sheffield, "Program of the Committee on Illegitimacy—Committee Report," National Conference of Social Work, *Proceedings* (Chicago, 1920), 78.

76. "Our Adopted Baby," *Woman's Home Companion* 43 (April 1916): 5. For similar sentiments, see also George Harrison Durand, "The Study of the Child from the Standpoint of the Home-Finding Agency," *PNCCC* (Indianapolis, 1907): 263; Neva R. Deardorff, "Research in the Field of Child Welfare Since the War," *Annals*

151 (Sept. 1930): 197, 202.

77. Romanofsky, "The Early History of Adoption Practices," 117–123; quotation on 119. See also Peter Romanofsky, "Professional Versus Volunteers: A Case Study of Adoption Workers in the 1920s," *Journal of Voluntary Action Research* 2 (April 1973): 95–101; Paula F. Pfeffer, "Homeless Children, Childless Homes," *Chicago History* 16 (Spring 1987): 51–65; Henry Dwight Chapin, *Hereditary and Child Culture* (New York, 1922).

78. See, for example, Louise Waterman Wise, in "Mothers in Name," *Survey* 43 (Mar. 20, 1920): 780, and Chapin, *Hereditary and Child Culture*, 204–205.

79. Ida R. Parker, *"Fit and Proper"? A Study of Legal Adoption in Massachusetts* (Boston: Church Home Society, 1927), 30–35, 40–41; Ruth Reed, *The Illegitimate Family in New York City* (New York, 1934), 38, 48, 88–90; Michael W. Sedlak, "Young Women and the City: Adolescent Deviance and the Transformation of Educational Policy, 1870–1960," *History of Education Policy* 23 (Spring 1983): 12.

80. Carrington Howard, "Adoption by Advertisement," *Survey* 35 (Dec. 11, 1915): 285–286; "Newspapers Cooperate in Adoptions," CWLA, *Bull.*, new ser., 6 (Jan. 15, 1927): 1, 5; Alberta S. B. Guibard and Ida R. Parker, *What Becomes of the Unmarried Mother: A Study of 82 Cases* (Boston, 1922), 59; Parker, *"Fit and Proper,"* 34–35; George B. Mangold, *Children Born Out of Wedlock: A Sociological Study of Illegitimacy; With Particular Reference to the United States* (Columbia, Mo., 1921), 82–83.

81. Pendleton, "New Aims in Adoption," *Annals* 151 (Sept. 1930): 155–156; Mangold, *Children Born Out of Wedlock*, 126–127; Murphy, "What Can Be Accomplished Through Good Social Work in the Field of Illegitimacy," *Annals* 98 (Nov. 1921): 131; A. Madorah Donahue, "Children Born Out of Wedlock," *Annals* 151 (Sept. 1930): 164; Donahue, "A Case of Illegitimacy, Where Mother and Child Have Been Dealt With Separately," *PNCCC* (Chicago, 1915): 125; Viviana A. Zelizer, *Pricing the Priceless Child: The Changing Social Value of Children* (New York, 1985), 196–198.

82. Slingerland, *Child-Placing in Families*, 168–169.

83. Carp, "Two Cheers for Orphanages," *Reviews in American History* 25 (June 1996).

ELIZABETH McKEOWN

Claiming the Poor

Catholic charities have been an important but largely overlooked element in the development of American welfare. Catholics have been present in the welfare system as both clients and providers. As American welfare moved from the informal and local initiatives of the nineteenth century to the legislative and administrative programs of the twentieth, the Catholic charities network has played a role in the evolution of policy toward poor children and families and has provided the Catholic church with an important avenue of access to public influence. The following essay reviews the foundations of this network in the United States between the Civil War and World War II.

Prior to the Civil War, American welfare was a local affair composed of a broad mix of public and private agencies and providers. The chief forms of public (statutory, tax-supported) welfare were the poorhouse, an institution borrowed from Great Britain, and "outdoor" or noninstitutional relief practices which had persisted from the colonial period. Private welfare agencies also sponsored both institutions and outdoor relief, though on a more modest scale, and the efforts of religiously motivated volunteers frequently acted as a stimulus for reform in the public sector. This mixture of state-sponsored and voluntary efforts created a legacy of "blurred and shifting boundaries" between public and private sectors of American welfare. Catholics have contributed heavily to that legacy.[1]

Although the public poorhouse failed either to improve persons or eradicate social ills, it was the harbinger of an extensive array of specialized institutions for dependent, delinquent, mentally ill and physically handicapped citizens that dotted the antebellum landscape. These institutions formed the backbone of an informal system of social welfare that also included hundreds of voluntary associations and organizations through which Protestant leaders attempted to rescue, reform, and discipline their less fortunate neighbors. The civic influence of these societies and the growing involvement of the state in poor relief prompted Catholics to organize their own forms of social provision.

Their reasons were obvious. Catholics constituted a decided majority of the class of "dependents and delinquents" who absorbed the attention and resources of public and private charity in most American cities between 1859 and 1900, and their numbers did not diminish dramatically until after World War II. From 1850 to 1880, Irish Catholic poor dominated the relief rolls and burdened the judicial systems of most large and medium-sized cities along the eastern seaboard. By the end of the century, Catholics from Italy and eastern Europe replaced the Irish as a leading cause of concern. The sheer numbers and the persistent foreignness and destitution of Catholic immigrants fueled the development of American welfare in the nineteenth century and shaped many of the specific practices of non-Catholic policy-makers and providers. Control, containment, and removal of poor people overwhelmed earlier strategies of rescue and reform.

Challenged by the activities of non-Catholics among their own poor, Catholics stepped up their efforts to care for their co-religionists. From the middle of the nineteenth century, Catholics began to organize parish-based outdoor relief for families and to specialize in welfare institutions for children, the sick, and the elderly. By the end of the nineteenth century, Catholic hospitals, protectories, schools, and orphanages dominated the landscape of institutional welfare. This growing network of Catholic institutions was staffed by the volunteer labor of religious communities of women, whose presence and practices were especially distinctive in industrial America. In addition to their lifetime commitment to the social work of the church, religious women embraced ideals of voluntary poverty and community of goods, and their lives offered a dramatic contrast to attitudes toward poverty expressed by the larger culture.

The work of the sisters was supplemented by hundreds of parish and ethnic organizations of the laity, who provided funds and volunteer support for Catholic relief and service initiatives around the country. Concerned to protect and improve the material and social standing of their co-religionists and of their church, Catholic workers also fervently maintained the more ancient traditions of Catholic charity. They and their lay counterparts shared an unswerving conviction that the ultimate aim of social provision was the salvation of souls—their own as well as those of their needier neighbors. Catholic motives and practices in social provision obviously represented a complex pattern of resistance and accommodation to modern American welfare, and "Catholic charity" remained a distinctive marker of Catholic identity and tradition in the larger culture. Faced with the challenge of progressive reform at the beginning of the twentieth century, Catholics stretched "charity" to embrace everything from the provisioning of officers for the new juvenile courts to the use of psychological tests on the needy and delinquent persons who came under their care and control. Charity expanded again to absorb the impact of the New Deal welfare state and the Great Society programs of the 1960s and 1970s.

Catholic charities, however, underwent significant alterations in organization and practice in response to the changing landscape of American welfare. Building on their strong local bases in parishes and institutions, Catholics created citywide, diocesan and national organizations and learned to wield influence in public financial and regulatory decision-making processes. They demanded inclusion in community chests and tax revenues, grounding their demands on claims about the importance of the "religious factor" in welfare programs. And they learned to deal with legal and regulatory challenges from public agencies, including state boards of charity, charity organization societies and citywide councils of social agencies and the new juvenile and domestic courts. Catholics also became an important factor as public welfare workers. They were appointed through political influence in the nineteenth century and through civil service qualifications and professional training in the twentieth.

Catholic providers persistently sought state funding for their work. Although they failed to win access to state support for their parochial schools, they fared better when they applied for public monies for children's institutions and protectories and hospitals. In the wake of the Great Society initiatives, Catholic charities emerged as the leading provider of government-sponsored welfare services in the country. By the 1990s, government funding accounted for more than two-thirds of the nearly $2 billion budget of Catholic Charities, U.S.A. In the process of this engagement with American welfare, Catholics overcame deep reservations about the role of the state in welfare provision and became consistent supporters of shared public-private responsibility and adequate public funding to alleviate ongoing poverty in the United States.

Public developments drove the Catholic agenda. The character of American welfare developed significantly after the Civil War, as the Union Army operated the Freedman's Bureau (1865–1876) to provide social and educational services for blacks in the South, and Northern cities benefited from community public health and welfare initiatives sparked by the volunteers of the United States Sanitary Commission. Thousands of Northern families welcomed public welfare in the form of the new veteran's pensions. These pensions represented the earliest form of categorical entitlement in American history and eventually became the single largest item in the federal budget.[2] There were also significant developments in welfare organization. States began to form official state boards of charity to provide supervision for the public institutions within the state. The composite nature of the welfare system continued to be visible in the new state boards, whose appointees remained volunteer citizens until well into the twentieth century. Catholics struggled to gain representation on these boards and in the new "quasi-public" oversight organizations like the State Charities Aid Association of New York and the local chapters of the Society for the Prevention of Cruelty to Children.

A growing interest in "scientific charity" presented a special challenge to Catholics. Beginning in Buffalo in 1878, non-Catholic reformers began to experiment with the British-inspired movement to bring private relief and reform agencies together in a cooperative management exercise. Under the generic title of charity organization societies (COS), independent voluntary relief agencies began to affiliate in citywide federations to coordinate and finance their efforts. Convinced that public welfare in the form of outdoor relief exacerbated both dependency and political corruption, the COS organizations campaigned to end it. They also urged the adoption of new measures to control the distribution of private relief. These included the investigation of all applicants for relief and the creation of central city registries to keep track of the recipients and to prevent the poor from receiving help from several sources at once. These proponents of scientific charity were quick to point out the deficiencies in Catholic welfare practice.

Catholics resisted these criticisms and were deeply suspicious of the new methods of scientific charity and the workers who administered it. Both poor and middle-class Catholics had reason to welcome the familiar and traditional practices of charity in the hostile environment of industrial America. Demands for careful record keeping and for the vigilant exchange of client information violated those traditions. The religious women who managed the child-caring institutions received needy children without inquiring too deeply into their backgrounds and kept them long enough to scandalize non-Catholic reformers. The sisters further violated the canons of scientific charity by sheltering pregnant women under fictitious names and placing children with foster parents without subjecting the parents to a thorough "social investigation." Lay men of the St. Vincent de Paul Society regularly provided food, fuel, and cash to needy families without a careful background check to determine if they had other sources of relief. Hospitals and homes for aged and handicapped persons responded to a nod from the local pastor or a plea from a member of their board rather than to a formal application from social service workers. Ethnic associations organized special "national" orphanages and most of the hundreds of local Catholic women's organizations supported neighborhood hospitals and orphanages and maintained face-to-face relationships with particular communities of religious sisters.

New York City provides prominent examples of the impact of the work of non-Catholic reformers on the development of Catholic social provision. The Children's Aid Society of New York was founded in 1853 by the Congregational clergyman Charles Loring Brace to improve the city by rescuing the children of the poor. It enjoyed considerable financial and civic support among New York's gentry for nearly a half century. The CAS-sponsored Newsboys Lodging House, and charity schools in the city featured religious and moral instruction, elementary education, and some industrial training. But the CAS also sponsored a much more controversial program of child removal. Between 1853 and 1880, Brace claimed to have transported more than 70,000 poor children from the city to rural areas. The CAS invented the "orphan train" and made "the West" a destination for thousands of New York's children.

Many of the children thus "rescued" by child-savers were Catholic or nominally Catholic, and the city's Catholic leadership reacted with strenuous objections and a major campaign to provide institutions within the city for the poor children of their own faith. As poor Catholic children received sustained attention from evangelical child-savers and charity organization societies in the last half of the nineteenth century, they became the focus of Catholic efforts in New York and the center of a national battle over methods, standards, and the roles of private and public welfare. In an effort to reclaim "their" children, New York Catholics deployed a substantial corps of volunteer and religious workers and established effective connections with City Hall and the State House. Their institutions and services for children became the mainstay of the network of New York Catholic charities and the leading influence in the creation of a national network of Catholic charities in the twentieth century.

Catholic success in maintaining religiously sponsored child-caring institutions with public support also fueled legislative debates in the city and state, and, when a new generation of reformers introduced new legislation, methods, and standards for welfare, the persistence of Catholic institutions became a prominent motivation behind the progressive "Home First" campaign to keep needy children in their own homes. By 1900, the old removal efforts designed to separate parents from their children were being replaced by proposals aimed at keeping dependent children in their family homes— and out of Catholic orphanages. Ironically, the institutional pattern that progressive reformers denounced had been made possible by the efforts of their own predecessors.

While agents of the Children's Aid Society were busy sending children "west" between 1855 and 1895, other reformers became determined to remove children from local poorhouses and to provide public funds for their support. In the 1870s, members of the New York State Board of Charities and the State Charities Aid Association undertook surveys and sponsored legislation to that end. The Children's Law of 1875 guaranteed public *per capita* payments for poor children institutionalized in the city, and a Catholic-sponsored rider stipulated that dependent children must be sheltered in institutions that reflected the religion of their parents. This legislation fueled the dramatic growth of Catholic child-caring institutions in the city, and enabled the sisters and their lay auxiliaries to provide a safety net for thousands of impoverished families. Their growing strength in Tammany Hall and consequent influence in Albany enabled Catholics to sustain the revenue stream created by Protestant reformers.

The "New York system" of mixed public and private child care had imitators in other cities, where local need and Catholic political access made congregate child-caring institutions popular. Alternatively, in cities like Boston and Baltimore, Catholics worked to become part of the establishment that governed foster care and child-placement programs at city and state levels.

Although they remained stubborn defenders of their institutions of charity, Catholics responded to the progressive welfare agenda after 1900 by reorganizing their agencies and professionalizing their practices. Two goals characterized their efforts. They sought to improve internal practices in Catholic charities and to enlarge the Catholic presence in public welfare policy formation. New York City remained the bellwether of these developments. In 1920 the archdiocese of New York inaugurated a major program of centralization and consolidated financing for its hitherto independent institutions and organizations. Archbishop Patrick J. Hayes also organized a statewide conference of Catholic charities to provide a vehicle by which the several Catholic bishops of New York state could bring more effective influence to bear on public welfare policy. Similar programs of centralization had begun in cities like Baltimore and Boston even before World War I. On the strength of these new "charities bureaus" or central diocesan agencies, Catholic leaders leveraged consideration for their institutions and organizations in policy discussions and effectively asserted their case for inclusion in community chests and tax revenues. But the centralization and professionalization of Catholic social provision greatly altered the original character of Catholic work, reducing both the freedom of the religious orders that founded and staffed the charitable institutions and the influence of the independent organizations of the laity that sustained them.

Catholic lay women, on the other hand, began to find salaried employment in diocesan charities and develop a new role as social work professionals in the early decades of the twentieth century. These new workers chose professional social work over the highly venerated life of the consecrated religious and were eager to assume responsibility for the religious welfare of their clients and to exercise a new blend of professional and pastoral authority in the church.[3]

They faced an uphill battle. Conservatives both inside and outside the church regarded professional social workers as agents of modernization and baneful influences on family life. This characterization was especially troublesome among Catholics, where a powerful ideology of family anchored Catholic social teaching and social practice. Beginning with *Rerum novarum*, the "labor encyclical" of Pope Leo XIII (1893), Catholic social doctrine rested on claims about the rights and needs of families. These claims provided the foundation for arguments about wage justice, the role of private property, and the responsibilities of the state. The family was intended for procreation and education of children. Parents had the duty of looking after both the eternal salvation and the social security of their offspring. Economic and social entitlements derived from these responsibilities, and family stability was crucial to Catholic social claims.

Consequently, the rising divorce rates, the growing popularity of birth control among the middle classes, and the "socialist" idea of companionate marriage that was becoming popular in twentieth-century America were major sources of concern to church leaders. The church taught that marriage was a sacrament and was therefore indissoluble. Fidelity between spouses was crucial to the primary aims of procreation and education of children. Birth control and sterilization were gross violations of the natural law and were therefore unacceptable. Agents of these views—often identified as "social workers"—were anathema among church leaders. One bishop summarized the connection succinctly: "Propagandists for birth control have seized upon the poverty resulting from low wages to advance their theories on family limitation. They have invaded the homes of the poor, either by way of literature or welfare workers . . .These zealots for birth control ignore the well-tested fact of experience that economic problems must be solved by economic means. In other words, wage control, not birth control, is the solution of poverty with its varied resultant evils"[4]

As they began to move into the middle class, however, Catholics seemed to be drawn along with other American to the "perverse practice." Rev. John Ryan admitted his fears to fellow priests: "Despite the optimistic and somewhat boastful language we sometimes affect when contrasting the conduct of our people in this matter with that of the people without the fold, we are forced to acknowledge in our colder moments that large sections of the Catholic population are considerably tainted." Drawing evidence from the confessional, from conversations with other priests, and from simple head-counting, he estimated that the number of children in Catholic families "of the middle and comfortable classes" in 1916 was little more than half the average of the previous generation.[5]

Similar suspicions ran all the way to the Vatican. In response to inquiries from Rome, Catholic University's Rev. John M. Cooper concluded that, while contraceptive practices were indeed "very widespread among our Catholics in the United States," the implied patterns of use varied greatly according to social class and income. Cooper suggested that the use was "very prevalent, perhaps 75% or at least 50%" among "well-to-do and educated" Catholics, while it was considerably less prominent among rural and foreign-born populations and unskilled workers. And since the Catholic population was "gradually, even rapidly, rising in the economic and educational scale," the prognosis was grim.[6]

Catholic social workers therefore stepped onto highly charged turf when they became involved with spiritual and material welfare of Catholic families. They assumed a double burden—of succeeding as welfare professionals and of serving as properly subordinate pastoral agents of the church. Seeking to save souls as well as mend lives, they were trained to employ the discipline of church sacraments in their routine casework and to make confession and communion a regular part of the treatment for those who applied for help. Their investigations of persons applying for aid included a routine check of baptismal and marriage records, and they inquired closely whether applicants went to church on Sundays and made efforts to send their children to Catholic schools. Social workers were also instructed to maintain a high level of "practical Catholicism" in their own lives, attending Mass and receiving the sacraments regularly and often bolstering their religious resources by taking vacation time to make a religious retreat. And they firmly resisted birth control, sterilization, and divorce.

In spite of the tight controls on their work, however, some Catholic workers were not shy about expressing their views on Catholic poor relief practices. Anne Culligan of St. Paul Catholic Charities argued, for instance, that Catholic workers should relinquish the goal of sequestering all Catholic poor under their care and control. Convinced that church-sponsored efforts could not begin to meet the need, she insisted that poor Catholics should not be penalized by being limited to inadequate Catholic resources. Breaking the traditional connection between religion and poor relief, Culligan argued that poverty was a community problem and that "the causes at the root of [Catholic] poverty are the same as in non-Catholic families." The burden of relief should be borne by the entire community, and she urged St. Paul Catholics to join the work of the local COS agency and to assume their share of the responsibility for social provision on a nonsectarian basis.[7]

In New York, social worker Mary Tinney also accepted the principle of public support for Catholic needs. "If we were able to take care of our own poor," she told co-workers in 1916, "we might assume full responsibility for them . . . But we do not take care of our own poor and we cannot." Commenting on the report that five of the eight thousand families relieved by New York's Charity Organization Society in 1915 were Catholics, Tinney concluded pragmatically: "It may be that we could not care for them, but as a matter of fact we did not . . . let us admit the fact and shape our policies accordingly."[8]

Both Culligan and Tinney were public employees. In the second decade of the twentieth century, Catholic women in growing numbers were working outside of diocesan agencies as employees of state and nonsectarian welfare organizations. Although these workers were drawn by higher salaries and wider opportunities in the public agencies, they generally maintained their commitment to Catholic teaching and their loyalty to the Catholic community. Their presence added a significant Catholic dimension to state boards of charity and to professional associations, municipal and state welfare organizations, and eventually to New Deal programs. New York Catholic social worker Jane Hoey, for example, was appointed to direct the Bureau of Public Assistance of the Social Security Board and to approve state plans for Aid to Dependent Children, while her colleague Mary Irene Atkinson became the director of the Child Welfare Division of the Children's Bureau. From their new federal positions, administrators like Hoey and Atkinson supported the growing role of the state in welfare provision but retained a strong emphasis in the parental and mentoring relationship characteristic of both Catholic charities and professional social work in the period. Social workers like these exercised a large influence on the role of Catholic charities in the emerging welfare state.[9]

Under the combined pressures of Catholic need and progressive welfare standards and practices, Catholics gradually began to develop a national organization and voice. It was a complex task requiring coordination of hundreds of dioceses and the achievement of effective local participation and a coherent voice at the national level. The National Conference of Catholic Charities (NCCC), founded in 1910, became the vehicle for that effort. Catholic charities leaders pressed for the creation of a national venue to extend the internal reorganization and give the movement a national visibility and voice. NCCC was an informal association of volunteers, professional social workers, and religious and diocesan clergy. Its national staff consisted of the secretary of the Conference and a single assistant. The base of NCCC power lay in the diocesan organizations of charity. Catholic Charities of New York City, Brooklyn, Buffalo, Rochester, and Albany, ensured New York's influence in NCCC activities, while the rapid growth of other urban Catholic charities organizations in Cleveland, Cincinnati, Toledo, Detroit, Chicago, St. Louis, Denver, San Francisco, and Los Angeles guaranteed them a prominent role. The office of diocesan director of charities quickly became a fast track for ecclesiastical promotion, and the number of former directors of charity in the American episcopacy increased markedly after World War I.

On the strength of its affiliated diocesan agencies, the NCCC's national secretary Rev. John O'Grady became a lobbyist for Catholic charities interests. He built up his influence in Catholic dioceses by cultivating his relationships with priests who were the directors of diocesan charities directors. These new charities executives were impressed with O'Grady's knowledge of welfare developments and with his demonstrated willingness to go anywhere in the country to offer them his counsel and advice. O'Grady used his Washington location to promote the charities organization movement in the dioceses, and he leveraged his position NCCC secretary and his knowledge of the situations in local Catholic strongholds to build a reputation in Washington.

John O'Grady's skills as an organizer and lobbyist were particularly tested during the New Deal. Although Catholics had fared well enough when American politics were largely a local matter, mastering the intricacies of special interest and reform politics on the national level represented a new challenge for Catholic charities. As the New Deal confronted them with initiatives that heralded a growing involvement of state and federal government in the lives of individuals and families, Catholic charities organizations struggled to advance their interests and to play a role in the formation and administration of federal welfare policies.[10]

The NCCC acted as policy advisor for local bishops and represented "the Catholic view" in state and national forums on public assistance, work relief, social security, housing, and youth. Diocesan directors became active participants in local and state initiatives for meeting the crisis; and, while Catholic social workers began to occupy significant positions in the state and federal welfare bureaucracy, conference secretary O'Grady became an eager promoter of Catholic charities' agendas on Capitol Hill.

O'Grady and his diocesan charities colleagues used the strategy honed earlier at local and state levels. They presented Catholic charities as the protector of the religious rights of Catholic welfare recipients in order to make a place for their agencies in the new public programs. Conceding the need for federal funding for social welfare, they sought legal protections for the religious identity of dependent children in the new public programs and attempted to establish Catholic agencies as administrators of federal and state welfare funds. In particular, they took a very active role in shaping the child-caring programs of the Social Security Act. When Roosevelt's cabinet-level Committee on Economic Security met to draft the social security bill in 1934, the National Conference of Catholic Charities engaged in a significant effort to shape the provisions of Aid to Dependent Children and Child Welfare Services in that legislation.

Behind a blitz of letter writing from diocesan agencies, and aided by connections with Catholic congressmen, NCCC pressure secured amendments limiting the child welfare services proposed by the Children's Bureau to primarily rural areas. More importantly, Catholic charities successfully negotiated to eliminate the possibility of *mandated* state participation in the financing of child-care services—an outcome which would have threatened the established local patterns of funding for Catholic child welfare where state laws prohibited the allocation of state funds to private institutions. The organization also succeeded in limiting the scope of Aid to Dependent Children. Under the ADC "kinship" clause, dependent children were defined as those who lived with their parents or with relatives within the second degree of kinship. This confined federal-state funding to the blood relatives of dependent children and forestalled a situation in which local governments providing per capita support for children in institutions would have a significant financial incentive to move children from institutions into foster families where they would be supported by ADC revenues rather than from the local public purse. Thus, while Catholic agencies remained barred from dispensing ADC funds directly to Catholic families, the final form of the social security legislation prevented ADC from being used for foster care and left traditional agencies responsible for the care of needy children who were unable to be sheltered by close relatives.

Meanwhile, there was a second contender for Catholic influence in national policy. The National Catholic Welfare Conference (NCWC) grew out of the Catholic war effort during World War I and remained involved in Catholic charities organization throughout the 1920s, but its ambitions extended well beyond the welfare of the poor. The NCWC was designed as an informal organization for consultation and action among the American bishops, and its leadership staked a claim to responsibility for the "welfare" of both church and nation. As its national agenda developed under the direction of its general secretary, Paulist John J. Burke, the NCWC provided a home for a group of Catholics who devoted themselves to what they called "the social question"—namely, the rights of labor, labor legislation and unions, and the role of the state. They anchored their analyses and recommendations in papal social encyclicals—Leo XIII's *Rerum novarum* (1891) and Pius XI's *Quadragesimo anno* (1931). Led by Rev. John A. Ryan, Social Action Department of the NCWC campaigned for a family wage and promoted labor legislation and sponsored industrial conferences aimed at bringing together representatives of labor and management to air grievances.

But the NCWC's initial connection to the Catholic charities movement failed to thrive. The activities of the NCCC during the New Deal greatly alarmed the NCWC leaders, who feared that the "charities conference" would become the dominant public voice of the church. In 1935, John Burke sent his deputy to the annual meeting of the National Conference of Catholic Charities in order to gain a first-hand impression of its strength. Michael Ready reported a disturbing trend. The NCCC now claimed the authority to speak for the bishops of the United States on social legislation. "I heard definite criticism of the N.C.W.C," Ready told his boss, ". . . [a] constant comparison of what the National Conference of Catholic Charities had done and what the N.C.W.C. had failed to do; what the National Conference of Catholic Charities on a given question had done well and what the N.C.W.C. on the same matter had done badly." Catholic charities leaders complained that the NCWC was inept in its dealings with Congress and that its representatives had "interfered disastrously" on social security legislation. "The most serious danger I sensed," Michael Ready concluded, "was the possibility of a definite alignment of a considerable group of bishops against the N.C.W.C. It seemed to me that some bishops were eager to get leadership and possibly national prominence, and they saw the National Conference of Catholic Charities as the organization that would give it to them."[11]

The tensions between the two organizations eased toward the end of the decade. John Burke died in 1936, and John O'Grady was removed from his position as dean of the School of Social Work at Catholic University in the course of the battle over modernization of the curriculum in the late 1930s. O'Grady continued to act as the national secretary for the NCCC, but the end of the New Deal seriously limited his role in national and state policy discussions.[12] By the end of the decade, economic relief became the clear responsibility of the new federal and state agencies. The poor were now directly eligible for government assistance through old age and child assistance programs and through the emerging public insurance programs for unemployment and old age. The federalization of welfare policy under SSA prevented the kind of direct influence in the formation and administration of state welfare policy that Catholics had enjoyed, for example, in the New York system. And Catholic women employed as administrators and social workers in the new public bureaucracies defended the rule of public administration for public funds and championed the role of the professional social worker in the lives of recipients of public assistance. While these Catholic social workers continued to believe that faith was a peerless asset in social life, they were also aware of the solid increase in the material security provided to poor Catholics by the state and enjoyed their own role in that improvement.

Under John O'Grady's leadership, the NCCC continued to pursue a slate of social issues including care for the elderly, housing and immigration, and community organization. NCCC spokespersons like O'Grady and Rose McHugh urged Catholic charities to develop its role as advocates for those who were newly eligible for state support. Reiterating the social teaching of the church, O'Grady insisted that "human needs constitute the primary title to material goods."[13] McHugh, who served as the assistant commissioner of welfare for the New York State Welfare Department before joining the Social Security Administration, argued that the English poor law tradition was contrary to Catholic teaching and that Catholic charities must become publicists for the poor, defending their legal right to assistance and to due process.[14]

The transformation of the Catholic charities network to include community organization and advocacy as well as direct services would take more than a quarter of a century.[15] Responding to the Great Society initiatives of the Johnson years, Catholic charities agencies took major steps to reconstruct themselves to serve a "new poor." By the 1990s, the local agencies affiliated with Catholic Charities, U.S.A.—the successor of the National Conference of Catholic Charities—spent $1.86 billion to support its social programs, and benefited from the talents of nearly 200,000 volunteers.[16] Its ability to continue to attract financial and human resources and to sustain grass-roots services and legislative advocacy makes the Catholic charities network a significant asset for the poor in contemporary America and underscores the importance of the voluntary sector in American welfare. Its distinctive character also makes Catholic charities a fascinating ingredient in the history of American social provision.

Notes

Copyright by Elizabeth McKeown, 1996. This essay draws on the extended account of these developments in Dorothy M. Brown and Elizabeth McKeown, *The Poor Belong to Us: Catholic Charities and American Welfare* (Cambridge, Mass.: Harvard University Press, 1997).

1. See Michael B. Katz, *In the Shadow of the Poorhouse: A Social History of Welfare in America* (New York, 1986): ch. 1, and Katz, *Improving Poor People: The Welfare State, the "Underclass," and Urban Schools As History* (Princeton N. J., 1995): ch. 1. The "blurred boundaries" comment is in *Katz, Improving Poor People,* 56–57.

2. See Theda Skocpol, *Protecting Soldiers and Mothers: The Political Origins of Social Policy in the United States* (Cambridge, Mass., 1992): Part I.

3. For a contemporary review of the problems surrounding the identity of professional social work in the early decades of the century, see Daniel J. Walkowitz, "The Making of a Feminine Professional Identity: Social Workers in the 1920s," *American Historical Review* 95 (October 1990): 1051–1075.

4. Bishop Aloisius Muench, *Proceedings of the National Conference of Catholic Charities,* (Washington, D.C., 1929).

5. John A. Ryan, "Family Limitation," *The Ecclesiastical Review* 55 (June 1916): 684–696.

6. John M. Cooper, *Memorandum on Prevalence of Contraception among Catholics of the United States* [1927]; Cooper to Monsignor George M. Leech, Secretary, Apostolic Delegation, Washington, D.C., January 30, 1927; and reply, February 1, 1927, John Cooper Papers, Archives of the Catholic University of America.

7. Anne Culligan, "How Far Should Catholics Care for Their Own Poor?" *Proceedings of the Sixth National Conference of Catholic Charities* (Washington, D.C., 1920): 93–103.

8. Mary Tinney, "Remarks on Adequate and Inadequate Relief," *Proceedings of the Fourth National Conference of Catholic Charities* (Washington, D.C., 1916): 141.

9. Male Catholic professionals also made careers in Catholic charity. The vast majority of the men were priests. They became directors of the expanding diocesan charity organizations, and "the charities" quickly became a favorite track for ecclesiastical promotion and preferment. These priest-executives of Catholic charities directed the activities of the female professionals, as Catholic charities took a central role in shaping the public presence of the church after World War I. Historian Robert Cross provided the following data on the fortunes of social workers in Catholic charities of New York at mid-century (although his use of the generic "layman" hides the fact that the lay workers are overwhelmingly women): "Catholic Charities, like most American Catholic enterprises, suffer from clericalism . . . Despite the rising number of skilled laymen and the deeply felt shortage of priests and sisters, the archdiocese of New York included no laymen among its 21-man administrative staff; of the 158 specialized agencies it maintains, only 33 are headed by laymen. Lay social workers must live with the expectation that they will not rise above the rank of casework supervisor; the large number of them now employed in positions of great responsibility by public and non-sectarian institutions constitutes a loss to Catholic charities, if a gain to society generally" Robert D. Cross, "Catholic Charities," *The Atlantic Monthly* (1962): 110–114.

10. Catholic response to the New Deal has received attention from Aaron I. Abell, *American Catholicism and Social Action* (Notre Dame, Ind., 1960); Francis L. Broderick, *Right Reverend New Dealer: John A. Ryan* (New York, 1963); George Q. Flynn, *American Catholics and the Roosevelt Presidency, 1932–1936* (Lexington,Ky.,

1968); and David O'Brien, *American Catholics and Social Reform: The New Deal Years* (New York, 1968).

11. Memorandum for Father Burke: Report on the 1935 Peoria Conference of the NCCC, by Rev. Michael Ready, Assistant General Secretary of the National Catholic Welfare Conference, October 15, 1935, Papers of the National Catholic Welfare Conference, Archives of The Catholic University of America. Ready and Burke had reason to be concerned that a new "alignment" was in the making in September 1935. The bishops of the United States were seriously split over the issue of the role of the United States in Mexico. One key prelate, Archbishop Michael Curley of Baltimore, had actively opposed the Mexican policy of Burke and his supporters in the NCWC since 1926, suggesting at one point that "gentle sacerdotal diplomats" like Burke should mind their own business. In January 1936, Curley resigned from the National Catholic Welfare Conference. For a full account of NCWC-Mexican relations, see Slawson: chs. 10 and 11; and Douglas J. Slawson, "The National Catholic Welfare Conference and the Mexican Church-State Conflict of the Mid-1930s: a Case of *Deja Vu*," *The Catholic Historical Review* 80 (January 1994): 58–96.

12. After World War II, O'Grady met Saul Alinsky and became interested in transferring Alinsky's methods to local Catholic charities organizations. Alinsky became enamored in return with O'Grady. The two met regularly in Chicago, and at one point, Alinsky signed a contract to write a book about the Catholic charities priest. A rough manuscript resulted but was never published, and the friendship eventually fell apart. O'Grady retired from the NCCC in 1961 after serving as secretary for forty years. See Thomas Tifft, "Toward A More Humane Social Policy: The Work and Influence of Monsignor John O'Grady," Ph.D. dissertation, Catholic University of America (1979), and John O'Grady to Saul Alinsky, April 3, 1954, in the Alinsky Manuscript, O'Grady Papers, Archives of The Catholic University of America.

13. John O'Grady, *The Catholic Church and the Destitute* (New York, 1929), 3.

14. Rose J. McHugh, "Functions of Catholic Charities in Assisting People to Obtain Their Rights Under the New Governmental Programs," *Proceedings of the Twenty-fifth National Conference of Catholic Charities* (Washington, D.C., 1939): 240–248.

15. Meanwhile, older tribalisms and entrenchments were much more visible. Speaking from a mid-century perspective, Robert Cross commented on "increasing Catholic contentiousness" and claimed that "a good many Protestants and Jews" were becoming exasperated because "Catholic charities were so preoccupied with the Church's position against divorce, artificial birth control and sterilization as to be indifferent to the worldly welfare of their clients. Where, as in New York City, this increasing mutual inclination to disagree over first principles was exacerbated by the organizational pride of strong Catholic, Protestant, Jewish and non-sectarian charities, a real retreat from previous patterns of cooperation occurred; the Health and Welfare Council, a federation of charitable agencies, broke up when in 1953 some Catholics insisted that no support be given Planned Parenthood work." Cross, "Catholic Charities," 113.

16. *Responding to Changing Times: Catholic Charities U.S.A., 1994 Annual Survey* (Washington, D.C., November 1995).

ELLIS W. HAWLEY

Herbert Hoover, Associationalism, and the Great Depression Relief Crisis of 1930–1933

When in the years to come, someone writes the history of private philanthropy in America, the winter of 1930–31 will stand as a red-letter era. No group of organizations and agencies ever strived more earnestly, more intelligently, and more devoutly to handle a stupendous problem than did the private organizations and agencies in our cities throughout the country.

— Frank Bane, 1931[1]

In recent debates over America's welfare state, one group of so-called "compassion conservatives" has argued that the potential for a superior substitute exists in the private sector. Recognizing the need for agencies of social adjustment and rescue, the group has insisted that the most effective way to provide these—the way that could meet real national needs efficiently while also strengthening individual and local responsibility, helping to "re-moralize" the social order, and applying the kind of personalized "tough love" that government bureaucrats cannot apply—is through a publicly encouraged network of the institutions making up "civil society." Such is the program, for example, set forth in Marvin Olasky's *Tragedy of American Compassion*, the book most commonly cited. And variations of the idea have been espoused by conservative activist Arianna Huffington, Bradley Foundation head Michael Joyce, Speaker of the House Newt Gingrich, and recent Republican presidential primary contender Lamar Alexander. The program was, in particular, at the core of Alexander's "citizenship agenda," as worked out in meetings hosted by Huffington and subsequently presented to the "conservative intelligentsia" at the Heritage Foundation.[2]

No evidence has been forthcoming that these people see themselves as following in the footsteps of Herbert Hoover. But the parallels between their prescriptions and those of the Hoover presidency during the Depression era relief crisis of 1930–1933 are striking. For Hoover and his associates, to be sure, the great concern was with preventing the creation of a dysfunctional welfare state like those established in Britain and Germany, not with scrapping one allegedly doing more social harm than good. But in both cases the broad indictments of welfare statism, the perceptions of a nonstatist alternative to atomistic individualism, the romantic images of voluntarism as more truly democratic than any governmental action, and the optimistic assessments of the private sector's capacity for beneficial social action were all basically similar. In both cases the central idea was to pull or coax an effective welfare system from the associative life of the private sector, using government as a facilitator of this process, and in this way to retain the essentials for continued freedom and progress.

This paper not only examines a crucial period in the making of America's welfare state but also explores historical experience seemingly relevant to current policy debates. It argues that there was a time when majority policy views closely resembled those of today's "compassion conservatives," that this led to wide-ranging efforts to create and make use of a private sector substitute for a welfare state, and that the failure of these under the circumstances of the time was a decisive factor in paving the way for the New Deal's welfare measures. More specifically, it will begin with a brief overview of how such thinking developed and became a part of Hoover's agenda by 1929. It will then focus on the kinds of programs that that thinking produced, looking particularly at White House involvements in social action and at the operations of the President's Emergency Committee for Employment (PECE) and the President's Organization on Unemployment Relief (POUR). And in a final section, it will trace the shifting views that would eventually lead to a more statist alternative. In addition, it will offer some thoughts about the lessons to be drawn from a fuller understanding of the experience.[3]

The beginnings of the story that would unfold in the early 1930s can be found in the kind of organizational growth that America experienced in the late nineteenth and early twentieth centuries. During this period the nation's antibureaucratic traditions kept its public sector bureaucracies from becoming any more than a "stunted tree." But its political culture was rich in elements conducive to private bureaucratization, seen not as "bureaucracy" but as entrepreneurial adaptation to a challenging environment; and these same elements tended to divert much of its search for new regulatory and welfare mechanisms into complex schemes of association building that could allegedly serve both private and public ends. Not only was there an immense growth of formalized business, professional, and occupational associations, with some effort to shape these into a government outside of government. There was also the rapid growth of a privatized welfare system, built around corporate service departments, charity organization societies, community and national welfare federations, social settlements, and a new breed of philanthropic foundations. And of importance to what would follow, the institutions involved were already advertising themselves both as constructive social adjusters and as defenders of public virtue against the evils flowing from traditional poor law administration and governmental bureaucracy.[4]

A major problem faced by those seeking improved governance through private sector institutions was that the new association building retained strong entrepreneurial as well as civic qualities. Much of the structure rested on appeals to narrow interests as well as appeals to good citizenship and desires for greater social control, and one component of the organizational output was a pluralistic proliferation of competing groups rather than units readily capable of fitting into an extra-governmental government.[5] Yet hopes of finding a new unifier for this "higher government"—either in a new business leadership, the new technocratic professions, or the new claimants to social scientific expertise—remained high.[6] And during the crisis produced by World War I, much of what had emerged from the pre-war wave of organizational formation had become a functional substitute for expanded government. In the words of Robert Wiebe, "the pieces fell into place with a neatness almost no one could have predicted."[7]

With the return to peace much of the war machinery was scrapped, and for a time there were strong attacks on some of the associational activity promoted during the war. Yet the idea that new regulatory and welfare needs could best be met through institutional formation in the private sector survived and came to dominate public policy during the 1920s. It was used to justify a new wave of promotional effort, undertaken particularly by foundation and corporate executives and their allies in government, the professions, and the social sciences. And hailed as indicating the idea's validity was the growth of corporate welfare and stabilization projects, a further flowering of community welfare funds, federations, and councils, further support for the professionalization of social work, and new demonstrations of what private sector agencies could do when mobilized to meet such emergencies as mass unemployment in 1921 and the Mississippi flood of 1927.[8] Although some critics deplored these developments as obstacles to genuinely needed governmental programs,[9] the dominant view stressed the greater professionalism and general superiority of the civic and social work being done in the private sector and saw it either as the way to avoid bigger government or as the way to keep a necessarily bigger government from damaging the wellsprings of national progress. As Governor Albert Ritchie of Maryland put it in 1926, most welfare work was far better done by private-sector agencies rooted in the "community" than by "state officials" in governmental bureaucracies; it was only through such agencies that existing levels of inspiration, competence, and efficiency could be maintained.[10]

By 1929, moreover, Herbert Hoover had become the most prominent of these would-be builders of an "associative state." As a war manager and war relief administrator, he had built large-scale regulatory and welfare systems heavily reliant on private sector resources. As the "great engineer," he had worked to advance his profession's claims to be an objective definer of progressive social behavior. As secretary of Commerce, he had helped to foster an expanded array of trade association activities and made them a part of his efforts to reduce industrial waste and remedy other market failures. As a champion of "social betterment" through applied social science, he had helped to launch new research projects and connect them to the expanding network of welfare associations. And as the man in charge of meeting national relief needs in 1921 and 1927, he had taken credit for putting together emergency organizations capable of coping with crisis situations while keeping government's role to a minimum.[11] Nor had Hoover allowed the gaps between ideal and practice in all of these endeavors to dampen his enthusiasm about the private sector's capabilities for meeting future national needs and thereby keeping the "American system" insulated from Europe's "hallucinations." Over the past twenty-five years, he declared in 1928, America had developed "a higher sense of organized co-operation," most of which either recognized a responsibility to the public or was "founded solely on public interest," and from which could come a "true self-government" comprising "more than political institutions."[12]

Such optimism was also evident as Hoover assumed the presidency. For him one major attraction of the office was the opportunity it afforded to continue the association building he had undertaken earlier. And once inaugurated, he quickly became involved not only in efforts to implement earlier designs for agricultural marketing associations and mechanisms of "economic balance." He also helped create a foundation-financed President's Research Committee on Social Trends and tried to make the Department of the Interior a national center for the promotion of better social work. In addition he planned a series of White House conferences intended to stimulate and guide the building of new or improved institutions of "social betterment."[13] America, he had said in 1928, was "in sight of the day" when poverty and the need for poor relief would disappear, when, if present policies were continued, there would be "a job for every man," and when a democracy, working through its societal as well as political institutions, would make it possible for all Americans to live fuller lives.[14] Neither he nor those with whom he was working had any expectations that America was about to experience its greatest unemployment relief crisis and in the end yield to some of the resulting demands for a greatly expanded welfare state.

Initially, moreover, Hoover did not believe that the stock market crash would produce a relief crisis. In its wake he called the nation's economic leaders into conference and secured pledges to maintain wages and minimize layoffs, expand construction, and avoid strikes and lockouts. In addition, he persuaded the United States Chamber of Commerce to set up organizations through which its constituent trade associations could work for pledge implementation, while also calling for governmental credit, spending, and tax policies that would support and supplement these private sector actions.[15] And by the spring of 1930, he was ready to claim that this "great economic experiment" in joint effort had "succeeded to a remarkable degree." On March 7 he released surveys indicating that "the worst effects of the crash on employment" were almost over, and speaking to the Chamber of Commerce on May 1, he asserted that employment was again rising and would continue to do so. For Hoover, "the great associations" representative of American economic life had again demonstrated their capacity to mobilize "individual initiative" in times of "stress," and the experience should now be studied "with a view to broad determination of what can be done to achieve greater stability for the future."[16]

The real need for emergency relief mobilization, so Hoover believed in mid-1930, was not in industrial centers but in rural areas affected by what Secretary of Agriculture Arthur Hyde called "the worst drought ever recorded in this country." Centered in the Ohio and Mississippi River valleys, the drought was producing severe distress accompanied by insistent calls for disaster relief. And in August of 1930, Hoover did respond by appointing a National Drought Relief Committee and getting the drought-area states to establish emergency committees of the sort used to mobilize private sector relief resources during the Mississippi flood of 1927.[17] In addition, the president took steps to secure better unemployment statistics and explore ways to stimulate more construction. But not until October was he ready to concede that a depression now raging "worldwide" was going to delay the recovery he had promised in the spring and require relief mobilization on the order of that undertaken in 1921 and 1922. The concession came in major addresses to the American Bankers Association and the American Federation of Labor, followed by an announcement on October 17 stating that a new Cabinet Committee would formulate plans for strengthening "Federal activities for employment," and by another on October 21 saying that Arthur Woods of the Rockefeller Foundation, the man who had headed the earlier relief mobilization, would be in charge of developing an appropriate organization.[18]

The organization that Woods put together in late 1930 consisted of a twenty-seven member presidential committee (the President's Emergency

Committee for Employment or PECE, with Woods as chair), a small central staff assisted by nine field representatives, and six functional sections concerned with relief matters, industrial cooperation, expanded construction, women's projects, employment statistics, and interpretive publicity.[19] The avowed purpose was to mobilize and deploy resources so as to provide aid for all the unemployed having "honest difficulties," preferably by giving them temporary or part-time work but if necessary through properly administered relief loans and grants. Yet care must also be taken to ensure that this did not diminish the sense of individual, family, and community responsibility that had protected America from European statism. This was one task of the private sector relief agencies now to be drawn into emergency service. And to help such agencies resist political interference with their work, public financing of the effort was to be minimal. Initially, the resources to be distributed were to come primarily from expanded charitable donations, decisions to hire that might normally have been put off until later, and work-sharing arrangements under which work would be taken from the employed and used to provide part-time jobs for the jobless.[20]

A key instrument for achieving these goals, as Woods and Hoover saw it, was a properly designed community committee, which PECE and collaborating state authorities would help to establish in every community suffering from unemployment. Initially, community organizers were advised to model their work on that described in a Russell Sage Foundation pamphlet or on that already undertaken in such "progressive" states as Ohio. But eventually explicit instructions were given, calling for committees that represented all groups and interests, operated through subcommittees specializing in each component of the operation (research, finance, employment, relief, and publicity), and had the standing to serve as coordinative planners, expanders of charitable giving, discouragers of harmful mass relief, and drawers of the necessary administrative resources from the area's existing welfare and business institutions. PECE would facilitate their operations, primarily through its promotive publicity, its provision of useful information, and its work with national organizations capable of shaping the behavior of their local units. But it was only through properly performing local committees that it could expect to meet emergency needs without doing damage to the nation's capacities for continuing progress.[21]

In the days that followed, moreover, the PECE, acting as a "trouble-shooter" and "booster engine," did oversee a whirl of activity from which came not only new committees but also much public relations effort, more intergroup cooperation, and some expansion of relief.[22] Working with and through the Association of Community Chests and Councils (ACCC), the Family Welfare Association of America (FWAA), the Red Cross, the Russell

Sage Foundation, and the religious-based charities, Porter Lee's relief division took credit for helping to build sound community programs alert to the newly urgent problems of mass transiency and eroding worker morale.[23] Working with and through business and engineering leaders, J. Douglas Brown's industrial division publicized model business relief plans and took credit for helping to redistribute work so as to give more families at least a share of it.[24] Working with and through the construction industries, Franklin Miller's works division strongly urged potential builders to take advantage of labor surpluses. Working with and through the media and the Association of National Advertisers, the PECE publicity section applied existing expertise on how to steer public opinion into the proper channels.[25] And working with and through the General Federation of Women's Clubs and other women's groups and agencies, Lilian Gilbreth's women's division sponsored home employment, subsistence gardening, and "wise spending" campaigns and urged women as "consumers" to "follow their dollars" and reward cooperating business firms.[26]

The effort, said PECE secretary Edward Hunt, proved that in America economic knowledge, human sympathy, and responsiveness to wise leadership were all widespread. And as Hoover saw it, the "gratifying degree of response" was enabling "local communities through their voluntary agencies" to fulfill their social duties.[27] Other statements, moreover, showed a tendency to view the experience both as a defense of Americanism and as a step toward a better managed prosperity. Among the PECE leaders, talk of emergency action often coexisted with talk of the new committees evolving into permanent managerial mechanisms, of business experiments with unemployment reserves evolving into a national system of employment planning and unemployment compensation, and of PECE acting as a midwife for the kind of private sector institutions that could minimize future unemployment. While deploring suggestions that the emergency be used to justify more government or create European-style economic councils, the Hooverites would use it to speed the coming of a private sector that could be both "free" and "progressive."[28]

Still, despite all the self-congratulation, relief needs kept growing,[29] and from Hoover's perspective rising pressure for governmental provision became an ominous threat potentially capable of bringing ruinous "raids" on the treasury and turning sound relief programs into wasteful, spiritually deficient, and character-destroying ones.[30] To ease the pressure, he and Treasury Undersecretary Ogden Mills urged that private sector agencies create a "national" relief fund that could move resources from less needy to more needy areas. But in the resulting negotiations, they found the Red Cross strongly resistant to moving much beyond disaster relief and the ACCC firmly committed to the principle of community rather than national funds.[31] All that Hoover could get was a special Red Cross drive for drought relief funds and some unpublicized Red Cross assistance in Appalachia's coal-mining towns, a program that was later taken over by the American Friends Service Committee with money from the Hoover-controlled American Relief Administration.[32] Such measures could not stem the demands for federal relief. And while Hoover managed in 1931 to keep the advocates of general relief appropriations at bay,[33] his battle against federal funding of poor relief in the drought areas ended in a public relations fiasco and grudging acceptance of a congressional appropriation of $65 million, mostly for feed and seed loans but some for rehabilitation assistance that could include food purchases.[34]

As the crisis deepened, moreover, some of those purportedly demonstrating the social capabilities of the private sector were beginning to argue that only governmental action could do the job, and that ways existed to make this acceptable. People who had once deplored the growing proportion of relief funds coming from city and state coffers were now urging larger appropriations and more public bureaucracy, especially for areas without community chests or Red Cross assistance. And with this came arguments that the potential harm could be minimized, in part by using quasi-private agencies rather than "poor law machinery" to administer the funds, and in part by encouraging public agencies to professionalize and become more like private charities.[35] Formalization of public-private cooperation had become desirable, and in mid-1931 PECE moved to establish formal cooperation with the American Association of Public Welfare Officials (AAPWO). That organization would now take the lead in promoting higher standards and professional training for public relief providers. Subsequently PECE helped it to secure $40 thousand from Rockefeller's Spelman Fund to begin such work. Chosen to head the effort was Frank Bane, who fittingly was both Virginia's public welfare commissioner and a PECE field representative.[36]

In other respects, too, PECE seemed headed in unintended directions. Internal rifts had developed over such matters as its advice on consumption and gardening, its attitudes toward jobs for married women, and its responses to cutbacks in other kinds of social work.[37] The PECE now seemed out of tune with a chorus of calls for legalized cartels as the way to sustain corporate profits and corporate welfare.[38] It had members, like Bryce Stewart and Joseph Willits, who strongly disagreed with Hoover's decision to veto Senator Wagner's bill authorizing federal funds for state employment exchanges. This, they said, was vitally needed, would not necessarily lead to "tammanyization" as the president feared, and would be far more effective than Hoover's substitute program of federal-state-private cooperation.[39] And beyond all this was a new reluctance to defend the agency and discount evidence of mounting distress. In March 1931 Woods began discussions with Hoover and others about the PECE's future, and in April, after it was agreed that Fred Croxton would become acting head, Woods resigned, left on a trip to Europe, and became an open advocate of federal relief grants to the states on the same basis as the grants for road building.[40] Another phase of Hoover's battle against welfare statism appeared to be ending, and decisions now had to be made about whether to continue the effort and if so, by what means.

In April 1931 Hoover and Woods thought that PECE might best be continued as an advisory committee attached to the Federal Employment Stabilization Board (FESB), an agency recently created to plan future public works. As they envisioned it, Croxton could become an assistant FESB director and as such continue to run the PECE complex. But subsequently, Hoover decided that more was needed, both to relieve distress and to save America from the follies being committed in Europe and being suggested at such places as the Chamber of Commerce convention and the annual meeting of the National Conference of Social Work.[41] Through presidential speeches, new Commerce Department initiatives, and renewed PECE work with trade associations, he set out to expose "the economic patent medicines from foreign lands" and strengthen commitments to the "American plan." He also reasserted the administration's opposition to wage cuts and got the ACCC to pledge cooperation in another national mobilization project.[42] And on August 19 he announced that Walter S. Gifford, president of the New York Charity Organization Society and former director of the wartime Council of National Defense, would head a new agency with which Croxton's work would be merged. Named the President's Organization on Unemployment Relief (POUR), the new body would "have charge" of unemployment relief measures during the coming winter and would, so Hoover said, make further talk about reviving the CND superfluous.[43]

As subsequently put together, POUR consisted of a central staff (mostly inherited from PECE), a 109-member advisory committee, field representatives in each state, and five working committees concerned respectively with relief mobilization and practice, industrial action, public works, and cooperating groups.[44] The first to be appointed, officially known as the Committee on Mobilization of Relief Resources, was headed by Owen Young and was given the task of taking over the mobilization project already being planned by PECE and the ACCC and providing for it a "background" of national support and stimulation. This was to be done between October 19 and November 25, 1931 and eventually it came to consist not only of further work with community and business organizers but also of benefit movie and sports performances and posters and billboards proclaiming "Of Course We Can Do It." The committee also collaborated with the media and advertising agencies to produce a suitable set of advertisements and news items and a series of national radio programs featuring such speakers as Charles Lindbergh, General John J. Pershing, and former president Calvin Coolidge.[45] The goal, it was stressed, was not a "national fund" but "maximum local funds" and proper channeling of America's "streams of human helpfulness," and again Hoover maintained that "the sum" of community efforts would "meet the needs of the Nation" and would do so in ways that accorded with the fundamentals upon which it was founded.[46]

As this effort proceeded, the other committees also took action. On October 5 Croxton's Committee on Administration of Relief, consisting largely of representatives from national charity and social work organizations,[47] began its efforts to improve relief practice, this time with an emphasis on preventing "hopeless migration," securing closer public-private "coordination," helping the AAPWO to upgrade public relief work, promoting school attendance and home food conservation, and preserving needed health, youth, and recreational services.[48] On October 8 Eliot Wadsworth's Committee on Cooperation with National Groups and Associations reported progress in getting a long list of national organizations to pledge support and have their local affiliates become parts of community units.[49] On October 29 Harry Wheeler's Committee on Employment Plans and Suggestions, made up of business leaders and economists, began promoting an "industrial program" calling for concerted resumption of normal buying, cooperative efforts to "unfreeze" credit, and renewed "job-giving" and "work sharing" with preference given to established family supporters.[50] And on December 16 James Garfield's Committee on the Program of Federal Public Works made suggestions for accelerating federal projects, but agreed with the president that seeking recovery through massive public works spending would do more harm than good.[51] Testifying before a Senate committee on January 8, 1932, Gifford asserted that sufficient resources had been mobilized and that resort to federal relief might well lead to withdrawal of some portion of these resources and hence to more suffering.[52]

Meanwhile, Hoover's effort to save America from foreign "patent medicines" was taking other forms as well. In statements that upset some POUR officials, he cited public health reports as proof that the American system had protected "the unfortunate" from "hunger and cold."[53] Through allies and surrogates, he moved to sharpen his distinctions between American and European "planning."[54] And insisting that the need now was "to restore the flow of credit which is the very basis of our economic life," he offered a program that eventually led to a private National Credit Association, a governmental Reconstruction Finance Corporation, a quasi-governmental Home Loan Bank System, and new lending powers for the Federal Reserve and Federal Farm Loan systems.[55] Yet little of the credit provided was used to create jobs, and as unemployment continued to grow so did public support for the federal relief being urged by such congressional "progressives" as Robert LaFollette, Edward Costigan, and Robert Wagner. In February 1932 the Senate voted down two rival bills, each authorizing $750 million for relief and public works. But as of March, despite Hoover's efforts to rally congressional leaders against the "dole," a similar bill was again being considered. And by May, as heart-rending stories of deprivation filled the press, new bills were appearing and federal aid was being declared essential by the very agencies that had been organized to avoid it. As an Iowa resolution put it, the federal government had to assume responsibility "since it alone can initiate the processes of controlled inflation, consumption, and taxation adequate to deal with both relief and business revival."[56]

In Congress, moreover, POUR's reputation was now such that new appropriations for its work had become unlikely. It suffered not only from a growing credibility gap but also from charges that it lacked compassion, was ill-informed, had "stimulated" little that would not have been done anyway, and was a part of Hoover's continuing effort to bypass Congress and "govern by commission." In 1930 Hoover had used Commerce Department money to fund PECE, and in 1931 he had secured a $150 thousand appropriation for POUR. But in 1932 his request for another $120 thousand met with strong opposition and claims that the agency he wanted funded was an "illegal and unauthorized" commission. No funds were included in the deficiency appropriation bill reported to the House of Representatives. And when Hoover's supporters tried to add them on the House floor, with Representative Edward W. Goss arguing strongly that POUR's stimulative activities, special campaigns, and work with business had all been of great value, the effort was unsuccessful. As the president saw it, the appropriation in question was "infinitesimal" in relation to the amount of resources that had been mobilized and put to use. But on July 8 the House voted to deny the request and thus allowed POUR's official termination to stand.[57]

By this time, too, Hoover had decided that limited use of his new credit institutions could be helpful in his battle to preserve the American relief system. Ironically, his new credit measures, especially the creation of the Reconstruction Finance Corporation (RFC), had intensified rather than eased the pressures for federal relief. The RFC, it was argued, should in fairness extend emergency credits to hard-pressed relief agencies as well as to needy banks and railroads. And when Senate minority leader Joseph T. Robinson and former war manager Bernard Baruch offered a plan in line with this sentiment, the president responded with his own proposal to make the RFC a financier of last resort for state relief operations and for previously deferred works projects that were both income-producing and capable of increasing employment. On May 12 he detailed what he had in mind, and a little over two months later, after repeated denunciations of congressional alternatives, strongly worded broadsides against "nonproductive" public works, and the veto of a bill found to be "so damaging" as to "bring far more distress than it will cure," he was able to secure essentially what he had proposed. Under the Emergency Relief and Construction Act signed on July 21, 1932, the RFC could lend up to $300 million to state relief programs and up to $1.5 billion for income-producing public works.[58]

In advocating and signing the measure, however, Hoover also made it clear that his hope was to save the American relief system, not replace it with an American version of the modern welfare state. Both the loans and the agency making them, he stressed, were emergency operations that would be unneeded in normal times, and resorting to the loans must come only "as a last extremity" in cases where there was an "absolute need and evidence of financial exhaustion." There must be no shirking of individual, family, community, and state responsibilities and no doubt that the loans for public works would be self-liquidating and could not be secured elsewhere. The new administrative machinery, moreover, was consciously put in the hands of people who agreed with the president. In effect, Fred Croxton and his staff from POUR took over the RFC's new Emergency Relief Division while Harvey Couch, an RFC director who had earlier been a central figure in Hoover's drought relief program, became the administrator for the public works loans. And not surprisingly, such administrators and the aides they continued to draw from private sector organizations were slow to find cases that merited RFC loans and quick to insist upon safeguards that would ensure administration according to their understanding of sound relief principles. By the end of Hoover's administration, $210 million had been loaned to the states for relief purposes. But most of these loans were not made until early 1933, and even by that time only $20 million had been advanced for self-liquidating public works.[59]

Hoover's determination to minimize federal relief and thus preserve "the spiritual impulses in our people for generous giving and generous service" was also apparent in new initiatives expected to maintain and continue what had been accomplished through the associational activities of charitable, civic, and business organizations. Although POUR was gone, Hoover persuaded former secretary of war Newton D. Baker to head a National Citizens Committee on Welfare and Relief Mobilization, which brought together the ACCC and some twenty-eight other welfare organizations. The committee met with the president at a White House conference on September 15 and subsequently coordinated another national campaign for charitable donations. In addition, RFC officials provided leverage for the campaign by suggesting that full participation in it was a prerequisite for federal aid.[60] And operating simultaneously, under the auspices of a new set of Business and Industrial Committees formed to promote the greater use of available credit, a new Share-the-Work Committee took over the task of persuading employers to implement work-spreading plans and their employees to accept them. Chaired by Walter Teagle of Standard Oil, the new organization maintained that "Job Security through Job Spreading" would release new "purchasing power," spawned numerous subgroups to preach its message, and claimed in March 1933 that over a million jobs existed because of the "work-spreading" it had helped to promote.[61]

While struggling to preserve the relief system that had developed in the private sector, Hoover was also considering arrangements that could limit governmental takeovers of other kinds of social work. He had assumed that this could be done when creating his Research Committee on Social Trends, and it had also been a theme at his subsequent White House conferences on child welfare and home building, each of which had produced a network of associations to promote the implementation of its recommendations. In addition, Secretary of the Interior Ray Lyman Wilbur had worked to produce similar machinery in the fields of health and education. And by 1932, Hoover was thinking of another national structure—similar in his mind to the Federal Reserve System, the Federal Farm Board associations, the Home Loan Banks, and the business and relief mobilizations—whose job it would be to push the "further development of cooperation" in the welfare field and thus "deny the extension of bureaucracy." More specifically, he considered a proposal from Inez Richardson, secretary of the child welfare conference, that funds be sought to establish a National Council on Social Development, conceived of as a nongovernmental body that would bring together, inform, and coordinate the organizational legacies of what Hoover and Wilbur had been building. No funds for such a council were ever secured. But the possibility was explored, and under other circumstances such an institution might have materialized as another of Hoover's barriers against welfare statism.[62]

Unfortunately for Hoover, the Depression, which he expected to end in 1930, 1931, and 1932, persisted throughout his administration and eventually brought to power governmental and private sector leaders who were ready to ignore his warnings and seek recovery and social stability through administrative and corporative state-building. By 1932 his effort to meet

national needs through the "further development" of cooperative and associational activities was regarded by most of his fellow countrymen as a demonstrated failure, showing in particular that the institutions upon which he
had relied were inherently incapable of meeting the kind of relief needs
generated by mass unemployment.[63] And ironically, in making the effort he
had helped to pave the way for the kinds of governmental growth that he had
worked so hard to prevent. He had not found a viable alternative for a welfare state, and contrary to his intentions his insistence on the need for an
alternative, his rationale for making public relief an accepted part of community programs, and his acceptance of federal relief loans through the RFC
had each moved the country another important step in the direction of the
New Deal's relief and social insurance programs. For three years his vision
of an associational order so developed as to "deny the extension" of statist
bureaucracies had strongly influenced the kind of machinery through which
relief was distributed, and initially the New Deal would find itself working
through this machinery and accepting its notions of what constituted good
relief practice. But the New Deal would also move on to much that Hoover
would strongly criticize, and it was in paving the way for this movement
that his actions between 1930 and 1932 were probably of greatest importance.[64]

Seen in retrospect, then, the Hoover administration's response to the unemployment relief crisis of 1930–1933 was at one and the same time an
extension of the Hooverian associationalism of the 1920s, a test of Hooverian
theories about American exceptionalism, and a new departure leading in
time to an American version of the welfare state. Initially, the response had
envisioned a crisis managed and overcome through a further development of
the kind of associational action hailed as successful during and after World
War I. But a number of the associations involved were reluctant to fill the
roles that the Hooverites assigned them, and while some made heroic efforts
to do so they found themselves unable to mobilize and deploy the necessary
resources. The response then shifted and became essentially one of seeking
ways to use public money without allowing this to undermine and corrupt
the privatized relief system thought to be a part of the American way. What
emerged in 1931 and 1932 was neither a full-fledged welfare state, a reversion to rugged individualism, nor a successful associationalism but rather a
curious and complex interpenetration of the public and private sectors, with
more and more funding coming from governmental taxes or credit but much
of it still administered through private associations, mixed committees, or
public agencies socialized to behave like their private sector counterparts.
    As of 1933, Hoover had managed to preserve a role for the institutional
network that he had hoped to develop into a superior substitute for the mod-

ern regulatory and welfare state. Welfare and business associations would continue to be assigned significant duties in the New Deal system of governance, in part due to the persistence of the antibureaucratic tradition so evident in Hoover's thinking; and after the New Deal a neo-Hooverian concern with curbing "creeping socialism" helped to produce another major growth of private-sector welfare programs and public-private partnerships.[65] Yet the role preserved for associational activities was hardly the one that Hoover had hoped to preserve when he established the President's Emergency Committee for Employment in 1930. Under the New Deal the funding of relief would become almost entirely governmental, the administration of it would eventually be shifted to public servants concerned with fulfilling a governmental obligation to its citizens, and America would adopt its own version of the social insurance systems pioneered by Britain and Germany.[66] New Era associationalism, it could be argued, helps to explain the stunted nature of the American welfare state as it emerged in the 1930s and 1940s. But Hoover's effort to block its emergence was a failure that had the unintended consequences of making New Deal state-building easier than it might have been, and in time the limited welfare state of the New Deal would evolve into the more expanded version characteristic of Lyndon Johnson's Great Society.[67]

The Hooverian experience, then, would seem to offer little encouragement to those who currently hope to supplant the welfare state with a private sector substitute. One might argue, to be sure, that Hoover's initiatives lack relevance, either because of the special circumstances created by the Great Depression or because his private sector lacked the potential of the one existing today.[68] But the experience was in line with what recent theoreticians of the voluntary sector have had to say about its inherent weaknesses, both as a producer and distributor of collective goods and as an entity that tends to become increasingly dependent on governmental financing.[69] What had emerged by the end of Hoover's administration was a clear foreshadowing of the public-private partnership that would re-emerge in the new welfare initiatives of the 1940s and 1950s and would remain at the center of an expanded welfare system in the 1960s and 1970s. But what had also emerged, in part because of Hoover's reluctance to recognize that the private sector was inherently incapable of meeting the demand for social services on its own, was a perception of "voluntary failure" that helped to produce a larger administrative state. And one suspects that this might well be the outcome of any serious attempt to carry out current proposals, rooted though they may be in a sense of "government failure" not in evidence in 1930.

Notes

1. Frank Bane, Address to American Association of Public Welfare Officials (AAPWO), June 15, 1931, in Croxton Office Files: AAPWO, Box 1098, PECE-POUR papers (selections from Record Group 73, National Archives), Hoover Presidential Library.

2. For discussions of the movement, see Rich Lowry and Ramesh Ponnuru, "Lamar? Come on!" *National Review* 48 (March 11, 1996): 51–53; Julian Wolpert, "Delusions of Charity," *The American Prospect,* 23 (Fall 1995): 86–88; and Wray Herbert, "The Revival of Civic Life," *U.S. News and World Report* 120 (Jan. 29, 1996): 63–67. The full citation to Olasky is *The Tragedy of American Compassion* (Washington, D.C., 1992).

3. The best available accounts of the Hoover relief operations are in Albert U. Romasco, *The Poverty of Abundance: Hoover, the Nation, the Depression* (New York, 1965), and Jordan A. Schwarz, *The Interregnum of Despair: Hoover, Congress, and the Depression* (Urbana, Ill., 1970). In addition, the published historical literature includes E. P. Hayes, *Activities of the President's Emergency Committee for Employment* (Concord, 1936); William H. Mullins, "Self Help in Seattle, 1931–32: Herbert Hoover's Concept of Cooperative Individualism and the Unemployed Citizens' League," *Pacific Northwest Quarterly* 72 (1981): 11–19; and Richard T. Ortquist, "Unemployment and Relief: Michigan's Response to the Depression during the Hoover Years," *Michigan History* 57 (1973): 209–236. None of these attempt to put the operations into the larger context of associationalism and its effects on public policy.

4. Louis Galambos, "American Bureaucracies in the Twentieth Century: Private Power and Public Interests" (1979), Unpublished paper in author's possession. See also Kenneth E. Boulding, *The Organizational Revolution: A Study in the Ethics of Economic Organization* (New York, 1953); Jerry Israel, ed., *Building the Organizational Society: Essays on Associational Actitivities in Modern America* (New York, 1972); James Weinstein, *The Corporate Ideal in the Liberal State, 1900–1918* (Boston, 1968); and Michael B. Katz, *In the Shadow of the Poorhouse: A Social History of Welfare in America* (New York, 1986), especially chapters 3, 6, and 7.

5. Strongly stressing this pluralistic component are Morton Keller's *Regulating a New Economy: Public Policy and Economic Change in America, 1900–1933* (Cambridge, Mass., 1990) and *Regulating a New Society: Public Policy and Social Change in America, 1900–1933* (Cambridge, Mass., 1994).

6. See especially Morrell Heald, *The Social Responsibilities of Business: Company and Community, 1900–1960* (Cleveland, 1970); Edwin T. Layton, Jr., *The Revolt of the Engineers: Social Responsibility and the American Engineering Profession* (Baltimore, 1971); John M. Jordan, *Machine-Age Ideology: Social Engineering and American Liberalism, 1911–1939* (Chapel Hill, 1994); and Robert D. Cuff, "We Band of Brothers: Woodrow Wilson's War Managers," *Canadian Review of American Studies* 5 (Fall 1974): 135–148.

7. Robert H. Wiebe, *The Search for Order, 1877–1920* (New York, 1967), quotation from page 296.

8. See Robert F. Himmelberg, *The Origins of the National Recovery Administration: Business, Government, and the Trade Association Issue, 1921–1933* (New York, 1976); Morrell Heald, "Business Thought in the Twenties: Social Responsibility," *American Quarterly* 13 (Summer 1961): 126–139; Edward Berkowitz and Kim

McQuaid, "Businessman and Bureaucrat: The Evolution of the American Social Welfare System," *Journal of Economic History* 38 (March 1978): 120–141; Cecil C. North, "The Community Fund and the Community," *Social Forces* 7 (September 1928): 90–97; Arthur E. Woods, "Whither Social Work?" *Survey* 50 (April 15, 1927): 74–75; Carolyn Grin, "The Unemployment Conference of 1921: An Experiment in National Cooperative Planning," *Mid-America* 55 (April 1973): 83–107; and Bruce A. Lohoff, "Herbert Hoover, Spokesman for Humane Efficiency: The Mississippi Flood of 1927," *American Quarterly* 22 (Fall 1970): 690–700.

9. See, for example, Abraham Epstein, "The Soullessness of Presentday Social Work," *Current History* 28 (June 1928): 390–395, and Kirby Page, "Is a New Feudalism Emerging?" *World Tomorrow* 10 (Jan. 1927): 31–33.

10. Albert Ritchie, "The State's Responsibility for Social Welfare," *Social Forces* (4 March 1926): 608–610. For discussion of the public vs. private question among professional social workers, see Raymond Clapp and M. C. Maclean, "The Effect of the Federation Movement upon the Relationship between Public and Private Welfare Agencies," *Proceedings of the National Council of Social Work* (1924): 519–530; Charles Johnson, "The Correlation of Public and Private Social Service," in *Proceedings NCSW* (1924): 29–33; and Frank J. Bruno and Ruth Taylor, "The Integration of Effort in Theory and Practice by Private and Public Agencies for the Common Good," in *Proceedings NCSW* (1924): 240–252.

11. See Ellis W. Hawley, "Herbert Hoover, the Commerce Secretariat, and the Vision of an 'Associative State,' 1921–1928," *Journal of American History* 41 (June 1974): 116–140; Alan Brinkley, "The New Deal: Prelude," *Wilson Quarterly* 6 (Spring 1982): 51–61; Jordan, *Machine-Age Ideology*, 110–128; Gary Dean Best, *The Politics of Individualism: Herbert Hoover in Transition, 1918–1921* (Westport, Conn., 1975); and the essays in Ellis W. Hawley, ed., *Herbert Hoover as Secretary of Commerce, 1921–1928: Studies in New Era Thought and Practice* (Iowa City, 1981).

12. Herbert Hoover, *The New Day* (Stanford, 1928), 32, 196–197. The allusion to Europe's "hallucinations" is from Hoover to Henry S. Pritchett, Nov. 18, 1921, Unemployment: NBER, 1921 folder, Commerce Files, Hoover Papers, Hoover Presidential Library.

13. Hoover's plans in these regards are described in David E. Hamilton, *From New Day to New Deal: American Farm Policy from Hoover to Roosevelt, 1928–1933* (Chapel Hill, 1991), 37–49; Guy Alchon, *The Invisible Hand of Planning: Capitalism, Social Science, and the State in the 1920s* (Princeton, 1985), 149–150; and Barry D. Karl, "Presidential Planning and Social Science Research: Mr. Hoover's Experts," *Perspectives in American History* 3 (1969): 347, 363–369. See also "President Hoover's Project for the Study of Government and Social Welfare," June 27, 1929, in Presidential Subject Files: Government Departments, Box 167, Hoover Papers; Ray Lyman Wilbur, "Memo on Conferences," May 2, 1929, in Presidential Subject Files: Child Health & Protection Conference, Box 97, Hoover Papers; Edward E. Hunt, "Recent Social Changes in the United States," Nov. 1, 1929, Box 24, Hunt Papers, Hoover Institution Archives, Stanford University; and Edward E.Hunt, "A Technique of Economic Balance," Box 18, Hunt Papers.

14. Hoover, *New Day*, 16–17.

15. See Romasco, *Poverty of Abundance*, 24–55; Robert Lamont, "The White House Conferences," *Journal of Business* 3 (July 1930): 269–271; "President's Conferences for Continued Industrial Progress," *Monthly Labor Review* 30 (Jan. 1930):

35–39; Chamber of Commerce of the United States, *Business Conditions and Outlook* (Washington, D.C., 1929); "Summary of Activities of the National Business Survey Conference," Jan. 23, 1930, in Presidential Subject Files: Chamber of Commerce, Box 91, Hoover Papers; and the press releases and other documents in Presidential Subject Files: Business Conferences, Boxes 86–87, Hoover Papers.

16. Office of the Federal Register, *Public Papers of the Presidents of the United States: Herbert Hoover, 1930* (Washington, D.C., 1976), 78–83, 171–179. Speaking to the Taylor Society on December 4, 1929, the economist Wesley Mitchell declared that "a more significant experiment in the technique of balance could not be devised than the one which is being performed before our eyes." *New York Times*, Dec. 5, 1929, 5.

17. David E. Hamilton, "Herbert Hoover and the Great Drought of 1930," *Journal of American History* 68 (March 1982): 850–858; *Public Papers: Hoover, 1930*, 321–330, 336–341, 344–347. Hyde is quoted by Hamilton, p. 850.

18. *Public Papers: Hoover, 1930*, 304–305, 311–315, 391–402, 411–415, 440–443. Since March of 1928, Paul Kellogg of the *Survey* had been urging Hoover to mount a replay of the Unemployment Conference of 1921, but Hoover had kept expressing the view that this was unneeded and could create unwarranted alarm about the unemployment that did exist. See Paul U. Kellogg to Edward E. Hunt, March 9, 1928; Dec. 19, 1929; Oct. 15, 1930, all in Folder 627, Survey Associates Papers, Social Work History Archives, University of Minnesota; and Kellogg to Hoover, April 18, 1930, Folder 622, Survey Associates Papers.

19. See "Staff Organization," in Central Files of PECE: General Organization, Box 1094, PECE-POUR Papers; National Archives, *Preliminary Inventory of the Records of the President's Organization on Unemployment Relief* (Washington, D.C., 1962), 1–2; and "Formation of the Committee," in Interview: E. P. Hayes and E. L. Bernays, Feb. 26, 1931, Box 1116, PECE-POUR Papers. The committee's name, especially the use of "employment" rather than "unemployment," was intended to emphasize continuity with Hoover's earlier efforts. Also, in spite of some effort to exclude people who had been "discredited" by their earlier predictions, many of the key positions in the organization were filled by individuals who had been involved in Hoover's earlier projects. Among these were Franklin T. Miller as the key figure in construction promotion, Joseph Willits as the person responsible for industrial relations, Lilian Gilbreth as head of the women's division, Edward L. Bernays as adviser on publicity, and Edward Eyre Hunt as the organization's secretary.

20. See statements by Hoover, Woods, and Lamont, *Public Papers: Hoover, 1930*, 437–443; Woods Press Conference, Oct. 29, 1930, in Presidential Subject Files: Unemployment, Press Conferences of Col. Arthur Woods, Box 341, Hoover Papers; "Established Policies," in Central Files of PECE: General Organization, Box 1094, PECE-POUR Papers; and "Principles of Organization and Administration of Welfare and Relief in Local Communities," in Croxton Office Files: General State Information, Box 1103, PECE-POUR Papers.

21. See Bryce Stewart, "Organization Plans and Procedure, Oct. 31,1930, and PECE, "Program and Organization," Nov. 7, 1930, both in Hayes Office Files: Untitled #5, Box 1116, PECE-POUR Papers; "Outline of Community Organization," April 3, 1931, in Appendix I, #2, Box 1152, PECE-POUR Papers; "Principles of Organization and Administration of Welfare and Relief in Local Communities," in Croxton Office Files: General State Information, Box 1103, PECE-POUR Papers;

and Department of Commerce, *Organization to Promote Employment in the State of Ohio, 1929 and 1930* (Washington, D.C., 1930).

22. James C. Lawrence, "Preliminary Report of PECE," Dec. 20, 1930, in Hayes Office Files: Untitled #5, Box 1116, PECE-POUR Papers; Woods Conversation with James B. Phelan, Nov. 6, 1930, in Central Files of PECE: Talks with State Governors, Box 1095, PECE-POUR Papers. Among activities undertaken at the local level were special fund drives, recreational promotions, self-denial days, clean-up and paint-up campaigns, "make work" programs, free employment services, and retraining in the schools. See, for example, Kendall Hoyt to Fred Croxton, July 9, 1931 (in regard to Baltimore), in Gifford Records: Baltimore, Box 1096, PECE-POUR Papers; and PECE, *Five "Made Work" Programs* (Washington, D.C., 1931), in regard to Rochester, Wilmington, Indianapolis, Milwaukee, and Chicago.

23. Porter Lee to Edward E. Hunt, Nov. 13, 1930, and Lee to Linton B. Swift, Nov. 21, 1930, both in Hayes Office Files: Untitled #4, Box 1116, PECE-POUR Papers; Lee to Woods, Dec. 11, 1930, in Hayes Office Files: B, Box 1114, PECE-POUR Papers; Lee to Woods, "Committee Policy on Care of Transients," Dec. 29,1930, in Hayes Office Files: Untitled #2, Box 1116, PECE-POUR Papers; "Work Relief," in Croxton Office Files: General State Information, Box 1103, PECE-POUR Papers. One of the division's principal activities was the publication of a "Community Plans and Action" series that eventually came to thirteen bulletins offering information and advice on differing aspects of relief organization and practice. A complete set of these is in Lee Office Files: Nos. 1–13 of *Community Plans and Action,* Box 1123, PECE-POUR Papers. Lee was also able to get foundation money for some of the new organizational and research activities of the FWAA and ACCC. See Fred Croxton to Linton Swift, May 26, 1931; Swift to Croxton, June 2, 1931; and Swift to Frederick C. Keppel, June 30, 1931, all in Hayes Office Files: Untitled #4, Box 1116, PECE-POUR Papers.

24. Kendall Hoyt, "Status of Work of Industrial Section," April 22, 1931, in Gifford Records: Memos to Mr. Croxton, Box 1097, PECE-POUR Papers; Hoyt, "Progress and Status of the Industrial Work of the PECE," June 4, 1931, Appendix I, #31, Box 1152, PECE-POUR Papers; "Special Survey of Employment Measures in Large Industrial Firms," July 10, 1931, in Gifford Records: Economic Information, Box 1096, PECE-POUR Papers; PECE Press Releases re Trade Association Cooperation and Loans to Those on Protracted Lay-offs, Feb. 21–22, 1931, Press Releases: Feb. 1931, Box 1144, PECE-POUR Papers; "Trade Association Plan," Croxton Files: Trade Association Executives Meeting, Box 1108, PECE-POUR Papers; J. D. Brown to Woods, Feb. 26, 1931, with "List of Organizations and Speakers for Radio Talks," in Hayes Office Files: Untitled #6, Box 1116, PECE-POUR Papers; Hayes, *Activities of PECE,* 66–81. The division's most visible activities were its sponsorship of radio talks by "progressive" industrialists, its urging of trade associations to acknowledge business obligations and establish cooperating committees, and its advocacy of share-the-work arrangements. To promote the latter, it produced and disseminated *A Survey of Unemployment Relief in Industry* (1930), *An Outline of Industrial Policies and Practices in Time of Reduced Operation and Employment* (1930), *Emergency and Permanent Policies for Spreading Work in Industrial Employment* (1931), and *Policies and Practices for the Stabilization of Employment in Retail Establishments* (1931).

25. "Public Works," in Hayes Office Files: Public Works Promotion, Box 1115, PECE-POUR Papers; Edward L. Bernays, "How National Advertisers Can Help in

the Present Emergency," Nov. 10, 1930, Presidential Subject Files: Unemployment, Press Releases of PECE and POUR, Box 342, Hoover Papers; "Specifications and Copy Requirements for Advertising Campaign for the PECE," in Arthur Woods Diary, General Accession 130, Hoover Presidential Library; Hayes, *Activities of PECE*, 151; Lawrence, "Preliminary Report of PECE," *loc. cit.* The publicity section saw its work as "educative" rather than "inspirational." It should, it was stipulated, avoid stirring emotions and urging people to "unwise actions."

26. "Activities of the Women's Division, PECE" and "Progress Report of the Women's Division," Dec. 26, 1930, both in Hayes Office Files: Untitled #12, Box 1116, PECE-POUR Papers; Gilbreth to Woods, April 28, 1931, Hayes Office Files: Women's Division, Box 1117, PECE-POUR Papers; "Wise Spending for the Family," in Women's Division Records: Budgets, Box 1131, PECE-POUR Papers; Gilbreth to Lucy Carver, March 27, 1931, Women's Division Records: Employer-Employee Relationship in the Home, Box 1134, PECE-POUR Papers; Gilbreth, "Follow Your Dollar Back to the Policies of the Businesses and Industries to Which It Goes," in Women's Division Records: Follow Your Dollar, Box 1132, PECE-POUR Papers; Hayes, *Activities of PECE*, 121–139. The "Follow Your Dollar" campaign was launched at the April 1931 convention of the General Federation of Women's Clubs, meeting in Phoenix, Arizona. In important respects it was a forerunner of the New Deal's Blue Eagle campaign in 1933. Mrs. Hoover also took a strong interest in the work of the PECE women's division and helped especially to publicize and promote relief work undertaken by the Girl Scouts. See Lewis L. Gould, "A Neglected First Lady: A Reappraisal of Lou Henry Hoover," in Dale C. Mayer, ed., *Lou Henry Hoover: Essays on a Busy Life* (Worland, Wyo., 1994), 172–175; PECE Press Releases, March 22 and 23, 1931, in Press Releases: March 1931, Box 1144, PECE-POUR Papers.

27. Radio Address of Edward Eyre Hunt, Dec. 12, 1930, Press Releases: Dec. 1930, Box 1143, PECE-POUR Papers; *Public Papers, Hoover, 1930*, 513.

28. See, for example, Woods's Address to the Indiana Commission for Relief of Distress Due to Unemployment, March 5, 1931, and his Address before the American Philosophical Society, April 23, 1931, both in Press Releases: March–April 1931, Box 1144, PECE-POUR Papers; "Prevention of Unemployment," Jan. 27, 1931, in Hayes Office Files: Chapter I, Box 1114, PECE-POUR Papers; J. Douglas Brown to M. B. Folsom, March 2, 10, and 27, 1931, in Industrial Division Records: Rochester Plan, Box 1129, PECE-POUR Papers; J. H. Willits to Woods, April 16, 1931, in Hayes Office Files: Untitled #6, PECE-POUR Papers; and Edward E. Hunt to Arch W. Shaw, Jan. 20, March 17, 1931, Box 37, Hunt Papers. The future, some thought, lay in Rochester where Eastman Kodak had persuaded the city's progressive firms to establish an unemployment reserve fund that would pay benefits during future layoffs, or in Indianapolis, Cincinnati, and Madison where emergency organizations had already become permanent committees.

29. The best estimates of unemployment in mid-1931 put it at slightly over 8 million (about 16% of the labor force), up from about 4.3 million in mid-1930. See Bureau of the Census, *Historical Statistics of the United States* (Washington, D.C., 1975), Part 1, p. 126.

30. This had become a central theme in Hoover's public discourse, particularly evident in his State of the Union message, his press conferences of December 9 and February 3, his statements in support of the Red Cross, and his Lincoln Day address

of 1931. See *Public Papers: Hoover, 1930*, 510–515, 556–557, and *Public Papers, Hoover, 1931*, 20, 32, 49–58, 71–76, 178–180, 260–262. See also "Relief," Jan. 22, 1931, in Hayes Office Files: B, Box 1114, PECE-POUR Papers.

31. James L. Feiser (Red Cross vice-chairman) to Staff, Oct. 22, 27, 31, Nov. 23, 25, 1930; DeWitt Smith to Staff, Nov. 1, 1930; Allen T. Burns, "National Committee on Unemployment and Drought Relief Funds," all in Drought Relief, 1930–31, Drawer 401.21, Red Cross Records (RG 200), National Archives; Feiser to D. H. Holbrook, Oct. 27, 1930; Feiser Memorandum, Nov. 17, 1930: Feiser to Staff, Oct. 30, 1930, all in Drought Relief, 1930–31, Drawer 401.02, Red Cross Records; Porter Lee to Edward E. Hunt, Nov. 3, 1930, Hayes Office Files: Untitled #4, PECE-POUR Papers; Hamilton, "Hoover and the Great Drought," 860–864; Nan Elizabeth Woodruff, *As Rare As Rain: Federal Relief in the Great Southern Drought of 1930–31* (Urbana, Ill., 1985), 41–44. Allen Burns, the ACCC executive director, initially favored a national fund and tried to help Hoover get one established. But he found that there was little support for it among the association's constituent organizations.

32. Arthur Woods, Memorandum of a Conversation with Hoover and Judge Payne, Feb. 11, 1931, in Central Files of PECE: Committee Memoranda—Woods, Box 1094, PECE-POUR Papers; Press Release, Jan. 18, 1931, in Presidential Subject Files: Drought—Press Releases, Box 119, Hoover Papers; Entries for Feb. 9, 10, 11, 16, 24, and April 4, 1931, Woods Diary; Woodruff, *As Rare As Rain*, 72–73; Fred Croxton Memoranda of May 8, 28, June 2, July 2, 6, 1931; Croxton to Max Mason, Nov. 16, 1931; Clarence Pickett to Croxton, Nov. 20, 1931, all in Croxton Office Files: AFSC, General, Box 1099, PECE-POUR Papers; "Report of Work of the AFSC in the Bituminous Coal Fields"; AFSC Coal Relief Section, "Statement of Receipts and Expenses to Aug. 31, 1932," both in Croxton Office Files: AFSC, Coal Field, Box 1098, PECE-POUR Papers. The American Relief Administration was a legacy of Hoover's European relief operations after World War I and had been used to fund some of his social betterment projects in the 1920s. From it the Friends received a total of $225 thousand. They also raised smaller sums from other sources and tried but failed to secure funding for rehabilitation work, disguised as social research, from the Rockefeller Foundation.

33. In Congress the leading advocates of federal relief for more than the drought areas were Senator Robert LaFollette, Jr., Senator Robert Wagner, and Representative Fiorello LaGuardia. Also being discussed were calls for much larger public works appropriations than the $150 million requested by President Hoover. These had come from such groups as the Unemployment League, the American Association for Labor Legislation (AALL), and the Emergency Committee for Federal Public Works as well as from corporate leaders like Gerard Swope of General Electric and business academics like Dean Wallace Donham of the Harvard Business School. In October 1930 Swope had urged the president to support a $1 billion program to be financed through a bond sales campaign similar to the Liberty Bond drives during the war, and shortly thereafter Donham proposed a "separate emergency budget" to be financed by "Emergency Re-Employment Bonds." See Woodruff, *As Rare As Rain*, 48–49, 66, 73; Udo Sautter, "Government and Unemployment: The Use of Public Works before the New Deal," *Journal of American History* 73 (June 1986): 80–81; James S. Taylor, "Statement on a Proposed Two or Three Billion Dollar Bond Issue," June 9, 1930, in Presidential Subject Files: Federal Government Aids during the Depression, Box 137, Hoover Papers; Swope to Hoover, Oct. 2, 1930, in Presidential Subject Files: Unem-

ployment, Box 271, Hoover Papers; Wallace B. Donham, "The Unemployment Emergency," in Presidential Subject Files: Unemployment Relief, Box 264, Hoover Papers; AALL Press Release, Dec. 31, 1930, Reel 71, AALL Papers, microfilm at Hoover Presidential Library.

34. Hamilton, "Hoover and the Great Drought," 865–875; Woodruff, *As Rare As Rain*, 66–95; C. Roger Lambert, "Food from the Public Crib: Agricultural Surpluses and Food Relief under Herbert Hoover," in Carl E. Krog and William R. Tanner, eds., *Herbert Hoover and the Republican Era: A Reconsideration* (New York, 1984), 164–168. During the debate Hoover was depicted as the president who "would feed Jackasses but wouldn't feed starving babies" and as the man who had used federal funds "to feed hungry Russians, hungry Bolsheviks, hungry men with long whiskers and wild ideas" but would not use them to feed hungry Americans.

35. See, for example, Porter Lee to Woods, Jan. 14, 1931, in Central Files of PECE: Committee Memoranda—Woods, Box 1094, PECE-POUR Papers; PECE Staff Meeting, January 15, 1931, in Publicity Section Records: Committee Meetings, Box 1137, PECE-POUR Papers; Fred Croxton to Woods, April 16, 1932, in Hayes Office Files: Untitled #2, Box 1116, PECE-POUR Papers; "Measures for Relief," June 4, 1931, in Hayes Office Files: Untitled #1, Box 1115, PECE-POUR Papers; Frank Bane, Address to AAPWO, June 15, 1931; Marietta Stevenson, "Recent Developments in Legislation for Public Relief of Unemployment," Dec. 1931, both in Croxton Office Files: AAPWO, Box 1098, PECE-POUR Papers; DeWitt Smith to Staff, Nov. 1, 1930, Drought Relief, Drawer 401.21, Red Cross Records; and E. G. Steger, "Public Money Through Private Agencies," *Survey* 67 (Oct. 15, 1931): 98–99. See also Josephine Chapin Brown, *Public Relief, 1929–1939* (New York, 1940), 63–70, 75–83; and Blanche D. Coll, *Safety Net: Welfare and Social Security, 1929–1979* (New Brunswick, 1995), 4–9. According to the statistics being used, private spending for relief had increased by 49.8 percent from 1929 to 1930 while public spending for relief had increased 152.7 percent. In America's seventy-five largest cities the public portion of relief spending had increased from 60 to 72 percent. These are in Croxton to Woods, April 16, 1931, and the Frank Bane address of June 15, 1931. One "middle course" held up as showing how to have "properly controlled" spending of public relief funds was that adopted in St. Louis. There a non political Citizens' Committee on Relief and Unemployment, organized by the mayor to represent government, business, the private-sector charities, and the public at large, had been empowered to select and hold accountable the agencies receiving and expending municipal funds. The St. Louis way is described in the article by Steger.

36. Fred Croxton to William J. Ellis, July 8, 1931; Letter to Guy Moffett, July 11, 1931, both in Croxton Office Files: AAPWO, Box 1098, PECE-POUR Papers; PECE, "For Staff Use Only," Aug. 12, 1931, in Industrial Division Records: Bi-Monthly Report, Box 1124, PECE-POUR Papers; POUR Press Releases of Aug. 20 and Sept. 1, 1931, in Press Releases: Aug.–Sept. 1931, Box 1145, PECE-POUR Papers; Hayes, *Activitiers of PECE*, 118. The AAPWO, concerned especially with enhancing the professional status and autonomy of public welfare administrators, had been founded in June 1930 at the meeting of the National Conference of Social Work in Boston. In addition, PECE encouraged the FWAA to set up a Pathfinding Committee on Governmental Relief Methods and took a new interest in establishing contacts with the Public Administration Clearing House and state conferences of social workers. See "Measures for Relief," June 4, 1931, *loc. cit.*, and FWAA, "Summary and Estimates

of Cost of Services Requested by PECE," Croxton Office Files: Family Welfare Association, Box 1102, PECE-POUR Papers.

37. As these controversies proceeded, PECE opted for "wise spending" over "buy now" campaigns, denied that its dietary and gardening recommendations adversely affected farm markets, endorsed preferential treatment for family breadwinners while refusing to approve the removal of married women from their jobs, and coupled its support for relief drives with warnings that the work done by educational, health, character-building, and recreational agencies was also vital to the nation's welfare and should be maintained. The ACCC was in the awkward position of having stressed relief appeals in its fund-raising campaigns while spending much of the money raised on other kinds of social programs. See "Wise Spending for the Family," in Women's Division Records: Budgets, and Louise Stanley to Alice Dickson, Feb. 24, 1931, in Women's Division Records: Agriculture, both in Box 1131, PECE-POUR Papers; PECE Press Release, April 5, 1931, in Press Releases: April 1931, Box 1144, PECE-POUR Papers; Edward Hunt to Lilian Gilbreth, Nov. 15, 1930; Gilbreth to Hunt, Nov. 19, 1930; Hunt to Dickson, Jan. 14, 1931; "Married Women Whose Husbands Hold Jobs," all in Women's Division: Memoranda from One Committee Member to Another, Box 1134, PECE-POUR Papers; Hayes, *Activities of PECE*, 132; Brown, *Public Relief,* 78–79; and "Principles of Organization and Administration of Welfare and Relief in Local Communities," Croxton Office Files: General State Information, Box 1103, PECE-POUR Papers.

38. In June 1931, for example, the Iowa Governor's Employment Committee resolved that since experts believed that "permanent relief lies in further development of business agreements" and since "business is moving in this direction," then the federal government should "take the initiative in this movement" and help to create a "national economic council" like "those which are already being developed by the leading nations of Europe." And similarly, at the U.S. Chamber of Commerce convention in May 1931, L. C. Reynolds of the American Writing Paper Company declared that "national control ought to be brought about through trade organizations" that were "clothed with legal authority" and "could be made quasi-governmental." See A. L. Urick to Fred Croxton, with accompanying resolution, June 9, 1931, in Central Files of PECE: Iowa, State Miscellaneous, Box 1095, PECE-POUR Papers; and L. C. Reynolds, quoted in *New York Herald Tribune*, May 1, 1931, clipping in Public Statements Back-up File, No. 1546A, Hoover Papers. See also Silas H. Strawn, "Shall Our Anti-Trust Laws Be Revised?" *Review of Reviews* 83 (June 1931): 69–70; and Himmelberg, *Origins of the NRA*, 125–127.

39. See Joseph Willits to Woods, Jan. 3, 1931; Bryce M. Stewart to Woods, Feb. 7, 1931; and "The Wagner Bill Veto," all in Hayes Office Files: Untitled #2, Box 1116, PECE-POUR Papers; Edward E. Hunt to Mary Van Kleeck, March 25, 1931, in Hunt Chronological Files: 1931, Box 1094, PECE-POUR Papers; Memorandum of March 3, 1931, stating "fundamental objections," in Presidential Subject Files: Unemployment—Wagner Employment Bureaus Bill, Box 342, Hoover Papers; *Public Papers: Hoover, 1931*, 132–138; Hayes, *Activities of PECE*, 141–146; and Schwartz, *Interregnum of Despair*, 36–41. Hunt defended the point of view taken by Hoover and Secretary of Labor William Doak, but Woods reportedly saw the veto as a "tragedy."

40. Entries for March 19, April 10, May 18, and May 28, 1931, Woods Diary; Woods Press Conference, April 27, 1931, in Hayes Office Files: Press Conferences,

Box 1115, PECE-POUR Papers; Romasco, *Poverty of Abundance*, 162–163; Sautter, "Public Works before the New Deal," 80.

41. Entry for April 10, 1931, Woods Diary; "Resolutions Adopted by U.S. Chamber of Commerce at Atlantic City, 1931," in Presidential Subject Files: Chamber of Commerce, Box 96, Hoover Papers; Gertrude Springer, "The Challenge of Hard Times," *Survey* 66 (July 15, 1931): 380–385; "We Cry Aloud for a Plan," *Review of Reviews* 84 (July 1931): 88. At the July meeting of the NCSW, where Croxton's presentation fell on "coolly critical ears," a number of speakers advocated unemployment insurance, federal relief grants, a national economic plan, and a continued shift of the relief burden to public agencies.

42. Herbert Hoover, "A Twenty-Year Plan for America," *Review of Reviews* 85 (July 1931): 40–41; Frederick M. Feiker, Address before the American Trade Association Executives, Sept. 24, 1931, in Feiker Papers: General Coorespondence, Box 81, Bureau of Foreign and Domestic Commerce Records (RG 151), National Archives; "Trade Association Plan," and "Report of Trade Association Executives Meeting," July 14, 1931, both in Croxton Office Files: Trade Association Executives Meeting, Box 1108, PECE-POUR Papers; Springer, "Challenge of Hard Times," 384; "Measures for Relief," June 4, 1931, in Hayes Office Files: Untitled #1, PECE-POUR Papers; Croxton Address to the ACCC, June 13, 1931, in Press Releases: June 1931, Box 1144, PECE-POUR Papers; *Public Papers: Hoover, 1931*, 363; Hayes, *Activities of PECE*, 115–116. The Rockefeller Foundation gave the ACCC $75 thousand to expand its field staff in preparation for the coming mobilization project.

43. *Public Papers: Hoover, 1931*, 387–389, 441–442. According to a later story, Gifford was reluctant to take the job and spent the entire time on the train back to New York trying to think of a way to get out of it. See Bryon Price, Oral History Interview, March 21, 1969, p. 7, Hoover Presidential Library.

44. "The President's Organization on Unemployment Relief: Statement of Organization and Activities," Appendix I, #43: Statement on Organization, Box 1152, PECE-POUR Papers; Statement of Walter Gifford, Aug. 25, 1931, and "Chronological Report of Activities of POUR," both in Croxton Office Files: News Releases—Organization, Box 1106, PECE-POUR Papers.

45. Statement of Walter Gifford, Sept. 1, 1931, in Croxton Office Files: News Releases—Organization, Box 1106, PECE-POUR Papers; "Progress Report by the Chairman," Sept. 18, 1931, in Gregg Office Files: Untitled: Sept. 17–25, 1931, Box 1150, PECE-POUR Papers; "Remarks of Gifford to Meeting of Committee on Mobilization of Relief Resources," Sept. 18, 1931, and Press Releases of Nov. 5, 8, and 18, 1931, all in Press Releases: Sept.–Nov. 1931, Box 1145, PECE-POUR Papers; "Report to the Director of POUR," Dec. 1931, in Relief Materials File, Owen D. Young Papers, Young Archives, Van Hornesville, New York; POUR Press Releases of Sept. 24, 27, Nov. 8, 1931, in Gifford Records: Mobilization of Relief Resources—Radio Programs, Box 1097, PECE-POUR Papers. Also playing leading roles in the campaign were advertising executive Bruce Barton and movie "czar" Will Hays.

46. See Gifford Statement, Aug. 25, 1931, in Croxton Office Files: News Releases—Organization, Box 1106, PECE-POUR Papers; "Remarks of Gifford to Meeting of Committee on Mobilization of Relief Resources," Sept. 18, 1931, in Press Releases: Sept. 1931, Box 1145, PECE-POUR Papers; "Welfare Work in the United States," in Hayes Office Files: Untitled #4, Box 1116, PECE-POUR Papers; and *Public Papers: Hoover, 1931*, 487–491.

47. Represented were the National Conference of Social Work, the Knights of Columbus, the Family Welfare Association of America, the Red Cross, the White House Conference on Child Protection and Health, the Young Women's Christian Association, the Salvation Army, the Association of Community Chests and Councils, and the American Association of Public Welfare Officials.

48. POUR, "Summary of First Meeting of the Committee on Administration of Relief," Oct. 5, 1931, in Croxton Office Files: Committee on Administration of Relief, Box 1101, PECE-POUR Papers; Croxton to Gifford, Oct. 16, 1931, in Gifford Records: Administration of Relief Committee, Box 1095, PECE-POUR Papers; POUR Press Releases of Oct. 5, 7, and 8, 1931, in Press Releases: Oct. 1931, Box 1145, PECE-POUR Papers. Among the new "guidance reports" issued were community bulletins on "back to school" promotion, the collection and distribution of clothing, and the use of "friendly visitors" to deliver food orders; a special bulletin on "Recreational Activities for the Unemployed"; *A Community Plan for Service to Transients* (1931), prepared by the National Association of Travelers Aid Societies; and "Regional Planning for Care of Homeless and Transient Men," which interestingly advised the inclusion of tobacco ("two packages a week") as part of the standard relief ration. Copies of these are available in Boxes 1095, 1123, and 1152 (Appendix I, #7 and #25), PECE-POUR Papers.

49. POUR Press Release, Oct. 8, 1931, in Press Releases: Oct. 1931, Box 1145, PECE-POUR Papers; "The President's Organization on Unemployment Relief: Statement of Organization and Activities," Appendix I, #43: Statement on Organization, Box 1152, PECE-POUR Papers. The list included the YMCA, the leading business service clubs, the American Federation of Labor, the National Association of Manufacturers, the Knights of Columbus, the American Railway Association, and the American Legion.

50. "Wheeler Committee Program for Promotion of Employment," Oct. 29, 1931, in Press Releases: Oct. 1931, Box 1145, PECE-POUR Papers; "From the Committee on Employment Plans and Suggestions," in Gifford Records: Employment Plans and Suggestions Committee, Box 1096, PECE-POUR Papers; Wheeler to Croxton, Dec. 9, 1931, in Central Files of POUR: Reports from the Field, Box 1095, PECE-POUR Papers. Also suggested but not pushed was the possibility of transferring surplus labor to farms on a "work for keep" basis.

51. "Report of the Committee on the Program of Federal Public Works," Dec. 16, 1931, in Croxton Office Files: Committee on Program of Federal Public Works, Box 1100, PECE-POUR Papers. New efforts to accelerate municipal projects had also been undertaken by a new public works section of the Chamber of Commerce with a staff provided by the industries and other interests involved. See "Public Works," in Hayes Office Files: Public Works Promotion, Box 1115, PECE-POUR Papers. The president had restated his views in his State of the Union message on December 8 and had some backing from the stand taken by the American Engineering Council. See *Public Papers: Hoover, 1931*, 588–589, 592–593; Sautter, "Public Works before the New Deal," 81–82.

52. "Testimony of Walter Gifford before a Subcommittee of the Senate Committee on Manufactures," Jan. 8, 1932, in Press Releases: Jan. 1932, Box 1146, PECE-POUR Papers. Gifford's subsequent defense of POUR, however, was not forceful enough for Hoover. According to press secretary Theodore Joslin, Hoover came to regard Gifford as a "weak sister" who made a "mighty poor" general in the battles

being waged and who should be replaced. See entries for Feb. 5, 17, 18, 21, 24, 1932, Joslin Diary, Box 10, Joslin Papers, Hoover Presidential Library.

53. *Public Papers: Hoover, 1931*, 391–398, 417–419, 584; Price, Oral History Interview, p. 7. Hoover relied particularly on an August 18 report from Surgeon General Hugh S. Cumming, which, in the president's words, showed that the public health had "apparently never been better than it has been over the past six months." On December 1 he also received further information and another memorandum from Cumming, this time claiming that health conditions were even better than they had been in August. See Cumming to Hoover, Dec. 1, 1931, in Presidential Subject Files: Public Health Bureau, Box 171, Hoover Papers.

54. Hoover gave no encouragement to the plans for "industrial government" through legalized cartels now coming from the Chamber of Commerce, the National Civic Federation, and former war administrators, and in September 1931 he got Senator Felix Hebert to denounce Gerard Swope's much publicized plan for government-backed cartelization as an un-American scheme for gigantic trusts and bureaucracies. In addition, he worked through former associates Julius Klein and Frederick Feiker, who now held positions in the Commerce Department, to depict government-endorsed trade association programs as true planning from "the bottom up" and in accord with American ideals. See Julius Barnes to Hoover, Sept. 4, 19, Oct. 5, 1931, all in Presidential Subject Files: Chamber of Commerce, Box 91, Hoover Papers; Julius Klein to Sheldon Cary, Oct. 2, 1931, and Klein to Oscar Cooley, Nov. 7, 1931, both in Office of the Secretary: General Correspondence, Files 81288 and 83057, Commerce Dept. Records (RG40), National Archives; "Chart of Essential Trade Association Activities," Oct. 1931; Committee on Planning to Feiker, Oct. 22, 1931; Feiker, "An American Economic Plan," Oct. 30, 1931, all in Feiker Papers: General Coorespondence, Boxes 78, 83, and 84, BFDC Records; and Hoover, Desk Memorandum on the Swope Plan (cir. Sept. 13, 1931); Hebert to Hoover, Sept. 15, 18, 1931, all in Presidential Subject Files: Business—Stabilization of Industry Plans, Box 92, Hoover Papers. See also Ellis W. Hawley, "Herbert Hoover and the Sherman Act, 1921–1933: An Early Phase of a Continuing Issue," *Iowa Law Review* 74 (July 1989): 1090–1093.

55. Romasco, *Poverty of Abundance*, 87–92, 186–198; *Public Papers: Hoover, 1931*, 466–468, 584–592 (quotation on 587); *Public Papers: Hoover, 1932* (1977), 1–4, 29–30, 66–67, 329–334. Hoover's advocacy of home loan banks preceded his new concern with credit restoration. He had called for consideration of them in his address to the Chamber of Commerce in 1930, and legislation to establish them had been a major subject of deliberation at the White House Conference on Home Building and Home Ownership in 1931. See *Public Papers: Hoover, 1930*, 176, 311–312; *Public Papers: Hoover, 1931*, 469–470, 525, 575–576.

56. Marietta Stevenson, "Recent Developments in Legislation for Public Relief of Unemployment," Dec. 1931, and "More Recent Developments in Legislation for Public Relief of Unemployment," March 1932, both in Croxton Office Files: AAPWO, Box 1098, PECE-POUR Papers; "Resolution of Industrial Committee of Iowa Conference of Social Work and Iowa Governor's Committee on Employment and Relief, May 14, 1932," in State Files: Iowa, Box 1110, PECE-POUR Papers; Haynes to Croxton, May 12, 1932, in Central Files of POUR: Reports from the Field, Box 1095, PECE-POUR Papers; Schwarz, *Interregnum of Despair*, 150–161; Brown, *Public Relief*, 103–123.

57. *Congressional Record* 75 (June 9, July 5, 8, 1932): 12485–12486, 13475, 14602, 14929–14930; Croxton to Phil Swing [undated but probably May or June

1932], in Hayes Office Files: Untitled #2, Box 1116, PECE-POUR Papers; National Archives, *Preliminary Inventory of Records of POUR*, 1–2. The charges that Hoover was trying to govern by "commission" and through "oligarchies of experts" while usurping the authority of the "legally constituted agencies" of government had been ongoing since 1929. See *Congressional Record* 72 (Feb. 21, 24, 1930): 4075, 4147; 75 (Feb. 18, 1932): 4247, 4528; Alva Johnston, "Mr. Hoover's Commissions Open New Era," in *New York Herald Tribune*, Jan. 30 and Feb. 1, 1930. For the administration's defense of Hoover's practice, see *Federal Commissions, Committees, and Boards* (Senate Document 174, 71st Congress, 1930), and Press Release on "Commissions and Committees," April 1932, in Presidential Subject Files: Commissions, Box 107, Hoover Papers.

58. *Public Papers: Hoover, 1932*, 210–214, 227–233, 237–241, 247–249, 276–281, 295–300, 305–311 (quotation on 311), 322–323; 47 *U.S. Statutes* 709, Public, No. 302; Schwarz, *Interregnum of Despair*, 162–172; Brown, *Public Relief*, 124–127; James Stuart Olson, *Herbert Hoover and the Reconstruction Finance Corporation, 1931–1933* (Ames: Iowa State University Press, 1977), 67–73; Harris Gaylord Warren, *Herbert Hoover and the Great Depression* (New York, 1959), 204–206. In the measure signed, the president said, Congress had finally agreed to eliminate such "obnoxious features" as federal "charity," "pork-barrel" loans "based upon population instead of need," loans for "nonproductive public works," and general loans for businesses and municipalities. During the debate he had also accepted legislation under which the Federal Farm Board could donate some of its holdings of wheat and cotton to the Red Cross.

59. *Public Papers: Hoover, 1932*, 213–214, 322–323 (quotations on 322); Olson, *Hoover and the RFC*, 76–86; Romasco, *Poverty of Abundance*, 223–226; Brown, *Public Relief*, 128–130, 134; William R. Brock, *Welfare, Democracy, and the New Deal* (Cambridge, 1988), 138–161. The AAPWO, now renamed the American Public Welfare Association, also worked closely with Croxton's Emergency Relief Division, especially in assisting the states to organize their investigative and administrative machinery.

60. *Public Papers: Hoover, 1932*, 429–433 (quotation on 430), 543–544; Allen Burns to Hoover, Aug. 4, 1932; "Summary Outline of Program for 1932"; and ACCC Bulletin #70, July 20, 1932, all in Croxton Office Files: Community Chest, Box 1101, PECE-POUR Papers; Olson, *Hoover and the RFC*, 80–81; Atlee Pomerene, *An Interpretation of the Relief and Construction Provisions of the Relief and Construction Act* (Washington, D.C., 1932); Warren, *Hoover and the Great Depression*, 207; Brown, *Public Relief*, 131–132. The campaign did raise private relief spending to a high point of more than $57 million in the winter of 1932–33. This still accounted for nearly one-fifth of all relief spending.

61. Teagle to Hoover, Aug. 19, 1932; Teagle to Julius Klein, Nov. 19, 1932; Hoover to Teagle, Nov. 21, 1932, all in Presidential Subject Files: National Conference of Banking and Industrial Committees, Box 210, Hoover Papers; "Work-Spreading," *Business Week* (Nov. 16, 1932): 12; *New York Times*, Aug. 28, 1932, 1; March 19, 1933, 17. A Banking and Industrial Committee had been organized in each Federal Reserve district in May 1932. In July a Central Banking and Industrial Committee was formed for coordinative purposes, and on August 26 the committees held a national conference in Washington, established an enlarged Central Committee chaired by Henry M. Robinson, and organized six subagencies for special activities, one of

which was the new share-the-work organization. See Edward E. Hunt, "Confidential History: National Conference of Banking and Industrial Committees," Box 17, Hunt Papers; *Public Papers: Hoover, 1932*, 350–352, 384–387, 390–396; and "The Government Ties Business into the Recovery Program," *Business Week* (Sept. 7, 1932): 5–6.

62. Hoover spelled out his thoughts about "cooperation" as a container of "bureaucracy" in his Madison Square Garden speech of October 31, 1932. See *Public Papers: Hoover, 1932*, 656–680 (quotations on 659). See also "Plan for the New York Speech," in Public Statements Back-up File, Item 2031, Hoover Papers; and Republican National Committee, *Social Service* (1932). More detailed descriptions of the association-building following the White House and Interior Department conferences can be found in "Action to be Taken on Better Homes and the Home Building Conference," June 1932; "Following Through: Follow-up Work of the White House Conference on Child Health and Protection," August 1932; National Advisory Committee on Illiteracy, News Release, March 24, 1930, all in Ray Lyman Wilbur Papers (Boxes 28, 51, 112), Hoover Institution Archives; and J. McKeen Cattell, "Education under the National Government," *School and Society* 34 (Sept. 5, 1931): 325–336. For the Richardson proposal and discussion of it, see Inez Richardson, "National Council on Social Development"; Wilbur to Hoover, May 26, 1932; and George Hastings to Wilbur, July 22, 1932, all in Wilbur File, Box 22, Papers of the White House Conference on Child Health and Child Protection, Hoover Institution Archives. Among the organizational legacies specified by Richardson were the White House Conference on Child Health and Protection, the President's Conference on Home Building and Home Ownership, the Committee on the Cost of Medical Care, the President's Research Committee on Social Trends, Better Homes in America, Inc., and the American Child Health Association. Wilbur thought that funds might be secured from the "Roosevelt Memorial people," but they were not receptive.

63. This was evident in the course and outcome of his bid for reelection. In addition, a social work community once strongly supportive of his associationalism had now changed its mind. At a Conference on the Maintenance of Welfare Standards, convened in November of 1932 by the American Public Welfare Association (formerly the AAPWO), the Public Administration Clearing House, and the University of Chicago's School of Social Service Administration, resolutions were adopted declaring that relief was the responsibility of local, state, and federal governments, that government had the ability to administer it, and that public funds should be administered by public agencies. These were also the views strongly expressed in the new congressional hearings on the relief issue in early 1933. See Schwarz, *Interregnum of Despair*, 193–204; Brown, *Public Relief*, 135–136; Brock, *Welfare, Democracy, and the New Deal*, 161–166.

64. The degree of continuity and discontinuity between Hoover's policies and the New Deal has continued to be a subject of historiographical controversy. Both he and the New Dealers stressed their differences in regard to what government could and should do, differences that were real enough despite a degree of exaggeration and distortion on both sides. But Hoover's break with classical theory concerning proper governmental behavior during a depression, his creation and subsequent expansion of the RFC, his invocation of various facets of the World War I experience, and his support of business, agricultural, and social planning have been used to argue that his

policies foreshadowed the New Deal and provided a foundation upon which it was built. For differing views of the matter, see Romasco, *Poverty of Abundance*, 231–234; Robert Sobel, *Herbert Hoover at the Onset of the Great Depression* (New York, 1975), ix– xii; Murray N. Rothbard, "Herbert Clark Hoover: A Reconsideration," *New Individualist Review* 4 (Winter 1966): 3–12; Frank Freidel, "Hoover and Roosevelt and Historical Continuity," in Mark Hatfield, comp., *Herbert Hoover Reassessed* (Washington, D.C., 1981), 275–291; and Ellis W. Hawley, *The Great War and the Search for a Modern Order* (New York, 1979), 223–226.

65. See Ellis W. Hawley, "The New Deal State and the Anti-Bureaucratic Tradition," in Robert Eden, ed., *The New Deal and Its Legacy: Critique and Reappraisal* (Westport, Conn., 1989), 77–90; and Robert Griffith, "Dwight D. Eisenhower and the Corporate Commonwealth," *American Historical Review* 87 (February 1982): 87–122.

66. The evolution of the New Deal system and its ideals of public service are traced in Berkowitz and McQuaid, "Businessman and Bureaucrat," 131–140; Brock, *Welfare, Democracy, and the New Deal,* 171–194, 278–369; Coll, *Safety Net*, 15–33, 47–102; and Brown, *Public Relief*, 145–170, 183–190, 301–326, 395–419. By 1937 relief expenditures from private funds constituted only about 1 percent of total relief expenditures, and after August 1, 1933, federal relief agencies insisted that the funds they provided be administered by public officials. Often, however, this meant the same people, since many of the social workers involved simply transferred to state and local public relief administration from private welfare agencies. As the private sector gave up its efforts to shoulder the relief burden, the agencies there found it necessary to rebuild support along other lines, which usually meant a continuing role for them in community planning, provision of nonrelief services, and casework aimed at securing better use of the relief being provided. Clearly, the New Deal system did a better job of meeting relief needs, but it should be noted that in terms of mobilization to provide jobs (as stressed by Hoover in 1930 and 1931) it was also a failure. Not until the 1940s were effective ways found to do this.

67. As students of the 1960s have noted, however, the expansion of the welfare state under Kennedy and Johnson did not bring a shrinkage of the non-profit sector. On the contrary, the state turned to nonprofit agencies as appropriate deliverers of the new services financed by public money, and the result was a considerable expansion of the nonprofit sector as well as a growth in governmental budgets. Indeed, by the 1970s the private nonprofit sector had, in the words of Lester Salamon, "become the principal vehicle for the delivery of government-financed human services, and government had, correspondingly, become the principal source of human service agency finance." In a sense, the relief system that had emerged by the end of Hoover's administration foreshadowed a general pattern that would eventually become characteristic of the American welfare system as a whole. Although his failure may have created a temporary opening for an American welfare state on the European model, passage through this remained so difficult that it was never negotiated. Instead, the United States has kept trying to devise substitutes that would be less threatening to cherished traditions, values, and vested interests. See Lester M. Salamon, *Partners in Public Service: Government-Nonprofit Relations in the Modern Welfare State* (Baltimore, 1995), quotation on p. 1.

68. Although Olasky never mentions Hoover, he does see the Depression period as being characterized by a different kind of unemployment and argues that by 1929

the mainstream private charities had become too bureaucratized, secularized, professionalized, and infected with socialist thinking to do the job that they had done in the 1890s. He also tends, however, to exaggerate the differences between the charities of the 1890s and those of the 1920s, downplaying the bureaucratic side of the charity organization societies. And from his discussion, it is never very clear why the private sector of today has more potential for ending public welfare than the one in 1929 had for preventing it. His major reasons for thinking that it has are its allegedly enhanced capabilities to see the evils of welfare statism and absorb the lessons of the past in devising an alternative. See Olasky, *Tragedy of American Compassion*, 80–115, 143–156, 223–233.

69. Lester Salamon argues that neither "market failure" nor "government failure" explains the kind of voluntary sector that has developed in twentieth-century America. Also at work has been "voluntary failure," due to the inherent inability of the voluntary system to "generate resources on a scale that is both adequate enough and reliable enough to cope with the human service problems of an advanced industrial society." And when such "failure" occurs, the long-range response has been to create a partnership that combines "the superior revenue-raising and democratic decision-making processes of government with the potentially smaller-scale, more personalized service-delivery capabilities of the voluntary sector." This became the way to reconcile a desire for public services with a deep-seated "hostility to the governmental apparatus that provides them" and was facilitated by an equation in the political culture of "civil society" action with the preservation of such cherished values as group and individual freedom, diversity, and a sense of community. See Salamon, *Partners in Public Service*, 33–49, 103–114, 185–199 (quotations on 42, 45, 114).

ALICE O'CONNOR

Neither Charity Nor Relief:
The War on Poverty and the Effort to
Redefine the Basis of Social Provision

In the 1960s the U.S. government declared war on poverty and in the process sought to bring about a permanent change in the relationship between the state, private charity, and the poor. To some degree, this effort can be seen as an extension of the broader historical shift that had been occurring in the United States and other industrial democracies since the nineteenth century, away from a reliance on the poor law tradition of localized charity and toward a system of rationalized state provision. But if the war on poverty was poor law reform, it was reform with a difference. An effort to extend the benefits of unprecedented mass prosperity and scientifically informed statecraft to those at the bottom of the social and economic ladder, the war on poverty represented an attempt to transform the very basis of social provision, to do away with the kind of morally charged categorizing that existed in both charity and public relief programs, and to create in its place a more neutral, rational system based on the principles of sound economic policymaking and on the concepts of equality and opportunity—to do away, that is, with the poor law mentality once and for all.

The war on poverty attempted to bring this transformation about in several different, sometimes divergent ways. First, there was an effort to define poverty as an economic problem and thus as a matter that should be addressed not through charitable benevolence and social casework but through economic policy. Second, there was an effort to constitute the poor as full political participants in society with a legitimate say in planning and organizing public and private benefit provision, rather than as charitable wards of the state. Third, there was an effort to extend the legal rights that most citizens enjoyed to the poor and, as part of that effort, to establish the receipt of public benefits as a right. Above all, through these efforts the federal government pledged to attack the "root causes" of poverty—thereby eliminating the traditional object of charity and public assistance altogether.

Despite their common genesis under the auspices of the war on poverty, these various efforts did not occur as part of a single, well-coordinated strategy and at times they even worked at cross-purposes. Nevertheless, they were informed by certain shared beliefs and assumptions that both motivated and constrained the policy strategies deployed in the war on poverty. One, which can trace its lineage to Progressive-era reform, was a belief in expertise as a kind of apolitical force for planned social change and a basis for rational policymaking. A second, rooted in the economic optimism that was so central to the politics and ideology of 1960s liberalism, was a belief that poverty could be eliminated without major changes in existing social or economic arrangements, primarily through a combination of economic growth, human capital investment, and socially rehabilitative intervention. Third was a belief that a war on poverty could be fought without directly confronting the issue of race, and indeed that an antipoverty program would represent a "race neutral" way of improving conditions for black Americans. Fourth was the assumption that, once mobilized, the resources and the political will would be available for as long as it would take to end poverty in America. All of these assumptions were embodied in a conceptualization of poverty as a social and economic anomaly in an otherwise affluent society, which occurred among an identifiable minority of "other Americans" who suffered from some identifiable handicaps, and that could be targeted for specialized analysis and policy intervention. The war on poverty began, then, with a premise that would ultimately serve to undermine its broader objectives: the idea that poverty was a problem of the poor.

Poverty and Political Economy

"The words 'poverty' and 'poor,' although on the threshold of revival, were not parts of the public language" wrote sociologist Hylan Lewis of the years immediately preceding the war on poverty. The problems were there, he went on to say, "but society chose not to see them—or at least not to call them that."[1] Instead, influenced by a combination of scientific sensibility and policy concern, the poor were recognized—if at all—as "low-income" families in hearings sponsored by Congressman John Sparkman in 1949, as residents of "distressed areas" in legislation that would eventually become the Area Redevelopment Act of 1961, or as the "structurally unemployed" in analyses that helped to provide the impetus for the Manpower Development and Training Act of 1962.[2] In sociological and anthropological literature they were the "lower classes," the "culturally deprived," urban "newcomers" or "disadvantaged" negroes. In economics poverty barely existed at all, "lost," as economist Theodore W. Schultze pointed out, "for want of a theory," or, as a prominent economist of poverty later said, relegated "to the dustbin" along with pauperism as a valid and useful conceptual category.[3] It came as something of a surprise, then, when "poverty" began to emerge as a subject of public and policy concern in the early 1960s. Even more surprising, it was economists, led by Keynesians at John F. Kennedy's Council of Economic Advisers (CEA), who were pushing to give the issue a prominent place on the president's 1964 domestic agenda.[4] In their hands, beginning with initial efforts at definition in 1963, poverty would become a legitimate subject for economic analysis and a target for national economic policy—and ultimately, overturning the biblical dictum, something that could be eliminated.

The CEA economists were by no means the first in recent memory to draw attention to poverty. The issue had actually been raised several years earlier by economist John Kenneth Galbraith, who in his best-selling 1958 book *The Affluent Society* called it a "national disgrace" and helped to stimulate a debate that would only later become immediately relevant to liberal policymakers.[5] The debate was over whether, as Galbraith, Swedish economist and author of *The American Dilemma* Gunnar Myrdal, and others claimed, there was a new, structural quality to contemporary poverty that made it immune to the simple solvent of aggregate economic growth being proposed by Kennedy's CEA. Rooted in a combination of economic restructuring stimulated by automation, persistent racial discrimination, a social welfare system that provided generously for the well organized but left whole categories of people behind, and geographic isolation, the "new poverty" separated an unskilled, disproportionately black minority of the population from the rest of affluent America and threatened to spawn a permanent group of "unemployable" people, an unskilled "underclass" that would be reproduced across succeeding generations. The new poverty, structuralists argued, called for significantly expanded redistributive social welfare spending, job creation, massive investments in education and targeted area development, and more aggressive antidiscrimination policies.[6] Their arguments were reinforced by civil rights leaders who, building on a long-standing tradition of black mobilization behind job guarantees, began in the early 1960s to call for a "domestic Marshall Plan" that would include job creation, income guarantees, and forceful measures to combat segregation, discrimination and the absence of capital in black communities. For Galbraith, dealing with poverty was also part of a larger effort to reorder political priorities, away from a liberal program that saw aggressive economic growth as the answer to all social problems and toward a program of "social balance" featuring a more rigorous public sector, controls on corporate power, and a more equitable distribution of wealth.[7]

While equally concerned about the persistent but "invisible" poverty problem, the economists in Kennedy's Council of Economic Advisers had a much more optimistic view of what a growing economy could do to solve it. Sustained economic growth and full employment—in this instance stimulated by a massive tax cut—remained "the two measures which can have the greatest effect in reducing poverty in the future," the CEA had maintained in its economic reports. Indeed, it was in a critique of Galbraith's notion that aggregate growth would not be effective against the new poverty that CEA staff member Robert Lampman, an economist from the University of Wisconsin, had earlier initiated what would become a career-long interest in issues of poverty and social welfare. In a paper commissioned by the Joint Economic Committee of Congress just after Galbraith's *Affluent Society* was published, Lampman had laid out the empirical basis for what would later become the CEA "aggregate growth" or "aggregationist" position, linking poverty not to structural economic change or permanent unemployment, but to slow growth and cyclical unemployment, and predicting that a return to the high growth levels of the postwar years would *by itself* reduce poverty rates from roughly 20 percent, where they stood in 1956, to 12 percent by 1976.[8] Although antidiscrimination and civil rights measures were important in clearing the way for black advancement, as antipoverty measures they were supplemental to the drive for growth and full employment, in the aggregationist view. Tight labor markets would stimulate employers to "break down the barriers of discrimination and overlook handicaps in a frenzy to hire any and all workers," Lampman wrote in an internal staff memo.[9] Moreover, Lampman and his colleagues shared a concern voiced by Truman CEA Chair Leon Keyserling, who warned against distinguishing "between the unemployment and growth problem on the one hand and the poverty problem on the other," on the assumption that the structuralist concept of the new poverty would lead to "casework" solutions and ultimately prove "self-defeating" for the real antipoverty cause.[10] From this perspective, keeping the poverty debate on a strictly economic basis was politically as well as intellectually strategic. Otherwise, economists ran the risk of losing ground to social welfare traditionalists who aimed to ameliorate rather than to eliminate the problem.

As Keyserling's comments indicate, the economists' position was coupled with considerable disdain for casework as a response to poverty—and to some degree for the profession of social work as well. The mainstream of the social work field had become increasingly professionalized and oriented to individual and family rehabilitation since the 1920s, and, despite an emerging movement within the profession to push for improved benefit levels and better coverage for poor families, rehabilitative services remained its main thrust in the early 1960s.[11] This rehabilitative emphasis had been reinforced in the Public Welfare Amendments of 1962, which, promising a major reorientation of the system, were aimed at containing rising welfare costs through significantly expanded preventive and rehabilitative services.[12] The economists were skeptical. As a tool for fighting or preventing poverty, they thought, casework services were both inefficient and largely beside the point. Nor, from a bureaucratic perspective, did the CEA staff trust the Department of Health, Education and Welfare (HEW) to reorganize its fragmented range of services into more comprehensive, self-help promoting interventions. As heads of a task force designated to plan the poverty initiative, the CEA economists looked for a mechanism that would enable them to "shake up" the old-line agency bureaucracies while effectively wresting control of the poverty issue from social work practitioners. They found their answer in an idea being promoted by a loose confederation of urban sociologists, foundation officials and community-based activists, and included in their approach a proposal for establishing local "community action agencies" designated to subsume the existing array of government services within a more comprehensive, coordinated local action plan. In combination with the expanded opportunities generated by the tax cut, community action would "break the cycle of poverty" and offer the poor a permanent escape from their plight.

Ultimately, the conceptual and legislative framework constructed by the CEA task force would strike a compromise among the various contingencies competing for a say in the war on poverty, beginning with a combination of structuralist and aggregationalist diagnoses of the poverty problem itself. Most of the poor would be the immediate beneficiaries of faster growth and higher employment, according to the CEA's Economic report of 1964, making the tax cut "the first requisite of a concerted attack on poverty." But growth and employment alone would not suffice, the Report went on to acknowledge, due to the "special handicaps" that characterized a certain subgroup of the population in poverty. "Policy will have to focus more sharply on the handicaps that deny the poor fair access to the expanding incomes of a growing economy." This included measures targeted at such "external" barriers as discrimination. For the most part, however, the programs suggested in the CEA framework were aimed at removing the "internal" barriers that, they believed, separated the poor from opportunity—and the benefits that would be brought about automatically by economic growth. The diagnosis was structural: the "new poverty" would not respond to growth alone. The solution—rehabilitate the poor without significant social or economic restructuring—was not. Over the objections of Secretary of Labor Willard Wirtz and others, the antipoverty package included training but no job creation and no mention at all of major redistributive measures. At the same time, the CEA Report was careful to distance itself from the kind of rehabilitation offered in traditional social services. The "human service" investments it proposed were largely educational and geared toward the labor market and were designed to enable poor Americans "to *earn* the American standard of living by their own efforts and contributions."[13] If the poor had a claim on the country, it was based less on compassion than on the national self-interest. "Humanity compels our action," the Report proclaimed, "but it is sound economics as well."[14]

The outcome of CEA task force deliberations reflected its members' abiding faith that economic growth would bring about higher employment rates and, when coupled with human capital investments and better service delivery mechanisms, would lead to significant reductions in poverty across the board. Attached to that faith was a strong bias against structural reform measures, in the belief that they were neither necessary nor politically feasible, and against traditional casework, in the belief that it treated symptoms rather than causes of poverty. A similar combination of economic confidence and political pragmatism informed the task force discussions about how the poverty problem should be defined for policy purposes, leading the economists to argue that it should be defined first, as lack of income which, in addition to making it a problem for economic policy, had the virtue of being narrow, concrete and "something we had some numbers on," according to Lampman; second, as an absolute rather than a relative (e.g., tied to the median income) cutoff point, on the theory that it was possible to target and eliminate absolute poverty while the relatively poor would by definition always be around; third, setting aside Lampman's own concern over the persistence of overall income disparities, as an issue of absolute deprivation rather than social and economic inequality, in the recognition that any mention of resdistribution would be political death for the new initiative. The result, later made official when the Office of Economic Opportunity adopted an official poverty line based on income standards calculated by Social Security Administration analyst Mollie Orshansky, was an "official" concept of poverty that, economists believed, represented a major political if not exactly a scientific achievement. The poverty line "enabled a quantification . . . of the changing number of poor people and hence of progress toward the goal of eliminating poverty," wrote Lampman, and it set a "rude and restrictive challenge" for those who would propose new policies: "what does it do for the poor?" Likewise, economist James Tobin predicted that future administrations would be "judged by their success or failure in reducing the officially measured prevalence of poverty."[15]

Having established the income-based definition of poverty, economists associated with the war on poverty set out to apply the tools of economic analysis to the actual battle. Their vehicle was the Office of Research, Plans, Programs and Evaluation (RPP&E) that was established as part of the new poverty agency, the Office of Economic Opportunity (OEO). Explicitly modeled on the Office of Systems Analysis at Robert McNamara's Department of Defense, RPP&E brought the techniques of cost/benefit analysis and econometric modeling to the tasks of policy planning and program evaluation, but most of all it sought to introduce the principles of empirically informed, rational decision making to the war on poverty. One of its chief innovations was to introduce the Planning, Programing and Budgeting System (PPBS), an approach to policy planning that had originally developed at the RAND corporation and the Department of Defense in the 1940s and 1950s. Adopted by the OEO and eventually mandated to the rest of the federal government in 1965, PPBS was a method for "setting goals, defining objectives and developing planning programs for meeting those objectives" or, as President Johnson more pithily described it in announcing the new mandate, a method for finding "new ways to do jobs faster, to do jobs better, and to do jobs less expensively."[16] The centerpiece of the new planning and decision-making system was a requirement that agencies submit long-range policy and budget projections, or Five Year Plans, to the Budget Bureau along with their annual appropriations requests.[17] It was in this context that the economists who staffed the OEO research office sought to follow through on the great promise of the war on poverty.

In a series of Five Year Plans submitted beginning in 1965, RPP&E analysts mapped out a comprehensive approach that, they claimed, would "end poverty in the United States as we define it today by 1976, 200 years from the declaration that the pursuit of happiness is among the inalienable rights of Americans." As presented in the 1966 Plan, the economists' approach to ending poverty would continue to rely principally on the strategies originally outlined by the Council of Economic Advisers: economic growth, human capital investments and services delivered through local community action programs. It would also add a measure that, if adopted as recommended, would represent a bold departure from existing social welfare practice and redirect antipoverty policy even further away from its old public assistance precepts and into the realm of economic policy. The proposal was to provide a guarantee of income support for all people below the poverty line, administered by the federal government in the form of a negative income tax, based simply on income need rather than on the maze of categorical requirements that governed the existing welfare system. In addition to de-localizing and de-categorizing the system of income provision, the negative income tax proposal would also overturn poor law tradition by providing for the "working" rather than just the "dependent" poor, eradicating what the economists saw as a major inequity in the system. Eventually, then, what the economists proposed as a mechanism for "ending poverty as we now define it" would also be a "substitute for the demeaning programs now lumped together under the head of Public Assistance." Nor should the administration fear that a basic income guarantee would cause people to stop working, they added, acknowledging the age-old barrier to providing aid to the laboring masses, because the tax could be designed to reward continued participation in the labor market without interfering with the prevailing market wage structure. "Well within our financial capacity," the new proposal would also be compatible with the expectations of a prosperous society. "We believe that the time is coming," the economists wrote, "when the American people will accept . . . a guaranteed minimum income at the poverty level as a right in a wealthy country and we propose to start moving in this direction now."[18]

The OEO analysts were not the only ones promoting the negative income tax at the time. Within two years of its first appearance in their Five Year Plan, the idea had received public endorsements from economists across the ideological spectrum, from the Chamber of Commerce and from a high-level panel of business executives appointed by President Johnson to study the issue. Nevertheless, its proponents within OEO were unable to garner political support from the president, who from the beginning of the poverty effort had made clear his opposition to any scheme that relied on expanded income maintenance. Only later, during the early years of the Nixon administration, did the idea receive any serious presidential backing and at that point it was welfare reform rather than eliminating poverty that served as its chief rationale. Even with below-poverty income levels and work requirements, however, Nixon's Family Assistance Plan went down to defeat following close votes in Congress. In subsequent years, the economists' vision of creating a rational, direct and equitable form of federal income support was partially realized in the form of expansions in the Food Stamp and Earned Income Tax Credit programs, but neither amounted to anything approaching a minimum income guarantee.

The economists were only partially successful, then, in their efforts to replace more traditional categorical and "demeaning" approaches to helping the poor with the more rational principles of modern economics. As a result of their efforts, poverty was officially defined as an absence of income and poverty did become the subject of a whole new area of economic expertise. They were unable, however, to summon political support for the idea that the combination of need, citizenship, and economic efficiency was argument enough to warrant a guarantee of income support. But in the end they also failed to transform the idea of poverty from one grounded in moral judgment to one grounded in scientific analysis. For the poverty warriors, influenced by their own economic faiths and by political considerations, resisted the possibility that the causes of poverty could be found in the economy itself and instead focused both policy and analytic attention on the "special handicaps" that presumably distinguished the poor from everyone else. Perhaps a problem for economics, poverty was not a problem of the economy. In place of the old categorization of deserving and undeserving poor, the economists had created a new one: those who could benefit from growth and those who could not.

Community Action: Empowering the Poor

At the heart of the poverty program lies a new form of dialogue between the poor and the rest of this society. First and foremost, this is to be a dialogue between *men*, between thinking, feeling human beings blessed with dignity and with those inalienable rights of life, liberty and the pursuit of happiness which form the core of our national credo. This is not to be a dialogue of manipulation, a new form of master-servant relationship, or worse still, a co-vert form of unilateral action which treats the poor as inanimate objects to be shaped in the image of the master class. The essence of this dialogue is to be found in the alteration of identities, the exchange and merger of perspectives of all its participants. Thus, the War Against Poverty is a call to action, to introspection, and to change for those who dwell in comfort as for those who dwell in misery and privation.[19]

—Sargent Shriver, OEO Director

While economists working in federal government agencies sought to bring the powers of economic growth and analysis to bear on the problem of poverty, a group of social scientists, activists and administrators who were primarily concerned with community-level reform were introducing a much different set of concepts into the new poverty initiative. Although they were allied with the economists in their critical stance toward public assistance and the existing social welfare bureaucracy, the architects of what became the Community Action Program were informed by much different theoretical perspectives about the nature of the poverty problem and the steps required to eliminate it. To community action theorists, poverty, much more than a lack of income, was embedded in a complex of social, cultural and institutional inadequacies that trapped the poor in a vicious "cycle" of deprivation and despair.[20] Economic growth could perhaps provide job opportunities for the poor, but "breaking the cycle" would require a more concerted and comprehensive effort to change the personal and "environmental" circumstances that prevented them from gaining access to those opportunities.

As subsequently spelled out in the process of planning the antipoverty legislation, these ideas became the basis for what would eventually come to be regarded as the most controversial—and little understood—provision of the war on poverty: the requirement, calling for "maximum feasible participation" of the poor in local community action agencies, that rested on the assumption that the first step in bringing about meaningful change was to alter the political relationship between the providers and the poor.[21]

Community action had its immediate origins in a series of experimental demonstration programs designed in response to the problems of juvenile delinquency and inner city decline in the late 1950s and early 1960s. Sponsored by the National Institute of Mental Health, the Ford Foundation and President Kennedy's Committee on Juvenile Delinquency, these demonstrations were concentrated for the most part in urban areas, and took place against the backdrop of industrial decentralization, white suburbanization, minority-group in-migration and infrastructural decay that had been fueling sporadic concern about a looming "urban crisis" for the better part of a decade.[22] The demonstration projects were informed by three strands of social scientific thought that, when brought together, formed a loose theoretical framework for the emerging community action movement. One, rooted in the "Chicago School" of sociology, argued that the various social processes implicated in urban change had a destabilizing effect on lower-class and immigrant neighborhoods located in the inner city core, undermining their capacity for effective social control and making them breeding grounds for the rise of deviant behavior and antisocial subcultural norms. In an experimental intervention known as the Chicago Area Project in the early 1930s, Chicago sociologists tried to reverse this process of community "disorganization" by working with neighborhood committees and "indigenous leaders"—and without the help of existing "helping" agencies—to develop locally generated fund raising and action plans to address delinquency, physical "blight" and other issues of community concern. Such approaches to localized capacity building were later incorporated by Chicago-trained social psychologist Leonard Cottrell into a concept of "community competence" that was used in developing criteria for choosing communities for federally supported antidelinquency demonstration projects in the early 1960s.[23] In Cottrell's vision, the "competent" community was one which was capable of functioning in a complex democratic society, capable, that is, of working in concert to analyze and achieve consensus about the nature of local problems and their solutions. The early Chicago-school experiments were also the springboard for a more radical, explicitly political model of community-based organizing, developed by Chicago sociology alumnus Saul D. Alinsky, which inspired some of the confrontational strategies used by a small number of community action agencies in the 1960s.

A second and related strand of thought that fed into the design for community action blended the Chicago-school concept of community disorganization with a structural theory of deviance proposed by sociologist Robert Merton, for an explanation of the origins of juvenile delinquency. As developed by Richard Cloward and Lloyd Ohlin in their influential book *Delinquency and Opportunity* (1960), the notion of "differential opportunity" depicted delinquency as a source of identity, status, and even upward mobility for poor youth whose isolation in slum communities presented them with severely constrained choices in life: limited to a few, mostly illegitimate "opportunity structures," delinquent youth were actually trying to achieve what the larger society recognized as success goals through the only means they had at hand. To make matters worse, the social institutions that were nominally supposed to act as avenues to opportunity—and especially the schools—had themselves become places where aspirations were denied and existing social inequalities were replicated. The basis of a project on New York's Lower East Side known as Mobilization for Youth, the Cloward/Ohlin theory pointed to the need to provide delinquent youths with access to legitimate opportunity structures, primarily by reforming local service and educational institutions but, equally important, by mobilizing neighborhood residents themselves for the total "reorganization of slum communities."[24]

A third strand of thought informing the early community demonstration projects blended an eclectic array of perspectives from urban planners, sociologists, social psychologists and mental health experts who, having conducted research and experiments of their own in urban communities, came together under the auspices of the National Institute of Mental Health beginning in the late 1950s to talk and write about the interconnectedness of the social problems they studied, which ranged from delinquency and mental health to housing and poverty. The researchers were also unified by a common frustration with society's inability to deal with what they called the "urban condition" which, though manifest in the overcrowded deteriorating slum communities where poverty and delinquency thrived, could, when properly situated within the "vast urban complexes" of which they were a part, be seen as symptoms of a much larger set of problems: the decline of central cities at the hands of industrial decentralization, suburban "sprawl" and the influx of poor minority migrants during the postwar years, and the resulting incapacity of outmoded municipal governing and social welfare institutions to deal with the new "vastness" and "complexity" of a "metropolitanizing" area. Particularly important in galvanizing the planners and social scientists for action was the example of the federal urban renewal program which, having started with the intention of clearing slums for purposes of residential and commercial redevelopment, was working out to be little more than a subsidy for downtown real estate developers who were more interested in removing than in rehousing the poor.[25] Addressed in their "totality," then, the problems of poor people in poor places called not for individual-level interventions in the traditional mode but for wide-scale "systems change," for innovation, and for efforts, as NIMH administrator Leonard Duhl wrote in 1962 *"to change ourselves* so that new overall patterns can evolve."[26]

While these different strands of community thought and action were varied in their targets and implications for social intervention, they did share a common frustration with the individualized, heavily "psychiatric world view" that characterized much of the social problem thinking and practice of the post–World War II period.[27] Nowhere was this sense of frustration more evident than in the animosity of urban sociologists toward professional social work and what they considered to be its misguided attempts to rehabilitate or cure individuals of antisocial behavior.[28] The social scientists engaged in community intervention also shared a commitment to applying their theoretical perspectives to planning and evaluating local action projects. By the early 1960s they were also becoming convinced that poverty was the "root cause" of the problems they were addressing and that poverty should be the target of their interventions.[29] When the Council of Economic Advisers got the go-ahead to begin antipoverty planning in earnest, the social scientists, foundation officials, urban planners, and federal bureaucrats who had been experimenting for the past several years were prepared with ideas and a set of practical principles for organizing local demonstration programs that became the basis of community action in the war on poverty. Communities, not just individuals, should be the targets for intervention and change; interventions should be planned in collaboration with communities, and not imposed from the outside. Interventions should also, in light of the complexity and interrelatedness of social problems, aim to be comprehensive, finding appropriate "entry points" from which integrated programs could be organized; and the providers—whether private foundations or government agencies—should act not as distant benefactors but as actively engaged "catalysts" for social and institutional change.[30] As a strategy against poverty, then, community action called for a new attitude toward the poor—as participants rather than mere beneficiaries—and toward the objectives of social provision—as change and empowerment—in place of the traditional assumptions of charity or public assistance.

From its first introduction into the antipoverty task force proceedings, community action was based on very different notions of what it was all about. Coming upon the idea rather late in the game when new ideas were in great demand, the economists in charge of the task force thought it made sense as a mechanism for delivering services more effectively and efficiently.

They were also attracted to the idea of giving local planning agencies a say in adapting federal programs to meet their own needs—and hoped in the process to learn more about the dynamics of poverty in different localities.[31] For those who had come up through the ranks of local experimentation, however, community action was all that and much more. Convinced by urban renewal and related experiences that real change would not occur without altering the power relationships in urban and rural areas, the community action veterans who were eventually recruited to plan and run the new program introduced two key provisions into the legislative and administrative requirements. One, that funds from Washington would be controlled not by official bureaucratic channels but by broadly representative local community action and planning agencies that were meant to bring public officials, private agencies, business, labor, neighborhood, and civil rights organizations together to develop comprehensive strategies for using them. The other, that the local plans be developed with "maximum feasible participation" of the poor.

Community action had scant opportunity to attempt the transformations its architects envisioned. Almost immediately upon releasing the first round of grants to local action agencies, the OEO officials charged with administering the Community Action Program met with strong—sometimes "savage"—resistance at the local level, and especially from the local officials whose control over federal resources was threatened by the new approach.[32] Angered by what they rightly saw as OEO's efforts to shake up the "status quo," a group of Democratic mayors, with Chicago's Richard J. Daley in the vanguard, flooded the White House with angry charges that the new agencies were in the hands of local subversives and worked up an anti-CAP petition within the U.S. Conference of Mayors.[33] Faced with a choice between a fledgling new agency and a traditional Democratic stronghold, President Johnson sided with the mayors and ordered a clamp-down and revisions in the program. Before the rein-in could take effect, though, a small but highly visible number of local community action projects were confronting the local establishment head-on, using strategies from Alinsky and the civil rights movement to organize the poor to fight for their own interests.[34] By the summer of 1965, just a few months earlier touted as the "vanguard" of the war on poverty, CAP, had provoked a hysteria of political reaction, complete with charges that it was fomenting "class warfare," and was considered a major source of embarrassment within the Johnson White House.[35] Having always viewed the program primarily as a mechanism for more integrated service delivery, administration economists who had initially supported the idea called for toning down or eliminating its "empowerment" emphasis, while redoubling its service coordination function.[36] When the economists in OEO requested significant expansion of the CAP budget for these purposes, however, the request was ignored and the budget was slashed instead. Congress followed with more restrictive measures in the following years, including an amendment giving governors veto power over community action plans. The message was clear: CAP had gone too far in its efforts to act as a "change agent" in the localities and in its efforts to recognize, as OEO critic Alinsky wrote, "that poverty involves poverty of power as well as poverty of economy."[37]

Despite the almost immediate fallout of political and economic support, CAP survived, albeit in much reduced form, until the Nixon administration replaced both it and the OEO with the block grants that attempted to reverse the historic trend toward federalization in the 1970s. CAP could also count several achievements in its relatively short life span: Head Start, legal services, neighborhood service and health centers, and several other smaller-scale innovations were started under its auspices. While less successful in stimulating across-the-board "systems change," CAP did have an impact on local social service institutions in poor communities, according to evaluations from residents and local officials alike, pushing them to become both better coordinated and, in communities where residents were independently organized to exert pressure for change, more responsive to the needs of the poor.[38] With its emphasis on resident participation and programs to train "paraprofessionals" from within the community, CAP also helped to change the face of the service bureaucracy in many localities, providing both employment and political opportunities for minorities in the public sector.[39] Nevertheless, at bottom CAP was a strategy for ending poverty that relied chiefly on providing more and better services for the poor and that, despite its conceptual roots in analyses of absent "opportunity structures" and the dislocations of urban change, did little to acknowledge or confront the shrinkage of job opportunities and the persistence of racial discrimination in poor communities. Instead, focusing its resources on eliminating the "internal" barriers posed by low education and human capital, the program was based on the premise that the problem was with the poor themselves.[40]

Social Rights and Legal Entitlements

A third set of efforts associated with the war on poverty sought to establish law as the basis for social provision and, as an approach centering on the legal rights of the poor, took place not in federal government agencies or in Congress but primarily in the courts. Once again combining a struggle for substantive goals with an attempt to change the relationship between the providers and the poor, these efforts revolved around three major objectives: to replace the tradition of indigent relief that prevailed in private-agency legal services with a system of public representation; to make the legal rights and representation enjoyed by most citizens available to the poor; and to develop the theoretical and legal basis for a right to economic security. The focal point for these efforts was the legal services movement in the war on poverty and the expanding field of poverty and public interest law it helped to stimulate.[41]

The legal services movement grew out of and brought about important changes in the much older tradition of free legal assistance represented by the Legal Aid Societies that were first established to serve poor immigrants in the nineteenth century. Generally funded by local bar associations and occasionally attached to settlement houses, legal aid societies relied heavily on volunteer and pro bono labor and for the most part were designed to provide basic services and no more. Aid was provided on the basis of indigency and need, and motivated by a combination of organized charitable benevolence and social obligation. It was also, in the eyes of later critics, used as a way of forestalling campaigns for the broader expansion of legal protections for the poor that were associated with labor and social reform movements. In contrast to the narrow services-oriented approach reflected in legal aid societies, the strategies that began to gain increasing momentum in the civil rights movement in the 1940s and 1950s did focus more explicitly on a broader agenda of legal reform and were premised on the belief that litigation was an effective and legitimate instrument of social policy and social justice. Through meticulous, often time-consuming use of strategic "test cases," civil rights lawyers—now acting as (poorly) paid professionals as well as pro bono volunteers—sought to expand the legally recognized rights of minorities to equal protection, social services, and opportunities. The legal services movement of the 1960s combined elements of both of these somewhat conflicting traditions. While some advocated an emphasis on providing comprehensive but basic legal services as part of the mission of local community action agencies, others emphasized the need for broader legal reform. With funding from the OEO and private foundations, the legal reformers established "back-up centers" in order to identify and pursue strategic cases for litigation while their colleagues in neighborhood-based law centers would continue the services approach.[42]

Although the civil rights movement was increasingly turning to issues of economic justice throughout the 1960s, it was an important development in legal theory that opened the way to a litigation strategy that took as its objective the legal recognition of a constitutional right to welfare or a guaranteed income.[43] In 1964 Yale law professor Charles Reich argued that an individual's access to such forms of government "largesse" as public assistance and social insurance should be protected as property rights since, in effect, they were distributed by government "as part of the individual's rightful share in the commonwealth."[44] Incorporating this perspective into their thinking, legal strategists began to build up a body of cases that would eventually bring them to the Supreme Court and create an opportunity to argue for a constitutional right to welfare benefits. The argument was rejected by the Court in 1970. However, that decision did establish the right of welfare recipients to a fair hearing before the state could deny or take away benefits, but it did not recognize welfare itself as a basic right.[45]

Despite the political opposition, heavy caseloads, and judicial resistance it enountered, the legal services movement made impressive gains within a relatively short period of time. Providing poor communities with full-time professional rather than part-time volunteer legal services, the movement helped to establish the right to equal legal representation for all kinds of services and treated the poor as clients rather than charity cases. The movement also brought about important changes in the practice of poverty law, stimulating new litigation strategies and theoretical perspectives in the area of legal reform, while also opening up opportunities for lawyers to work in collaboration with local organizers and grass-roots groups in poor communities. While there was by no means a consensus on strategy within legal and organizing circles, they joined together in mutual recognition of the importance of establishing rights rather than charitable or state benevolence as the basis of provision.[46] And the litigation strategists did make progress, albeit incremental, toward this goal, with court victories that together helped to make the legislative "entitlement" to benefits for all who were eligible a reality. In addition to the recognition of a right to a fair hearing, poverty lawyers won cases restricting state practices such as unannounced "man in the house" searches on the grounds of invasion of privacy and struck down the residency and other arbitrary requirements used by states to keep their welfare caseloads low.[47]

The lawyers were not able, however, to establish a constitutional right to welfare or to economic security, nor did they effectively mobilize behind a legislative strategy for improved benefits and services as some within the movement were urging.[48] While suffering the consequences of political, judicial, and ideological opposition to their goals, they were also hampered by their own focus on individual rights. Partially successful as a means of recognizing the right to basic legal protections, this strategy did not offer the basis for establishing the poor as a discriminated-against group, nor, more importantly, for establishing poverty itself as a form of economic and social discrimination that denied basic citizenship rights and opportunities. Within

the legal strategy itself, then, poverty remained a matter of individual deprivation rather than structurally generated inequality, poor welfare recipients
remained artificially isolated from their counterparts in the low-wage labor
market, and provision remained a matter of state obligation rather than an
economic right shared by all.[49]

Eliminating Poverty

Viewed in historical perspective, the nation's commitment to eliminating
poverty was extremely short-lived, as was the belief that it could actually be
accomplished. As early as the spring of 1965, the poverty warriors at OEO
were being asked to curb their already inadequate budgets so that resources
could be freed up for the Vietnam War. By the end of that year, even the
most "hardheaded" economists were pleading with President Johnson to re-
think his curbs on domestic spending, lest his administration signal a "retreat" from a battle so recently launched.[50] Convinced that the country had
both the know-how and the resources, many veterans of the battle began to
conclude that what they were facing was a failure of political will.[51] With
the election of Richard Nixon in 1968, the already dwindling war on poverty came to an end, while containing inflation and welfare reform replaced
eliminating poverty as the central goals of economic and social policy. A
decade after it had all begun, policy analysts would look back and conclude
that, despite such considerable achievements as the passage of Medicare
and Medicaid, the creation of an income floor for the elderly, and reductions
of overall poverty rates to half their former levels, the Great Society's war
on poverty had not, finally, been won—but neither was the battle over.[52]

The Great Society's attempt to strike a fatal blow against poverty met
with many political roadblocks, but it was also limited by its own failure, at
the conceptual as well as the policy level, to link the poverty problem to its
roots in the economy and in social and racial inequality. Recognizing the
connections, the poverty warriors nevertheless continued to define the problem in terms of individual deficits, convinced that remedial interventions
would give the poor the wherewithal to reap the infinite benefits of economic growth. For all its promise as a bold departure from the past, then, the
war on poverty was in some ways quite traditional: its aim was not to transform society, but to transform the poor. That irony in what one observer
called the "Great Society's poor law," has taken on a new twist today, as the
war on poverty has come to symbolize a misguided "radical" tradition that a
new generation of reformers is trying to overturn, when in fact their own
effort to dismantle even the limited apparatus of federal economic, state and

legal provision established since the 1930s amounts to a change far more radical in scope than anything contemplated by the poverty warriors: a return to the localities, to charity, and to morality in providing for the poor. In short, a return to the poor law tradition.[53]

Notes

1. Hylan Lewis, "The Family: New Agenda, Different Rhetoric," *Children of Poverty, Children of Affluence* (New York, 1967), 1.

2. James T. Patterson, *America's Struggle Against Poverty 1900–1994* (New York, 1995), 94–95, 127–129; Henry J. Aaron, *Politics and the Professors* (Washington, D.C., 1978), 11–145; Sar A. Levitan and Robert Taggart, *The Great Society's Poor Law: A New Approach to Poverty* (Baltimore, 1969), 3–48.

3. Theodore W. Schultze, "Investing in Poor People: An Economist's View," in *The Economics of Poverty*, (Washington, D.C., 1964); Robert Lampman, Oral History Interview, LBJ Library.

4. Carl M. Brauer, "Kennedy, Johnson and the War on Poverty," *Journal of American History* 69 (June 1982): 98–119.

5. John Kenneth Galbraith, *The Affluent Society* (Boston, 1958).

6. For examples of structuralist arguments, see Galbraith, *The Affluent Society*; Gunnar Myrdal, *Challenge to Affluence* (New York, 1965); Oscar Ornati, *Poverty Amidst Affluence* (New York, 1968). A more extensive discussion of the structuralist arguments is in Alice O'Connor, "From Lower Class to Underclass: The Poor in American Social Science," (Ph.D. diss., Johns Hopkins University, 1991), chap. 5.

7. Galbraith, *The Affluent Society*, 332.

8. Robert Lampman, *The Low Income Population and Economic Growth in the United States* (Washington, D.C., 1959).

9. Lampman to Walter Heller, June 10, 1963, Legislative Background: Economic Opportunity Act of 1964, LBJ Presidential Library, Box 1.

10. Keyserling, quoted in Patterson, *America's Struggle Against Poverty*, 112.

11. James Leiby, *A History of Social Welfare and Social Work in the United States* (New York, 1978); John Ehrenreich, *The Altruistic Imagination* (New York, 1985).

12. James L. Sundquist, "The Origins of the War on Poverty," in Sundquist, ed. *On Fighting Poverty* (New York, 1969), 15–16.

13. Council of Economic Advisers, *Economic Report of the President* (Washington, D.C., 1964).

14. Ibid., 56.

15. Robert J. Lampman, "What Does it Do for the Poor? A New Test for National Policy," *Public Interest*, (1973): 81; James Tobin, quoted in Robert H. Haveman, *Poverty Policy and Poverty Research* (Madison, Wisc., 1987), 56.

16. Lyndon Johnson, quoted in Walter Williams, *Social Policy Research and Analysis: The Experience in the Federal Social Agencies* (New York, 1971), 5.

17. Bureau of the Budget, "Planning, Programming, Budgeting," Bulletin 66–3,

(October 1965), LBJ Library, OEO Microfilm Collection, Reel 1.

18. Office of Economic Opportunity, *National Anti-Poverty Plan* (June 1966) Section IV, 1–3; Introduction, iv, LBJ Library, Shriver Papers.

19. Sargent Shriver, *Poverty in Plenty*, Proceedings from a Conference at Georgetown University (Washington, D.C., 1964), 10.

20. For a succinct statement of how the "cycle of poverty" idea informed community action, see John Wofford, "The Politics of Local Responsibility: Administration of the Community Action Program, 1964–1966" in Sundquist, *On Fighting Poverty*, 73.

21. For various accounts of how "maximum feasible participation" became part of the Economic Opportunity Act of 1964, see Adam Yarmolinsky, "The Beginnings of OEO," in Sundquist, *On Fighting Poverty*, 34–51; Daniel P. Moynihan, *Maximum Feasible Misunderstanding* (New York, 1969); Allen J. Matusow, *The Unravelling of America: A History of Liberalism in the 1960s* (New York, 1984), 244–245.

22. Alice O'Connor, "Community Action, Urban Reform, and the Fight Against Poverty," *Journal of Urban History*, 22 (July 1996): 586–625.

23. A classic statement of the "disorganization" thesis is Clifford R. Shaw, *Delinquency Areas: A Study of the Geographic Distribution of School Truants, Juvenile Delinquents and Adult Offenders in Chicago* (Chicago, 1929). For a discussion of Chicago school influences on later juvenile delinquency demonstration programs, see Daniel Knapp and Kenneth Polk, *Scouting the War on Poverty* (Lexington, Ky., 1971), 25–28. Leonard S. Cottrell, "The Competent Community," Speech delivered at the University of North Carolina, November 30, 1972, included in Summary Planning and Materials, Brandeis Conference on the war on poverty, JFK Library.

24. Richard Cloward and Lloyd Ohlin, *Delinquency and Opportunity* (New York, 1960), 211, quoted in Knapp, *Scouting*, 33; Robert Merton, "Opportunity Structure: The Emergence, Diffusion, and Differentiation of a Sociological Concept, 1930s–1950s," *The Legacy of Anomie Theory; Advances in Criminological Theory*, 6 (1985), 44–53.

25. Marc A. Weiss, "The Origins and Legacy of Urban Renewal," in J. Paul Mitchell, ed., *Federal Housing Policy and Programs, Past and Present* (New Brunswick, N. J., 1985), 253–276; James Q. Wilson, ed., *Urban Renewal: The Record and the Controversy* (Cambridge, 1966).

26. Leonard Duhl, ed., *The Urban Condition* (New York, 1963).

27. S. M Miller and Frank Reissman, "Social Change vs. the Psychiatric World View," in Miller and Reissman, eds., *Social Class and Social Policy* (New York, 1968), 261–274.

28. Herbert J. Gans, "Urban Poverty and Social Planning," in Paul F. Lazarsfeld et al., eds., *The Uses of Sociology* (New York, 1967), 437–476.

29. Sundquist, "The Origins of the War on Poverty," in *On Fighting Poverty*, 7–8; O'Connor, "Community Action," 611–612.

30. O'Connor, "Community Action"; Peter Marris and Martin Rein, *Dilemmas of Social Reform: Poverty and Community Action in the United States* (New York, 1967).

31. "Outlines of a Proposed Poverty Program," Memorandum to Department Secretaries from Kermit G. Hall and Walter Heller, January 6, 1964, Wilbur Cohen Papers, Wisconsin State Historical Society, Box 149, folder 6.

32. William F. Haddad, "Mr. Shriver and the Savage Politics of Poverty," *Harper's*,

231 (December, 1965): 43–46.

33. Matusow, *The Unravelling of America,* 246–250.

34. Thomas F. Jackson, "The State, the Movement and the Urban Poor: Political Mobilizing in the 1960s," in Michael Katz, ed., *The "Underclass" Debate: Views from History* (Princeton, N. J., 1993) 418–422.

35. Wofford, "The Politics of Local Responsibility," in Sundquist, *On Fighting Poverty.*

36. Matusow, *The Unravelling of America,* 250.

37. Saul D. Alinsky, "The War on Poverty—Political Pornography," *The Journal of Social Issues* 21 (1965): 41.

38. For a summary of CAP evaluations, see Alice O'Connor, "Evaluating Comprehensive Community Initiatives: A View from History," in James P. Connell, et al., *New Approaches to Evaluating Community Initiatives* (Washington, D.C., 1995), 39–47.

39. For a critical discussion of the political implications of this outcome, see Jackson, "The State, the Movement and the Urban Poor," in Katz, *The "Underclass" Debate,* 420–421.

40. O'Connor, "Community Action," 591–593. For a sharp critique of community action's failure to address racial inequality, see Charles Silberman, *Crisis in Black and White* (New York, 1964), 351–354

41. Much of the discussion below relies on Martha F. Davis, *Brutal Need: Lawyers and the Welfare Rights Movement, 1960–1973* (New Haven, 1993). For a useful review of the first ten years of the legal services movement, see also Ellen Jane Hollingsworth, "Ten Years of Legal Services for the Poor," in Robert H. Haveman, ed., *A Decade of Federal Antipoverty Programs: Achievements, Failures, and Lessons* (New York, 1977), 285–315.

42. Davis, *Brutal Need,* 22–39; Hollingsworth, "Ten Years," 293–294.

43. Davis, *Brutal Need,* 37, 99–118.

44. Michael B. Katz, *The Undeserving Poor: From the War on Poverty to the War on Welfare* (New York, 1989), 108–109; Charles Reich, quoted in Katz, *The Undeserving Poor,* 109.

45. Davis, *Brutal Need,* 99–118.

46. Ibid., 40–55; 142–145.

47. Katz, *The Undeserving Poor,* 107–108.

48. Davis, *Brutal Need,* 119–142.

49. Edward Sparer, "Discussion," in Haveman, *Decade of Federal Antipoverty Programs,* 324–327.

50. OEO Administrative History, LBJ Library, 610–612; Walter Heller to LBJ, "What Price Great Society?" December 21, 1965, LBJ Library, White House Central Files, Confidential Files, Box 98.

51. Sundquist, "The End of the Experiment?" in *On Fighting Poverty,* 235.

52. Haveman, *A Decade of Federal Anti Poverty Programs*

53. Levitan and Taggart, *The Great Society's Poor Law.*

DONALD T. CRITCHLOW

Implementing Family Planning Policy: Philanthropic Foundations and the Modern Welfare State

The expansion of the welfare state in the Johnson and Nixon administrations created a seeming paradox that remains apparent in the contemporary liberal regime: The rapid growth of nonprofit, voluntaristic sector occurred at the same time federal social policy became increasingly centralized and active. The parallel development of the centralized welfare state and the voluntary sector was no coincidence. The growth of federal social programs mobilized the nonprofit sector, while in turn the nonprofit sector, through policy innovation and program implementation, helped legitimize the modern welfare state.

Thus, as the traditional federal system that had existed since the founding of the nation eroded in the 1960s, when the federal government extended its powers at the expense of state power, the nonprofit sector was called upon to help design, implement, and administer social programs that had once been within the jurisdiction of the public sector.[1] As a consequence, the nonprofit sector expanded in the 1960s at the very time that the federal government enlarged its powers over the states. As one leading student of the nonprofit sector noted, "the voluntary sector, rather than constituting an alternative to the welfare state, was largely its creation."[2] The result produced an unusual phenomenon—government centralization produced greater nonprofit sector voluntarism.

In the years between 1965 and 1980 the American social welfare state underwent a significant transformation. During these years, the welfare state was expanded to include a new national health insurance plan for the elderly and the poor (Medicare and Medicaid), employment and training programs for the unemployed, and social service and housing aid for the disadvantaged. From 1965 through 1980, government spending on social welfare grew by 263 percent in inflation-adjusted dollars. Federal spending expanded from 11.5 percent of the gross national product in 1965 to 19.5 in 1976, before falling slightly to 18.5 percent in 1980. From 1965 through 1975, the great growth of these expenditures came from the creation of new programs. Furthermore, beginning in 1967, federal government spending on social welfare surpassed state and local government expenditures for the first time.[3]

The expansion of the welfare state, as Lester Salamon has observed, promoted the emergence of a government nonprofit partnership.[4] Increasingly in the 1960s, the federal government turned over the delivery of services to private nonprofit organizations. The federal government generated the funds but then turned actual delivery of services over to other public state and local organizations and private organizations. The private, nonprofit sector became a major beneficiary of this system of services. These services included hospital care to the elderly, support for research, and new social service and community development programs. By the 1980s, the federal government alone provided $40 billion in support to the private nonprofit sector, while state and local governments provided additional amounts from their own resources.

Federal demand enabled the nonprofit sector to grow by leaps and bounds. Indeed, in 1940 there were only 12,500 charitable, tax exempt organizations. By 1990, there were over 700 thousand, with most of this growth taking place after the 1960s.[5] While the federal government centralized social policy through congressional mandates, administrative and legislative regulations, and new funding arrangements, the delivery and implementation of these programs were placed in the hands of state and local governments and nonprofit organizations.

The result of this new welfare system—the second welfare state, if you will—blended public and private action. This "mixed" welfare state that emerged in the late 1960s and 1970s marked a creation unique to the United States, reflecting a deep-seated American tradition of associative enterprise that combines self-reliance and private voluntarism with communitarianism and government activity. An important feature of this second welfare state was the important role left to private, nonprofit organizations and to nongovernmental institutions in serving essentially public goals.[6]

The emergence of the second welfare state in the last three decades, contrary to the concerns of those who feared that government would replace the nonprofit sector altogether, created a vibrant nonprofit sector. Government, in turn, came to rely on this sector to design programs, undertake demonstration projects, implement new programs, contract with other private agencies, and provide outside consultation and independent review agencies and activities.

As this second welfare state emerged, the nonprofit sector was called upon to play a number of distinct functions. Nonprofit organizations served as *funding intermediaries* distributing funds to other parts of the nonprofit sector, *service providing organizations* involved in health care, education, counseling, adoption assistance, and *political action agencies* supporting particular pieces of legislation or candidates for political office. Of particular importance to this study is the role played by service-providing organizations. By providing public services, these nonprofit organizations developed a symbiotic relationship with the federal government. Although Americans contributed an average of $123 per person to various charitable causes in 1990, representing about 2.2 percent of the gross national product, considerably higher than most other countries, government grants, contracts and reimbursements accounted for 31 percent of nonprofit service organizations income. In turn, only 18 percent of total income that nonprofit organizations receive comes from private giving.[7]

The role of the nonprofit sector in the second welfare state has only begun to be explored by scholars.[8] Only a few scholars, those mostly interested in the so-called "independent sector," noted that a unique relationship had developed between the federal government and nonprofit organizations. As these scholars began to develop a basic taxonomy of nonprofit organizations, a debate emerged concerning whether nonprofit organizations are integral to government, indeed, even "inventions" of the modern welfare state, or whether these nonprofit organizations, as one student framed it, serve "a special niche in the organization universe because of their devotion to higher purposes."[9] Much of this debate framed the ramifications of this nonprofit-government symbiosis as an either-or proposition. Either the nonprofit sector is an invention of the new welfare state, or the nonprofit voluntarism presents an alternative to a failed welfare state.

An exploration of the involvement of the nonprofit sector, specifically the foundation community, in the development and implementation of family planning policy in the 1960s and 1970s presents a more complex view of the relationship between the nonprofit sector and federal government. Clearly, at least in this policy area, nonprofits simply did not emerge as passive creations necessitated by federal programming. Indeed, policy experts at the Rockefeller Foundation, the Population Council, and the Ford Foundation, as well as policy activists for the Planned Parenthood Federation of America and the Population Crisis Committee played a significant role in putting family planning on the policy agenda, drafting family planning regulations and legislation, and then implementing family planning programs. Their involvement in family planning policy reinforces the importance of the nonprofit sector to the development of the modern welfare state. At the same time, however, the activities of the Population Council and the Ford Foundation in developing and implementing family planning programs also reveal the limitations inherent in the second welfare state. In the end, both the

Population Council and the Ford Foundation withdrew from active participation in family programs in the United States when they discovered cooperation with the federal government was hampered by bureaucratic infighting, squabbling between local, state, and federal agencies, and intrusive government oversight. In the end, as family policy in the Johnson and Nixon period suggests, the new welfare state created a symbiosis between the public and private sectors, but this relationship remained uneasy, with neither party feeling fully comfortable with the other.

Prior to the 1960s, the federal government's involvement in family planning remained minimal. Nonetheless, family planning became an integral part of Johnson's war on poverty in the 1960s and was rapidly expanded in the 1970s as the Nixon administration sought to grapple with the "welfare mess." Both the Johnson and the Nixon administrations sought to use family planning as a means of addressing social problems concerning poverty, rising out-of-wedlock births, and income inequality in the United States. In order to employ family planning as a tool in welfare policy, the Johnson administration initially provided matching grants to state and local welfare agencies to develop family planning programs. In 1967, however, Congress enacted legislation through amendments to the Social Security Act that mandated state funding for family planning programs.

Throughout this decade, a well-organized population movement, composed of policy experts and activists, played a critical role in placing family planning on the political agenda. This population movement, supported by such philanthropic foundations such as the Population Council and the Ford Foundation, and private organizations such as Planned Parenthood of America, remained actively involved in each stage of the policy process from innovation through implementation. While population advocates remained divided as to strategy and urgency, there was a consensus that world and American populations were growing too fast and in haphazard ways. Their efforts set a context for the policy debate, helped formulate regulatory and legislative changes, and served to implement family planning services for federal, state, and local government agencies that often lacked an adequate family planning infrastructure.

An intensive lobbying effort by these organizations encouraged the Johnson and Nixon administrations to see family planning as vital to federal social programs. Beginning in the 1950s, key leaders from these organizations began to encourage federal officials within the executive office, the federal bureaucracy, and Congress to establish federally funded domestic and international family planning programs. At critical junctions in this campaign, leaders from these philanthropic organizations worked with the White House, the federal bureaucracy, and Congress to draft and support family planning legislation, while at the same time mobilizing public opinion in favor of federal funding of birth control programs. Indeed, the federal government's involvement in family planning would not have occurred as rapidly or intensely without the support of the foundation establishment and the population control movement.

Once having initiated family planning programs, however, the federal government turned to philanthropic organizations such as the Population Council and the Ford Foundation to establish pilot and demonstration family planning programs. These experimental programs, intended to serve as models for large scale programs, revealed the problems inherent in family planning itself and the inevitable tensions between government funding agencies and private organizations. Demonstration programs consistently revealed an inability to target poor populations, high incidence of dropout rates once programs were established, and a failure to find adequate methods of birth control acceptable to program recipients. Tensions arose between government funding agencies, operating under strict federal guidelines and through complex bureaucracies, and private organizations that sought programmatic and administrative flexibility in establishing their programs. By the early 1970s, the Population Council and the Ford Foundation abandoned servicing domestic family planning programs. Still, although both organizations continued to fund family planning projects domestically and internationally, the Population Council and the Ford Foundation disassociated themselves from activism and emphasized their earlier commitment to basic research in the medical and social sciences. This emphasis on research—a return to their original mission—entailed downplaying the activism witnessed in the mid-1960s and early 1970s, but reflected problems they had encountered in administering family planning programs sponsored by the federal government. At the same time, the perceived failure of these programs, internationally and domestically, led the foundation community and the population movement to retreat from family planning as a sole means of solving larger social and economic problems, including income disparity, the oppression of women, and racism.

Throughout this period, philanthropic organizations including the Population Council, Planned Parenthood, the Ford Foundation, and the Population Crisis Committee played a critical role in formulating family planning policy. The origins of the population movement lay in the post–World War II period when many social scientists foresaw an impending population crisis that threatened international economic development, world peace, and domestic tranquility. For these population experts, the Second World War revealed all too dramatically the tragic implications of what could happen when population outdistanced food and natural resources. This population movement as it emerged in the postwar period included a spectrum of opinion that divided as to the urgency of the population problem. On one side of this spectrum stood representatives of John D. Rockefeller 3d's Population Council, the Rockefeller Foundation, and the Ford Foundation that prided themselves on their scientific objectivity and their belief that while the population problem remained critical, the issue needed to be addressed gradually through political elites and high government officials. At the other end of the spectrum, activist groups such as the Population Crisis Committee, founded by millionaire Hugh Moore, viewed the population explosion as a national and global emergency that needed to be addressed immediately and, if necessary, with radical, coercive measures. Between the two ends stood groups such as Planned Parenthood of America that viewed the population issue primarily in terms of individual freedom and the right of families, especially women, to determine the spacing of their children. While these groups often coordinated their lobbying efforts, tensions among the groups found expression throughout this period. In turn, these differences as to urgency and strategy were represented in the federal government. The executive branch of the government during the Johnson and Nixon administrations, ever aware of the potential of political backlash, tended to pursue a gradualist approach to legislation and family planning programs. On the other hand, federal bureaucrats in Health, Education, and Welfare (HEW) and the Agency for International Development (AID) saw population control in more urgent terms.

In 1942, the Children's Bureau began quietly providing grants to state and local health departments for family planning services under Title V of the Social Security Act, but these programs remained narrow in scope. As the 1950s drew to a close, however, the population movement sought to lobby American policymakers to pursue more activist public policies. During the Eisenhower years, family planning, much like welfare, simply was not on the policy agenda. Indeed, a survey of public family planning programs conducted by Planned Parenthood in 1956 revealed that only seven states, mostly in the South, had birth control available to women for postpartum checkups.[10] Furthermore, when General William Draper, at the urging of Hugh Moore, tried to place family planning on the agenda in his "Report of the President's Committee to Study the United States Military Assistance Program," issued in 1959, Eisenhower rejected this aspect of the report.[11]

The advent of the Kennedy administration brought new opportunities for the population lobby to redirect policy. Population activists such as Mary S. Calderone of Planned Parenthood felt that Kennedy would be anxious to show he was not dictated to by the Catholic Church on policy matters.[12] Initial strategy called for bringing the United States government slowly into family planning through foreign aid. Population Council officer Frank Notestein observed that "Even without being directly involved in the birth control field there is a host of things our government can do which will be of great assistance to the recipient nations in fostering their own birth control programs."[13]

Early in the Kennedy administration, population activists initiated a series of meetings with the former president of the Rockefeller Foundation, Secretary of State Dean Rusk, Assistant Undersecretary of State Robert Barnett, National Security Adviser McGeorge Bundy, and other government officials. In these meetings, Population Council staff encouraged the promotion of family planning, but warned of a "danger of a backfire" from Roman Catholics, if this issue became too public. As a consequence, it was agreed that the population issue should be "stirred up" within the administration, without "going as far as advocating anything that would arouse strong vocal opposition in Congress."[14]

Concerned with potential political backlash, the Kennedy White House, while aware of these meetings, made a conscious decision to remain "neutral" on the population issue by not advocating a specific policy or specific program. Kennedy's reluctance to press the issue too quickly, therefore, kept the population issue on the back burner.[15] Instead, administrative officials began to test the waters in press conferences and public addresses mentioning a growing population problem. At the same time, Congress moved slowly forward by appropriating funds especially for family planning clinics in the District of Columbia.

The turning point in population policy came with the advent of the Johnson presidency. Working closely with the population lobby, although not dominated by it, the Johnson administration sought to link family planning to welfare assistance and to its foreign assistance programs.[16] Still the population issue remained "touchy." Public attitudes appeared to be changing on the subject, but ever the wary politician, Johnson did not want to get too far ahead of public opinion, and he feared alienating the Roman Catholic Church hierarchy if he moved too quickly.

Realizing that the family planning issue remained a sensitive one, the administration pursued an incrementalist approach. For example, AID provided assistance only in the development of health services, population censuses, and population surveys. Domestically, HEW still had not developed a formal policy on family planning, although a number of states primarily in the South had developed family planning programs. Similarly, Katherine B. Oettinger, director of the U.S. Children's Bureau, reported to Planned Parenthood that her agency was not pushing a birth control program with "great vigor," but she hoped that states would request Maternal and Child Health program funds for birth control. Claiming to be "rather ignorant" about fertility control she requested from PPFA a list of affiliates and medical staff to call upon for advice.[17]

Within Congress, the administration sought to establish a bipartisan foundation to move the issue further along.[18] In 1965, eight family planning bills were introduced in Congress and Senator Ernest Gruening (D-Alaska), a longtime advocate of family planning, opened hearings to urge that family planning be made available on a universal basis as a right to parents. In pursuing a bipartisan approach, the White House supported General William Draper's work with Republican congressional leaders to come out in support of family planning. In late 1966, Republican leaders drafted a statement on the population problem that called for a bipartisan approach to the problem.

In January 1966, the newly appointed Secretary of HEW, John Gardner, who had replaced Anthony Celebrezze the previous July, issued for the first time departmental regulations that made funds available to the states for family planning. The Johnson administration perceived these new regulations as "an important step" in linking the public assistance to family planning. Moreover, alarmed by the growing rate of out-of-wedlock births among poor blacks, the Johnson administration believed that new HEW regulations would "embolden" state and local agencies to ask for federal funds and technical assistance. When the Roman Catholic bishops backed away from opposing the HEW regulations, the administration was itself emboldened in pressing forward on the issue.[19] That May, Gardner created a new post, Deputy Assistant Secretary for Science and Population, headed by Dr. Milo E. Leavitt. Nevertheless, HEW's commitment to family planning remained minimal. In 1967, HEW employed only ten full-time professional staff members assigned to family planning.

Nevertheless, forty states by 1967 provided family planning services. At this point, appropriations for family planning remained modest, even as the OEO had launched fifty-five projects designed to provide family planning information and services to indigent women. These services were located in housing projects, churches, and local health centers, but services were still restricted to married women living with their husbands.[20] Moreover, the Children's Bureau had a budget of only $45 million in formula grants to states for family planning. In addition, the Public Health Service and the Office of Education administered modest family planning and sex education programs.[21] These various programs tied family planning into an integral part of Johnson's war on poverty. As one White House aide told Johnson, on "the value of family planning as a *social measure* . . . family planning is a crucial part of community efforts to reduce poverty and dependency. Office of Economic Opportunity researchers have concluded that family planning is probably the most effective anti-poverty program currently available."[22]

The Children's Bureau, along with the OEO, was one of the key agencies involved in federal family planning programs. In 1967, the bureau's family planning budget was increased to $50 million through its maternal and child health and maternity and infant care programs. Approximately 200 thousand women received support through these two programs, but the bureau was hamstrung by restrictions that limited matching grants to state and local agencies. This policy excluded voluntary agencies such as Planned Parenthood. Furthermore, although many states had established family planning programs, these efforts were uneven. The most active programs were in the South, while northern states such as Illinois and New York only had programs in their largest cities. In turn, South Dakota, Vermont, and Wisconsin provided no family planning services at all.[23] While federal officials noted these differences, they did not offer an analysis as to the disparity in between the states. One obvious explanation must rest in the influence of Roman Catholics in industrialized northern states, a feature that federal officials were not going to focus on readily in their reports.

By 1967, the administration was ready to press the population issue further when Johnson boldly declared in his State of the Union address that "next to the pursuit of peace, the really great challenge of the human family is the race between food supply and population increase . . . The time for concerned action is here, and we must get on with the job."[24] While Johnson referred primarily to overseas involvement, policy activists translated this call into a domestic agenda. In the summer of 1967, a review of HEW programs conducted by Frederick Jaffe (Planned Parenthood), Oscar Harkavy (Ford Foundation), and Samuel Wishik (Columbia University) led to the creation of a new position of Deputy Assistant Secretary for Population and Family Planning to be headed by Katherine Brownell Oettinger, former head of the Children's Bureau.[25]

Meanwhile, Congress enacted legislative changes that marked a critical turning point in federal family planning policy abroad. The Foreign Assistance Act (1967), under Title X, earmarked $35 million for family planning. The second piece of domestic legislation proved even more important, the Social Security Amendments of 1967. Proposed by congressmen George Bush (R-Texas) and Hermann Schnebele (R-Pennsylvania), the law earmarked that at least 6 percent of appropriated funds were to be designated for family planning projects through the Maternal and Child Health Services and the Maternal and Infant Care projects under HEW.[26] Under the amendment, states were required to make family planning available to all adult welfare recipients by July 1975. Specifically, this new legislation required state welfare agencies to develop family planning programs in order to prevent or reduce the incidence of out-of-wedlock births. Moreover, the amendment allowed the federal and state governments to grant family planning funds to private organizations such as Planned Parenthood.[27]

At the same time, Title XIX (Medicaid) of the Social Security Act was amended to provide family planning services for all married women eligible for Aid to Families with Dependent Children (AFDC). Because of the federal government's limited capacity for delivering family planning services, Congress hoped that Medicaid would provide provisions for family planning to the poor.

This legislation marked a profound shift in family planning policy, but it went generally unnoticed when the U.S. Senate became caught up in a debate over a workfare program proposed in the administration-backed bill.[28] As a consequence, the debate over the Social Security Amendments (1967) focused on this aspect of welfare reform—workfare—instead of family planning per se. In the end, workfare would be dropped from the final welfare bill, while comprehensive child and maternal health care was enacted. At the same time, the administration's legislative strategy opposed legislation proposed by Senator Ernest Gruening (D-Alaska) and Senator Joseph Tydings (D-Maryland) that explicitly called for categorical family planning grants and proposed a White House sponsored conference on family planning. White House congressional liaison Philip S. Hughes warned that "Our problem is that we don't need any legislation and that support of any bill specifically directed at birth control problems may actually set us back if it encounters serious obstacles in Congress." Similarly, Hughes feared that a White House Conference might "polarize public opinion, particularly at any time prior to the Pope's final decision on birth control."[29]

Nonetheless, a quiet revolution had occurred that went generally unnoticed by the public and the critics of family planning. The Office of Economic Opportunity issued new guidelines that gave local Community Action Program agencies the option of establishing their own eligibility criteria for family planning programs that no longer frowned on providing services to single women or those not living with their husbands. By late 1968, OEO was supporting 160 family planning programs in 36 states, Puerto Rico, and the District of Columbia. Additional services were provided through the OEO-funded Comprehensive Neighborhood Health Centers.[30]

Meanwhile, HEW appropriations through the Children's Bureau and other agencies were rapidly expanded. Maternal and child health service grants to states rose from $1.5 million in 1965 to $2.5 million in 1969. Special project grants for maternal and infant care, including family planning grants, rose from a mere $350,000 in 1965 to $21 million by 1969. Grants through the Children's Bureau maternal and child health care program and the maternity and infant care programs provided grants for family planning services for 300,000 women.[31] More importantly, under Title IV of the Social Security Amendments of 1967, states were mandated to offer family planning services to appropriate AFDC recipients. To fund these programs the federal government awarded matching grants at a rate of 85 percent through 1969, and 75 percent subsequently. In turn, other parts of the act provided funds for demonstration projects related to the prevention and reduction of dependency through family planning programs, family planning for the mentally retarded, medically indigent, Cuban refugees, American Indians, Alaska natives, and migrant agricultural workers and their families.[32]

Nevertheless, even as HEW officials touted the success of these programs, they worried that not enough was being done to contain, as one HEW staff member put it, a "burgeoning" population that threatened to overwhelm health care and social services. HEW officials complained that only a small portion of the 5.2 million poor women in need of family planning were being covered because of limited funding.[33] Although demographers challenged the figure of 5.2 million—a figure that had been arrived at by Planned Parenthood—it was clear that family planning programs were experiencing serious problems.[34] Surveys showed that in some programs there was a drop out rate of nearly 50 percent among clients. Furthermore, out-of-wedlock births were skyrocketing. Since 1950, there had been an increase of 83 percent in reported out-of-wedlock births.[35]

The election of a Republican to the White House elicited fears in population circles that family planning might fall off the presidential agenda, especially with the publication of *Humanae Vitae*, Pope Paul VI's encyclical issued in the summer of 1968 that reconfirmed the immutability of natural law doctrine.[36] They need not have worried, however. Nixon's concern with the spiraling rise in dependency and high incidence of out-of-wedlock births led his administration, guided by domestic advisor Daniel Moynihan, to see family planning as an instrument that could control welfare costs.[37]

On July 18, 1969, Nixon sent a message to Congress requesting that "we establish as a national goal family planning services within the next five years to all those who want them but cannot afford them." He asked for an increase for family planning to rise to $150 million within the next five years. He also called for the establishment of a President's Commission on Population Growth and the American Future, advocated by Rockefeller.[38]

Responding to Nixon's initiative, Congress enacted the Family Planning Services and Population Act (1970). Throughout the legislative process, the population lobby played a critical role. Planned Parenthood helped quarterback the hearings before the Senate subcommittee on Labor and Public Welfare, chaired by Thomas Eagleton (D-Missouri), leading the Senate to pass the bill unanimously.[39]

When John W. McCormick (D-Massachusetts), the seventy-eight-year-old Speaker of the House and a devout Catholic, tried to bottle the bill up in the House committee, the recently appointed chairman of the Population Crisis Committee, General Andrew O'Meara, also a Catholic, went to Cardinal Terence Cooke of New York to apply pressure on McCormick to release the bill from the committee. With McCormick's support, the bill was voted out of committee and passed the House, 298–32.[40]

The law established an Office of Population Affairs and a National Center for Family Planning Services in HEW. Moreover, Congress authorized $382 million for family planning services, research, personnel training, and educational activities. The act also established the long-sought Commission on Population Growth and the American Future.

Although Johnson and Nixon had created a legislative mandate to provide federal funding for family planning services, the government was forced to rely heavily on private health and local family planning clinics to deliver these services. Indeed, the war on poverty health programs awarded approximately 40 percent of its grants to Planned Parenthood. As a consequence Planned Parenthood, as well as private clinics, many of them that emerged from the women's health movement, became the principal vehicles for delivery of government financed family planning services to poor women.[41]

The involvement of philanthropic foundations in public policy and American politics brought its own set of problems, however. A critical report by the Treasury Department on tax abuses by philanthropic foundations issued in 1965 fueled congressional critics such as populist Wright Patman (D-Texas).[42] The Ford Foundation's support for voter registration drives in the South and school redistricting in Manhattan incensed conservative critics.[43] Further controversy came when it was discovered that in 1967 the Ford Foundation awarded grants to eight members of the staff of the late Senator Robert F. Kennedy (D-New York), with the personal approval of the foundation's new president McGeorge Bundy. Bundy's arrogant defense of these grants in early 1969 before the House Ways and Means Committee, then considering an omnibus tax reform bill, did little to assuage conservative critics. John D. Rockefeller 3d was able to thwart the most punitive parts of the House bill by issuing a separate report. He orchestrated the report through the Rockefeller-financed private Commission on Foundations and Private Philanthropy, chaired by Peter G. Peterson. Nonetheless, Congress enacted the Tax Reform Act (1969) that corrected many of the worst tax abuses of charitable organizations. These attacks revealed the Ford Foundation's vulnerability to accusations that it was not simply a nonpartisan, philanthropic institution interested in objective research.

From 1952, when the foundation first entered the population field, through 1977, when it reevaluated its activity in this area, the Ford Foundation committed $222 million to population work, the largest share (56 percent) going to reproductive sciences and contraceptive work.[44] While most of the Ford Foundation's activity involved international family planning and support for basic reproductive research, Ford became increasingly involved in domestic family planning programs. As early as 1962, the foundation's trustees affirmed their intention "to maintain strong efforts in the United States" in order to "achieve a break-through on the problems of demography, the motivational factors in family planning, and the political and social consequences of population control."[45] Even after it became evident that the Johnson administration was committed to family planning as a critical component of the war on poverty, the foundation worried that family planning services would not become "available to the extent implied by existing policy statements."[46]

This concern led the foundation to begin making small grants to support demonstration programs intended to improve the delivery of contraceptives and to catalyze major federal support for family planning. By initiating these demonstration programs, foundation officers believed that Ford's involvement in international family planning programs in developing countries should not detract from the importance of domestic interests. "As attention is turned to the question of social control of fertility in developing countries," a foundation report declared in 1968, "emphasis should also be given to population policy in the United States . . . As we prescribe for Delhi, so must we take account of Detroit."[47]

Beginning in 1966, the foundation made its first domestic grants totaling about $2 million. The purpose of these grants was to support experimental programs intended to improve delivery services, not to underwrite ongoing programs. Ford's most dramatic involvement in family planning came in Louisiana where the Ford Foundation supported the work of Dr. Joseph Beasley that led to the development of a statewide family planning program. Beasley's program quickly became touted as a model for family planning programs throughout the country and even internationally. With this first flush of success, Ford Foundation officers congratulated themselves on the role private philanthropy could play in supporting public programs. When charges of political corruption and misappropriation of funds began to circulate, however, the foundation distanced themselves from the program. The

Louisiana experiment provides an illustration of how anxious family planners were to implement programs to the point of overriding caution.

In 1965, more than half of Louisiana's black population, which constituted 30 percent of the state's general population, were poor. More than a fourth of the black families received public assistance.[48] Until 1965, the state of Louisiana did not have a single family planning clinic nor did Planned Parenthood have a single chapter in the state. That year, Beasley, a physician at the Tulane Medical School, established the Tulane Center for Population and Family Studies for the sole purpose of conducting a state survey on contraceptive practices among the indigent population. He focused his efforts on Lincoln Parish, a rural county where 43 percent of the women were in the lowest income group, and accounted for 94 percent of the illegitimate births. His studies showed that for every one dollar spent for family planning, the state would save over thirteen dollars on welfare costs. He realized that an argument linking reduced welfare costs by providing family planning services to poor black women would appeal to policymakers.

Armed with his findings, Beasley convinced the state attorney general to reinterpret the criminal code to allow for family planning services through county public health care agencies. Meanwhile, he carefully cultivated the Catholic Church hierarchy in the state to support his program. After a series of meetings—which critics later maintained were held in some of New Orlean's finest restaurants over bottles of old wine—the church officials took a position, that "We will not endorse, but we will not oppose." Beasley's first grant to establish a family planning program in Lincoln Parish came in 1965 from the HEW through the Children's Bureau. In 1967, the Ford Foundation awarded an additional $300 thousand to Beasley to assist his family planning program. This small demonstration program quickly proved a success as family planning services were extended to 75 percent of all poor women in the parish. Within two years, he claimed, births to indigent women declined 44 percent, compared with the decline of 25 percent in the four surrounding parishes. At the same time there was a corresponding decrease in total out-of-wedlock births and fewer births to teenagers. (Later critics charged that these figures were misleading since decreased fertility and out-of-wedlock births were evident throughout the state.)

In July 1967, he successfully extended his work to metropolitan New Orleans. Within the year HEW approved a $1.75 million grant to develop a statewide program. Operating with continued support from the Ford grant, specifically awarded for this purpose, Beasley was soon managing eighty-eight clinics in sixty-three parishes, reaching over 40 thousand women. The foundation provided funds for research, development, and evaluation, but suspicions began to arise regarding the accuracy of Beasley's figures. Nonetheless, by 1970 his program received another matching grant of $1.2 million from HEW for family planning. When the grant was held up by the HEW bureaucracy, Ford provided emergency funds to continue the "demonstration" aspects of the program. That the Ford Foundation had to supplement Louisiana's state programs in 1970, while federal funds were tied up in the HEW bureaucracy, only indicated some of the difficulties of a federal system of social programming. The Ford Foundation was forced to intervene because, in the words of a foundation officer, "this large scale federal funding is both inflexible and unpredictable from one year to the next."[49]

By 1972 Beasley had opened 148 clinics. During these years his program administered fifty-five grants from diverse public and private sources. Federal funds amounted to about $14 million. The organization employed 533 people, many of them black community outreach workers, and met an average monthly payroll of $260 thousand. Beasley moved to incorporate his operation into the Family Health Foundation that expanded its focus to comprehensive community health programs, early child education, and national and international family planning, supported by U.S. AID and Ford Foundation grants. The Louisiana program was replicated in Illinois and other states. One Ford Foundation officer concluded, Beasley has proved "beyond a doubt that the combination of strong leadership, sophisticated management techniques, high quality services, and adequate funding ensure a high degree of family acceptance in urban and rural areas. It is a useful model not only for other parts of the United States, but to some extent for other countries as well."[50] Pilot projects were proposed for Brazil, Colombia, Mexico, and Venezuela. The Family Health Foundation produced its own movie, *To Hunt with a Cat,* to promote its project. Beasley became a national spokesperson for family planning and was elected chairman of the Board of Directors of Planned Parenthood, appointed to a visiting endowed chair of population and public health at Harvard Medical School (funded by Hugh Moore), and served as a consultant to the World Health Organization, the State Department, the Agency for International Development, and the World Bank. There was even talk of a Nobel Prize.[51]

Yet as the Louisiana program expanded there developed a constant need for funds to keep the programs running. The liberalization of federal funds on a new nine-to-one match to state funds, and the liberalization of eligibility to include teenagers allowed Beasley to expand his client base further. Growing out-of-wedlock births among teenagers became a concern of the Family Health Foundation, as studies revealed that women under 21 years of age were four and one-half times as likely to incur an unintended pregnancy, while illegitimate births in the public hospital skyrocketed 40 percent from 1967 to 1970.[52] This insatiable demand for funds to keep the machine operating opened the foundation to political manipulation and attack.

In 1971, black militants began charging that the program was a racist program aimed at genocide in the African American community. At the same time, outreach workers in project areas reported intermittent harassment from Black Muslims. At one community meeting, one outreach worker repeated that it was disrupted by Muslims who accused her of being a "pill-pusher" and "a traitor to her race."[53] Neighborhood black political organizations such as Southern Organization for United Leadership (SOUL) and Community Organization for Urban Politics (COUP), funded by OEO and Model City, demanded patronage. Beasley promoted his critics into top management and hired other nationalist critics and their relatives in other positions. A system of kickbacks to black contractors and relatives of the governor Edwin Edwards was put into place. Talk of corruption became widespread.

Finally in December 1972 the Louisiana State Medical Society presented preliminary evidence that the Family Health Foundation had taken money from OEO and HEW for the same purposes. Four months later in April 1973 a federal grand jury requested by the medical society was convened. U.S. Attorney General Gerald Gallinghouse, charged Beasley with misuse of federal funds, mail fraud, obstruction of justice, and making false statements. Launching what Gallinghouse called the "most extensive investigation in the history of the state," the inquiry widened to include besides Beasley, Family Health Foundation officials, the governor's brother Marian, and top administrators of Tulane Medical School. Neither the Rockefeller nor Ford Foundations were accused of involvement in what became known in the state as "Our Own Little Watergate."

Federal and state investigations revealed that state politicians and their relatives had taken trips on foundation planes to Latin America, Washington, and other places; that the foundation had rented office space in Washington, D.C. as a base for lobbying the thirty-eight agencies that supported it and that in doing so it had spent federal money for entertainment, foreign travel, liquor, flowers, and apartments. Questions were raised about the misuse of private donations from the Rockefeller and Ford Foundations for federal matching grants. One audit revealed that political contributions had been made to two governors, two state senators, and a State Supreme Court justice. In the midst of this investigation, the Family Health Foundation placed Senator Joseph Tydings on retainer for $40 thousand a year and Harry Dent, former counsel to President Nixon for $20 thousand a year. Beasley tried also to fight back by buying television time to appeal for community support. It did little good. In the end the federal government found that $6.2 million had been improperly used. After three separate trials involving a variety of charges, Beasley was sentenced to two years in prison. After serving seventeen months in prison, his medical license was revoked. Beasley took a position in Health and Nutrition at Bard College in New York, where Ford Foundation grants permitted him to work on prenatal nutrition. To many in Louisiana, he remained a Robin Hood who had tried to help the poor, only to become ensnared in the Byzantine tangles of Southern politics.

The Louisiana experiment in family planning proved to be the most dramatic example of the political pitfalls that awaited the family planner on the state level. Bureaucratic entanglement was common and could frustrate the most conscientious of administrators. This was all too apparent in the Ford Foundation's experience in supporting Planned Parenthood programs in New York City. This experience represented the more typical experience for family planners in these years, although it proved to be no less successful than did the Louisiana program, albeit for different reasons.

In New York City, the Ford Foundation helped fund the activities of Planned Parenthood of New York City (PPNYC) in working with local and state agencies to develop family planning programs. In Harlem, the PPNYC coordinated local antipoverty agencies and local municipal hospitals in writing grants to the Human Resources administration. In Long Island PPNYC established the first permanent family service in the community, while helping to organize a clinic in South Brooklyn. In addition, PPNYC assigned a full-time staff nurse to provide assistance in setting up a clinic in south Brooklyn. Using a grant from the Ford Foundation, PPNYC trained personnel in thirty-nine different public and private agencies, and provided an orientation program for 641 family planning workers.

Nonetheless, PPNYC found itself quickly overextended and in deep financial problems. These problems were exacerbated when a feud erupted between the state Department of Social Services and the state Department of Health over the control of Medicaid funds. As a result of this fight, PPNYC did not receive Medicaid payments for services provided to lower-income women eligible for reimbursement. The dispute between the two state departments was so acrimonious that both sides refused to talk with each other, so private agencies were left in the lurch without Medicaid accreditation. These financial problems were further complicated when PPNYC's annual fund-raising campaign in 1967 fell far short, after a dispute with the national Planned Parenthood-World Population over fund raising. In 1970, the Ford Foundation was called upon to bail out PPNYC with another major grant to provide technical assistance to government agencies in family planning, including the training of administration and community personnel, technical assistance for community sponsored services, and identification and preparation for family planning programs throughout the city.

Still, by 1970, New York City's Human Resources Administration in cooperation with PPNYC had established sixteen community-based facilities, providing services to 40 thousand poor women, a threefold increase in six years. Nevertheless, a survey of these clinics showed that much of the personnel assigned to these clinics lacked proper training. Moreover, for all of its activities, PPNYC estimated that over a half-million indigent women still lacked access to family planning.[54] An obvious conclusion was that public agencies were incapable of providing personnel and services for indigent women, but that private agencies such as Planned Parenthood were a poor substitute for what these public agencies lacked.

Foundation officers found other kinds of problems in Baltimore. In 1971, the Ford Foundation provided a $250 thousand three-year grant to Planned Parenthood of Maryland to establish an experimental program aimed at preventing out-of-wedlock teenage pregnancies. By 1968, out-of-wedlock births in Baltimore had risen to 15 thousand births per year, even though the overall birth rate in the city was declining. Especially disconcerting was that among non-white girls sixteen years and younger, 20 percent had one or more out-of-wedlock births. Designed by Dr. Thomas Saski of the Department of Population and Family Health at Johns Hopkins University, the program targeted the racially mixed area of west Baltimore where out-of-wedlock birth was a particularly acute problem. The program set up an advisory council with representatives from the Urban League, Planned Parenthood, the Johns Hopkins School of Hygiene, the Baltimore City Health Department, as well as police, clergymen, educators, and antipoverty programs.

The program sent field workers into the schools and local neighborhoods to set up sex education programs. At the end of three years, field workers reported that "Programs of sex education and family life values in twelve to eighteen year olds in hard core poverty areas have been strikingly unsuccessful as out-of-wedlock births continued to rise." Field workers attributed the failure to the lack of adequate educational techniques and audio-visual materials, but the problems appear to have been deeper than just techniques and materials. White teenagers participating in the racially mixed programs quickly dropped out. Average attendance within the programs remained small, with most of the participants only attending once. Moreover, most of the girls that remained were the ones who were not sexually active. As the sexually active girls told one interviewer, they did not enroll in the program because they "could take care of themselves." In the end, the program was deemed a failure, although the Ford Foundation went ahead and funded another large grant for a similar program to the New York City Board of Education. One foundation officer lamented that "it is of course unfortunate that lessons learned in the Baltimore project were not fully available at the time the staff work was being done on the grant for the program in New York."[55]

These demonstration programs reveal the problems inherent in delivering family planning services to the poor: Even when access to family planning services were available, participation remained low, dropout rates high, and complaints about the side effects of contraception—whether oral or mechanical—were persistent. The net effect was that out-of-wedlock births continued to climb, while family planning appeared to have little affect in addressing deeper social problems underlying domestic poverty.

Even when family planners touted the success of these programs, they worried that not enough was being done to contain, as one HEW staff member put it, a "burgeoning" population that threatened to overwhelm health care and social services.[56] Surveys showed that in some programs there was a dropout rate of 50 percent among clients. Similarly, a detailed study of federally financed family planning programs in the St. Louis region showed dropout rates on average were 38 percent. The rate coincided with general rates of women discontinuing use of contraceptives. For example, a Princeton National Fertility Study estimated that approximately 6.4 million women have used oral contraceptives since 1960, but of these, one-third of them had discontinued its use, largely because of unpleasant side effects.[57] A study of Minnesota women using oral contraceptives showed that over half had discontinued use within five years of initation.[58]

One of the most innovative programs designed to address some of the problems—rising out-of-wedlock births, inability to reach target populations, poor delivery systems, and low retention—came from a Population Council demonstration program, funded by HEW and OEO, that utilized major metropolitan and university hospitals to target inner-city recently postpartum women for contraception and sterilization.[59] Concerned with the federal government's inability to deliver contraception services either directly or through funding state and local agencies, HEW officials turned to the Population Council in 1971 to establish a demonstration family planning program that would use the existing health infrastructure, metropolitan hospitals, to ensure that family planning reached into the inner city. The idea that postpartum women would be most open to enrolling in a family planning program or undergoing sterilization had been developed by the Population Council in its international family planning programs. Early experiences in family planning programs suggested to HEW officials that locating family planning programs in postpartum clinics was economical and efficient.[60]

Although funded by OEO in 1968, the Population Council had developed its postpartum program two years earlier. The program had started with a few hospitals in developing countries and quickly expanded to twenty-six hospitals in fifteen countries. The effectiveness of this program suggested that a similar program might be developed in the United States. In early spring 1968, a series of meetings were initiated by John D. Rockefeller 3d with the representatives of leading medical schools, the Ford Foundation, the Urban League, deans of nineteen major medical schools, Planned Parenthood, and OEO/HEW officials to develop a demonstration postpartum program. At these meetings OEO officials felt a national family planning program was "unrealistic and unworkable" given the current delivery system. Specifically, Philip R. Lee, assistant secretary for HEW, noted that direct funding of programs had proved much more effective than working through various local and state departments of health.[61]

By November 1968, the Population Council had prepared a detailed proposal for setting up the family planning program. The program called for thirteen medical schools to extend family planning services for the poor in their respective communities. Aimed at reducing teenage pregnancies and illegal abortions, the hospital program targeted patients hospitalized for delivery or abortion or who were in postpartum clinics.

The administration of the program appeared clear on paper. The Office of Economic Opportunity provided the funds for the project; the Population Council administered the program; and the hospitals extended family planning in their communities through postpartum clinics. "The medical school center, with its broad base of knowledge and medical manpower," the proposal declared, "has the greatest capability of all health care providers to direct a truly comprehensive family planning program."[62]

In order to ensure flexibility, each school was allowed to structure its own program within the general guidelines. For example, medical schools at Case Western University, Emory University, Johns Hopkins University, University of Florida, and West Virginia University worked closely with county health and local family planning clinics, while Albert Einstein Hospital, Yale University, New York Medical College, Temple University, and Wayne State University coordinated their efforts with local departments of health and welfare, as well as local OEO programs. Many of the hospitals established sex education programs through local boards of education or local Neighborhood Youth Corps agencies. All the programs were expected to involve community neighborhood associations and to have community representatives on the board, as dictated by OEO policy.

The program appeared innovative, designed to incorporate a variety of approaches while promising an opportunity to expand the program to hospitals and medical facilities across the country. Moreover, the program offered a solution to the lack of infrastructure that federal officials in HEW and OEO saw as detrimental to a national family planning program. Through federal and nonprofit sector cooperation, the program provided a means of addressing growing social problems related to poverty, teenage birth, illegal abortions, and inadequate sex education.

Nonetheless, for all its promise the program got off to a rocky start. Although HEW/OEO officials expressed deep enthusiasm for the program, funding was delayed in what the Population Council saw as bureaucratic incompetence at the HEW. After one meeting in a series of lengthy meetings, one Population Council representative reported in a confidential memorandum, "All in all, a worthless meeting, hastily arranged by HEW, even though considerable lead time was given, and without adequate preparation on their part." So upset was he by these bureaucratic delays, Bernard Berelson, president of the Population Council, wrote HEW official Phillip Lee that "I feel bound to report to you how disappointed and personally distressed I am at the outcome. In view of the department's statements about the high priority given to population and family planning matters, I had hoped that such difficulties would be overcome."[63] In turn, Berelson felt that the medical school group was being "used" by Katherine Oettinger, head of HEW family planning, to protect her budget from congressional cutbacks.[64]

After nearly two years of planning and bureaucratic wrangling, the project was launched in June 1969 with a $1.9 million grant. The guidelines established by the OEO, however, proved burdensome for both the Population Council and the medical schools. From the outset problems arose between the Population Council and OEO when contract letters failed to go out to the medical schools. While OEO officials assured the Population Council that it understood that it would be integral to all "policy deliberations," OEO criticized the council for inefficiency for not providing five copies of quarterly reports to be submitted by the fourteen hospital projects. In turn, the medical schools complained about having to issue monthly reports that were administratively burdensome and costly. At the same time, reimbursements from OEO were often delayed so that medical schools and the Population Council were placed in the position of having to cover $913 thousand in reimbursements to the projects in the first year.[65] Moreover, OEO continued to complain that the medical schools were not including representatives from the communities they were serving and were not serving the poor. As a consequence, the Population Council often felt that it was caught in the middle between overly demanding and hostile federal bureaucrats who did not understand the projects and medical schools that were upset by the lack of support. The consequence was that the Population Council, as one officer wrote, was getting it in "the neck from both sides. We get the chores of doing OEO's budget cutting dirty work and their administration."[66]

Meanwhile, the medical school projects had run into a number of difficulties that revealed the problems of administering family planning projects in poor communities. A review of the program by the Westinghouse Learning Corporation issued early in the 1970s disclosed myriad problems inherent in the programs. Westinghouse reported that medical school officials particularly resented OEO restrictions on sterilization and abortion because they hurt family planning projects, even though a number of projects continued to perform abortions and sterilizations. At the same time, many of the projects had met with "active resistance by racial and religious elements" within the community.[67]

For example, the Harlem Hospital and Columbia Presbyterian Hospital came under attack by militant blacks for running a "genocidal program." In a pamphlet published by the United Black Front, a community group, the projects were accused of not informing young blacks of the "dangerous after-effects of birth control pills or abortions." The United Black Front accused the hospitals of pursuing a policy set by "City Elders of Protocol" who feared a growing black population. The inflammatory pamphlet declared, "Under the supervision of Dr. Donald P. Swartz, a Zionist sympathizer, abortions are now being performed on our young Black women of Harlem on a massive basis . . . Dr. Swartz has successfully murdered more than 800 unborn Black babies in less than two months time." The United Black Front declared, "either we get off our rear ends, on our own, and fight for our survival as a people, or else just lay down and die."[68] While the Population Council felt that "Black Power" resistance was only episodic, family planning needed to change its "sales image by broadening community representation.[69]

Other projects came under attack as well. The University of Chicago Medical School project drew heavy criticism from black leaders who raised similar charges of "genocide." Moreover, the Westinghouse study found that many of these projects continued to perform sterilizations and abortions, although this went against federal guidelines. The Johns Hopkins project under Hugh Davis, the inventor of the Dalkon Shield, openly pursued a policy of sterilization and abortion. Davis noted that 16 percent of women using his East Baltimore clinic had selected surgical sterilization. "Sterilization in the female," Davis declared, "has been made simple, economical, and exceedingly convenient, and the acceptance in our patients is a testimonial to the ready availability and effectiveness of the procedure. We hope that improved methods of sterilization, abortion, and birth control will become more widely available."[70] Support for postpartum sterilization found favor at the Wayne State University family planning project in Detroit and the Emory University project in Atlanta, in clear violation of OEO guidelines.

These violations only exacerbated tensions between the OEO and the

Population Council. OEO officials demanded that funds not be used for abortion and sterilization. At the same time, OEO officials criticized projects for not including community representatives on their boards and for not implementing projects that targeted the poor. For example, Emory University's program served only college students. When the OEO tried to set a series of conditions for renewing the grant in early 1970, the Population Council informed OEO it was dropping out of the project. The project continued for another year, but the Population Council's withdrawal doomed the project.

By the mid-1970s, both the Population Council and the Ford Foundation had withdrawn from active participation in family planning programs in the United States. Within both organizations, officers felt that active involvement in providing family planning services had detracted from their missions to provide basic medical and social science research and to develop policy innovations. At the same time, the expansion of public state and local family planning programs no longer necessitated the direct involvement of the Population Council and the Ford Foundation in family planning programming. Moreover, foundation officers concluded that the time and money spent in developing these programs had been wasted.

Although the family planning experiment with the Population Council and the Ford Foundation was short-lived, the federal government, nonetheless, continued to rely heavily on the nonprofit organizations, such as Planned Parenthood Federation of America, to provide family planning services. Indeed, approximately 40 percent of PPFA's annual budget came from federal funds. Yet the politicization of family planning following the *Roe v. Wade* (1973) decision placed PPFA at the center of a political maelstrom.[71] As a consequence, PPFA has found its own program development and flexibility restrained by federal restrictions. In this way, the nonprofit sector, as it has developed a symbiotic relationship to the public sector in the modern American welfare state, has found itself no longer so private and less immune from the vicissitudes of partisan politics.

Notes

This article draws from the author's forthcoming book on federal family planning policy to be published by Oxford University Press in 1998.

1. The expansion of grant-in-aid conditions in the public assistance program is discussed in Martha Derthick, *The Influence of Federal Grants: Public Assistance in Massachusetts* (Cambridge, Mass., 1970). For the erosion of the federal system in the 1960s, see Martha Derthick, "Crossing Thresholds: Federalism in the 1960s,"

Journal of Policy History 8:1(1996): 64–81. Derthick's work casts new meaning on what scholars have described as the "new federalism," as it emerged in this period. New federalism, as a reform idea and structure projected by its proponents, was a system that sought to balance federal mandates and funding with state and local interests. See Timothy Conlan, *New Federalism: Intergovernmental Reform from Nixon to Reagan* (Washington, D.C., 1988).

2. Peter Dobkin Hall, *Inventing the Nonprofit Sector and Other Essays on Philanthropy, Voluntarism, and Nonprofit Organizations* (Baltimore, 1992), 7.

3. These figures are drawn from Lester M. Salamon, *America's Nonprofit Sector: A Primer* (Baltimore, 1992), 45–46.

4. Salamon, *America's Nonprofit Sector*, 46.

5. Hall, *Inventing the Nonprofit Sector*, 14.

6. The role of nonprofit institutions in the modern welfare state has only begun to be explored. An excellent beginning point in understanding the new welfare state is Neil Gilbert, *Capitalism and the Welfare State: Dilemmas of Social Benevolence* (New Haven, 1983) and Sheila B. Kameran and Alfred J. Kahn, *Privatization and the Welfare State* (Princeton, 1989). An important study of the nonprofit sector is Eleanor L. Brilliant, *The United Way: Dilemmas of Organized Charity* (New York, 1990). Also, Steven Rathgeb Smith and Michael Lipsky, *Nonprofits for Hire: The Welfare State in the Age of Contracting* (Cambridge, 1993). Lester M. Salamon has explored the nonprofit sector in a number of studies including, *America's Nonprofit Sector: A Primer* (Baltimore, 1992) and Lester M. Salamon and Alan J. Abramson, *The Federal Budget and the Nonprofit Sector* (Washington, D.C., 1982). Useful essays on the nonprofit sector are found in Lester M. Salamon, ed., *Beyond Privatization: The Tools of Government Action* (Washington, D.C., 1989).

7. These figures are found in Lester M. Salamon, *America's Nonprofit Sector*, 25–26.

8. An important exploration of the nonprofit sector is Hall, *Inventing the Nonprofit Sector*.

9. Hall, *Inventing the Nonprofit Sector*, 14. The view that nonprofits are integral to government is found in Lester Salamon, "Partners in Public Service: The Scope and Theory of Government Nonprofit Relations," in W. W. Powell, ed., *The Nonprofit Sector: A Research Handbook* (New Haven, 1988), 89–117; and Henry Hansmann, "Economic Theories of the Nonprofit Sector," in *The Nonprofit Sector*, 27–42. This debate suggested profound ideological and political consequences. Both liberals and conservatives alike viewed the nonprofit, voluntary sector as more flexible, responsive, and democratic than the federal bureaucracy. Yet, if the nonprofit sector was a creation of the federal government this suggested than the nonprofit, voluntary sector could not exist without the infusion of subsidies, earned revenues, and contracts from the public sector. Cuts in federal social spending thereby implied downsizing the nonprofit sector, the very place fiscal and social conservatives hoped to bolster as a replacement for federal welfare state. Furthermore, this relationship suggested that nonprofits enjoyed less flexibility in policy development and program implementation.

10. Miriam F. Garwood to Dr. William Vogt, July 5, 1956, Subject file, Public Health, Planned Parenthood Federation of America Papers (PPFA), Smith College (hereafter PPFA).

11. For a discussion of the issue within the Eisenhower administration, see Draper

Committee, President's Committee to Study the United States Military Assistance Program (MAP) 1958–1959, Boxes 1–17, the Dwight D. Eisenhower Library.

After leaving office, Eisenhower came to believe that the population problem was one of the "most critical problems facing mankind," warning of "riotous explosions" at home and abroad unless the problem was faced head-on. Still, in 1959, he believed it was not "the function of the federal government to interfere in the social structures of other nations by using . . . American resources to assist them in a partial stabilization of their numbers." By 1965, however, Eisenhower was willing to support family planning abroad as well as within the United States. He specifically recommended that if welfare were not tied to family planning, "then history will rightly condemn us." We find ourselves, he wrote, in a "curious position of spending money with one hand to slow up population growth among responsible families and with the other providing financial incentive for increase production by the ignorant, feeble-minded or lazy." Dwight D. Eisenhower to Senator Ernest Gruening, June 18, 1965, Post Presidential papers, 1961–1969, Eisenhower Library.

For Eisenhower's views on family planning see Clifford Roberts to William H. Draper, February 28, 1966, Special Name Series, Box 16; William H. Draper to Dwight D. Eisenhower, December 21, 1963, Office files, Box 33; Dwight D. Eisenhower to William H. Draper, December 30, 1963, Office files, Box 33; William H. Draper to General Dwight D. Eisenhower, December 26, 1964, Office files, Box 33; William H. Draper to Dwight D. Eisenhower, December 8, 1964, Office files, Box 33; William H. Draper to General Dwight D. Eisenhower, November 18, 1964, Office files, Box 33; William H. Draper to General Dwight D. Eisenhower, September 28, 1964, Office files, Box 33; William H. Draper to General Dwight D. Eisenhower, March 6, 1964, Office files, Box 33; and Dwight D. Eisenhower to H. J. Porter, November 20, 1964, Office files, Box 49 in Dwight D. Eisenhower Library.

For Moore's influence on the Draper Report, see Hugh Moore to General William H. Draper, April 25, 1959, Box 17; and Hugh Moore to William H. Draper, July 9, 1965, Box 17, Moore papers.

12. Mary S. Calderone to Cass Canfield, June 24, 1960, Canfield files from 1960, PPFA.

13. Frank W. Notestein to Louis T. Rosenberg, November 16, 1961, RG 2, Box 45, Rockefeller Archives (hereafter RA).

14. While the Population Council cultivated relations with the Kennedy administration, Cass Canfield and General Draper from Planned Parenthood conducted a series of meetings with other Kennedy officials including Dean Rusk, McGeorge Bundy, Walter Rostow, Averill Harriman, and George McGhee. It was also agreed to "educate" key members of Congress. Cass Canfield to Winfield Best, February 20, 1962, RG IV3B4.6 Box 122, RA.

15. Minutes of Population Council Staff (April 5, 1962), RG IV3 B4.6, Box 128; and Cass Canfield to Frank Notestein, March 6, 1962, RG IV3B4.6, Box 122; in RA. Lester R. Gordon to the White House, November 25, 1963, National Security Files, Box 38, Lyndon Baines Johnson Library (hereafter LBJ Library).

In late 1962, Richard N. Garner, speaking before the Economic and Financial Committee of the United Nations General Assembly declared that "The United States is concerned about the social consequences of its own population trends and is devoting attention to this problem." Richard N. Garner, Deputy Assistant Secretary for

International Affairs, "Population Growth: A World Problem" (December 10, 1962), National Security Files, Box 38, LBJ Library. This speech was published in a State Department pamphlet, "Population Growth: World Problem—Statement of U.S. Policy" (Washington, D. C., 1963).

16. Cass Canfield of Planned Parenthood reported that administration officials were discussing steps to "activate the government in population matters" after the 1964 election. Hugh Moore to John D. Rockefeller 3d, October 26, 1964, Box 17; and Philip R. Lee, Director, AID Health Service to Hugh Moore, June 18, 1964, Box 17, Moore papers.

17. Richard Day to Allan Guttmacher, April 12, 1965, Subject File, Children's Bureau, PPFA.

18. Douglass Cater to the President (December, 6, 1966), Central Files, Welfare, Box 1, in LBJ Library.

19. The importance of the new HEW regulations to the Johnson administration is discussed in Harry C. McPherson, Jr. to the President, January 5, 1966, Douglass Cater File, Box 66, LBJ Library.

When the Catholic bishops protested, HEW delayed sending out its new regulations. After a series of meetings, the bishops proved, "quite conciliatory." Wilbur Cohen told Johnson, "There's a moral in that." The Johnson administration, however, feared "flack" from the Catholic block in Congress by Hugh Carey or Clem Zablocki. Harry C. McPherson to Bill Moyers, January 28, 1966, Douglass Cater file, Box 66, LBJ Library.

20. An overview of national family planning programs operating on the federal level is provided in a Ford Foundation pamphlet, Gordon W. Perkins and David Radel, *Current Status of Family Planning Programs in the United States* (New York, 1966), located in the Ford Foundation Archives (hereafter FA).

21. The Public Health Service provided family planning through its comprehensive health services for Native Americans, Alaskan natives, and dependents of uniformed services personnel. In turn, the Office of Education had funded 645 projects for developing family life and sex education projects. The U.S. Department of Health, Education and Welfare, *Family Planning, Fertility, and Population Dynamics* (September 1966) (Washington, D.C., 1966).

22. Douglass Cater, "Family Planning Services in Public Health Programs," September 1966, Douglass Cater File, in LBJ Library.

23. Arthur J. Lesser, Memorandum, July 25, 1967, Children's Bureau Records, Box 1142; and Joseph H. Meyers, Commissioner of Welfare to Mr. Wilbur Cohen, July 19, 1967, Children's Bureau Records, Box 1142, National Archives.

24. Lyndon B. Johnson, "State of Union Address, (1967)," *Public Papers of the Presidents of the United States; Lyndon B. Johnson, 1963–1969*, (Washington, D.C., 1963–1969).

25. Oscar Harkavy, Frederick S. Jaffe, Samuel M. Wishik, "Implementing DHEW Policy on Family Planning and Population: A Consultant's Confidential Report," September 1967, in Oscar Harkavy File, FA.

26. Both Bush and Schnebele had close associations with the family planning movement. Bush's father, Prescott Bush had promoted birth control as a Senator from Connecticut and Schnebele had been Nelson Rockefeller's college roommate. U.S. Congress, Senate Committee on Finance, *Social Security Amendments of 1967; Hearings on H.R. 10280* (Washington, D.C., 1967).

For John D. Rockefeller 3d's involvement in this legislation see Douglass Cater to John D. Rockefeller, May 8, 1968, Ervin Duggan Office Files, Box 12, LBJ Library.

27. For the importance of this new legislation see Katherine B. Oettinger to John Gardner, October 11, 1967, Children Bureau Records, Box 1142; Dr. Philip R. Lee to John Gardner, December 6, 1967, Childrens Bureau Records, Box 1142; and Arthur J. Lesser to Don Haider, April 8, 1968, Children's Bureau Records, Box 1143, National Archives.

28. The proposed workfare program gained the support of the House, which wanted punitive measures to freeze aid to mothers of children born out of wedlock, but immediately drew opposition from liberals in the Senate, led by Senator Robert Kennedy, state and local welfare administrators, and the Catholic Church. James Jones to Harry McPherson, April 4, 1967, Legislative files, Box 165; W. Rommel to Harry McPherson, September 30, 1966, Legislative files, Box 165; Wilbur J. Cohen, to Lyndon Baines Johnson, July 14, 1967, Legislative files, Box 164; and Douglass Cater to Joseph Califano, December 22, 1967, Legislative files, Box 164, in LBJ Library.

29. Philip S. Hughes to Harry McPherson, February 1, 1967, Legislative files, Box 164, LBJ Library. Without administration support, the Gruening and Tyding bills were doomed. United State Congress, *Population Crisis; Hearings Before the Subcommittee on Foreign Aid Expenditures of the Committee on Government Operations on S. 1676 Eighty-Ninth Congress, First and Second Sessions* (Washington, D.C., 1966).

30. Office of Economic Opportunity, *Family Planning* (Washington, D.C., 1969), 2.

31. Department of Health Education and Welfare, "Report on Family Planning Activities; A Report to the House Committee on Appropriations," (1968), in Ervin Duggan Files, Box 12, LBJ Library.

32. Secretary of HEW, John W. Gardner, "Family Planning Policy," January 31, 1968, Douglass Cater Papers, Box 66, LBJ Library. Also, Mrs. E. Switzer to Katherine B. Oettinger, January 22, 1968, Children's Bureau Files, Box 1142, National Archives; Katherine B. Oettinger, "Family Planning Program Objects," Douglass Cater Files, Box 66, LBJ Library; and Philip R. Lee, "Report of the Special Study Group on the Provision of Family Planning Services," October 1968, Wilbur Cohen File, LBJ Library.

33. Dr. Carl S. Schultz to HEW Secretary, "Constraints in the Development of Domestic Family Planning Service," July 29, 1968, Children's Bureau Records, Box 1142, National Archives; and Dr. Arthur J. Lesser, "Family Planning, Present and Proposed Activities, FY 1968–1969," n.d., Children's Bureau Records, Box 1143, National Archives.

34. Judith Black, "The Fallacy of the Five Million Women: A Reestimate," *Demography* 9:4 (November 1972), 569–588.

35. Arthur J. Lesser, "Children's Bureau Family Planning Programs," October 3, 1967, Children's Bureau Records, Box 1143, National Archives.

36. Rockefeller kept a close watch on the early Nixon administration to see where the new president stood on family planning. He was pleased to note that Katherine Oettinger's position as Assistant Secretary of Health and Population was continued in the new administration with the appointment of Louis Hellman, a longtime advocate of family planning. Bernard Berelson, "Memorandum Regarding Conversation with Carl Shultz," March 10, 1969, RG 5, RA.

Rockefeller wrote to HEW Secretary Robert Finch and presidential adviser Daniel Patrick Moynihan, "In my opinion the present administration has a real and exciting opportunity" to make the transition from concern to action in family planning. "There is so much that needs to be done and time is running out," he wrote on another occasion. Rockefeller to Daniel Moynihan, February 13, 1969, RG 5, RA; Rockefeller to Daniel Moynihan, March 26, 1969; and Rockefeller to Lee A. DuBridge, Science Adviser to the President, March 26, 1969, John D. Rockefeller 3d Papers (in process), RA.

37. Joan Hoff in her revisionist history of the Nixon administration, *Nixon Reconsidered* (New York, 1994), especially pp. 119–129, downplays Moynihan's role in domestic affairs, but the archival evidence shows that Moynihan played a critical role in promoting family planning in the administration. He helped draft the legislation, guide it through Congress, and then served as the presidential liaison to the Rockefeller Commission on Population Growth and the American Future. Hoff does not discuss family planning within the Nixon administration. Also, on the inner workings of the Nixon administration see A. James Reichley, *Conservatives in an Age of Change: The Nixon and Ford Administrations* (Washington, D.C., 1989) and Rowland Evans, Jr. and Robert D. Novak, *Nixon in the White House: The Frustration of Power* (New York, 1970).

38. Working with the administration, Rockefeller successfully lobbied Congress for legislation establishing the commission. Congress also enacted the Family Planning services and Population Act (1970) that established a National Center for Family Planning Services in HEW and authorized over the next three fiscal years $382 million for family planning services. Rockefeller and the White House staff carefully tracked legislation creating the new commission. In this regard, Rockefeller was pleased to report that congressman George Bush had "facilitated handling of the bill by arranging its transfer from the Mills committee to the Committee on Government Operations." Ronald Freedom to Rockefeller, October 1, 1969, John D. Rockefeller 3d papers (in process), RA.

Also, U.S. Congress, Senate, *Family Planning Services: Hearings Before the Subcommittee on Public Health and Welfare of the Committee on Interstate and Foreign Commerce on H.R. 15159, H.R. 9107, H.R. 9109, H.R. 19109, and H.R. 15691*, Ninety-First Congress, Second Session (Washington, D.C., 1970). The "Statement of House Republican Task Force on Earth Resources and Population" is reprinted in the hearings, 199–200. See also, Thomas B. Littlewood, *The Politics of Population Control* (Notre Dame, 1977).

39. U.S. Congress, *Family Planning and Population Research, 1970 Hearings Before the Subcommittee on Health of the Committee on Labor and Public Welfare Ninety-First Congress* (Washington, D.C., 1970); also Thomas B. Littlewood, *The Politics of Population Control*, 53–57.

40. Hugh Moore to A. W. Schmidt, December 31, 1970, Box 17, Moore Papers.

41. See Lester M. Salamon, *Partners in Public Service: Government-Nonprofit Relations in the Modern Welfare State* (Baltimore, 1995).

42. U.S. Congress, *Treasury Department Report on Philanthropy*, House Committee on Ways and Means, 8901, February 2, 1965 (Washington, D.C., 1965).

43. John Ensor Harr and Peter J. Johnson, *The Rockefeller Conscience: An American Family in Public and Private* (New York, 1991), 289–300; and Waldemar Nielson, *The Big Foundations* (New York, 1972).

44. Ford Foundation, "The Foundation's Strategy for Work on Population," Confidential Memorandum, June 1977, FA.

45. Ford Foundation, "Policy Paper on Population," March 28/29, 1963, FA.

46. Gordon W. Perkins and David Radell, *Current Status of Family Planning Programs in the United States* (New York, 1966).

47. Ford Foundation, "Ford Foundation's Activities in Population," August 1968, Oscar Harkavy files, FA.

48. For a fascinating account of Beasley and the Louisiana family planning program, see Martha C. Ward, *Poor Women, Powerful Men; America's Great Experiment in Family Planning* (Boulder, 1986). This discussion draws heavily from Ward's fine account of the Louisana family planning program. Also, Thomas B. Littlewood, *The Politics of Population Control* (Notre Dame, 1977), 88.

49. Ford Foundation, "Ford Foundation's Activities in Population," August, 1968, Harkavy files; Ford Foundation, "Tulane University; Partial Support of a Family Planning Demostration Program for New Orleans and State of Louisiana," March 30, 1970, RG 670-0140 (microfilm), FA. Also, U.S. Senate, *Family Planning and Population Research, 1970* (Washington, D.C., 1970), 66–70.

50. David Bell to McGeorge Bundy, "Support to Family Planning Programs: Demonstration of New Orleans and Louisiana Family Planning," June 32, 1972, FA.

51. Ward, *Poor Women*, 73.

52. Ward, *Poor Women*, 82–83.

53. Ward, *Poor Women*, 91–97, quotation 93.

54. David R. Gwatkin to Oscar Harkavy (April 30, 1968), and Planned Parenthood of New York City, Inc. File, January 28, 1968, RGA 680-0770, FA.

55. "Support for an Education and Contraceptive Service Program for Teenagers in Cooperation with Baltimore Urban League and Johns Hopkins University, February 28, 1971, in Planned Parenthood Association of Maryland, Inc. File (microfilm); and Robert S. Wickham to Oscar Harkavy, August 28, 1975, Evaluation of Grant 680-0200, in Planned Parenthood Association of Maryland File, FA.

56. Dr. Carl S. Schultz to HEW Secretary, "Constraints in the Development of Domestic Family Planning Service," July 29, 1968, Children's Bureau Records, Box 1142, National Archives; and Dr. Arthur J. Lesser, "Family Planning, Present and Proposed Activities, FY 1968–1969" (n.d.), Children's Bureau Records, Box 1143, National Archives.

57. Health, Education and Welfare, *Child Health and Human Development: Research Progress. A Report to the National Institute of Child Health and Human Development* (Washington, D.C., 1972), 42–44.

58. Cited in Richard Albert Rielly, "Family Planning Service Programs: An Operational Analysis of the City of St. Louis, Missouri," (Ph.D. thesis, School of Medicine, Washington University, May 1972); Barbara Seaman, *The Doctor's Case Against the Pill* (New York, 1969); Jean Sharpe, "The Birth Controllers," and Barbara Seaman, "The Dangers of Oral Contraception," in Claudia Dreifus, ed. *Seizing Our Bodies: The Politics of Women's Health*, (New York, 1978), 57–74 and 75–85.

59. In 1967, the Children's Bureau called for an extension of a program focused on young unmarried mothers to reduce "recidivism" among unwed mothers of school age that would interrupt "the cycle of failure" that led to dependence of welfare and continued reproduction of illegitimate offspring." Arthur J. Lesser, "Children's Bureau Family Planning Programs," October 3, 1967, Children's Bureau Records, Box 1143, National Archives.

By 1972, however, surveys showed recidivism in the programs was a major problem. See, Health, Education and Welfare, *Child Health and Human Development: Research Progress. A Report of the National Institute of Child Health and Human Development* (Washington, D.C., 1972), 42–44.

60. U.S. Department of Health, Education, and Welfare, *Family Planning Service Programs: An Operational Analysis* (Washington, D.C., 1970), 73. Also, Howard C. Taylor, "A Family Planning Program Related to Maternity Service," *American Journal of Obstretrics and Gynecology* (July 1966): 726–731.

61. The schools involved in the program included Case Western University, University of Chicago, Columbia University, Emory University, Johns Hopkins University, University of Florida, Albert Einstein Hospital, Harlem Hospital, New York Medical College, University of Pittsburgh, University of Pennsylvania, Temple University, Wayne State University, and West Virginia University. "Summary of Meeting to Consider the Proposal Family Planning via the Medical Schools," April 5, 1968; "Minutes of June 28th Meeting at the University Club to Review a Proposal to Bring Family Planning to the Urban Poor via the Medical Schools," June 28, 1967; "Summary of Meeting to Consider the Proposal on Family Planning," August 18, 1967; OEO-Postpartum Program, Population Council Files, RA.

62. "Family Planning Via Medical Schools: A Proposal Prepared by the Population Council," November 1968, in OEO/Postpartum Program Files, Population Council, RA.

63. Population Council, "Summary of Meeting to Consider the Proposal on Family Planning Via the Medical Schools," May 28, 1968; Bernard Berelson to Philip R. Lee, May 29, 1968; Bernard Berleson to Files, Telephone Conversation with Katherine Oettinger, April 15, 1968, OEO/Postpartum Project, Population Council File, RA.

64. Bernard Berleson to Files, "Telephone Conversation with Katherine Oettinger," April 15, 1968, Population Council Files, RA.

65. George Contis to Frank Shubeck, November 21, 1969; and Cliff Peace to Joel Montague, "Impasse on OEO Program," December 1, 1970, Population Council, RA.

66. WBW to BB, February 24, 1970, Population Council, RA.

67. Westinghouse Learning Corporation, "The Office of Economic Opportunity, Population Council, Medical Schools, Family Planning Programs Assessment, Summary Report, 1970," in Population Council, RA.

68. United Black Front, "An Analysis of Our Communities' Trinity—Health, Education and Labor. As It Affects Us, with an Emphasis on Health and Education," Copy in Population Council File, RA.

69. Population Council, Progress Report, June 15, 1969 to December 31, 1969, Population Council, RA.

70. Hugh B. Davis, "Transcript of Speech" (1971), Population Council, RA.

71. For a discussion of the politics of family planning in the 1980s see Michele McKeegan, *Abortion Politics: Mutiny in the Ranks of the Right* (New York, 1992).

JAMES T. PATTERSON

"Reforming" Relief and Welfare: Thoughts on 1834 and 1996

Anyone who is even casually familiar with writings on the history of social welfare policies in Great Britain and the United States understands that scholars have long emphasized the powerful continuity of attitudes and laws that stigmatize the poor and "blame the victim." Thus Joel Handler, in his revealingly titled book, *The Poverty of Welfare Reform*, complained in 1995 that "welfare policy . . . still lies in the shadow of the sturdy beggar." He added, "the disjuncture between what is legislated and what is needed . . . is not new . . . social policy has been stuck in the same misconceptions for almost 650 years."[1]

Not surprisingly, Frances Fox Piven has echoed this view. In August 1996 she wrote an op-ed piece entitled "From Workhouse to Workfare," wherein she lambasted President Bill Clinton's decision to sign the welfare "reform" of 1996. This law abolished a highly visible sixty-one-year-old cash assistance program, Aid to Families with Dependent Children (AFDC), that then supported some 12 million poor people. "The United States government," she wrote, "is eagerly following the 1834 script by ending Federal responsibility for welfare . . . We may have to relive the misery and moral degradation of England in the 19th century to learn what happens when a society deserts its most vulnerable members."[2]

Handler and Piven perceive greater continuity than is warranted by the historical record; social policies have changed considerably over time.[3] Still, they alert us correctly to the durable power of public officials who have opposed the granting of generous public assistance and who—especially since the 1830s—have tried hard to transform the poor into more productive people. At a few especially troubled times in history, governmental "reforms" reflecting such approaches have attempted boldly to overhaul and transform the provision of relief for the needy.

As Piven argued, two of the most striking of these times have been the early nineteenth century in Britain and the past twenty-five years or so in the

United States—at the beginning and (some think) the end of the industrial age of western civilization. In both eras, a wide spectrum of "experts" and policymakers installed what they hoped would be sweeping changes in social policies. As President Bill Clinton has put it in our own times, the goal of such efforts is to "end welfare as we know it"—a phrase that was so often repeated during his first presidential term that White House aides came to refer to it simply as "EWAKI."[4] Questions therefore arise: how comparable are these two eras of "reform" in history? What common forces, if any, might encourage us, like Piven, to put these widely separated events in the same box? What differences might prompt us to shy away from such an effort?

It was of course in 1834 that Parliament amended the Elizabethan poor laws, which had in effect guaranteed many poor people access to parish-administered public relief. The "new" poor law in 1834 (contrary to Piven's assertion) did not abrogate all rights to relief, nor did it establish time limits on how long a person might continue to receive public aid. But the much-debated reform did seek to cut back "outdoor relief" (aid given outside of institutions) for the "undeserving" poor—that is, able-bodied, nonaged adults who were receiving public assistance—and to require them either to find jobs or to scrape along in workhouses, which were expected to proliferate as part of a grand centralization of existing procedures. Once in workhouses, many of the "undeserving" were to be separated from their families and forced to subsist under conditions of "less eligibility" than people who were employed in the market economy. The harshness of life in the work-house, reformers thought, would drive many of the "undeserving" to scramble for employment, thereby cutting the costs of public relief and—some hoped—reviving the work ethic and personal morality.[5]

The claim that a similarly sweeping movement for "reform" has wholly succeeded in the United States during the past twenty-five years is obviously premature.[6] Still, some useful comparisons between the backgrounds to 1834 and 1996 can be made. As in the 1820s and 1830s, critics of welfare programs in our own time grew ever bolder over an extended period of time, mainly after the 1960s.[7] By August 1996, a host of state experiments (notably in Wisconsin, Michigan, New Jersey, and Ohio) were already being put in place. These efforts, like the reform of 1834 in Britain, sought to cut costs and to restore a work ethic and a public morality that many people feared were fading away.[8] Following Republican triumphs in the election of 1994, leaders of both parties, appealing to what they assumed was powerful popular sentiment, competed to see who could do a more thorough job of dumping the most hated parts of the welfare system—notably AFDC—on the scrap heap of history.[9] Many, like Piven, think that they succeeded in 1996, for the new law—unlike the reform of 1834—did away with nationally guaranteed cash public assistance to needy families with dependent children and set various limits on the amount of time that recipients might continue to get help.[10]

Now, historians know enough not to equate passage of a law with meaningful change. Reformers in the 1830s, for instance, barked a little more fiercely than they managed to bite. They won a battle but perhaps not the war. Scholarship on the reform of 1834 has shown that many officials implemented the new law in a more humane and paternalistic manner than critics had anticipated. These officials balked at depriving the "undeserving" of outdoor relief, which—in part because it was usually cheaper than institutional ("indoor") care—remained a very important feature of the British system. Some local authorities, citing the costs of construction, refused to build new workhouses or to enlarge ones that already existed. Private philanthropy, moreover, increased over time, ameliorating suffering in a number of areas. For all these reasons the poor law of 1834, like many legislated "reforms" in history, had effects somewhat different from those that its advocates—or its detractors—had expected.[11]

America's "reformers" in the past thirty-odd years have also found it easier—so far—to make loud denunciations of public welfare than to transform it. Efforts in the 1960s to reduce the long-range costs of welfare, including the bolstering of social services in 1962 and the "war on poverty" of 1964, had little impact. The numbers of people on AFDC swelled in the 1960s and early 1970s, and new means-tested programs, such as Medicaid, Food Stamps, and Supplemental Security Income (SSI), came into being, aiding varying groups of the needy and increasing costs to taxpayers.[12] The major federal reform of the 1980s, the Family Support Act of 1988, focused on getting states to move the poor from the welfare rolls to the workplace.[13] But for a variety of reasons, among them a recession that led to low levels of state funding, this effort, too, had little effect.[14] The same was true of the forty-three welfare "waivers" that Presidents Ronald Reagan, George Bush, and Clinton gave to the states by August 1996—rhetoric notwithstanding, most of these changes in welfare administration had small impact on the majority of poor people.[15]

Some of those who commented on the passage of the welfare act of 1996 wondered at the time whether even this much-touted law would have truly large consequences.[16] Mickey Kaus, a well-informed writer, exclaimed, "I don't know what's going to happen, and nobody else does either." These observers admitted that no one had a clear idea of how the states would react to the law, which appeared to offer a fair amount of leeway for experimentation. In particular, it seemed impossible to predict how many recipients of welfare would be affected by the time limits and lifetime caps on benefits, two of the most hotly debated features of the new legislation, or to know whether jobs could be found to support the large numbers of people who faced the loss of their benefits within two years.[17]

Conservatives and others, dismissing in 1996 what they thought were hysterical reactions among advocates for the needy, were especially loud in pooh-poohing liberal predictions of disaster. A *Boston Globe* columnist, Jeff Jacoby, wrote, "welfare, all the screeching notwithstanding, isn't being dismantled. It isn't even being overhauled. It is being ever so slightly tightened."[18] Douglas Besharov of the American Enterprise Institute declared, "After you get done with all the rhetoric—from both sides—this bill hardly forces states to do anything. States that want to 'end welfare as we know it' now have the tools to do so, but states that want to continue the *status quo* can do that, too. Real welfare reform is now up to the states."[19] To Jacoby and Besharov, the welfare act of 1996 promised to scrap some of the worst aspects of the old system but did not threaten the well-being of truly deserving people.

In the months following passage of the law, many of its supporters became ever more confident that it would not harm the poor. To begin with, they stressed that the block grants offered a "windfall" to states. [20] This was because the act based the size of such grants on the substantial cost of supporting AFDC in early 1994, when case loads had been at an all-time high. In the wake of the more bullish economy after 1994, case loads dropped significantly.[21] Block grants—"windfalls"—therefore were expected to augment the benefits of many continuing welfare recipients and to enable states to help legal immigrants and others who might otherwise have been deprived (under provisions of the law) of SSI or Food Stamps.[22] Some states, welcoming their "windfalls," began to develop programs for job training, job placement, and day care—all of which promised to promote the major goal of the legislation: moving people from welfare to work. Representative E. Clay Shaw, Jr., a Florida Republican who had helped to write the law, exclaimed happily in February 1997, "So many people have been throwing rocks at us and saying we're going to starve kids. And quite simply, they're wrong. The law's working. And it's working right from the beginning."[23]

Liberals were far less optimistic about the "reform" of 1996. State officials, they insisted, can never escape politically powerful demands from taxpayers to reduce expenditures, especially outlays for the support—or even the training—of "undeserving" welfare recipients. These liberals noted that many state legislatures in 1997 enacted time limits for receipt of welfare that were *shorter* than the maximum of two years envisioned by the federal law.[24] Other states seemed ready to use their "windfalls" for purposes only distantly related to the problems of the poor. Liberals added that some 50 percent of the 4 million or so adults on AFDC were long-term recipients who for one reason or another were functionally unable to hold a job: these people—and their children—would suffer greatly if forced off the rolls. Critics of the welfare "reform" of 1996 wondered above all whether the market—even an expansive one—could ever create enough decent-paying jobs (and provide for child and health care) for former recipients of AFDC: this responsibility, they argued, could be assumed only by the federal government. These critics asked finally, what happens if a recession descends? They answered their own question: the block grants authorized by the law would prove to be disastrously insufficient.[25]

Still, it was also not at all clear in 1996–1997 that popular attitudes would acquiesce in a major rollback of welfare in the future. Contemporary public opinion polls, as in the past, offered ambiguous findings on this subject—so much depended on the wording and language of the questions asked—but continued to suggest that the majority of American people do not wish to abandon the poor. State officials, confronting such attitudes, might well think twice before depriving people, especially "deserving" groups such as the disabled, the elderly, and children, of various forms of support.[26] The conservative editors of the *Weekly Standard* wondered in August 1996, "Is there a state government anywhere in the country vicious enough to fashion a welfare program that produces long bread lines of homeless children? Are there voters anywhere in [the] country who would tolerate such a result? We don't believe it." [27] Reflections such as these suggested that something like pre-1996 policies—"welfare as we know it"—might well survive in many American states.

The reform sentiments leading to the new poor law of 1834 and the rollback efforts of the 1980s and 1990s nonetheless stand out as landmark *symbols* in the history of Anglo-American public assistance. In both eras, well-placed "experts," policymakers, and political leaders grew increasingly dissatisfied—not suddenly, but over considerable periods of time— with the existing systems of public assistance. In Britain these elites did not need to worry about securing democratic support—few people had the franchise in 1834. In the United States, however, advocates of reform managed to mobilize a fairly broad-based political coalition. In September 1995, thirty-five of forty-six Senate Democrats joined Republicans to pass a major rollback of welfare, 87 to 12. President Clinton endorsed the bill at the time, even though he and his aides knew of a study estimating that it would push an additional 1.1 million American children into poverty.[28] The act that passed in 1996 contained conservative provisions that would have seemed astonishing a few years earlier. (Welcoming the law, GOP presidential nominee Robert Dole chortled, "the first 100 days of the Dole administration have begun 97 days early.")[29] The title of the bill was revealing: the Personal Responsibility and Work Opportunity Reconcilliation Act of 1996.

Opponents of "reform,"both in the 1830s and in our own times, were in no way caught napping. Then and in 1995–1996 they assailed the proposed changes. Thomas Carlyle, while critical of waste in the pre-1834 system, called the new law the epitome of a "pig philosophy" that reduced everyone to the "cash nexus." Benjamin Disraeli observed angrily that England had announced, "poverty is a crime."[30] Equally scary predictions of doom accompanied debate and passage of the act of 1996. "This is not reform," the *New York Times* editorialized, "it is punishment."[31] Leading the fight against the rollback, Senator Daniel Patrick Moynihan of New York denounced it as "the most brutal act of social policy since Reconstruction."[32] The columnist E. J. Dionne branded the measure a "horror of a bill . . . The bill's premise is that if we kick poor people and their kids around a little more, maybe they'll go to work. Then again, maybe they won't. We have no idea. But, hey, maybe the savings from this bill can pay for a little election-year tax cut."[33]

As these critics stressed, many of the ideas underlying the reform of 1996 echoed those of reformers in 1834: the distinction between a "deserving" and "undeserving" poor, opposition to cash relief for the "undeserving," and the quest for a system based on less eligibility. Perhaps most strikingly similar is the idea that public policy can rehabilitate "traditional" families, restore "old-fashioned" values, and promote better "character." This is what Gertrude Himmelfarb has approvingly identified as the quest for "remoralization." Welfare measures, perhaps more than any other policy, expose this quest, which represents a profoundly moral strain in Anglo-American thinking about the good society.[34]

How do we account for these two eras of "reform" in history? Are the causes mainly similar or dissimilar? The answer is that some of the most frequently observed similarities in these causes hold up pretty well, others less so.

One common explanation for the rise of "reform" sentiment in both eras highlights the costs of public assistance and the role of angry, impatient taxpayers—or rate-payers as they were called in 1834. These concerns have clearly mattered. Poor rates doubled in England between 1775 and 1800 and then doubled again between 1800 and 1817. The so-called Speenhamland system, which began in Berkshire in the 1790s and spread to some southern counties by the 1830s, intensified criticism of existing policies, for it called upon parish officials not only to help the poor who did not have work but also to supplement the wages of low-paid agricultural laborers, thereby guaranteeing families—partly at rate-payers' expense—a minimum income as calibrated by the cost of bread. Karl Polanyi credited the Speenhamland procedures with establishing a "right to live." But he had harsh things, too, to say about them, which he said "pauperized" people and created a "fool's paradise."[35] Carlyle worried that the Speenhamland system provided "indiscriminate" aid to people.[36]

Economists and philosophers, led by Thomas Malthus, further complained that poor relief steadily increased the numbers receiving assistance and thereby added to the costs incurred by rate-payers. Worse, these critics thought, poor relief policies depressed wages (because employers knew that public subsidies would provide for their workers), harmed productivity (because laborers supposedly had nothing to gain by working hard), increased the cost of food (because of the decline in productivity), and therefore lowered the real wages of the poor (because they had to pay more for food).

As if these were not problems enough, Malthusians thought that people on relief were thereby encouraged to have more children, thus intensifying a coming crisis exacerbated by rapid population growth amid finite resources. Well before 1834, the idea that the poor laws imposed high "costs" was shared by many (though not all) "experts" on the subject. These costs, in turn, were thought to be dragging down the economy as a whole, portending an increasingly bleak future for England. What scholars today call "economic knowledge," in short, did much to shape the reform of 1834.

Similar concerns about costs and taxes—concerns that reflect the continuing power of classical liberalism in Anglo-American thought—have gripped advocates of rollback in the United States since the 1960s. On the state level, taxpayers' revolts, notably in California in 1978, sent a loud message to politicians who might otherwise have supported generous social programs. On the national level, conservatives and others have deplored the cost of welfare expenditures, especially for Medicaid and SSI, which rose considerably in the 1970s and thereafter.[37] Moreover, federal taxes supporting other social policies, notably Social Security and Medicare, jumped enormously over these years, eating substantially into the paychecks of people.

As innumerable observers have pointed out, however, concerns over costs were somewhat exaggerated in both periods. The Speenhamland system took hold only in a relatively small number of places—no longer in Berkshire by 1834—and probably had little overall effect. Though the costs of public aid did fall in many rural regions after the reform of 1834, the main reason was probably not the provisions of the new law, but economic growth, which over time helped to improve conditions in many areas. The fact that private philanthropy for the poor increased considerably after 1834 suggests, more-over, that rate-payers were scarcely hard-pressed, or blind to the need to help the dependent. They had concerns, to be sure, but they did always not center in pocketbooks.

In the United States, scholars have tirelessly (and accurately) tried to make people understand that means-tested aid has been a relatively small item in overall federal spending in our own times.[38] While the costs of some means-tested programs, notably Medicaid and SSI, increased in the 1970s, 1980s, and 1990s, this was not the case after 1976 with AFDC. The number of people on AFDC in fact decreased between 1992 and 1996, from 14.1 to 12.8 million people. The overall federal tax burden remained stable in the 1980s and 1990s and is light by comparison with burdens in other industri-alized nations. The reach of the American welfare state, indeed, continues to be relatively small in many respects, notably in the realm of health care. Even as rollbackers worried about the costs of helping the poor, the federal budget deficit, which is considerably smaller per capita than those in other leading world economies, was falling—from 5 percent of national income in 1992 to 2.2 percent in early 1996.[39] Most writers on poverty and welfare in modern American history agree that the costs of means-tested welfare do not impose much of a burden on taxpayers or create significant problems for the economy as a whole.[40] What is relevant in antiwelfare thinking nowa-days—as in the 1820s and 1830s—is not so much the reality of costs, which have been modest, but rather the *perception* of costs. That is a different story, to be addressed later.

A second explanation of agitation for "reform" in both eras focuses on popular fears of social unrest and disorder, which are said to sharpen al-ready ugly stereotypes about poor people, to arouse backlash, and thereby to weaken humanitarian responses.

This explanation, too, cannot be dismissed. The Swing riots of 1830, led by agricultural laborers opposing the introduction of threshing machines, provided a backdrop of social unrest of which English reformers in 1834 were well aware. Some contemporaries worried about the "ragged poor" in the big cities and about the rise of "Two Nations."[41] In our own times, critics have associated welfare with frightening increases in violent crime, riots, and out-of-wedlock pregnancy. This image of poor people, especially poor black people, as a restless "underclass" might have been expected to frighten lawmakers into buying social peace with more generous welfare benefits.[42] America's poor in the 1990s, however, have lacked resources, organization, and political power. Many Americans, emboldened by these weaknesses, have therefore felt free to cite the "pathological" condition of the "underclasses" as reason enough to roll back the welfare state.

This interpretation, however, also carries us only so far. As Himmelfarb and others have emphasized, the momentum for repeal of the Elizabethan poor laws and the Speenhamland system had accelerated before the Swing riots. Concerns about the "ragged poor," while mounting by 1834, did not much affect the reformers.[43] In the United States, popular alarm about violent crime indeed increased enormously after the mid-1960s. And revulsion against the "underclasses" surely reinforced cries for cuts in AFDC. Yet the demand to roll back welfare in our own times seems to stem from considerably broader fears than these and to be aimed less at violent males than at unmarried mothers, especially black mothers, whose supposed sexual promiscuity prompts the loudest and most frightened public responses. Indeed, rates of violent crimes have subsided a little in the United States during the 1980s and 1990s, yet the push for "welfare reform" has seemed to become ever stronger over time.[44]

While trends in costs, crime, and unrest do not fully explain the demands for "reform" of welfare, they direct us to a central point that seems relevant in both the 1830s and in recent times: the development of widespread and often pessimistic *perceptions* of *future* economic and social decline.

First, the economic worries. Those who pressed for abolition or reform of the English poor law system in the early nineteenth century were living in an economy that was undergoing what Karl Polanyi later called a "great transformation." The rise of market-based capitalism was rapidly overturning economic relationships, especially in the countryside. Large numbers of unemployed drifters seemed to be wandering into parishes and seeking aid. Factories were beginning to increase in number. These trends created rising unease about life in the future. Not only Malthusians (whose ideas did not in fact carry the day in 1834) but also many others worried about the capacity of the culture to cope with these changes.[45]

Comparable jeremiads have been commonplace in our own times, especially in the economically unsettled years of the 1970s, 1980s, and early 1990s. Economists and politicians in these years warned repeatedly that overseas competitors were more efficient and hard-working and that the American dream of upward mobility was dying.[46] Federal budget deficits, while reduced after 1993, still seemed elephantine in the mid-1990s in contrast to the "good old days" of the 1950s and early 1960s. Laments, from liberals as well as conservatives, mounted over the supposedly disastrous impact on the economy of large-scale immigration.[47] Many Americans in the early 1990s, like some (not all) reformers of the Elizabethan poor laws in the early nineteenth century, perceived an economic system at risk of substantial decline in the future. As Theodore Marmor and his collaborators put it a few years ago, criticism of American welfare policies crested in the 1980s on waves of growing awareness of "the economy's poor performance and the accompanying sense of national disintegration."[48]

Central to these perceptions of economic decline is a selective use of history, which is thought to offer "lessons."[49] Doomsayers in the 1830s and the 1990s had come to believe that older ways were better, and that liberal changes in relief and welfare policies had made things worse.[50] Thus, many reformers in the 1820s and 1830s insisted that a key villain of the piece was the Speenhamland system, which they said distorted a less-flawed, earlier manner of dealing with the poor. Similarly, many contemporary advocates of rollback in the United States think that the 1950s and early 1960s represented something of a Golden Age in which economic growth was ascending, only to be arrested by such "disasters" as the "war on poverty" and a big rise in the number of people on AFDC.[51]

Social fears, both in the 1820s and 1830s and in recent American history, reveal even more about the quest for revision of welfare than do economic concerns. The coalition of reformers in the 1830s was composed not only of economic thinkers but also of evangelicals who worried deeply about the morals of the poor, indeed of society at large.[52] Other people at that time grew alarmed that women were moving into the job market in larger numbers, thereby, it was assumed, damaging family life. In our own times, concerns about the decline of the "traditional" family have darkened the mood of rollback. Here, too, religious ideas have figured prominently in debates. In both eras, morally concerned people insisted that the poor must somehow be induced, or forced, to *behave* in a proper fashion.

To stress the role of such perceptions is not to say that they are wholly off base, particularly those in our own time. The American economy has indeed sputtered in many years since the early 1970s.[53] Social problems, too, are real. The incidence of poverty among women and children in the United States has increased since the early 1970s and is considerably higher than in other industrialized nations.[54] And concerns about American family life in the 1990s rest on statistics of seismic proportions. As Moynihan despaired during debates over welfare reform in 1996, the rise in out-of-wedlock birth rates, which by then had reached 50 percent in New York City, "has hit us like a cyclone, and in our confusion we are doing mad things."[55]

Still, it is also true that certain *kinds* of economic and social knowledge—heavily influenced by the ideas of conservative economists—seem to dominate debate in times of "reform" and rollback, crowding out other versions and in some ways simplifying complexities. In our own times, for instance, much of this knowledge has been especially alarmist in tone, gripping a great many articulate "experts," receiving wide attention in the media, capturing opportunistic support from politicians, and appealing (or so it has seemed) to large numbers of citizens active in the electoral process.[56]

Careful writers have of course tried to expose flaws in such apocalyptic worldviews and to offer carefully nuanced descriptions of contemporary socioeconomic change in the United States.[57] Observers ranging in ideological position from Moynihan to David Ellwood to Lawrence Mead have stressed how little we really know about the causes of changes in America's family patterns—that is, that our social and economic knowledge has limits.[58] Other writers have offered well-informed rebuttals to negative stereotypes about welfare recipients.[59] Yet advocates of rollback nonetheless persuaded Congress in 1996 that welfare widens a spectrum of horrors ranging from idleness to promiscuity. Like the reformers in 1834, they insisted that changes in the law can shape human behavior and restore the good old days. As Glenn Loury has said of such thinkers, they seek to "turn back the influence of modernity."[60] It is of course ironic that many people who place so much faith in the power of public policy to change people call themselves conservative.

A focus on similarities between the 1830s in Britain and the 1990s in the United States, however, can easily blind us to significant differences. These differences are numerous, varied, and important. One concerns the policy-making process. English politics in the early nineteenth century were largely class-based, excluding not only the poor but also the working classes from parliamentary decision-making. It is therefore difficult to argue that the reform of 1834 reflected anything like "public" opinion. Rollback in the United States, by contrast, may be said to reveal a considerable swing to conservatism, one that grew in political power after the mid-1960s.

A related difference involves the attitudes of reformers in both eras to the potential of central government action. In the 1820s and 1830s reformers drew upon rising faith in the capacity of the state in order to champion centralized change of practices that had been rooted in local control. Led by experts like Edwin Chadwick, they were self-assured, self-conscious social engineers, optimistic about the expertise they imagined they had. Rather like American advocates (in the 1960s and 1970s) of guaranteed annual income programs, they thought they could streamline and therefore make more efficient the administration of public aid. And the streamlining would come from the central government, which would break the hold of local parishes in the management of relief. By contrast, American rollbackers since the 1960s have been highly critical of centralized solutions. Pessimistic about a lot of things—notably the wisdom of the federal government and the psychology of the poor—they demanded (or seemed to demand) much greater decentralization. In these ways the rhetoric of the reformers—promoting national power in 1834, denouncing it in 1996—could hardly have differed more profoundly.

Another difference relates to the dimming after 1973 in the United States of popular expectations about future progress, expectations that had expanded enormously during the economically prosperous 1950s and 1960s.[61] These expectations, boosted by exaggerated claims among liberals in the Lyndon Johnson years, led many people at that time to believe that government had Big Answers to Big Problems. That, of course, was not always the case, and the burden of oversell has thereafter hung like a millstone around the neck of contemporary liberalism. Conservative thinkers and interest groups, aided by well-endowed think-tanks, have ridiculed the oversell and thereby ripped big holes in the fabric of liberal thought.[62]

Expectations about the American economy, meanwhile, grew so grand by the mid-1960s that they were virtually certain to outpace the capacity of the economy to maintain high rates of growth. When "stagflation" descended in the 1970s, popular anger, rage, and backlash escalated rapidly. Since then Americans have seemed especially ready to believe the doomsayers, many of whom get great attention from the sometimes sensationalist media.[63] The larger pessimism of our own times—in part well founded, in part a reaction against the grand expectations of the 1950s and 1960s—has intensified already corrosively negative feelings against politics in general, and against federal social policies in particular.[64]

The pessimism has also afflicted liberals. As Gareth Davies and Robert Kelso have argued in recent books, liberals began shifting gears in the late 1960s and early 1970s. Before that time liberals like Johnson had stressed that social policy should improve economic opportunity. Government should offer a hand up, not a hand out. It should open doors, not lay down floors. This was an essentially optimistic faith that credited poor people with some agency of their own. By the 1970s, however, the uncertain economy was shaking popular nerve. Liberals, losing faith in the potential of expanding opportunity, emphasized instead the responsibility of government to offer protection to the unfortunate. "Entitlements" began to swell. Some liberals left the impression that the poor, rendered helpless in a free-falling economy, did not need to shoulder responsibilities themselves. Needless to say, this impression made for poor politics, which is why Clinton distanced himself from it.[65] As did many lawmakers on Capitol Hill in 1996, for whom "liberalism" of this stripe was perceived as virtually un-American.

Still another difference separating the worlds of the 1830s and the 1990s is obvious: divisiveness over issues of race and gender in the America of our time is vastly sharper than it was in 1834, when reformers worried mainly about the deleterious impact of the old system on "undeserving" whites, the majority of them male. Since the 1960s, by contrast, poverty in the United States has increasingly been perceived to be a "black" (or black ghetto) phenomenon—one that especially damages the moral behavior of black women. Many of the travails of contemporary American liberalism, indeed, stem from these perceptions, and more broadly from the effect that an ever more racialized politics has had on the Democratic party. President Johnson, of course, made the fateful choice to identify his party with the aspirations of black people, thereby aiding the civil rights movement. In the long run, however, his choice widened deep fissures in the party. Much of the subsequent intensity of popular hostility to "welfare" can be understood by looking at the way that racial antagonisms have shattered the liberal political coalition.[66]

These differences block any effort to draw completely comparable pictures of the politics of 1834 and 1996. History, after all, rarely repeats itself. What remains comparable, however, is the power of *perceptions* in both eras—perceptions that promoted nervous predictions about the future economic viability and moral health of society. A culture in which "experts" and key policymakers are receptive to social and economic knowledge of that sort is one in which poor people, especially those deemed to be "undeserving," may bear the brunt of changes in public policy.

Reformers in 1834 did win a battle, and they did so again in 1996. Whether today's victors will win the war—that is, whether the "reforms" of our own times will have the impact that angry liberals foresee—remains to be seen. After all, the advocates of change in 1834 did not entirely win their war. Still, there is no doubting the *symbolic* meaning of what happened in both eras. As Handler and Piven observed, the influence of rollbackers of our own times, like that of the reformers in Britain during the 1820s and 1830s, exposes the continuing power of unflattering perceptions about the "undeserving" and reveals an apparently timeless faith that laws can be crafted that will make better people of the poor.

Acknowledgments

Thanks to Edward Berkowitz, Anthony Brundage, Sarah Phillips, Susannah Ottaway, Perry Curtis, and Hilary Silver for comments on earlier versions of this paper.

Notes

1. Joel Handler, *The Poverty of Welfare Reform* (New Haven, 1995), 4–8. Other recent critical approaches to the history of Western welfare policies include Frances Fox Piven and Richard Cloward, *Regulating the Poor: The Functions of Public Welfare* (rev. ed., New York, 1993), esp. 3–42; Herbert Gans, *The War Against the Poor: The Underclass and Antipoverty Policy* (New York, 1995), 23–26; Michael Katz, *Improving Poor People: The Welfare State, The "Underclass," and Urban Schools as History* (Princeton, 1995), 60–98; Mimi Abramovitz, *Regulating the Lives of Women: Social Welfare from Colonial Times to the Present* (Boston, 1988); Linda Gordon, *Pitied But Not Entitled: Single Mothers and the History of Welfare* (New York, 1994); and Ruth Sidel, *Keeping Women and Children Last: America's War on the Poor* (New York, 1996).

2. *New York Times*, August 1, 1996. Approximately one-third of these recipients were adults, the rest children under the age of eighteen. As this essay will emphasize below, Piven was wrong to imply that the law of 1834 ended national involvement in relief policy. On the contrary, it greatly *strengthened* national engagement.

3. See, for example, Ann Shola Orloff, *The Politics of Pensions: A Comparative Analysis of Britain, Canada, and the United States, 1880–1940* (Madison,1993); Dietrich Rueschemeyer and Theda Skocpol, eds., *States, Social Knowledge, and the Origins of Modern Social Policies* (Princeton, 1996); and Michael Lacey and Mary Furner, "Social Investigation, Social Knowledge, and the State: An Introduction," in Lacey and Furner, eds., *The State and Social Investigation in Britain and the United States* (New York, 1993), 3–62.

4. David Ellwood, "Welfare Reform As I Knew It," *The American Prospect* (May/June 1996), 22–29.

5. The huge literature on the background, passage, and impact of the 1834 law (which was preceded by a number of experiments) includes Karl Polanyi, *The Great Transformation* (Boston, 1944), esp. 77–85, 223–225; Samuel Menchner, *Poor Law to Poverty Program: Economic Security Policy in Britain and the United States* (Pittsburgh, 1967), 93–129; Gertrude Himmelfarb, *The Idea of Poverty: England in the Early Industrial Age* (New York, 1984), 4–12, 27–28, 147–152, 523–533; Himmelfarb, *The Demoralization of Society* (New York, 1995), 128–142, 241–242; J. R. Poynter, *Society and Pauperism: English Ideas on Poor Relief, 1795–1834* (London, 1969); and Anthony Brundage, *The Making of the New Poor Law: The Politics of Inquiry, Enactment, and Implementation, 1832–1839* (New Brunswick, 1978).

6. As I revise this paper in October 1997, I recognize that it will be some time before we can confidently assess the effects of the "reform" of 1996.

7. Theodore Marmor, Jerry Mashow, and Philip Harvey, *America's Misunderstood Welfare State: Persistent Myths, Enduring Realities* (New York, 1990), 173–174, 216–221; Abramovitz, *Regulating the Lives of Women*, 358–363.

8. Handler, *The Poverty of Welfare Reform*, 95–108.

9. Some very costly social welfare programs were safe from such dumping, including Social Security and Medicare. Both of these target the elderly; neither is means-tested. See footnote 16 for provisions of the act of 1996.

10. The historical background to the law of 1996 is mainly captured in contemporary magazines and newspapers. But see Mary Jo Bane and David Ellwood, *Welfare*

Realities: From Rhetoric to Reform (Cambridge, Mass., 1994), esp. 1–27, 143–162; Edward Berkowitz, *America's Welfare State from Roosevelt to Reagan* (Baltimore, 1991), 120–149, 189–197; Sheldon Danziger, Gary Sandefur, and Daniel Weinberg, eds., *Confronting Poverty: Prescriptions for Change* (Cambridge, Mass., 1994); Michael Katz, ed., *The "Underclass" Debate: Views from History* (Princeton, 1993); and William Kelso, *Poverty and the Underclass: Changing Perceptions of the Poor in America* (New York, 1994).

11. Important sources include Mark Blaug, "The Myth of the Old Poor Law and the Making of the New," *Journal of Economic History* 23 (1963): 151–184; Blaug, "The Poor Law Re-examined," *Journal of Economic History* 24 (1964): 229–245; Robert Humphries, *Sin, Organized Charity, and the Poor Law in Victorian England* (New York, 1995); Jose Harris, "Economic Knowledge and British Social Policy," in Mary Furner and Barry Supple, eds., *The State and Economic Knowledge: The American and British Experiences* (New York, 1990), 379–435; and especially Donald Winch, "Economic Knowledge and Government in Britain: Some Historical and Comparative Reflections," *The State and Economic Knowledge*, 40–70. See also Anthony Brundage, "Private Charity and the 1834 Poor Law," in this volume.

12. SSI, established in 1972, provides federal assistance to many needy people who are disabled or elderly. It centralized federal-state categorical assistance programs that had been started under provisions of the Social Security Act of 1935. Like Social Security, SSI is indexed to keep pace with changes in consumer prices. AFDC, also established by the Social Security Act, remained (until abolished in 1996) a noncentralized federal-state program, and was not indexed; its beneficiaries (mostly low-income women and their dependent children) were perceived as less "deserving" than the disabled or elderly.

13. Among the advocates of change in these years were Charles Murray, *Losing Ground: American Social Policy, 1950–1980* (New York, 1984); (less stridently) Lawrence Mead, *The New Politics of Poverty: The Nonworking Poor in America* (New York, 1992); and Mickey Kaus, *The End of Equality* (New York, 1992). More recently, Marvin Olasky, *Renewing American Compassion* (New York, 1996). See also Kelso, *Poverty and the Underclass*, noted above.

14. James Patterson, *America's Struggle Against Poverty, 1900–1994* (Cambridge, Mass., 1995), 231–232; Marmor et al., *America's Misunderstood Welfare State*, 114–124; Bane and Ellwood, *Welfare Realities*, 125–130, passim; Handler, *The Poverty of Welfare Reform*, 76–79.

15. Handler, *The Poverty of Welfare Reform*, 92–94.

16. The act, which states were supposed to adapt to no later than October 1, 1997, abolished AFDC and replaced it with federal "block grants" (totaling $16.4 billion per year) to states, which were then expected to develop and fund (with the aid of the block grants) their own welfare-to-work programs: the act earmarked no federal money for jobs, job training, job placement, or day care. To supplement the block grants, states were required to spend at least 75 percent as much per year on public assistance (and promotion of jobs) as they had done in 1994. Other provisions of the act required able-bodied family heads on welfare to work within two years or face the loss of federal aid, and limited federal support for welfare benefits to most families to a lifetime total of five years ("hardship" exceptions were authorized for a maximum of 20 percent of adult recipients). States were permitted to set shorter time

limits, both for individuals and for families. The law further barred states from using block grants to provide cash payments to unmarried parents under the age of 18 unless these young parents stayed in school and lived with an adult. Other provisions (set for implementation at various times in 1997) authorized states to cut off SSI, Medicaid, and Food Stamps to most legal immigrants during their first five years in the United States; established stricter standards concerning the administration of SSI benefits to disabled children; and tightened rules concerning the eligibility for Food Stamps of adults who are not raising children. Savings were expected to total around $55 billion over the first six years of the new system—$23 billion of them in cuts of Food Stamps and $22 billion in cutbacks of benefits once available to legal immigrants. It was estimated that the act would affect 100,000 to 200,000 of 965,000 disabled children who had previously received SSI, 500,000 legal immigrants who had been on the rolls of SSI, and one million recipients of Food Stamps (some of them legal immigrants). The law called upon states to have 25 percent of former welfare recipients working by late 1997 and 50 percent by 2002; states that fail to meet these targets could expect to face (modest) cuts in their block grants. As these provisions make clear, the goals of the "reform" of 1996 were similar to those of the poor law of 1834 and the Family Support Act of 1988: to save money and to move people from welfare to work. For a solid summary of clauses affecting immigrants, see William Primus, "Immigrant Provisions in the New Welfare Law," *Focus* (Fall/ Winter 1996–1997): 14–18.

17. *New York Times*, August 2, 1996. The "shot-in-the-dark," "anything-is-better-than-what-we-have-now" approach to welfare reform in 1996 was one of the most remarkable aspects of the effort. It reflected huge frustration over welfare policies, especially AFDC, that had mounted since the 1960s.

18. *Syndicated in the Providence Journal-Bulletin*, August 7, 1996. For a similar view see "Victory," *Weekly Standard*, August 12, 1996, 9–10. This article maintained that only the seven states without waivers (states that had merely 5 percent of the welfare population) needed to adhere to the law's stipulation that heads of families on welfare go to work after two years on the rolls.

19. *Providence Journal-Bulletin*, August 4, 1996. See also "Actions by States Hold Keys to Welfare Law's Future," *New York Times*, October 1, 1996.

20. Estimated at $1.3 billion by the *New Republic* in a confident editorial, "It's Working," March 24, 1997, 9.

21. The *New Republic* estimated the drop in case loads between March 1996 and March 1997 at 18 percent. This drop, combined with the continuation in early 1997 of 1994 levels of federal welfare spending, meant that the average welfare family in early 1997 (assuming states did not divert the block grant money or slash their own spending) could receive in 1997 an estimated $5,662, as opposed to $3,624 in 1994 (Estimate in *Washington Post*, Feburary 14, 1997).

22. Indeed, many states in early 1997 took steps to assist legal immigrants (and recipients of Food Stamps) so as to protect them from some of the cuts authorized in the law of 1996. Congress, too, later softened these blows.

23. *New York Times*, Feb. 2, 1997.

24. As noted earlier, the law was permissive to states in this as well as in many other respects. It promises to result in considerable state-by-state variations in policies affecting the poor.

25. See Peter Edelman, "The Worst Thing Bill Clinton Has Done," *Atlantic Monthly* (March 1997): 43–58; Rebecca Blank, "The Effect of the 1996 Welfare Reforms," October 1996, Center for Urban Affairs and Policy Research, Northwestern Univ.; Jason DeParle, "Mugged by Reality," *New York Times Magazine* (December 8, 1996): 64–67, 99–100; and Jeffrey Katz, "Small Change," *New Republic*, (December 9, 1996): 14–15.

26. Consider also the important role of state welfare bureaucracies: these, accustomed to serving needy people, present formidable obstacles to the demolition of public aid. On this point, see Blank, "Effect of Welfare Reforms."

27. "Victory," *Weekly Standard* (August 7, 1996): 9.

28. *New York Times*, September 28, 1995, December 23, 1995; Jason DeParle, "Welfare, End of," *New York Times Magazine* (December 17, 1995): 64–65; Paul Offner, "Flippers," *New Republic* (Feburary 12, 1996): 10–11.

29. Robert Kuttner, "Clinton Didn't Have to Cave in on Welfare," *Providence Journal-Bulletin*, August 10, 1996.

30. Himmelfarb, *Idea of Poverty*, 523–528; Himmelfarb, *Demoralization*, 132–133.

31. *New York Times*, August 1, 1996.

32. Jacoby, Cited in *Providence Journal-Bulletin*, August 7, 1996.

33. *Providence Journal-Bulletin*, August 6, 1996.

34. See also James Wilson, *The Moral Sense* (New York, 1993); William Bennett, *The Book of Virtues: A Treasury of Great Moral Stories* (New York, 1993); and Barbara Dafoe Whitehead, "Dan Quayle Was Right," *Atlantic Monthly* (April 1993): 47–84. A sharp critique of such moralism in the American past is James Morone, "The Corrosive Politics of Virtue," *The American Prospect* (May/June, 1996): 30–39.

35. Polanyi, *The Great Transformation*, 77–85.

36. Himmelfarb, *Idea of Poverty*, 12. His concerns were exaggerated; as noted below, the system probably did not have much effect.

37. The cost of the major means-tested programs in constant dollars—from federal, state, and local sources—rose three and a half times between 1968 and 1988, mostly between 1968 and 1973. (These figures count AFDC, Food Stamps, Medicaid, and SSI.) Marmor et al., *America's Misunderstood Welfare State*, 90–92.

38. The real value of AFDC benefits, which in 1996 accounted for around one per cent of the federal budget, declined by some 30 per cent from the early 1970s until then. Federal and state spending for the program, stable in recent years, amounted in 1996 to around 14 per cent of the sum spent on Medicare and 9 per cent of the budget for the Pentagon. All means-tested spending in 1996 accounted for roughly 10 per cent of the federal budget. *New York Times*, August 2, 1996.

39. "Budget Myths," *New York Times*, January 12, 1996.

40. See, for example, the arguments of Murray, *Losing Ground*; as well as those of Bane and Ellwood, *Welfare Realities*; and Marmor et al., *America's Misunderstood Welfare State*.

41. Himmelfarb, *Idea of Poverty*, 152–153, 527–529.

42. The argument, of course, in Piven and Cloward, *Regulating the Poor*.

43. Mounting fears about the "lumpen" and the "dangerous classes" mostly came after, not before 1834, in Great Britain.

44. For an authoritative account of recent trends in American crime, see James Q. Wilson, "Crime and Public Policy," in Wilson and Joan Petersilia, eds., *Crime* (San Francisco, 1995), 489–511 (and other essays in the volume).

45. Himmelfarb, *Idea of Poverty*, 137–139.

46. See especially Katherine Newman, *Falling from Grace: The Experience of Downward Mobility in the American Middle Class* (New York, 1989); and Bennett Harrison and Barry Bluestone, *The Great U-Turn: Corporate Restructuring and the Polarizing of America* (New York, 1988).

47. One such liberal is Michael Lind, *The Next American Nation* (New York, 1995).

48. Marmor et al., *America's Misunderstood Welfare State*, 7.

49. Furner and Supple, *The State and Economic Knowledgd*, 13.

50. See especially Olasky, *Renewing American Compassion*.

51. Allen Matusow's book, *The Unraveling of America: A History of Liberalism in the 1960s* (New York, 1984), set the stage for scholarly receptivity to some of these ideas when he asserted in 1984 that the war on poverty was "destined to be one of the great failures of twentieth-century liberalism" (220). Charles Murray's widely noted book, *Losing Ground*, appeared in the same year. Although it differed substantially from Matusow's, it reached an equally pessimistic conclusion about the capacity of public policymakers to do the right thing. For a spirited critique of doomsaying see Michael Elliott, *The Day Before Yesterday: Reconsidering America's Past, Rediscovering the Present* (New York, 1996).

52. Harris, "Economic Knowledge."

53. Frank Levy, *Dollars and Dreams: The Changing Nature of American Income Distribution* (New York, 1987); Sheldon Danziger and Peter Gottschalk, eds., *Uneven Tides: Rising Inequality in America* (New York, 1993).

54. Lynne Casper, Sara McLanahan, and Irwin Garfinkle, "The Gender-Poverty Gap: What We Can Learn from Other Countries," *American Sociological Review* 59 (August 1994): 594–605.

55. *New York Times*, August 2, 1996. It was later reported that these rates fell in 1995 for the first time in more than twenty years, but they had become so high by that time that concerns about family life remained intense.

56. Lacey and Furner, "Social Investigation," 7–8, note the different levels of "economic knowledge." I follow these distinctions here.

57. See especially Isabel Sawhill and Daniel McMurrer, "American Dreams and Discontents: Beyond the Level Playing Field" (Washington, D.C., 1996), which asks thoughtful questions about trends in social mobility and life chances.

58. Isabel Sawhill, "Poverty in the U.S.: Why Is It So Persistent?" *Journal of Economic Literature* 26 (Sept. 1988): 1073–1119; Mead, "Poverty: How Little We Know," *Social Service Review* 68 (September 1994): 322–350; Moynihan, "Congress Builds a Coffin"; Ellwood, "Welfare Reform As I Knew It." See also Katha Pollitt, "What We Know," *New Republic* (August 12, 1996): 20.

59. Mary Jo Bane and David Ellwood, "Slipping into and out of Poverty: The Dynamics of Spells," *Journal of Human Resources* 21 (Winter 1986): 1–23; John Schwarz and Thomas Volgy, "Above the Poverty Line—But Poor," *The Nation* (February 13, 1993): 191–192; Christopher Jencks, "What Is the Underclass—and Is It Growing?" *Focus* (Spring-Summer 1989): 14–26; Jencks and Kathryn Edin, "The Real Welfare Problem," *The American Prospect* (Spring 1990): 31–50; Handler, *The Poverty of Welfare Reform*, 45–52.

60. *New York Times*, August 4, 1996.

61. The central theme of my book, *Grand Expectations: The United States, 1945–1974* (New York, 1996).

62. Peter Steinfels, *The Neoconservatives: The Men Who Are Changing America's Politics* (New York, 1979); Donald T. Critchlow, "Think Tanks, Antistatism, and Democracy: The Nonpartisan Ideal and Policy Research in the United States, 1913–1987," in Lacey and Furner, eds., *The State and Social Investigation*, 279–322; Marmor et al., *America's Misunderstood Welfare State*, 13–17.

63. Critical evaluations of such doomsaying include, besides Elliott, H. Erich Heinemann, "The Downsizing Myth," *New York Times*, March 25, 1996; and Robert Samuelson, "Productivity Takes Up Savings Slack," *Providence Journal-Bulletin*, June 18, 1996.

64. E. J. Dionne, *Why Americans Hate Politics* (New York, 1991).

65. Gareth Davies, *From Opportunity to Entitlement: The Transformation and Decline of Great Society Liberalism* (Lawrence, 1996); Kelso, *Poverty and the Underclass*, 282–294. See also Hugh Heclo, "The Sixties' False Dawn: Awakenings, Movements, and Postmodern Policy-Making," *Journal of Policy History* 8 (1) (1996): 34–63; and Ira Katznelson, "Knowledge About What? Policy Intellectuals and the New Liberalism," in Rueschemeyer and Skocpol, *States, Social Knowledge, and Origins*, 17–47.

66. Thomas Edsall with Mary Edsall, *Chain Reaction: The Impact of Race, Rights, and Taxes on American Politics* (New York, 1991).

Index

Contributors

Thomas M. Adams: A director at the National Endowment for the Humanities, Dr. Adams has published *Bureaucrats and Beggars: French Social Policy in the Age of the Enlightenment*.

Anthony Brundage: Professor of history at California State Polytechnic University in Pomona. His books include *The Making of the New Poor Law: The Politics of Inquiry, Enactment, and Implementation* and *England's "Prussian Minister": Edwin Chadwick and the Politics of Government Growth, 1832–1854*.

E. Wayne Carp: Associate professor of history at Pacific Lutheran University and the author of *To Starve the Army at Pleasure: Continental Army Administration and American Political Culture* and *Secrecy and Disclosure: A History of Adoption in America*.

Donald T. Critchlow: Editor of the *Journal of Policy History*, his books include *The Brookings Institution: Expertise and Influence in a Democratic Society*; *Studebaker: The Life and Death of an American Corporation*; and *Intended Consequences: Birth Control, Abortion, and the Federal Government* (in press).

Ellis W. Hawley: Professor emeritus of history at the University of Iowa. He has written extensively on issues of public policy, including *The New Deal and the Problem of Monopoly: A Study in Economic Ambivalence*; *The Great War and the Search for a Modern Order: A History of the American People and their Institutions, 1917–1933*; and *Herbert Hoover and the Crisis of American Capitalism*.

Elizabeth McKeown: Professor of theology at Georgetown University, she is the author of *War and Welfare: Catholics and World War I* and most recently is coauthor with Dorothy M. Brown of *The Poor Belong To Us: Catholic Charities in American Welfare* .

Kathryn Norberg: Associate professor of history and director of the women's studies program at the University of California, Los Angeles. Her works include *Rich and Poor in Grenoble, 1600–1814.*

Alice O'Connor: Assistant professor of history at the University of California, Santa Barbara. She is currently completing a book on the history of poverty research and its role in social welfare policy since the 1920s.

Charles H. Parker: Assistant professor of history at Saint Louis University. He is the author of *The Reformation of Community: Social Welfare and Calvinist Charity in Holland, 1572-1620* (forthcoming, September 1998).

James T. Patterson: Professor of history at Brown University, he is particularly interested in the late twentieth-century United States. His most recent work is *Grand Expectations: The United States, 1945–1974.* He has also written *America's Struggle against Poverty, 1900–1994* and *The Welfare State in America, 1930–1980.*

Brian Pullan: Professor of history at the University of Manchester, his research is primarily in early modern Italian poor relief. He has written *Rich and Poor in Renaissance Venice: The Social Institutions of a Catholic State*; *Crisis and Change in the Venetian Economy in the Sixteenth and Seventeenth Centuries*; and *A History of Early Renaissance Italy for the Mid-thirteenth to the Mid-fifteenth Century.*